KT-233-960

Friendship and Peer Relations in Children

8

R

₪ 4 JUN 2002

THE LIBRARY

UNIVERSITY OF
WINCHESTER

KA 0147769 2

Friendship and Peer Relations in Children

Phil Erwin

Manchester Metropolitan University, UK

JOHN WILEY & SONS

Chichester · New York · Brisbane · Toronto · Singapore

Copyright © 1993 by John Wiley & Sons Ltd,
Baffins Lane, Chichester,
West Sussex PO19 1UD, England

All rights reserved.

No part of this book may be reproduced by any means,
or transmitted, or translated into a machine language
without the written permission of the publisher.

Other Wiley Editorial Offices

John Wiley & Sons, Inc., 605 Third Avenue,
New York, NY 10158-0012, USA

Jacaranda Wiley Ltd, G.P.O. Box 859, Brisbane,
Queensland 4001, Australia

John Wiley & Sons (Canada) Ltd, 22 Worcester Road,
Rexdale, Ontario M9W 1L1, Canada

John Wiley & Sons (SEA) Pte Ltd, 37 Jalan Pemimpin #05-04,
Block B, Union Industrial Building, Singapore 2057

KING ALFRED'S COLLEGE
WINCHESTER

155.
418
ERW   01477692

Library of Congress Cataloging-in-Publication Data

Erwin, Phil.
    Friendship and peer relations in children / Phil Erwin.
        p. cm.
    Includes bibliographical references (p.   ) and index.
    ISBN 0-471-92584-5 (ppc)
    ISBN 0-471-93877-7 (paper)
    1. Friendship in children. 2. Interpersonal relations in children
    I. Title.
    BF723.F68E78   1993   92–29620
    155.4′ 18—dc20   CIP

British Library Cataloguing in Publication Data

A catalogue record for this book is available from the British Library

ISBN 0-471-92584-5 (ppc)
     0-471-93877-7 (paper)

Typeset in 10/12 Times from author's disks by Dobbie Typesetting Ltd, Tavistock
Printed and bound in Great Britain by Biddles Ltd, Guildford and King's Lynn

Contents

Foreword

Over the last ten years or so the field of research into social and personal relationships has grown by leaps and bounds as a variety of scholars has discovered the ways in which such relationships underpin much of life and has sought to understand their dynamics. The field has been discovered to be composed of scholars from many different disciplines, some concerned with societal forces that shape relational activity, some investigating the development of a child's conception of friendship or experience of sociality in the playground, others focusing on the cognitions that make up a part of the activities of conducting relationships.

There is almost no social behaviour that does not bear upon relationship and vice versa – it is even, as some are beginning to argue (e.g. Gergen & Gergen, 1992; Shotter, 1992), very probable that our conceptions of the nature of individuality, self, and communication between people are likely to trace their way back to an understanding of relationships. Thus, as children venture out of the home and into school or from school into society they are taking with them some important lessons about themselves in relation to others; lessons that have been slowly learned and developed in the experiences that they take with them from place to place and learning environment to learning environment (Duck, 1991).

Despite the growth in the work on relationships as a whole and the growth of work into the origins of children's relational behaviours and knowledge, the two have largely grown in parallel and only a few attempts have been made to generalise from one domain to another (e.g. Fogel, in press). Recent efforts to extend attachment theory from infancy to adult romantic relationships (Hazan & Shaver, 1987) have been a successful instance of such attempts to connect the two domains. Efforts to understand the ways in which mothers reflect on their own childhood relationships and project them into the rearing of their own children (Putallaz, Costanzo & Klein, in press) are other instances. As another example, Hinde & Stevenson-Hinde (1986) have researched the continuities between relationships in the home and relationships in the school for children's behaviours of relating. By and large, however, there have been few attempts to connect the literature on adults and the literature on children in either direction, or to attempt to comprehend the relational endeavour as having any global singularity across the lifespan of the individual self.

Phil Erwin's book begins the effort of tying our knowledge of adult friendships to our knowledge of children's friendships, on the one hand, and of connecting knowledge about one part of childhood to other parts later in life. It thus provides a major service to the two relatively unconnected fields. The author identifies a number of important commonalities in the two literatures and deals with processes well studied in one area in terms of processes less well studied in the other (for example his discussions of similarity and physical attractiveness). The author reviews an enormous amount of research in a variety of fields yet gives a good coherent sense of the forces acting on children's friendships, their behaviour in such friendships and their notions of their own value to other people. His proposals are not only interesting in themselves but provide a beacon for future scholars that will light our way to a greater understanding of the role of personal relationships in the lives of individuals and the ways in which such relationships and relational learning tend to produce the socialised adults that make up a successful society.

References

Duck, S. W. (1991). *Friends, For Life*, 2nd edn, Hemel Hempstead: Harvester Wheatsheaf [US Edition: *Understanding Relationships*, New York: Guilford].

Fogel, A. (in press). *Developing Through Relationships: Communication, Self, and Culture in Early Infancy*, Hemel Hempstead: Harvester Wheatsheaf.

Gergen, M. & Gergen, K. (1992). Attributions, accounts and close relationships: close calls and relational resolutions. In J. H. Harvey, T. L. Orbuch & A. L. Weber (Eds), *Attributions, Accounts and Close Relationships*, New York: Springer-Verlag, pp. 19–39.

Hazan, C. & Shaver, P. R. (1987). Romantic love conceptualized as an attachment process. *Journal of Personality and Social Psychology*, **52**, 511–524.

Hinde, R. A. & Stevenson-Hinde, J. (1986). Relating childhood relationships to individual characteristics. In W. Hartup & Z. Rubin (Eds), *Relationships and Development*, Hillsdale, NJ: Erlbaum, pp. 27–50.

Putallaz, M., Costanzo, P. & Klein, T. (in press). Parental childhood social experiences and their effects on children's relationships. In S. W. Duck (Ed.), *Understanding Relationship Processes 2: Learning About Relationships*, Newbury Park: SAGE.

Shotter, J. (1992). What is a "personal" relationship? A rhetorical–responsive account of "unfinished business". In J. H. Harvey, T. L. Orbuch & A. L. Weber (Eds), *Attributions, Accounts and Close Relationships*, New York: Springer-Verlag, pp. 19–39.

Steve Duck
University of Iowa, USA

Preface

Just over 12 short years ago there were no notable books specifically on the subject of children's friendships. There were chapters that were beginning to open up the theoretical territory, and empirical research was entering a boom phase, but the area was fragmented and researchers were reticent to draw hasty conclusions. In a very short period of time this picture was to change dramatically with the publications of notable early works such as Zick Rubin's (1980) excellent and very readable *Children's Friendships*; Foot, Chapman & Smith's (1980) *Friendship and Social Relationships in Children*; and Asher & Gottman's (1981) *The Development of Children's Friendships*. Since then the field has flourished and there is no shortage of books. So why, you may ask, yet another book on the topic? A brief look along the book shelves answers this question. Most of the existing books are edited, highly specialised texts. In this book I have tried to take a broader approach than is usual. Broader in the sense of its target audience and of its perspective. In terms of its target audience, I hope that it will be found useful by readers not just from psychology – though there should be plenty to interest them – but also from associated disciplines and professional areas.

Although I report a great deal of research, some of it in great detail, I have tried to avoid jargon and psychological nit-picking. Research is examined for its general quality and its implications. Often it is the sheer weight and diversity of evidence that is convincing rather than the methodological rigour of any individual study. In the sense of a broader perspective, I have tried to show that relationships are an integral part of children's broader social and psychological functioning. Rather than drawing strict lines around those aspects of processes related to relationships, I have outlined broader influences. What is the point, for example, of knowing that social comparison is important in relationships if there isn't a basic appreciation of why social comparison is important, how it may change developmentally, and how it fits in with other aspects of the child's life?

In this book I adopt a topic-based approach to issues associated with children's friendships. In their general sweep the chapters are arranged in a developmental order – in the sense both of age and relationship growth. Children's initial attachments to parents are examined before their peer relationships. The antecedents of early attraction are examined before factors which are more significant for long established friendships.

Chapter 1 focuses on the early attachment of infants to their parents and how these are important for later peer relationships and adjustment. Chapters 2 through 6 are detailed examinations of the antecedents of children's peer relationships. Chapter 2 examines the impact of children's social cognitive abilities on their relationships. These abilities mediate children's experience of their social world. To this extent they underpin all of the other factors that are examined in subsequent chapters. The effects of physical attractiveness, sex roles, social skills, and cultural norms in relationships occur because of the child's perception and interpretation of social cues. Chapter 3 continues this cognitive theme by examining one of the most researched and intrinsically interesting antecedents of attraction: physical appearance. This is an early and potent source of information that is available to potential friends. Only if the other child is a sufficiently attractive partner is interaction likely to ensue. And then the child's social skills, background, and character will become important. These are discussed in detail in the next three closely related chapters. Chapter 4 moves the level of analysis from cognitive abilities to overt behaviour and social skills. To relate successfully to peers, children must not only accurately perceive and understand the demands of their peer relationships, they must be able to enact appropriate responses. Failure here is likely to leave the child isolated and unable to initiate or sustain satisfying relationships. Chapter 5 examines self-disclosure, a specific social skill that has received considerable attention in the literature on adult relationships. The communication of personal information is recognised as an important tool used to build relationships. Although self-disclosure is no less significant in children's relationships than adults', it has so far received considerably less attention from researchers and acknowledgement by authors. Chapter 6 examines the nature and function of information that is gathered in relationships, whether by self-disclosure processes, direct observation, relationships, or other indirect sources. The focus here is on social comparison processes and the role of similarity of attitudes and personality in relationships. This brings the analysis full circle in that it returns to cognitive factors.

The broad picture of relationships painted by the first six chapters of this book leaves a number of loose ends which are tied up in Chapters 7 and 8. Chapter 7 looks at sex differences and the commonly reported sex segregation in children's relationships. This is an interesting and controversial area that also informs the debate about sex differences in adult patterns of relating. Chapter 8 reviews the social and physical context of relationships. In particular it examines how children's home neighbourhoods and school classrooms affect their relationships. The effects of these contexts is often marked, indicating that the environmental context of relationships is worthy of considerably more attention than it typically receives.

Chapters 9 and 10 represent the most recent focus of research on children's relationships. They examine how and when they go wrong, and how they can be repaired. The practical application of relationships research and theory is clearly showing an area that is coming of age. These are topics of major significance and social relevance. None the less, these are also areas that have only recently attracted substantial amounts of research attention and so, while there are interesting findings to report, they are also tantalisingly incomplete. I hope these chapters will serve as an invitation to some readers to join the quest to understand and help children in their relationships.

My first introduction to the area of personal relationships was a lecture by Steve Duck. For this and subsequent encouragement and support, including comments on an early draft of this book, I owe him a great debt of thanks. To my counselling supervisor, Peter Pumfrey, I also owe considerable thanks; this training changed my perspective and priorities considerably and so influenced the later parts of this book. I am grateful to numerous other colleagues for copies of papers and the privilege of discussing their work with them. Thanks are especially due to Teresa, for her tolerance and support during my long period of self-imposed isolation during the writing of this book, and for protecting this solitude from Titch, a rather boisterous Jack Russell terrier!

Phil Erwin
February 1992

1 Attachment, child rearing practices and early relationships

The young child seeks and explores new relationships within the framework of expectations for self and others that emerges from the primary relationship.

(Sroufe & Fleeson, 1986, p. 52)

The early bond or attachment of a child to a parent or primary caregiver exerts a major influence on later relationships. It is on the foundation of this primary relationship that the conduct and expectations of all other relationships are built. As Maccoby & Martin (1983, p. 72) put it: "At each stage the quality of prior relationships must have an impact on the quality of relationships that can grow out of the child's developing capacities for interaction. But the nature of the cross-age linkages is something that is only beginning to be explored." This chapter examines the child's early relationship with his or her caregiver and its impact on later peer relationships. Though attachment is a long-established area of psychological research, it is an area with many controversies. Even the definition of attachment can be controversial. Is attachment a bond of affection that *causes* the child to behave in certain ways or is the term simply a metaphor that is useful to summarise a diverse set of behaviours which characterise the caregiver–child relationship? Having considered this fundamental question the chapter then provides a basic background of attachment theory and research. How children become attached to their parents, how the quality of attachment may vary, and how attachment can be measured. All of these issues are important, but more significant for our purposes are their potential implications for later relationships. Although these implications have been discussed since the earliest days of attachment theory, it is only relatively recently that intense, systematic research effort has started to produce substantial and convincing evidence. It is this research that forms the focal point of the chapter. An important part of this evidence pertains to the mechanisms by which quality of attachment affects competence in later relationships. In part, evidence suggests that the child's experience of attachment affects his or her general social orientation, though there is also evidence that some specific skills are acquired within parent–child relationships and generalised to subsequent peer relationships. In this youthful area of research patterns are beginning to emerge, but there is still substantial controversy. The limitations of research, due to social circumstances and methodological shortcomings are reviewed. Lastly, patterns of parenting beyond initial attachment are examined to show the continuing importance of sensitive parenting throughout childhood.

Background

In Erikson's (1968) theory of psychosocial development a series of stages are proposed, each of which entails a distinct task or crisis to be resolved if the child is to achieve a balanced, mature sense of identity. The stage encompassing the first year of life is portrayed as a key time for relationships. This is the stage of trust versus mistrust, a notion similar to Ainsworth et al.'s (1978) distinction between secure versus insecure attachment. The development of a secure attachment and a sense of trust requires physical comfort and security, the products of sensitive, responsive parenting (Bowlby, 1969). Trust in infancy sets the stage for future patterns of relating; it produces a general and persisting expectation that the world in general is a good and pleasant place and that relationships are satisfying and reliable. In contrast, poor attachment may result in an anxious, over-dependent child with a lifelong inability to maintain mutual trust in relationships. These notions are similar to the ideas put forward by Sroufe and his associates, succinctly summarised in the quotation at the beginning of this chapter.

Considerable research effort has been devoted to examining the connection between early attachment and later relationships, mostly focusing on the mother–child relationship of middle-class Americans and Europeans. Though not full explanations or adequate as excuses, the basic reasons for this emphasis are quite simple. First, most research in the area is conducted by American and European psychologists. Second, in these cultures variants of the nuclear family (a unit consisting of two generations, parents and children) are the norm. In this context the mother is most often the primary caregiver and hence the most likely candidate for the child's initial attachment. Third, middle-class culture and populations are most visible and accessible for study.

The cultural and evaluative judgements implicit in much of the child-rearing literature do not necessarily apply to other groups or cultures. What constitutes social, psychological and economic success will be defined within a given social and cultural milieu. "A mother child relationship that produces successful adults in one situation will not necessarily do so in another" (Bretherton, 1985). A good parental style is one which promotes the development of characteristics which will facilitate the achievement of culturally designated and valued goals. These often differ in industrial or pre-industrial societies and also between sub-cultures within a society. For example, Ogbu (1981) has noted that children in the urban ghettos of America need to learn behaviour patterns very different from those of their middle-class counterparts if they are to survive and prosper. Success is determined more by gang membership or by being generally "street-wise", knowing how to fight and hustle, rather than by scholastic performance. In contrast to the authoritative parenting often advocated by middle-class psychologists, and well suited to middle-class families, ghetto parents tend to be extremely warm and affectionate to their infants but tend to use an authoritarian style of parenting, which is often severe, inconsistent, power assertive, and uses physical discipline. This is likely to encourage behaviours which, while frowned on by the middle classes, is highly adaptive in the ghetto: assertiveness, self-reliance, and a mistrust of authority figures.

Research has focused on the child's attachment to his or her mother largely because this reflects patterns of parenting within Western society; it does not imply that the child's attachment to the mother is qualitatively different from that with other figures. Other figures can, and increasingly commonly do, also take on this role. Neither does the significance of the primary attachment reduce or deny the impact of later attachments, possibly to the father or siblings and, as is becoming increasingly recognised, more complex family dynamics (Ladd, 1991). For example, research indicates that if one secure attachment has definite benefits for later social relationships, having two is even more advantageous. Toddlers securely attached to both parents are more relaxed and socially responsive when interacting with a strange adult than are children who are insecure with one or both parents (Main & Weston, 1981).

To examine the impact of early attachment on later relationships in detail it is first necessary to define attachment and explore factors which affect the quality of this first relationship. It is to these issues that the next sections are devoted.

Defining attachment

Above all, attachment is a useful integrative concept. It allows a parsimonious explanation for the relationship between various attachment behaviours and the continuity of these behaviours over time and space. But to what extent do these attachment behaviours allow us to infer some underlying unitary construct? On this point opinions differ markedly. The term attachment has been used in two fundamentally different ways by different writers.

The original use of the term attachment, heavily influenced by Freudian and ethological perspectives, was to refer to a strong and enduring emotional or affective *bond* of the individual to one or a few significant others (Bowlby, 1958, 1969). ''Affectional bonds are characteristic of the individual, not the dyad . . . I define an 'affectional bond' as a relatively long-enduring tie in which the partner is important as a unique individual and is interchangeable with none other. In an affectional bond there is a desire to maintain closeness to the partner.'' (Ainsworth, 1989, p. 711).

So, from this perspective attachment is seen as a unitary force that drives and directs the behaviour that it subsumes. It is seen as indicated by behaviours that serve to maintain proximity with the attachment figures. Attachment in this sense represents an extremely intense form of relationship, an emotional bonding, it is not to be confused with general sociability which is positive behaviour toward a much wider range of social figures, which is much less emotionally involving, and often considerably less permanent.

Other authors have been less willing to infer individual emotional bonds on the basis of patterns of social behaviour. From this perspective the term attachment behaviour ''has been used to denote particular classes of responses that occur in dyadic relationships'' (Cairns, 1972, p. 35), such as separation anxiety and proximity seeking. This sees the term attachment as a metaphor for certain characteristic forms of interaction rather than a cause of these patterns. Attachment behaviours are seen as a reflection of the consequences which they produce for the child. The extent of separation crying serves as a good example of this approach. On one level this can be interpreted as a good indicator of the disruption of an attachment bond, yet by altering the effects that it produces – the responses of parents – it is possible to alter this pattern of responding and hence apparent attachment (Gewirtz, 1976). This alternative perspective allows attachment to be seen as a property of some patterns of interaction, rather than as a characteristic of an individual, it is a co-ordination and mutual dependence or determination in interaction (e.g. M. K. Rosenthal, 1973). It is to a more detailed examination of attachment as a reciprocal relationship that the next section is devoted.

Attachment as a relationship

Attachment is not a static, immutable state but a dynamic relationship, the result of a history of interaction between the infant and the parent. This implies that *both* participants play crucial roles in establishing and maintaining this relationship. On the part of the more skilled participant, the parent, the fundamental basis of a strong and secure attachment appears to lie in the acceptance, sensitivity, and responsiveness to the child (Benn, 1986; Sroufe & Fleeson, 1986). The child affects attachment mainly because of his or her characteristics and the effect that these have on the responsiveness of the parent. The contribution of each of these figures to the attachment relationship will be considered in turn, though we should first note their behavioural consequences. Secure attachment is characterised by well synchronised reciprocal, rewarding interactions. Insecure attachments typically show interactions which are either minimally involved and unresponsive or intrusive (Isabella & Belsky, 1991).

A significant contributor to the mother's responsiveness to her infant is her own family experiences. Mothers from disrupted families (for example, where parents were divorced) are likely to show lower levels of interaction with their children (Hall, Pawlby & Wolkind, 1979). The impact of the mother's background on her responsiveness to the child implies that maternal sensitivity is a relatively stable and predictable attribute. Research suggests that it is possible to identify women who are likely to be sensitive and responsive as mothers even before their child is born. In a study of women in mid-pregnancy, Heinicke et al. (1983) found that those women that were warm and outgoing, high in ego strength (a measure of adaptive functioning and self-esteem), and confident in visualising themselves as mothers tended to make highly sensitive and responsive parents. Where sensitivity to the child does change or show variations over the course of infancy, this is often associated with important changes in family circumstances. In a study by Pianta, Sroufe & Egeland (1989), sources of family stress, such as unemployment or illness, were found to lead to reductions in maternal sensitivity. Positive, supporting relationships with family and friends produced increases in sensitivity.

The mother's reactions to her child, and consequently the quality of the relationship that is established, is also affected by the infant's appearance, temperament and responsiveness. In this way both participants contribute to the attachment relationship and the influence is reciprocal. The role of the child's characteristics was shown in the study by Pianta, Sroufe & Egeland (1989), mentioned above. Positive temperamental characteristics in daughters and low levels of affect and sociability in boys were associated with increased parental sensitivity. Presumably the effects children's characteristics have on their parents may lie in sex-role stereotyping. The quiet, reserved boy may be regarded as in need of compensatory attention to encourage more active, assertive behaviour. This again serves to highlight the potential impact of sociocultural factors on attachment. In slightly older children, a study by Buss (1981) confirmed the interplay between child temperament and parental behaviour. When offering assistance to a child engaged on a task, the parents of five year olds previously categorised as active were more likely to physically intervene in the child's ongoing activity but had difficulty in establishing a good working relationship. Interactions tended to become hostile power struggles. Parents with less active children were likely to have more positive and peaceful encounters.

Overall, the evidence seems clear. Attachment is not an ability or characteristic possessed by an individual. It describes a relatively stable though malleable relationship between two mutually influencing partners.

Becoming attached

The process of becoming attached has been subjected to detailed study and description in extensive research programmes by both Schaffer & Emerson (1964) and Ainsworth et al. (1978). The very young child does not appear to show attachment as such but does show patterns of preference and behaviour which will facilitate the later formation of an attachment relationship (Bowlby, 1969). In the first few months of life the infant encourages the proximity of other people, and especially the caregiver, by means of a variety of basic abilities and behaviours. The newborn child responds to the sound of the human voice and can even discriminate and prefers the mother's voice (DeCasper & Fifer, 1980). There is also an increasingly detailed preference for face-like visual stimuli (Schaffer, 1971). On the part of the parent, behaviours such as sucking, smiling, clinging, crying, and visual attention are interpreted as signs of content, confirmation that she or he is functioning well and is appreciated as a caregiver. These feelings of efficacy in the parent in turn promote a desire for further interaction and so encourage and maintain physical contact and sensitivity. From about six weeks old the child shows a preference for social rather than non-social stimuli and, having learnt the consequences of his or her natural behaviours, uses some of them, such as smiling and crying as social signals in order to attract attention. Despite this evidently social orientation, at this age there is as yet no consistent preference for one specific caregiver rather than another.

Over the next six months or so infants gradually become more discriminating in their attachment behaviours. By about three months of age, photographs of the mother are recognised and preferred to those of strangers (Barrera & Maurer, 1981a, 1981b). Proximity-promoting behaviours are still directed at a variety of people, though infants react more positively to the people that regularly take care of them.

At about six or seven months of age the child's social development is marked by a major milestone, the formation of the primary attachment. This is crucially dependent on the child's cognitive development, the acquisition of the concept of object permanence. With the achievement of the concept of object permanence the child understands that an object or person removed from sight does not cease to exist. Caregivers are missed when absent, they may be looked for, and the child may loudly protest being deprived of their presence (Schaffer, 1971). Attachment behaviours are now starting to be directed to a single, major caregiver and a fear of strangers is typically evident. At this age the child is able to crawl about and so directly approach the caregiver rather than simply trying to attract attention. The greater mobility of the child also means that the caregiver is now used as a secure base for exploration; at times of perceived threat, such as the approach of a stranger, safety and proximity can be rapidly restored through directly approaching the caregiver.

Following on from initial attachments, at about nine to twelve months of age, stranger anxiety starts to decline and there begins a generalisation of attachment to include other figures that are significant in the child's life, such as the father and siblings. The child's explorations also become more extensive and, on encountering a new person, object or situation, the attachment figure may be used for social referencing, their reactions providing a guide as to appropriate behaviour (Klinnert et al., 1986).

This section has examined the development of attachment. The validity and usefulness of research on attachment ultimately depends on the reliability and accuracy with which it can be measured, and this is the topic of the next section.

Measuring attachment

In biological terms, attachment serves to protect the young and hence maintain the species. The attachment figure is a secure base for the child's exploration of a potentially threatening world, and as a source of comfort at times of stress and fear. According to Bowlby, attachment is indicated by frequent interaction and attempts to maintain proximity. These characteristics provide the possibility of behavioural measures of attachment.

To be a useful construct, attachment must be operationally defined in terms of specific behavioural indices, though many authors have questioned the adequacy of such measures. Cohen (1974) has argued that few of the commonly used indices (such as crying on separation, following, and gaze) have been unequivocally demonstrated to be reliable and, most importantly, selective indicators of attachment that can discriminate between an attachment figure and some other familiar, non-feared person. In a detailed critique Masters & Wellman (1974) have questioned the temporal, cross-situational and cross-behavioural consistency of attachment behaviours. The authors conclude that

> ... there is little stability and functional equivalence among many attachment behaviours. A child who looks frequently at his mother on one day does not necessarily do so on the next. A child who vocalizes frequently to his mother does not necessarily cry lengthily when she leaves. They suspect that a child

who cries when his mother leaves the laboratory does not necessarily cry when she leaves at home. (Masters & Wellman, 1974, p. 228).

The strange situation test

Despite the many reservations that have been voiced over the consistency and stability of behavioural indices of attachment, the concept has been staunchly defended. There has been a good deal of research showing clear *patterns* of attachment behaviours in specific situations (Lamb, 1974). An influential and commonly used measure of attachment for children between about 12 and 18 months of age has been proposed by Ainsworth and her associates (Ainsworth et al., 1978). These authors argue that quality of attachments to caregivers can be measured by means of a technique known as the strange situation test, a standardised procedure of up to 21 minutes which subjects the infant to gradually increasing levels of stress. The child's behaviour during the various test episodes, such as their levels of exploratory activity, reactions to strangers, reactions to separation, and behaviour on being reunited with the caregiver, allowed three general categories of attachment to be distinguished: secure attachment, insecure–avoidant attachment and insecure–resistant attachment. These attachment classifications are described in detail later in this chapter.

For the strange situation test to have validity it must reflect behaviour in other circumstances, outside of the laboratory. Research on the strange situation test became popular because it did appear to have predictive validity. The observed interaction of the mother and child at home in the first few months of the child's life does appear to be closely related to subsequent behaviour in the strange situation test (Ainsworth et al., 1978).

For any test to be useful it must also be reliable: if the same child is tested twice, then similar results should be produced on each occasion. Without reliability, the question of validity is meaningless. Fortunately, the strange situation test does appear to be able to reveal strong consistency in patterns of attachment. Studies have found that children securely attached at one year of age were similarly attached at 18 months and six years of age (Main, Kaplan & Cassidy, 1985).

Attachment classification may well change with changes in family circumstances that affect maternal care, such as changes in the mother's employment status (Thompson, Lamb & Estes, 1982), but this is another issue; few would argue that the attachment relationship is supposed to be immutable. First we must consider the argument that some apparent differences in attachment are exaggerated or confounded by differences in the child's temperament. The relationship between the child's temperamental characteristics, interaction with the caregiver, and attachment is a complex issue which is examined next.

Temperament or attachment?

Despite the large amount of research based on the strange situation test, it has not gone uncriticised as a measure of attachment. Several authors have argued that the child's behaviour in the test is a reflection of temperamental characteristics rather than quality of attachment (Chess & Thomas, 1982; Kagan, 1984). An important consequence of ascribing differences in behaviour largely to the impact of innate temperamental factors is the implication that they should be relatively stable. The infant would be expected to be resilient and show similar adaptations across time, a variety of social figures, and despite wide differences in styles of parenting (Kagan, 1987). From this perspective the significance of early attachment for later relationships and social competence has been exaggerated; the description of the insecurely attached infant could equally well serve to describe the temperamentally difficult child.

Some of the strongest evidence for the role of constitutional factors in temperament and sociability comes from genetic studies. Identical (monozygotic) twins are moderately similar in their levels of temperament whereas fraternal (dizygotic) twins show little or no similarity (Buss & Plomin, 1984), a pattern that has been observed even in children as old as ten years of age (Scarr, 1968). Temperament generally shows moderate levels of stability across the childhood years (Rothbart, 1986), but is clearly highest in early childhood. Despite the undoubted consistency deriving from a genetic component to temperament, there is also an undeniable and accumulating impact due to environmental factors. A rather nice example of the joint importance of genetic and environmental determinants of temperament comes from Scarr & Kidd (1983), who found that adopted children were as similar in temperament to their genetically unrelated adoptive parents as to their biological parents.

As Sroufe (1985) points out, if we take into account the observed independence of the quality of a child's attachments to different parents and changes in attachment with family circumstances, the temperament explanation of attachment behaviours looks increasingly improbable. The balance of evidence suggests that temperament is an important factor affecting attachment, but it would be unwise to overlook or underestimate the impact of environmental influences. It is impossible to explain a child's attachment behaviours, as shown in the strange situation test, solely in terms of individual congenital characteristics. In contrast, the concept of attachment implies a potentially greater malleability in the mother–child relationship and can easily account for these findings.

Important studies have directly examined the relationships between infant temperament, caregiving behaviour and infant social behaviour, and found caregiver responsiveness to be the most reliable predictor of later quality of attachment (Goldberg et al., 1986). Infant behaviour in the early weeks of life, such as levels of crying, does not show temporal stability or predict later attachment; maternal responsiveness in the same period does (Blehar, Lieberman & Ainsworth, 1977). Child abuse, maltreatment and neglect are commonly associated with insecure attachments (Paterson & Moran, 1988; Youngblade & Belsky, 1989). Hinde (1987) reports an interesting study by Engfer (1986) in which a lack of maternal sensitivity was more closely associated with four- and 18-month-old children being labelled as difficult than were any of the characteristics of the child. This in itself is fairly interesting, but an even more interesting finding of this study was that difficulty of the child at 43 months of age was better predicted by peer co-operativeness ten months earlier than by any maternal characteristics. Apparently maternal sensitivity is important in determining which babies are labelled as difficult, and these expectations may then act as a self-fulfilling prophecy with children coming to behave accordingly. Far from temperament determining attachment, it starts to appear that consistency in temperament and sociability are crucially dependent on consistency in the status of the attachment relationship (Thompson & Lamb, 1984).

A unified perspective

The quality of attachment reflects the history of a relationship, and temperament is but one of several contributing factors. Securely attached children may show very different and individual patterns of temperament. They can vary considerably in their levels of responsiveness and irritability, and show very different activity levels (Sroufe, 1979). The way the caregiver responds to the infant, rather than the child's temperament as such, plays the major role in determining the quality of infant attachment.

Few authors would actually wish to see attachment and temperament as exclusive influences. The significance of a child's temperamental characteristics is determined by the way in which they interact with specific aspects of the environment. The characteristics of infants may actually promote specific patterns of child care from parents. It has been suggested that children are generally resilient and will typically adapt to their environment, though extremes of temperament themselves promote changes in that environment, such as in patterns of caregiving (Buss & Plomin, 1984). Irritable children may exhaust their parents and reduce their tolerance and levels of responsiveness, or else may foster over-control or indulgence. The temperamentally difficult infant is thus more likely to form an insecure attachment with his or her caregiver (Goldsmith, Bradshaw & Riesser-Danner, 1986). Where an insecure attachment is formed, Belsky & Rovine (1987) suggest that the child's temperamental characteristics then affect whether this is avoidant or resistant.

With increasing age, attempts to separate the relative importance of temperament and parental sensitivity are increasingly pointless. As Sroufe & Fleeson (1986, p. 52) note, "Once the infant has been involved in the attachment relationship, its inherent dispositions are both subsumed and transformed by the relationship. These dispositions cannot be reclaimed as the infant moves forward to new relationships. Congenital temperament, could it be assessed, in large part ceases to exist as a separate entity." Later relationships grow out of current relationships, in the sense of a natural dialectic. Temperament and relationship histories are totally intertwined, they are not carried forward separately but are synergistically combined; through their mutual and interacting impact they provide each child with a unique and qualitatively distinct working model of relationships.

Having considered the nature of attachment, and how this may be measured by the strange situation test, the next section considers the effects that these early relationships, and stranger anxiety, for subsequent peer relationships.

Attachment, stranger anxiety and peer sociability

Most infants react positively to strangers until the primary attachment is formed; shortly after this comes a fear of unfamiliar individuals (Schaffer & Emerson, 1964). Some support for a cognitive developmental explanation of this stranger anxiety comes from Jacobson (1980), who showed that a child's level of development was closely related to the appearance of stranger anxiety. Infants scoring highest on a cognitive test at ten months of age were most wary of strange peers at one year of age, those scoring lower showed a later peak in stranger anxiety. With the ability to form a stable schema for the faces of regular companions comes a fear of those individuals that are unrecognised (Kagan, 1972). The appearance of a stranger typically produces behavioural responses such as avoidance, anxiety, crying, increased proximity seeking, and clinging to the caregiver. These reactions do show a degree of flexibility, they are affected by the physical setting of the encounter, the presence or absence of the mother or a familiar companion, and the stranger's appearance and behaviour. The avoidance responses to the approach of a strange adult initially show a developmental increase in strength but then decline over the course of the second year as the schema for recognising adults is generalised.

As our primary interest in this book is the children's relationships with their peers it is interesting to note that infants do not typically show anxiety about a strange child until their second year (Lewis & Brooks, 1974), considerably later than for a fear of adults. This discrepancy has been the subject of empirical research and provides insights into the basis of stranger anxiety and peer relationships. In a follow-up to their earlier study, Brooks

& Lewis (1976) investigated whether the earlier negative reaction to adults than to children could be due to the physical size of the stranger. Infants were exposed to a strange adult, child, or an adult midget the size of the child. There were more negative reactions to the adult strangers, regardless of physical size. It appears that the adult facial appearance is more important than physical size as a basis for stranger anxiety.

The lesser contact that a child of eight or so months has with peers in comparison to adults may mean that the schema for faces is initially limited to adults. As the child becomes more mobile and contact with other children increases the schema is likely to be elaborated and apprehension to strange peers occurs (Kagan, Kearsley & Zelazo, 1975). This cognitive explanation receives some support from Kagan, Kearsley & Zelazo's finding that children with group experience showed less inhibition with unfamiliar peers.

Quality of attachment

On the basis of responses in the strange situation test, Ainsworth et al. (1978) argued that infants differed in the type or quality of their attachments to caregivers. Three main categories (and potentially eight subgroups) of attachment were distinguished: secure attachment, anxious-avoidant attachment, and anxious-resistant attachment. Each of these patterns of attachment is supposedly the product of specific parenting styles (Ainsworth, 1979). These will now be outlined.

Secure attachment

Secure attachment is typically the result of sensitive and responsive child care. Parents of securely attached infants are typically warm and emotionally expressive (e.g. Egeland & Farber, 1984). They appear to enjoy touching and close contact with the infant, they are sensitive to their child's signals and needs, and they encourage the infant to explore and communicate. This provides a model for the child's expectations of other relationships. The securely attached child appears open and receptive to contact initiated by the mother, and behaves as if the mother is expected to respond to his or her needs and social overtures. Although the child appears to enjoy proximity she or he is not clinging and also uses the mother as a secure base for active exploration, maintaining contact through periodic glances in the mother's direction. The securely attached child shows a clear preference for the mother in comparison to strangers. While the mother is present the child is outgoing to strangers and even enjoys being picked up by others; the child moves freely back to play when put down again. The child is visibly upset if separated from the mother; on her return the child can be comforted if distressed, the mother is greeted warmly and with evident pleasure. Studies typically report 50–70% of one year olds as securely attached.

Insecure–avoidant attachment

These mothers are often rigid, self-centred people, perhaps even showing depressive tendencies (e.g. Radke-Yarrow et al., 1985), who are likely to be psychologically distant and rejecting of their babies, especially if the child is perceived to be troublesome. The mothers of anxious–avoidant infants do not show the same level of involvement with their infants as the mothers of securely attached children. These mothers are likely to be less tolerant and more irritable, especially for any disruption that the child causes to their own lives and plans. This often manifests itself in a lack of responsiveness to the child's demands and a tendency to eschew physical contact. The mother's positive behaviours and interactions with the child are often limited and brief (Tracy & Ainsworth, 1981). The child learns to reciprocate the mother's behaviour. Though these children do not resist the mother's efforts to make contact, they do not actively seek it and the mother is largely ignored. The mother's behaviour does not encourage the child to regard her as a secure base and so the child shows little interest in exploring his or her world when with the mother. Neither does the child show marked signs of distress when separated from the mother. On the mother's return the child may avoid contact or turn away and ignore her. The child is not especially wary of strangers and seems in large measure to treat them the same as the mother – often ignoring or avoiding them. Studies typically report about 20–25% of one year olds as showing this pattern of attachment.

An interesting paradox about this attachment classification is that it can also be the result of mothers being too attentive (Isabella & Belsky, 1991). With an over-enthusiastic mother who provides continuously high levels of stimulation, regardless of whether the child wants this or not, avoidance becomes a means of regulating insensitive and excessive pressures for social interaction.

Insecure–resistant attachment

The mothers of these children do attempt to provide close physical contact; they often appear to have problems in interpreting the infant's needs and establishing synchronised patterns of interaction. They appear inconsistent in their caregiving. The child also shows ambivalent patterns of behaviour, at times appearing dependent and clinging and at other times avoiding or even fighting against contact. The child appears anxious, reluctant to explore and, even with the mother present, very suspicious of strangers. The resistant child is very distressed if the mother departs, but on being reunited both seeks and shows resistance to being comforted. The child appears angry about the enforced separation and on reunion with the mother shows this by rejecting her social overtures, possibly even showing aggressive behaviour such as pushing the mother away and trying to hit her. The end result of this conflicted behaviour is that the child remains near the mother but resists any attempts to initiate physical contact. This type of attachment appears to characterise about 10% of one year olds.

This type of attachment is more likely in infants that were temperamentally difficult babies, being excessively irritable or unresponsive (Waters, Vaughn & Egeland, 1980). Though care must be exercised in attributing too decisive a role to temperamental characteristics, many such infants do become securely attached, indicating the need and benefits of a sensitive matching of caregiver behaviour to infant temperament (Thomas, Chess & Birch, 1970).

Quality of attachment and later relationships

The quality of children's attachments to their parents varies and lays important foundations for their later ease and sociability with other children and adults. "Relationships seem to exert powerful influences over the individuals participating in them, and also to shape future relationships" (Sroufe & Fleeson, 1986, p. 67). Each infant has a different set of expectations, commonly termed a working model, of relationships which are derived from his or her early attachments (Bowlby, 1969). These expectations include information such as whether people respond to the infant's cries for help, and whether attention and affection are reliably available.

Although the working model of relationships that children derive from their early attachments can change with experience, Bowlby (1980) argues that they are not in constant flux. This provides the consistency and yet flexibility which allows for developmental changes in attachment behaviours (Bretherton, 1985). Once developed these working models of attachment act as heuristic devices, helping to shape and explain experience. The working model is likely to provide a direct guide for our social behaviour, to determine our approach to resolving interpersonal conflicts and problems, and to affect which social information is perceived as relevant and hence noticed and remembered. "The young child seeks and explores new relationships within the framework of expectations for self and others that emerges from the primary relationship" (Sroufe & Fleeson, 1986, p. 52).

The idea that attachments in infancy find their reflection in the later relationships of the child and adult has proved to be a popular topic of research recently. One line of research suggests that the child that has experienced neglect develops a model as being personally unworthy of any better treatment from others and as unable to influence their behaviour (Paterson & Moran, 1988). An important point to emphasise here is that the child appears to learn *both* sides of his or her attachment relationships. Thus the adult is able to enact the role of parent because of personal childhood experiences (Bretherton, 1985). In essence, the individual attempts to create in each new relationship aspects of the pattern with which she or he is familiar. One consequence of this idea is extremely important: it implies that patterns of neglectful and deprived parenting may be recreated in each successive generation of a family.

From this view, the crucial significance of the child's first attachment would be difficult to overemphasise. From this beginning comes the foundation on which the child's working model of relationships is built. It implies that there is a direct relationship from one set of earlier social experiences to the next. Relationships are seen as hierarchical, current relationships being built on the accumulated experiences of all those that have gone before. Though later experiences affect relationship expectations they will always be coloured by the earlier adaptations.

Attachment and children's peer relationships

The continuity of attachment with subsequent relationships is most clearly demonstrated in those peer relationships which are formed soonest after the primary attachment. These are less coloured by other relationship experiences.

Quality of attachment is well documented as predicting the expression and control of affections throughout the preschool years (Sroufe et al., 1984). A study by Matas, Arend & Sroufe (1978) found that infants securely attached to their mothers at 18 months old were less likely to ignore the mother and more likely to comply with maternal requests at two years of age. These children were also more effective with their peers at two years of age. They were more likely to participate in bouts of symbolic play, were more enthusiastic, happier, less aggressive, more persistent, spent less time off-task, and were less easily frustrated. In contrast, insecurely attached children were more likely to cry or whine, to appear unhappy and to resist and be aggressive to the parent. These children showed continued differences in adaptation throughout the subsequent kindergarten years (Arend, Gove & Sroufe, 1979).

A number of studies confirm that infants securely attached to their mothers at 12–19 months of age also show positive patterns of social behaviour three or four years later in the nursery school. Children from a background of secure attachment are likely to be confident, curious, skilful and less dependent (Erickson, Sroufe & Egeland, 1985). They are also likely to be more socially-oriented and empathic, and act in a more co-operative, friendly and outgoing manner to other infants and adults. They consequently tend to be more popular and have more friends (LaFreniere & Sroufe, 1985).

At this stage it is appropriate to examine in detail some of the major research showing the impact of early attachment on later peer relationships. The relatively small number of studies conducted in this area have attempted to ascertain either how early attachment affects the child's affective orientation to peer interaction, or how it teaches the child specific interaction skills and a sense of trust. Each of these will be examined in turn.

Social orientation

The approach adopted by studies in this section has focused on the confidence and expressiveness of children and how this correlates with their attachment history. In a study by Waters, Wippman & Sroufe (1979) infants rated as securely or anxiously attached to their mothers at 15 months of age were observed again at 42 months old during play with peers at nursery school. On 11 out of 12 measures of peer competence, and 5 out of 12 items measuring personal competence (termed ego strength or effectance by the authors), the securely attached group were rated higher than the insecurely attached group. These children were more likely to initiate play activities with other children and to be involved in peer interaction. The securely attached children also appeared to be more skilled in these social exchanges. Parents are more effective models and more effective in coaching their children about social relationships in the context of a warm and secure parent–child relationship. Although it was not the largest difference between the two attachment groups (cf. Jacobson et al., 1986), the most significant difference between attachment groups on peer interaction items referred to the extent to which other children sought the child's company. It is interesting to note that a subsequent study by Jacobson & Wille (1986) also reported that in the initial encounters of two- to three-year-olds with unfamiliar peers, attachment status at 18 months of age related more to the child's attractiveness as a partner than to his or her own behavioural interest in interaction. Secure children were likely to receive more positive responses from their peers than were avoidant children. Ambivalent children actually received more disruptive, resistance and conflict responses from peers.

In an interesting study by Pastor (1981) each of 13 secure, 12 anxious–avoidant and 12 anxious–resistant infants between 20 and 23 months old was paired with an unknown securely attached infant. The attachment of these infants to their mothers had been determined by the strange situation test at 18 months of age. Each child's behaviour to his or her mother and to the other infant was recorded. This section focuses on the findings relating to peer interactions. Infants that had been rated as secure showed more sociability and peer orientation, they made more social bids and ignored fewer peer bids compared to the insecure children. Secure children were also better at redirecting their behaviour after a conflict over a toy. The parents of securely attached children facilitated the peer interaction by responding appropriately while their child was with a playmate. In contrast, recent research indicates that the mothers of four year olds that had been classified as insecurely attached at 20 months are more adult-centred and more likely to use coercive, power-centred methods of controlling their children (Booth, Rose-Krasnor & Rubin, 1991). These findings highlight the continuity of the literatures on attachment and styles of parenting, despite the relatively independent development of these two areas of research. To return to Pastor's (1981) findings, the anxious–avoidant toddlers were active participants in the play sessions but were rated more negatively in their orientation to peers and elicited more aggression from their partners. In contrast, the anxious-resistant infants appeared considerably less skilled with peers; they were visibly distressed by the situation, made few peer offers and tended to ignore those made to them.

The research examined so far clearly shows the impact of attachment on the acquisition of social skills and social orientation, but it does not reveal the effect of mutual quality of attachment on the quality of later longer-term relationships. Recent research has addressed this issue. A study by Park & Waters (1989) found that the quality of a best friend relationship is also influenced by the attachment histories of both partners. In this study pairs of four-year-old friends were observed during free play. Where both members were classified as securely attached the interaction was more harmonious, less controlling, more responsive, and happier than was the case in pairs where one member was insecurely attached. This is an important extension to previous research; it shows that the impact of attachment histories on social interaction is not limited to superficial initial encounters.

Interaction skills

A study by Lieberman (1977) examined the role of security of attachment to the mother and peer experience on peer competence at three years old. Parents of securely attached children were more likely to provide social experiences with peers. Both the mother–child relationship and the peer experience affected subsequent competence with unacquainted peers. Children whose attachments to their mother were rated as secure showed a more positive social orientation, they showed higher levels of reciprocal interaction (such as sharing and showing or pointing), and lower levels of negative, aggressive behaviour. Experience with peers mainly improved interaction skills centring around co-ordinated verbal exchanges. The child's responsiveness and number of chains of exchange were both correlated with peer experience.

Even within the category of secure attachment subgroups have been delineated on the basis of the balance been exploration and attachment behaviours. These subgroups seem to find their reflection in patterns of later peer relations. Infants showing higher levels of proximity and contact seeking with the mother show less frequent and sophisticated interaction with peers than children that explore more freely and show more distal attachment behaviours toward the mother, such as looking and talking (Easterbrooks & Lamb, 1979).

The maternal precursor hypothesis

The maternal precursor hypothesis suggests that patterns of sociability and peer interaction skills are initially developed in the relationship with the mother without taking the child's security of attachment into account. This is examined in Chapter 4, in the context of a broader consideration of the nature of relationship skills. Specific patterns of maternal interaction are predictive of positive social behaviour, assertiveness and sadness in preschoolers (Denham, Renwick & Holt, 1991), but to what extent does the relationship with the mother facilitate the learning of specific skills which are then transferred to relationships with peers rather than merely the establishment of general patterns of sociability? The evidence for any large-scale learning and then direct transfer of specific skills from the relationship with the mother to that with peers seems limited (Lamb & Nash, 1989). Rather than the learning of specific skills, alternative explanations for the influence of early attachments on later relationships have been couched in terms of their impact on the affective tone of a toddler's peer interactions (Jacobson et al., 1986), or possibly their possible effect on the child's pattern of social problem solving (Pettit, Dodge & Brown, 1988).

This question of whether skills are learned in one relationship and then simply transferred to another is difficult to assess because of a number of methodological differences between studies. For example, studies of peer interaction in young children have not been consistent in whether interaction was observed in the presence of the mother or not, and the amount of interaction the mother is permitted if she is present. Both these factors significantly affect the child's observed social behaviour.

Even in studies without the problems outlined above, direct comparisons of a child's behaviour with his or her mother and peers is not without its difficulties. Aside from the obvious difference in ages, mothers are likely to be the most familiar social figure to the young child, and to interact with the child in ways which are very different from his or her peers. The mother tends to play a dominant, interpretive role in her early relationships with the child, and purely social interchanges are less common than with peers (Vandell & Wilson, 1982). The child's level of skill appears relatively sophisticated because of the interaction skills of the mother. In similar vein, apparent skill with peers is significantly affected by the level of competence and sociability of any peer (Vandell & Wilson, 1982).

To examine in more detail the extent to which a child's peer relationships originate in the relationship with the mother, it is necessary to consider the functions that these skills serve in these different relationships. This is examined in the next section.

The uses of skills

An important issue in the transferability of skills concerns the functions that these behaviours are supposed to serve. Although some individual behaviours are common to both domains, and a correlation in their frequency in both domains suggests some relationship (Vandell, 1980), several researchers have examined a variety of specific social behaviours as well as the frequency and structure of interactions and found no evidence that social skills emerged first in interaction with the mother and only later with peers (e.g. Vandell & Wilson, 1982; Bakeman & Adamson, 1984, 1986).

From only a few weeks of age infants behave differently from mothers and strange peers (Fogel, 1979). When alone with the mother the infant appears relaxed and shows varied and finely detailed patterns of behaviour. In contrast, behaviour to a strange peer generally involves gross movements of the arms and body. This existence and use of different sets of skills with mothers and peers appears to be maintained through later childhood, possibly reflecting the different nature and purposes served by each of these relationships. For example, when both mothers and unfamiliar peers are available, infants were more likely to look at and vocalise to peers and more likely to touch and remain close to the mother (Vandell, 1980). In older children rough and tumble play is likely to be mainly with peers but the parent is still sought for nurturance and security.

Common skills

Despite the differences in the patterns of the child's parent and peer interactions, it does also appear that some patterns of social behaviour are common to both relationships. As Lamb & Nash (1989) conclude, children appear to use whatever skills they have available with whatever partner.

Skills and experience in all social domains are likely to affect each other (Hay, 1985).

Even newborn babies can show a synchronisation of their behaviour with that of an adult. For example, they can synchronise their head movement with the approach or withdrawal of an adult's head (Peery, 1980). These routines are typically relatively common experiences to the child. Through these interactions both the caregiver and child learn to be responsive and to synchronise their behaviour. The child comes to understand that the other person's attention or responses are contingent on his or her own behaviour and that as this mutual synchrony is mastered relationships become more satisfying for both partners.

These early synchronised interactions serve an important basis for learning the rules of later interaction. The mother's role in these early interactions has been termed scaffolding (Bruner & Sherwood, 1976). Scaffolding is a phenomenon more common with parents than with peers or siblings (Vandell & Wilson, 1987), it provides a framework within which social interaction can take place and facilitates the development of the child's interactional skills. Scaffolding will typically take the form of parents responding to the child's social and non-social acts in ways that promote further responses from the infant. For example, in a game of peek-a-boo the child may initially play a rather passive role as the mother hides and then reappears and shows surprise, but as the child becomes more sophisticated she or he becomes an increasingly active and enthusiastic participant. Infants with more extensive scaffolding and turn-taking experience with their parents are more likely to engage in similar turn-taking interactions with their peers (Vandell & Wilson, 1987).

Patterns of adaptation

The studies examined in the preceding sections paint a clear picture of the effects of different types of early attachment on later functioning in peer relationships. The child that was anxiously attached as an infant is likely to demonstrate continuity in his or her patterns of adaptation to playmates in preschool. In later peer relationships the child still comes laden with the baggage of his or her own history. "We cannot assume that early experiences will somehow be cancelled by later experience. Lasting consequences of early inadequate experience may be subtle and complex . . . But there will be consequences" (Sroufe, 1979).

Anxiously attached children are likely to show lower levels of social competence and to present behaviour problems (Erickson, Sroufe & Egeland, 1985). Children with anxious–avoidant attachments tend to be hostile and negative, distant, and not seek teachers even if injured or otherwise stressed

(Sroufe, 1983). A study by Troy & Sroufe (1987) even suggests that the presence of victimisation in preschooler dyads is associated with a history of avoidant attachment; bullying appears to reflect characteristic relationships histories for both the victim and the victimiser (Olweus, 1980). Anxious–resistant children show ineptness in peer interaction, more chronic low-level helplessness and dependency, and be constantly near or orientated to the teacher (Sroufe, 1983). They often score higher than anxious–avoidant or securely attached children on measures of social dominance and social participation, but their impulsive behaviour is less effective in that they are also likely to be rated lowest in peer status (LaFreniere & Sroufe, 1985).

A long-term study that has followed some children for over a decade has found that these differences in social competence are relatively stable characteristics. Ten year olds with a background of secure attachment scored significantly higher on "ego-resiliency", self confidence, and an overall measure of competence; they scored significantly lower on dependence, were less often isolated and less likely to be the passive recipients of aggression (Sroufe & Jacobvitz, 1989). This shows a considerable degree of consistency with the earlier findings from the study of 3–5 year olds.

Attachment and relationships in adolescence and adulthood

Although most research looking at the consequences of parental attachments for peer relationships has focused on preschoolers and children of elementary school age, the findings of this body of research do seem to be consistent with the existing research on adolescents. Attachment to parents does appear to promote competence in adolescence and ultimately in adulthood. Adolescence is a time of rapid expansion of the individual's social world. Although it is a period where great significance is invested in the peer group, parents none the less continue to provide an anchor for adaptive exploration and effective coping with the many new and conflicting demands that are experienced (Cooper & Ayers-Lopez, 1985). Quality of relationships with parents may continue to be more important for well-being than those with peers, and maternal support is a major factor in the adolescent's self-esteem (Greenberg, Siegel & Leitch, 1983). In a study of late adolescents, Kobak & Sceery (1988) found first-year college students classed as having secure attachment were rated as less anxious, more "ego resilient", and less hostile by their peers, and perceived their relations with family and friends as more supportive. In a study by Gold & Yanof (1985) adolescent girls that identified strongly with their mothers were also more likely to have the best same-sex peer relationships.

Another line of research on post-infant attachment has focused on romantic love. A model of romantic love based on the idea that romantic attachments parallel the secure, anxious–ambivalent, and avoidant types of child–parent attachments was proposed by Hazan & Shaver (1987). They reported that the relative frequency of these three styles of attachment are approximately the same in adults and infants. Subsequent studies have largely confirmed a relationship between these self-reported attachment styles and the subjective experience of love (Feeney & Noller, 1991), though refinements have also been proposed in the theoretical analysis. One development, by Bartholomew (1990), suggested that styles of attachment could be conceptualised in terms of two underlying dimensions: the individual's model of Self and Other. This opens the door to the suggestion that for many purposes it is more useful to think of attachment in terms of a relative placement on these two dimensions rather than simply a small number of types such as secure or insecure (Brennan, Shaver & Tobey, 1991). While such typologies are easier to deal in diagnostic and social policy terms, they undoubtedly obscure some of the rich variety of forms that attachment takes.

The ways in which adults describe their childhood attachments and their experience of love show impressive parallels. But we must be cautious in how we interpret this evidence. Two closely related problems prevent the simple conclusion that a child's early attachments establish a pattern for his or her later romantic relationships. First, the evidence for a direct continuity rather than simply a similarity between patterns of childhood attachment and romantic love is sparse. Second, there are problems with relying on people's recollections of childhood relationships. Experiences in current relationships may well colour our memories of earlier relationships (Miller, 1989). At the very least it seems likely that our perceptions of current and past relationships affect *each other*.

The above lines of research show the increasing influence of attachment concepts on our general thinking about personal relationships across the whole lifespan. These developments in attachment theory and research are important for at least two reasons. First, they establish important continuity to our understanding of relationships. Second, they establish important connections and hence open up new bodies of literature to research in each of the previously discrete area of research.

The primary role of the attachment relationship

Depending on which textbook you read you will probably be left with one of two impressions. One view is that it is well established that the attachment relationship to a large extent determines subsequent peer relationships. Alan Sroufe is a convincing exponent of this view and, as we have seen, there is indeed substantial evidence that can be cited to support this conclusion. An alternative view argues that this conclusion is premature, that there are methodological problems with many of the studies that lead to this conclusion, and that the role of other factors, most notably the child's temperament, can account for many of the reported findings (Lamb & Nash, 1989). Lewis & Feiring (1989) conclude that "In general, the theoretical belief that early infant–mother security of attachment relates to later friendship patterns is not well supported by the empirical findings" (p. 250). As you will gather if you compare this quotation with those from Sroufe that are mentioned in this chapter, the debate over the impact of attachment on later relationships is far from settled.

The study by Jacobson & Wille (1986) has been cited as empirical evidence that does *not* show a relationship between attachment security and later peer relationships (Lewis & Feiring, 1989). If, however, this study is examined carefully, it actually appears supportive of a link between attachment status and quality of later peer relationships. Jacobson & Wille (1986) present data showing that early attachment affects the behaviour of children in such a way as to influence their attractiveness as a partner for interaction. By age three, securely attached children were more attractive and more positively responded to by their peers than were insecurely attached children; anxiously attached children received either fewer positive responses or more disruptive responses and peer resistance. Although this study has been severely criticised on methodological grounds (Lamb & Nash, 1989), its results appear to be at best supportive of a link between attachment security and later peer relationships, or at worst are ambiguous rather than negative.

A more subtle criticism of research on the maternal precursor hypothesis is Hartup's (1986) observation that it has largely attempted to establish a connection between a child's early relations and his or her individual characteristics later in life – rather than the form and functioning of later relationships (smoothness, stability, mutuality); this latter connection is considerably less clear. This is valid point which future research should address, though it does not detract from the findings of existing research which indicate that attachment experiences does influence the individual's ability and motivation in relationships later in life. Indeed, no simple correspondence in the form or functions of relating across the lifespan need necessarily be expected. Previous relationships affect current relationships because they affect the individual's subjective model of relationships. In Sroufe & Fleeson's (1986) eminently quotable words, "It is assumed that relationships are not constructed afresh, nor are new relationships based on the simple transfer of particular responses from old relationships. Instead, it is assumed that previous relationships exert their influence through the attitudes, expectations and understanding of roles that they leave with the individual" (p. 53).

Later attachment

As children progress beyond infancy and through the early years of childhood there are notable advances in their physical and cognitive abilities and these appear to be mirrored in an expanding social interest and ability. In the one year old, proximity seeking is a prime indicator of attachment. In the following year or two children are considerably more mobile and can talk sufficiently to base their attachment on more subtle, distant forms of contact. During the preschool years the overall level of proximity-seeking behaviour declines. Simple perspective-taking abilities and improved communication skills enable something of the meaning and reasons for separation to be taken into account and hence lessen its impact. As these abilities become more sophisticated and the children's confidence in them increases so does their tolerance of separation (Ainsworth, 1989). Most children are now comfortable playing on their own in another room, though attachment is still clearly shown in the patterning of behaviour, such as greetings, and at times of stress when these young children will still seek out the parents for succour. Even six year olds can be reliably rated for security of attachment based on their behaviour during a reunion after a brief separation from the parents. The attachment classifications obtained by this method correlate with strange situation test assessments of the child as an infant (Main & Cassidy, 1988), and with the child's competence at school (Cohn, 1990).

At elementary school age, involvement with peers becomes markedly more important for the child and considerably less time is spent with the parents (Hill & Stafford, 1980). Attachment behaviours become less physical, less dependent on proximity, and more subtle. Older children are able to take the attachment bond for granted, they understand the significance of time and distance in relationships, and do not become overly concerned about the non-immediate accessibility of parents (Bowlby, 1965). Freed from the worries about the permanence of the parental attachment, children are now able to direct their energies to relationships outside the home. From 9–19 years of age, levels of intimacy and social support from the parents declines while that with peers increases. As levels of tension in the parent–child relationship increase and ultimately peak in early to mid-adolescence, relationships with parents become increasingly concerned with routine matters, such as the management of time and behaviour rather than attachment (Hunter & Youniss, 1982; Furman & Buhrmester, 1992).

Despite the presence of competing peer attractions, the continuing importance of parental attachments throughout childhood should not be discounted. Parental attachments remain of paramount, if less obvious, importance throughout childhood. This is clearly revealed in exceptional circumstances, for example homesickness. Throughout childhood parents are still seen as a consistently high source of nurturance, and quality of attachment to parents seems to be more closely related to a sense of well-being and happiness than is quality of relationships with peers (Greenberg, Siegel & Leitch, 1983). Though the increasing autonomy and independence of later adolescence and early adulthood does reduce the monopolistic significance of parental attachments in the individual's life, it is doubtful that it is ever fully relinquished (Ainsworth, 1989). Unfortunately research on attachment in older age groups has proved difficult due to problems in establishing universal criteria by which it can be assessed and of establishing that later criteria are still measuring the same construct as the earlier strange situation criteria.

No relationship is an island . . .

As already noted, to a large extent research on attachment has focused on the mother–infant relationship and has paid relatively little attention to the roles of other social figures. And yet it is now becoming widely acknowledged that it is unwise to consider the mother–infant relationship outside of its broader socioemotional and economic contexts (Cohn, Patterson & Christopoulos, 1991). For example, marital tensions may leave mothers more negatively orientated toward their infants, or alternatively seeking compensatory satisfaction in the parental role (Belsky, 1981).

The child's relationships with the mother and peers are also likely to be reciprocally influencing (Lamb & Nash, 1989). Children with experience of peers in a playgroup show changes in their patterns of relationships with their parents. These children become both more socially sensitive and responsive to their parents and more likely to assume the initiative in opening an encounter (Vandell, 1979).

Relationships exist not only in relation to other current relationships but also in the context of previous relationships. A number of studies are now starting to accumulate evidence about cross-generational effects on attachment and parenting styles. For example, mothers experiencing major difficulties with their toddlers are themselves likely to have had poor relations with their parents (Frommer & O'Shea, 1973). In an interesting study by Main, Kaplan & Cassidy (1985), the parents of infants whose attachment had been determined by the strange situation test were interviewed to ascertain their working models of attachment. Parents perceiving their earlier relationships as secure also tended to have a secure attachment with their own children; infant avoidance of parents following a separation was related to the parents' reports of rejection in their own childhoods. Resistance in the mother–child relationship was associated with continuing anger and conflict about the mother's own parents. Parents from a background of neglect or abuse may themselves be inclined to misinterpret natural infant behaviours as difficult or rejecting and be at risk for mistreating their child (Youngblade & Belsky, 1989). Despite the many criticisms and alternative explanations which could be raised against many of these findings, they serve to highlight important questions and concerns for anyone interested in the welfare of children.

Child rearing patterns and children's social behaviour

The impact of the parents' behaviour on the child extends considerably beyond the formation of the primary attachments, though beyond the first year the character of their relationship with the child changes considerably. As the child becomes more mobile, better able to regulate his or her own behaviour, and independent, the parents are less dominant and all-encompassing as the initiators of interaction and the suppliers of care and entertainment (Maccoby & Martin, 1983). They start to increasingly feature as teachers of rules and standards of behaviour. Erikson (1963) terms the task or crisis at this psychosocial stage of development as being autonomy versus shame and doubt. Autonomy, initiative and feelings of competence are increasingly important to the child and yet must also be limited to the bounds of social propriety. Excesses in either direction are likely to leave their permanent mark on the child.

In a study of three- and four-year-olds Baumrind (1967) found that the child-rearing styles of parents were closely related to the characteristic behaviour patterns of their children. Three groups of children were initially distinguished on the basis of their patterns of self-control, approach avoidance tendencies, self-reliance, subjective mood, and peer affiliation tendencies. The parenting styles of these children was then contrasted in terms of levels of parental control, maturity demands, nurturance, and parent–child communication. Three main styles of parenting were distinguished, though in terms of their characteristic levels of responsiveness and control they actually represent a continuum. These three broad styles of parenting have been termed: authoritarian, authoritative, and permissive (Baumrind, 1971). However, if parental styles are reflecting two independent intersecting dimensions, levels of parental control and levels of parental responsiveness, then one would expect four rather than three types of parenting to be possible. A logical extension of Baumrind's typology has been the addition of a further class of permissive parenting, the neglecting type (Maccoby & Martin, 1983).

The significance of these various styles of parenting is their implication for the future styles of behaviour and adjustment of the child. They teach both specific skills and patterns of social problem solving (Pettit et al., 1991). These various styles of parenting and their consequences will be examined next. The interested reader may also wish to compare these descriptions with those outlined for the various types of attachment. The effects from these two sources are undoubtedly closely connected. This should not be surprising, as we have already emphasised the crucial role of the caregiver's behaviour in the formation of attachments. Indeed, later maternal behaviour is related to and predictable on the basis of earlier assessments of attachment (Matas, Arend & Sroufe, 1978).

Authoritarian parenting

Authoritarian parents are typified as "detached and controlling, and somewhat less warm than other parents" (Baumrind, 1971, p. 2). They are likely to establish an immutable and broad set of rules and codes of behaviour which must be strictly and unquestioningly obeyed. These rules are not open to negotiation and violations are likely to be punished. Compliance appears to be a more important goal for the parents than the persuasion of a rightful argument. The emphasis on the power differential in the relationship and a lack of responsiveness can detract from the warmth expressed in this style of parenting. This lack of warmth in the parent–child relationship may then in turn produce a child with low self-esteem, moodiness and anxieties about social comparison. The lack of personal initiative afforded the child by the parents can also result in a child that is isolated and has difficulties in initiating and maintaining social interaction with peers (Attili, 1989).

The use of power assertive discipline or the withdrawal of love may also lead to a self-centred orientation which inhibits prosocial behaviour and fosters aggression and hostility (Brody & Shaffer, 1982; Parke & Slaby, 1983). If the use of discipline is not skilfully managed the child can become anxious and timid, or alternatively aggressive and uncontrolled (Patterson, 1986). This style of parental control has significant cognitive as well as behavioural ramifications. Children experiencing power assertive styles of discipline actually expect their unfriendly, assertive methods of resolving peer conflicts (such as threatening to hit the other child) to be successful (Hart, Ladd & Burleson, 1990). And, of course, the child who expects such a strategy to work is hardly likely to try an alternative.

Authoritative parenting

This a flexible, responsive and nurturant style of parenting. Authoritative parents are "controlling and demanding; but they were also warm, rational and receptive to the child's communication" (Baumrind, 1971, p. 1). This style encourages independence but within a framework of discipline. Necessary limits and expectations are explained and justified, though these may be questioned by the child or even renegotiated. Within these parameters compliance with the spirit of any restrictions is expected and, if necessary, enforced non-punitively. Aggression and antisocial behaviour are discouraged; transgressions are discussed, with appropriate consideration of changes in future behaviour and restitution for current damages. This style of parenting promotes high self-esteem; the child learns to be questioning but responsible and friendly, to relate to others and take account of their view, and to be independent, responsible, and socially resilient. These parenting characteristics and the positive, prosocial characteristics they promote in children have been associated with later psychological well-being, social adjustment and peer popularity (Roopnarine, 1987).

Permissive parenting

Permissiveness resulting from the parents' indulgence of the child is "noncontrolling, nondemanding, and relatively warm" (Baumrind, 1971, p. 2). The parent is accepting and responsive to the child, but imposes relatively few limits and controls. One possible consequence of this is that even aggressive, impulsive behaviour is condoned. Rebelliousness has been treated as acceptable and the child learns little regard for rules and standards of behaviour. Such uncontrolled and possibly aggressive behaviour is likely to be highly aversive to peers and so these children are often unpopular or rejected. An alternative outcome of indulgent, overprotective parenting, especially of boys, may be that children are sociable but overdependent and reserved with peers, constantly seeking the approval of adults (Kagan & Moss, 1962).

The neglecting style of parenting accords a permissiveness that stems from a large degree of indifference and unresponsiveness to the child on the part of the parent. In extreme cases this culminates in physical abuse and psychological hostility toward the child (Egeland & Sroufe, 1981). More than any other style of parenting, the neglecting parent is associated with consistently negative outcomes in many areas of psychological functioning. Maltreated children may become self-blaming and even justify the way they are treated by their parents on the basis of their own bad behaviour (Dean et al., 1986). These children are likely to show low self-esteem, aggressiveness and disobedience, and to be more impulsive and moody as adolescents. In extreme cases the psychological unavailabilty of the mother culminates in "increasing deficits in all aspects of psychological functioning by age 2" (Maccoby & Martin, 1983, p. 49). The implications of this style of parenting, if such it can be termed, are potentially devastating.

Conclusion

Research on the impact of early attachment on future peer relationships is relatively sparse. This is unfortunate, though interest in the area does appear to be increasing rapidly. What evidence does exist highlights the potential significance of the child's early relationship with the caregiver. Warm, responsive parenting early in life, and continuing into later childhood, appear to be crucial influences on the child's social orientation and expectations of relationships. Current relationships are not constructed in isolation but are coloured by other past and present relationships.

2 Social cognition and person perception

Intimacy implies not only revelations of self and tenderness but also a
reasonably subtle set of social inference processes and role-taking abilities.
(Hill & Palmquist, 1978, p. 27)

A fundamental principle emphasised by many psychologists has been that social behaviour is mediated by perceptual and cognitive processes, by the child's interpretation of social cues (e.g. Dodge et al., 1986). These interpretations allow children to control their social world by enabling them to predict the behaviour of others, control their own behaviour, and regulate social interactions. The basis for an individual's actions cannot be fully understood without taking these social cognitive processes into account. A simple example will make this point clearer: if a child interprets a second child's behaviour as friendly then she or he is likely to respond to it differently than if she or he interprets exactly the same behaviour as aggressive or accidental. From a psychological perspective an important task is to understand the bases for these different interpretations and the consequent decisions regarding appropriate action. It is to issues such as these that this chapter is addressed. Social cognition is concerned with "how children conceptualize other people and how they come to understand the thoughts, emotions, intentions, and viewpoints of others" (Shantz, 1975, p. 258).

In the study of children's peer relationships three interrelated aspects of social cognitive development stand out as having received special attention and it is on these that this chapter will focus. The first topic, empathy and role-taking, emphasises the importance of being able to see objects and events from another's point of view if one is to relate to them effectively. The second topic concerns the child's level of understanding of the concept of friendship, the rules, obligations, and benefits of the relationship. This will affect whether the actions of others are interpreted as friendly and hence significantly influence the subsequent course of a relationship. The third topic is concerned with the attributions children make for the causes of social behaviour. The determination of intentionality, that a behaviour or act was freely chosen and not due simply to luck or circumstances, is a crucial factor in evaluating another's behaviour relative to the expectations and obligations associated with friendship. In combination these three topics emphasise that to relate to others successfully the child must acknowledge their independent perspective and interests, possess expectations or criteria to distinguish friendship behaviour from other social behaviour, and be able to understand the causes of their behaviour to the extent that this affects its interpretation.

Empathy

Empathy has been defined in various ways. Most current conceptions emphasise that empathy consists of both a cognitive and an affective component, though some authors do give more emphasis to one aspect or the other (Feshbach, 1978). It is the affective component that distinguishes empathy from role-taking. A role-taking ability is necessary for full empathic understanding, but they are by no means the same phenomenon. Three main compdnents of empathy have been distinguished (Feshbach, 1978): (1) the ability to discriminate and label the affective states of others, (2) the ability to assume another's perspective and role, and (3) an emotional capacity and responsiveness. Empathy is the ability of the child to match his or her own feelings with those of another person, though this does not imply that she or he necessarily experiences the same emotion. On some occasions we do indeed experience emotion alongside another person, but equally we sometimes simply imagine their feelings (Harris, 1989). With equal levels of understanding there are marked variations in empathy. For example, it is likely to be greater toward others of the same age, sex, or ethnic background (Feshbach, 1978). This distinction would seem to indicate the utility of distinguishing between an affective role-taking ability and empathy, though Harris simply uses it to argue that empathy is a stance rather than any deep insight. A useful working definition that emphasises the affective nature of empathic understanding, but does not limit it to the experience of identical emotions has been proposed by Hoffman (1987). This conceptualisation regards empathy as simply the experience of a similar or congruent emotion, as "an affective response more appropriate to someone else's situation than to one's own" (Hoffman, 1987, p. 48).

Empathy and cognition

Empathy plays a significant role in interpersonal communication, interaction and friendship formation. Establishing developmental changes in the nature of empathy has consequently been recognised as an important research task.

Simple empathy precedes a more sophisticated role-taking ability and forms the foundation from which it is differentiated. Egocentric children vicariously experiencing the arousal of others will be unable to distinguish it from their own arousal. In attempting to understand themselves and their own reactions they will consequently be learning to understand and distinguish themselves from others. Their arousal will provide initial cues about what others are feeling and motivate them to explore these further (Hoffman, 1981b). Cognition and affect are inextricably intertwined in empathy and the understanding of others. "Though an affect, empathy has a fundamental cognitive component . . . the level of empathy depends on the level of cognition; and empathy development corresponds, at least partly, to the development of a cognitive sense of others" (Hoffman, 1988, p. 509). Perhaps not surprisingly, studies of the development of empathy show that to a large extent it does mirror the general development of cognitive abilities. There is a gradual move from an emphasis on the immediate, superficial and obvious toward an emphasis on inference and abstract qualities. These social cognitive considerations form an important basis for Martin Hoffman's theory of the development of empathy, a major contribution to our understanding of the phenomenon. This theory will be examined in detail in due course.

Empathy as innate

It has been argued by Hoffman (1981a) that to the extent that prosocial behaviour facilitates social organisation and co-operation, and consequently has survival value, there is likely to be an evolutionary selection of individuals able to recognise and experience the emotions of others – in other words, to respond in an empathic manner. There is some evidence that a basic empathic ability is innate. A simple form of empathic responding is evident even in the newborn child. This is shown in a study by Sagi & Hoffman (1976). Infants less than 36 hours old listened either to another infant crying, to a computer simulation of the crying, or were left in silence. The young children that heard the real crying showed more physical agitation and crying than the children hearing the simulated crying or silence. These interesting results, which have been confirmed by Martin & Clark (1982), have significant implications. As Hoffman argues, the human cry is distinctive and recognisable to the human infant. More significantly, infants show (and Hoffman argues, feel) the distress of the other infant. To return to Hoffman's point about the evolutionary advantage of empathy, the contagion of a crying response could be an effective survival mechanism as it would be more likely to attract the attention of adults in times of distress and threat.

Further evidence that a basic empathic ability is innate comes from the study of twins. Identical (monozygotic) twins possess the same genetic make-up and so if empathy is innate they should show similar levels. Of course it is also conceivable that such twins have a different family and social experiences from non-twins, but research has often attempted to cancel out these environmental differences by making comparisons with fraternal (dizygotic) twins. In a study by Matthews et al. (1981) a test of empathic concern was given to 230 pairs of middle-aged fraternal and identical male twins. The identical twins showed moderately similar levels of empathic concern, there was little evidence of this in the fraternal twins. These results provide some support for the idea that empathy has a heritable component, though the evidence is far from conclusive. Although the twins had lived apart for many years they had none the less been raised together and so differences in the socialisation of identical twins could still account for the results of this study. For example, the parents of some identical twins dress their children the same and stress mutual interests and activities.

Development of empathy

The argument that there is an innate basis for empathy does not deny the fact that empathy also changes developmentally, due to differences in socialisation. With more sophisticated cognitive abilities and the ability to take another's perspective the children come to understand the basis of their empathic feelings more fully. In young children, role-taking abilities are limited and situational factors are the crucial determinants of empathic responding (Hughes, Tingle & Sawin, 1981). Children as young as three years of age can recognise the affective reactions of other people in simple, familiar situations (Borke, 1971), and preschoolers show more empathy with a peer made unhappy in a situation that they themselves have experienced (Barnett, 1984). This seems to be a primitive form of empathy possibly reflecting stereotypes or the child's memory of similar events that have happened to him or her and the associated emotional reactions. Older children show an increasing ability to use personal and psychological reasons rather than situational descriptions as the basis for their explanations of another's emotions and their own empathic responses.

A systematic attempt to account for the development of empathy has been provided by Hoffman (1988). This theory proposes that there are four stages in the development of empathic understanding. In the first year of life there is a global empathy, the automatic matching of emotion. For example, children often cry in response to hearing another infant crying. This stage reflects the very young children's lack of discrimination between themselves and others. Stage two of Hoffman's theory portrays the child of approximately 1–3 years old as displaying an egocentric empathy. Distress in others provokes a feeling of distress in the child him or herself. His or her attempt to alleviate the other's distress may consist of offering comfort in the form the child personally would seek. An example given by Hoffman is of an 18-month-old child fetching his own mother to comfort a crying companion even though the other child's mother was also present. The third stage lasts until adolescence and sees the emergence of a true empathic understanding of another's feelings. The other's feelings are partially matched and responses become increasingly subtle. This empathic ability becomes increasingly sophisticated over the primary school years and by middle childhood the child can cope with the simultaneous display of contradictory emotions. For example, a child may empathise with another's plight but also appreciate that in some circumstances the other would rather not be helped, perhaps because this would cause embarrassment. These apparently sophisticated reactions are still, however, limited to concrete situations. Observational studies of preadolescents often show a link between empathy and prosocial behaviour but also often fail to reveal such a link if hypothetical stories are used (Eisenberg & Miller, 1987). The final stage in the development of empathy, beginning in adolescence, brings with it a more general appreciation of the other's life experience. At this stage, a high level of empathic understanding gives the adolescent a deep-felt appreciation of the long-term effects and implications of an individual's life circumstances, such as the death of a family member, and there can also be empathic concern for entire groups or classes of people, such as the poor or handicapped. As relationships at this age increasingly emphasise intimacy and involvement, the level of empathic understanding of adolescents also has important implications for how their peers evaluate their social competence (Ford, 1982). Higher levels of empathic understanding are associated with greater popularity and more satisfying peer relationships. This is discussed in more detail later in this chapter.

Role-taking

Role-taking is an important basis for children's negotiation of their social reality, self-concept, and social relationships. A quarter of a century ago the child's role-taking abilities were regarded as minimal. As Flavell (1966, p. 164) noted, "Young children possess extremely rudimentary role-taking skills. Yet the ability to put oneself in another person's shoes is a prerequisite to effective social relations". More recent research sees the young child's abilities as considerably more sophisticated. Even young preschoolers are now recognised as having a basic understanding that another's perspective differs from their own. In a study by Denham (1986) many children of two and three years of age were correctly able to identify the emotions represented by puppets enacting a series of vignettes. In some of the vignettes the puppets expressed emotions in accord with the way most children would feel (e.g. fear during a nightmare) while in others they expressed the opposite emotions. Even in those instances where the displayed emotion was inappropriate the children were still relatively accurate in identifying it – though often emphasising that they wouldn't feel that way! Many other authors provide similar evidence that young children show at least a basic level of role-taking ability in their everyday life. This is shown, for example, by three year olds adapting the complexity of their speech when speaking to handicapped or younger children (Shatz & Gelman, 1973; Guralnick & Paul-Brown, 1984).

The culmination of cognitive developmental processes in role-taking is observed in adolescence – but with potential teething problems. As Elkind (1967) has noted, the onset of the capacity to think in terms of abstractions combined with new and sophisticated role-taking abilities often produce a period of egocentrism characterised by a failure to distinguish between the events to which the individual's own thoughts are directed and those to which the thoughts of others are directed. Many adolescents go through such a phase. Other people are seen as being as concerned with the individual's attributes as is the individual, and there is a lack of recognition that personal experiences have their counterpart in the experiences of others. This leads to heightened self-consciousness and concern about what others think. To young adolescents their zits are assumed to be of as much interest and concern to their social network as they are to themselves!

Selman's theory of role-taking

A number of theories of role-taking and social cognitive development have been proposed, the most detailed and influential of which is that of Robert Selman. Selman's theory is based on the notion that in order to understand and relate to others it is necessary to appreciate that they possess a different perspective from our own and to comprehend the relationship between these different perspectives. His research is unusual in being theory guided rather than data driven (Selman, 1981). Selman investigated the development of children's social cognitive abilities by means of a series of semi-structured interviews. Children were typically presented with a social dilemma, a story without an ending, and then led into a discussion around a set of key questions. This allowed the researchers to probe the meanings of answers given by children in response to the dilemmas rather than simply relying on their own interpretation of the simple responses. In short, it recognised that children of different ages often use the same words in an answer but intend to convey very different meanings. A sample dilemma and its associated key questions is presented below. In this case the sociomoral dilemma is for 4–10 year olds.

Holly is an 8-year-old girl who likes to climb trees. She is the best tree climber in the neighbourhood. One day while climbing down from a tall tree, she falls off the bottom branch but does not hurt herself. Her father sees her fall. He is upset and asks her to promise not to climb trees any more. Holly promises.

Later that day, Holly and her friends meet Shawn. Shawn's kitten is caught up in a tree and can't get down. Something has to be done right away, or the kitten may fall. Holly is the only one who climbs trees well enough to reach the kitten and get it down, but she remembers her promise to her father.

The role-taking questions for this dilemma were:

1. Does Holly know how Shawn feels about the kitten?
2. How will Holly's father feel if he finds out she climbed the tree?
3. What does Holly think her father will do if he finds out that she climbed the tree?
4. What would you do in this situation?

(Selman, 1976, p. 302)

Stages in the development of role-taking

Based on his extensive research Selman (1976) proposed a five-stage model of the development of children's social cognitive understanding, which he has also applied specifically to the understanding of friendship (Selman, 1980). These are outlined briefly below. For further detail and discussion of these developmental stages and their implications see Robert Selman's (1980) excellent book *The Growth of Interpersonal Understanding*.

Stage 0 Egocentric role-taking (approximately 4–6 years of age). The child is unable to distinguish his or her perspective from that of another (e.g. that of Holly in the story).

Stage 1 Social–informational role-taking (approximately 6–8 years of age). The child recognises that another will have a different perspective to him or herself if they are in a situation but is still unable to consider both perspectives simultaneously. The child considers that with appropriate information another person will also come to the same "correct" view. When asked if Holly's father would be angry if he found out that she had climbed the tree a child at stage 1 might well reply that he would if he did not know her reason for doing so but with appropriate explanation would understand her reasons.

Stage 2 Self-reflective role-taking (approximately 8–10 years of age). The child understands that each individual has a unique perspective due to his or her personal values and orientation. A major development marking this stage is the child's ability to reflect on his or her own behaviour from the other's perspective or to reflect on a relationship from an outsider's perspective. A child at this stage would appreciate that different fathers would react differently to the situation outlined in the Holly story.

Stage 3 Mutual role-taking (approximately 10–12 years of age). At this stage the child is able to recognise the relationship of his or her own social perspective to that of some average group member and can adopt a metaperspective – i.e. can appreciate that others are aware of what his or her view is.

Stage 4 Social and conventional system role-taking (from approximately age 12–15 years and over). At this stage the child shows an ability to take into account general social considerations, rules and norms and can reflect on these. Others are recognised as complex and subjective but also as possessing organised and consistent patterns of personality and behaviour.

Research has confirmed that level of role-taking ability does correlate with age and that these stages do form a true developmental sequence. To investigate the sequential invariance of these stages, Gurucharri & Selman (1982) analysed the data from 41 children that had been followed for a period of five years, from initial ages ranging between six and twelve years. Results supported Selman's hypothesised order of developmental levels. Over the five-year period all the children showed an increase in their level of social cognition. There was a sequential progression through the stages and children that lagged at one point of testing were likely to make up any shortfall by a subsequent time of testing.

Role-taking and other abilities

A considerable amount of research has noted cross-domain continuities in the development of social-cognitive abilities, logical abilities, and social skills. There is an increasing acknowledgement that social development and cognitive development do not simply develop in parallel but are inextricably intertwined and reciprocally influencing (Kohlberg, 1969; Piaget, 1977). Through working together children are able to perform cognitive operations which were beyond each child's individual abilities. This is consequently an important means of acquiring new cognitive operations (Doise & Mugny, 1984). Conversely, a child's level of cognitive development is an important determinant of his or her social behaviour, such as types of play (Rubin & Maioni, 1975). To further examine this issue of mutual influences on development it is first

necessary to briefly outline a major influence on thinking in these areas –
Piaget's theory of cognitive development.

· In Piaget's (1970) theory, termed Genetic Epistemology, a series of
cognitive developmental stages are outlined. The child below about six or
seven years of age (i.e. at the level of preoperational thinking) is seen as
egocentric, as unable to take the perspective of another or to go beyond the
superficial and most salient perceptual aspects of a situation. In the
appropriate terminology, the child is unable to decentre. By contrast, as the
egocentrism of the preoperational child gives way to concrete operational
thinking these abilities become evident and the child shows conservation, a
concept of invariance despite changes in appearance, and a better ability to
classify aspects of his or her world. The final stage in Piaget's theory, formal
operational thinking, goes beyond immediate, concrete reality and allows
the child to think in more abstract terms, in terms of hypothetical possibilities.

Research has examined the continuity between various logical and social
cognitive abilities. For example, a study by Rubin (1973) found that the ability
to decentre formed the basis of a high interrelationship among a set of
measures including conservation, role-taking, and communicative, cognitive,
and spatial egocentrism. Despite the complexity of the notion of intelligence,
there is also a correlation between this construct and role-taking ability (e.g.
Pellegrini, 1985a).

Empirical studies also show the stages of friendship reasoning outlined
Selman to be closely related to, but not identical with, a child's level of
cognitive development (Keller & Wood, 1989). In a study by Keating & Clark
(1980), a direct comparison was made between the child's cognitive
developmental level and level of role-taking ability. Eighteen out of 22 (82%)
subjects categorised as being at Piaget's stage of concrete operational thinking
were at Selman's social–informational or self-reflective stages of role-taking.
This is roughly what might be expected. One would also expect that children
at the level of advanced concrete operational thinking or early formal
operational thinking would be at Selman's stages three and four (self-reflective
and social and conventional system role-taking) and for 84 out of 121 subjects
(69%) this held true – 31 (26%) of the remaining subjects were still at the
self-reflective stage of role-taking. Finally, one would expect that subjects
with well-established formal operational thinking would be at Selman's level
four, social and conventional role-taking. Four out of eight subjects (50%)
were, a further three (38%) were at the preceding stage of mutual role-taking.
Overall these results suggest a close affinity between general cognitive
development and interpersonal role-taking ability but they also suggest that
it is appropriate to regard these as separate and distinct domains. The
relatively weaker relationship for later stages of development than for earlier
stages reflect that, beyond a minimum level, factors other than simply
cognitive processing ability are significant for performance in interpersonal

role-taking. As Muss (1982, p. 501) concluded, "At this point we are not justified in assuming that cognitive problem-solving skills can easily be transferred and applied to social problem-solving skills".

Methodological considerations

The meaning of many studies of role-taking is unclear because of methodological problems. Studies have shown the association between various role-taking skills to be very variable (Kurdek & Rodgon, 1975), which demonstrates the complex nature of the construct and the potential for bias due to a number of task demands and subject characteristics. Studies by Pellegrini (1985a) and Keller & Wood (1989) report that subject characteristics such as social class can have a marked effect on role-taking performance.

Comparisons of several widely used role-taking tasks have found consistent and marked differences in their difficulty (Kurdek, 1977). Many role-taking tasks possess poor convergent validity (do not correlate well with other role-taking tasks), and two widely used tasks that have been examined in detail, those of Rothenberg (1970) and Chandler (1973), even showed low levels of internal consistency (Rubin, 1978). In short, role-taking ability measured by one task is not especially predictive of role-taking ability as measured by a second, different task, and some tasks appear to be measuring more than one ability!

Subsequent research has attempted to model and delineate the potential multiplicity of factors that contribute to social role-taking. In an experimental examination of Selman's model, Schofield & Kafer (1985) found that the difficulty of a role-taking task was affected by the familiarity and concreteness of the situations presented in role-play dilemmas. The authors used these findings to question a strict form of Selman's structural–developmental approach and argued that they are more consistent with a gradual generalisation of social cognitive abilities, moving from an ability to use the skills in only familiar and concrete situations to being able to apply them even in abstract and unfamiliar situations.

It appears that there is more to role-taking than simply reducing egocentrism. A lack of egocentrism is a necessary but not a sufficient condition for the demonstration of role-taking skill. It is to some aspects of the child's social experience that we now turn in order to examine their relationship to the development of role-taking skills. As the extant literature indicates that social interaction and social cognition represent reciprocal influences, each will be examined in turn. First, the effects of social interaction on the development of role-taking abilities, and then the influence of social cognition and role-taking on the child's social behaviour and relationships.

Social interaction and the development of role-taking

In his book *The Moral Judgement of the Child* Piaget (1977) argues that play is a crucial factor in the development of a child's role-taking abilities. Rubin & Pepler (1980) review evidence relating to this position and also conclude that fantasy and thematic play do indeed promote improvements in role-taking skills. The equal status of peers allows differences in perspective to be aired, and playing different roles highlights discrepancies in perspective which must be resolved if play is to continue.

Some basic evidence for the importance of social interaction in the development of role-taking comes from research by Bridgeman (1981). In this study fifth graders worked interdependently in six-person groups that required the co-operation and participation of all group members to achieve study goals. After eight weeks these children showed improved role-taking skills; children taught by other methods showed no such increase. This shows the potential cognitive benefits of peer interaction, though other research suggests that some forms of contact and types of relationship are better than others at promoting role-taking.

In a study by Nelson & Aboud (1985) third and fourth graders were formed into pairs of either friends or non-friend acquaintances. The social knowledge of each child was then individually assessed in a pre-test requiring answers to six moral dilemmas on interpersonal issues. For example, one dilemma was "What is the right thing to do if a boy [girl] much smaller than you starts to fight with you?" The pairs of children were then required to discuss one of the issues. Friends were more critical of their partners than were non-friends, and provided more explanation of their position. After the discussion each child was individually interviewed to note any change in their solution to the moral dilemma. Results indicated that initial disagreement on the solution to the dilemma produced a greater level of change in solutions than did initial agreement. There was no marked difference in the amount of change for friendship versus non-friendship groups, though there were qualitative differences in the changes observed. Friends were more likely to change to more mature solutions than were non-friends. At least part of the basis for this effect seems to be due to the fact that either partner is likely to change solutions in the non-friend pairs whereas in the friend pairings it is likely to be the partner with the less mature solution that changes. Conflict with friends provides an important driving force which helps children to realise the limits of their outlook and develop more mature social problem-solving skills.

Social cognition, communication, and social relations

Empirical attempts to establish the relationship between social cognitive abilities, communication, and other social variables have made considerable headway in recent years. Over a series of studies a group of researchers have produced a compelling outline of the possible patterns of relationship between a number of variables and children's peer relationships (Applegate et al., 1985; Burleson, Delia & Applegate, 1990; Clark & Jones, 1990; Delia & Applegate, 1990). The variables examined included social class, maternal and child social cognitive abilities, maternal and child communication quality, and children's peer relationships.

If the results of the above studies are combined, an interesting picture of the role of social cognition in children's peer relationships emerges. Social class primarily exerted its effect through the mother's social cognitive development, her perceptions of social contexts and peoples. Maternal social cognitive skills in turn directly predicted the quality of communication with the child, it was positively related to the mother's use of reflection-enhancing modes of discipline and nurturance (encouraging the child to reflect on the consequences of actions and the psychological qualities of others). Quality of maternal communication, the use of reflection-enhancing messages, was in turn related to the child's social cognitive skills. The child's social cognitive skills then predicted his or her level of person-centred, adaptive communication which predicted success in peer relations. This account serves an important function in emphasising that the role of social cognition in children's peer relationships can only be understood in its dynamic social and historical context.

Though the above account is an important step forward in our understanding of the origins of social cognitive influences on children's peer relationships, it also serves to highlight how much more research remains to be done. Most of the above pattern of relationships between variables was established in young school-children, it is conceivable that it will show developmental changes. For example, in their study of first and third graders Burleson, Delia & Applegate (1990) found maternal communication predicted children's communication skills and peer acceptance over the two years of his study. In the second year of the study the child's own communication skills predicted peer acceptance. The authors suggested that this indicates the increasing significance of the child's skills as these improve; maternal behaviour was most predictive in younger children.

Effects of role-taking on social relationships

This chapter has argued that role-taking and empathy are closely related to other aspects of social functioning. Dramatic changes are evident in children's peer relationships as their role-taking skills develop. It is to an examination of these changes that we now turn, a more detailed consideration of the role of social cognitive factors in relation to social skills and the structuring of ongoing social interaction is given in Chapter 4.

As children's role-taking abilities improve, so they are able to sustain increasingly sophisticated forms of friendship. The stages in the development of role-taking outlined by Selman (1980) can be used to provide a characterisation of children's patterns of friendship at different developmental stages. As Selman's work shows, the young egocentric child, at stage zero of social role-taking, will see his or her friends simply as people who live nearby or are playmates. At stage one the child is able to recognise that his playmates have different emotions and intentions. A friend becomes anyone trying to do nice things for another. By stage two the child recognises that friendship implies a reciprocal relationship, sharing, mutual respect, kindness and affection. The pre-adolescent at stage three has an awareness of the personality and preferences of the peers and a friend becomes a person with similar interests and values, someone with whom there is mutual support and the sharing of intimate, personal information. Finally, the young adolescent at stage four is entering an era in which relationships show both interdependence and intimacy, and yet also a respect for the other's autonomy. The general picture is of children's friendships becoming increasingly selective and increasingly other-centred with age.

Research on children in grades three to eight has confirmed a correlation between their level of interpersonal understanding (social role-taking) and popularity (e.g. Spence, 1987), though this effect is weaker for groups below this age range (Le Mare & Rubin, 1987). Greater sophistication on role-taking skills is also associated with an ability to maintain close friendships. Children with friends show higher levels of affective role-taking than those without friends (McGuire & Weisz, 1982).

The better ability of good role-takers to infer the needs of others and consequently to have the option to respond more flexibly in role performance explains their social success and popularity. They appear more similar and rewarding to those with whom they interact. This is rather neatly shown in a study by Hudson, Forman & Brion-Meisels (1982). Second-grade children classified as having high or low role-taking ability were videotaped teaching two same-sex kindergarten children how to make caterpillars with construction paper. The interaction between the kindergarten children and their second-grade tutors differed on a number of dimensions, most notably in terms of their reactions to indirect requests for help. Tutors with a high level of role-taking ability were more sensitive to subtle and indirect indications when help was needed. For example, straining with scissors and frequent glances at a tutor with a high level of role-taking ability were likely to elicit a query as to whether the pupil needed help, "high role takers rarely overlooked such indirect requests" (Hudson, Forman & Brion-Meisels, 1982, p. 1327). Tutors with a low level of role-taking ability were unlikely to respond to problems unless confronted directly and explicitly; they were likely to respond to indirect cues with a smile, perhaps not recognising them as a request for help. Again, the inevitable conclusion is that social and cognitive development are inextricably intertwined.

More mature levels of understanding about relationships are associated with lower levels of aggressiveness and more prosocial behaviour in peer interactions, such as sharing and helping (Selman, 1980). Both these characteristics are important for children's friendship and probably underlie Kurdek & Krile's (1982) finding that children in grades three to eight scoring high for understanding individuals and friendship were more likely to be involved in a mutual friendship than were their lower scoring counterparts.

Understanding friendship

Children's role-taking abilities have important consequences for the expectations that they will hold about their relationships. These friendship concepts have been a major area of research on children's friendships. This section examines the developmental changes which occur in children's concepts about friendship. The concern of this section is twofold. First, to examine the mechanisms by which information is gathered and impressions are formed. Second, to describe the content of children's impressions of their peers, and especially their friends – what characteristics they pay attention to.

The concepts children hold about friendship have obvious implications for the sorts of information that they are able to use as a basis for their relationships – though these parallels are often presented as self-evident truths rather than as empirical facts. Research on relationship concepts considerably predates and has far outstripped research examining how these concepts affect the dynamics of actual relationships. Research of this latter form has been a relatively recent endeavour and few correlations between relationship concepts and patterns of interaction have been empirically demonstrated (Hartup, 1983). Such demonstrations are essential as there is often little or no correspondence between why children say they behaved in a certain way and the actual factors that influenced their behaviour (Bigelow, 1982). Clarification of the relationship between children's social cognitive abilities and their social behaviour is likely to take many years and necessitate the consideration of a number of additional factors. As a first step, Berndt (1981c) argues that normative factors must also be taken into account. He proposes a method for investigating these links which is based on Fishbein & Ajzen's (1975) Theory of Reasoned Action, a model of the relationship between attitudes and behaviour (or behavioural intention) which takes into account social and personal norms and the individual's motivation to comply with these.

Despite researchers' different theoretical orientations and methodological approaches, ranging from free descriptions, adjective rating scales, repertory grids, and resolving social dilemmas, through to detailed semi-structured interviews, the extensive literature on children's and adolescents' descriptions of their peers is remarkably consistent. "With age, increases occur in the number of interpersonal constructs used, the flexibility and precision with which they are used, the complexity and organisation of information and ideas about one's friends, and the recognition of certain attributes as characteristic of friends as distinguished from acquaintances" (Hartup, 1983, p. 138).

Some of the most systematic and well thought-out early research on children's descriptions of their friendships was conducted by Brian Bigelow and John La Gaipa, and their research is described in detail below to give a flavour of the methods and findings of this area.

Friendship expectations

In their initial study Bigelow & La Gaipa (1975) had school-teachers conduct a class exercise in which children in grades one through eight (about 6–14 years of age) had to think about their best friends of the same sex and write an essay on what is expected of a best friend that was different from other acquaintances. These essays were divided into their constituent statements which were content analysed on 21 dimensions. Some examples of these dimensions will make this process easier to visualise. A very basic dimension was "help – friend as giver" (e.g. "He gives me candy"). A more sophisticated category, typical of middle-childhood was "acceptance" (e.g. "Can argue and still be friends"), while "intimacy potential" (e.g. "Can tell her my secrets") was only used by children approaching their teens. Sixteen of the 21 dimensions showed increase with age, three showed no changes, and two declined in usage. The authors noted the grade at which the various categories of friendship expectations (FEs) first regularly appeared and concluded that "These age-related FE changes appear to indicate a transition from egocentric to sociocentric and sociocentric to empathic FEs" (p. 858). In discussing the limitations of their study Bigelow & La Gaipa acknowledged that it would be premature to regard the observed developmental changes as representing discrete stages. To examine this a second study was conducted.

In his follow-up study Bigelow (1977) tested the sequential invariance of his proposed stages in the development of friendship expectations. If they do constitute genuine developmental stages, each building on the achievements of its predecessors, then it is essential that they only occur in a specific sequential order. This study used 6–14-year-old Scottish and Anglo-Canadian school-children. The children again wrote essays on the expectations that they held for friends that were different from other acquaintances. These were again content analysed. The use of Scottish and Canadian children enabled a cross-cultural comparison to be made, which confirmed a high level of consistency in the age of onset of use of friendship expectation dimensions. This does not, of course, deny that different cultural and ethnic groups give more or less emphasis to specific behavioural expectations (Rotheram-Borus & Phinney, 1990). The finding of an invariant sequence in which dimensions of friendship expectations develop is important in showing the influence of cognitive developmental factors rather than simply the influence of socialisation practices which vary from one culture to another.

As in the first study, not all dimensions of friendship expectations increased with age. Most notable amongst those that were frequently mentioned but did not show developmental increases in either the Scottish or Canadian samples were ego reinforcement and reciprocity of liking. The basic psychological support provided by these aspects is a fundamental function of a wide variety of relationships and across a wide age range. Eleven categories of friendship expectation increased with age in each sample. These 11 categories are given below – the grade of onset, as given in Bigelow & La Gaipa (1975), is shown in brackets:

1. common activities (2)
2. help – friend as giver (2)
3. evaluation (3)
4. propinquity (3)
5. character admiration (4)
6. acceptance (4)
7. incremental prior interaction (4)
8. loyalty and commitment (5)
9. genuineness (6)
10. common interests (7)
11. intimacy potential (7).

This provided initial support for the notion of stages in the development of friendship expectations. Further confirmation came from the finding of a grade and rank order in the proposed developmental sequence. When children did mention categories outside of their developmental level these were usually from lower developmental levels – these would be expected to be within their cognitive abilities whereas more advanced categories would be expected to be less well understood. The final stage of analysis delineated developmentally discrete clusters of friendship expectations that comprised the developmental sequence. Results confirmed that the associations between categories indicated a three-stage model of friendship expectations. An important point to emphasise here is that more sophisticated stages do not imply that information that was important at previous stages is subsequently ignored, rather it is superseded. The term 'stage' is not intended to imply abrupt qualitative transitions in the way that children talk about friendships; they are a convenient shorthand for emphasising the dominant and most sophisticated levels of friendship concept that are typically provided by children at a given developmental level. Descriptions by older children continue to contain many references to factors such as physical appearance, but they also go beyond this in their references to abstract traits and characteristics. Current concerns extend and build on the child's developmentally earlier abilities.

Despite using methods very different from Robert Selman's, Bigelow & La Gaipa have arrived at very similar results and conclusions. Their work is, however, limited by the lack of attention to children below school age. This omission was rectified in studies by Hayes and his associates (Hayes, 1978; Hayes, Gershman & Bolin, 1980), and it is to these that we turn next.

Preschoolers

In a programme of research by Donald Hayes, Bigelow's analysis of the development of children's friendship expectations has been extended to the relationships of preschoolers between 36 and approximately 66 months of age. In his initial study, Hayes (1978) found that propinquity, common activities, general play, evaluations, and physical possessions were all reliably used as reasons for friendship. Rule violation, aggression and aberrant behaviour were used as a basis for disliking. Hayes went on to suggest, though his evidence at the time was not conclusive, that reciprocal friendships are based on evaluation and common activities/play. Unilateral relationships (where child A nominates child B as best friend but child B does not nominate child A best friend) are based on physical possessions and propinquity. This interesting twist in the tale gained some support from a follow-up study by Hayes, Gersham & Bolin (1980) in which it was found that reciprocal friendships did indeed differ from unilateral friendships in placing significantly greater emphasis on evaluation and common activities, though there were no significant differences on other dimensions.

Levels of relating

Developed at about the same time as Bigelow's theory, another influential approach to the study of the development of children's concepts of social relationships, including friendship, was proposed by James Youniss and his associates (Youniss & Volpe, 1978). Youniss emphasises that developmental changes in friendship and peer relations are constructive. New concepts build on and extend old concepts; there is an intimate connection between new an old cognitive structures. In short, developmental changes represent transformations and elaborations of meaning. This Piagetian analysis emphasises the growth of operational thinking in relationships, of concepts based on abstract, reversible actions. This is an important point which we shall return to shortly.

The model of social relations presented by Youniss represents a development and synthesis of Piaget's (1977) theory of cognitive development and Sullivan's (1953) theory of interpersonal relations. This synthesis stresses that the objects of social knowing are not individuals, the self and others, but rather the interpersonal relation that exist between them. The development of friendship concepts represents more than a simple progressive adding of new concepts about others throughout the life course, it is an abstraction of the general forms of relations that exist between individuals. It is these properties that define and distinguish relations one from another. As noted by Oppenheimer & Thijssen (1983, p. 69), "Concepts about processes leading to friendships form an integral part of concepts about friendship". Youniss is concerned with the whole field of a child's social relations, but stresses the importance of friendship as a relation between two equals. Peer relationships involve the mutual or reciprocal construction of a relation and are consequently seen as important in enabling the development of co-operation, respect and sensitivity. This contrasts with many other relationships in which the distribution of power (and hence the determination of the course of the relationship) is unequal, such as with parents.

According to Youniss, to understand any social relationship, including friendship, it is necessary to understand the operations (actions) on which it is based. The actions necessary to establish, maintain or dissolve relationships are central to their definition. To investigate this Youniss conducted a series of studies examining children's definitions of friendship, its natural history, and associated norms for interaction. Children of different ages were asked what actions (operations) were necessary to initiate and maintain social relationships. For example, subjects could be asked what actions would show that they liked someone.

Despite a methodology different from either Bigelow's or Selman's, Youniss' findings concerning children's understanding of the meaning of friendship were very similar. Younger children emphasised the quality of ongoing interaction, its concrete reward–cost features and material or social benefits; older children emphasised factors such intimacy, trust, and respect. More detailed analysis suggested that the major changes in friendship concepts could be explained in terms of a notion of reciprocity. The elaboration of this simple concept provides a common underlying basis for the multitude of changes which characterise the development of a broad range of friendship norms and concepts. Youniss stresses that development in relationships entails an increasing understanding of the relationship between interpersonal acts and psychological states (e.g. that friendship can make a lonely or sad person happy). Six to eight year olds know the actions necessary for friendship, such as sharing goods and playing together, and see these in simple, rule-based terms. Reciprocity is simple and concrete. A friend's contribution to an interaction matches that of his or her companion. Positive contributions will maintain relationships and negative contributions will lead to their dissolution. The violation of a friendship requires the restoration of appropriate behaviour. By pre-adolescence the notion of reciprocity has been extended to more specific activities and psychological characteristics; co-operation and mutual respect is the norm. Adjustment to partners is a mutual exercise and equality is an important consideration. The idea of the friend as an irreplaceable person is also beginning to emerge as a further form of reciprocity. The emphasis is moving to qualities of the person rather than actions and similarity on these abstract characteristics is sought. In adolescence reciprocity is transformed to encompass the notion of a shared identity; a sense of mutuality, of "we" rather than "you" and "me". Loyalty, support and the sharing of burdens and secrets become significant. When such relationships are violated this must be acknowledged before they can be repaired.

Having considered a variety of approaches to explaining children's friendship concepts, it is encouraging to note the degree of consistency in their findings. Despite the limitations of individual research programmes, taken together these results portray a clear picture of the child's understanding of friendship and represent a sound base on which future research can build.

Developmental stages in friendship descriptions

The previous sections have examined two major approaches to explaining the development of children's descriptions of their friendships. These have been remarkably consistent in the picture that they paint concerning the stages in the development of friendship concepts, and also fully in accord with Selman's model of role-taking examined earlier. To summarise and integrate these various approaches, a series of distinctive main stages in the development of children's friendship concepts will each be examined in turn, in order to bring out their distinctive and increasingly sophisticated character. For convenience the terms coined by Bigelow (1977) will be used to label the stages. The statements used as examples of typical descriptions are drawn from the research of Erwin (1983).

The first "egocentric" or "situational" stage lasts until about seven or eight years of age and emphasises the concrete, external features of others. The child at this stage is self-centred and concerned with immediate actions and consequences. Descriptions of friends and friendship often emphasise rewards and costs, propinquity, shared activities, physical appearance, and possessions. Typical statements from such children's descriptions of their friends are: "he plays football with me", "she's always moaning", "he lives near me". Any dispositional and evaluative terms tend to be used in a global sense. *Apparent* trait terms include "kind", "good", "smart", and "mean", though these are used more as a description of recent behaviour rather than as lasting or general traits (Rholes & Ruble, 1984); they are not a sufficient basis for friendship and an attractive toy or sweets is likely to be a great boost to popularity.

The second stage lasts until about 11 years of age and has been characterised as "sociocentric" or "normative"; reciprocity and sharing are evident and the emphasis is on the values, rules and obligations of relationships. This is the era in which Sullivan (1953) hypothesised that a close chum relationship would be so important. In line with this, children are showing a recognition of the idea that others possess enduring personality characteristics that are evident across many situations, but also that there are situational variations – i.e. differentiation. Descriptions start to give a greater emphasis to psychological dimensions, to inner traits and qualities, and on reciprocity (give and take, doing things together) in relationships. For example "she'll just sit and do work all day", "he's big-headed", "she's very stubborn". One ten year old after due thought commented of her friend that "she shares more things" – younger children are more concerned with simply being given things. There are even indications of an awareness of the role of similarity as a basis for friendship. One ten year old commented "she's like me a lot".

In adolescence a third and final stage in the development of children's description of their peers emerges. This "empathic" or "internal-psychological" stage emphasises intimacy and trust, self-disclosure and personal dispositions. Within this stage the interpersonal cognitive system continues to grow by means of increasing organisation and integration. This enables more comparisons of traits, of one person with another, and a greater recognition of inconsistencies and exceptions. There is an ability to combine discrepant information and more refinement of descriptions (Shantz, 1983). A teenager is able to recognise that a friend can be "shy and social", or "kind-hearted" and yet also "catty sometimes". Complex psychological characteristics such as "easy-going", "generous", and "someone you can talk to" can be attributed to others.

As Bigelow & La Gaipa (1980, p. 19) noted, a sequence of three developmental stages in the development of children's friendship concepts "is perfectly consistent with the prelogical, concrete–operational and formal–operational distinctions employed in Piagetian theorizing". The acknowledgement, albeit very cautious, of the possibility of a stage-like progression in the development of friendship expectations is an important aspect common to the theories of Bigelow, Selman, and Youniss.

Attribution processes

In the previous section we examined how children describe their friends. It is important to understand not only what aspects of others are regarded as important bases for children's friendship at different ages but how these characteristics come to be attributed to others. This topic has been accorded considerably less attention. This section examines how information relevant to establishment and maintenance of children's relationships is gathered, inferred, and possibly biased by their social cognitive processes.

The processes involved in attributing intentions and dispositions to others have been accorded substantial attention by researchers in social psychology but, apart from a few early studies, systematic research by developmental psychologists is a relatively recent endeavour, perhaps only dating back as far as the mid-1970s (Fincham, 1983). We are currently gaining insights into what children are capable of in terms of attribution, less clear is the extent to which these abilities reflect how they actually process social information in the real world. As Lalljee, Watson & White (1983) point out, explanations for causes are influenced and can be explained on three main levels. In terms of cultural and sub-cultural norms, interpersonal demands (e.g. the need to maintain a relationship or to ascribe blame), and the intrapersonal processing of information. The vast majority of research on attribution has focused on this last factor, especially by developmental psychologists, for whom understanding social and individual changes throughout the lifespan is a prime concern. Despite its obvious significance, there is a paucity of research on the attribution processes in children's ongoing relationships.

For children to operate effectively in their social world they need to be able to anticipate the behaviour of others. This requires an element of understanding and control over the social events that they experience. In their striving to achieve this Heider (1958) portrayed people as naive psychologists attempting to analyse the causal origins of behaviour. The development of the ability to attribute traits and dispositions to others is an important factor underpinning close friendships. It is shortly after this ability appears in common use, about the age of nine, that the close chum relationships of middle childhood become possible and evident (Sullivan, 1953).

From their earliest interactions with their world, children experience the co-occurrence of events and through this, and socialisation practices, are encouraged to think about their actions and experiences in cause–effect terms. Young children rarely use causal language, but it is a common finding that their language often underestimates their actions and abilities. In a simple situation, where there are a small number of possible explanations for an event, preschoolers do show an awareness of people as causal agents. From at least three years of age there are a variety of rules available to the child for making causal attributions. These range from simple temporal or spatial contiguity of cause and effect, through to an analysis of their patterns of covariation (Shultz et al., 1986).

Despite the seemingly wide variety of rules available to the child for making causal attributions, their abilities are fairly simple ability at this age. Three year olds are aware that people must be present to be the cause of an event, and that behaviour must precede an event to be its cause (Sedlak & Kurtz, 1981), but their everyday understanding of causality is based mainly on the association of events rather than a more complex relationship between factors. The attributional error made by many preschoolers is to assume that most social behaviour is intentional.

During the preschool years and into the early elementary school years the child becomes increasingly proficient at distinguishing accidental from deliberate and involuntary acts (Shantz, 1983). In its most sophisticated form this means that the child comes to appreciate that consistencies in behaviour reflect underlying traits and dispositions. In this context, dispositions and traits provide the consistency that makes possible a relatively stable, predictable, and controllable world. The establishment of dispositional causes for social behaviour represents a considerably more complex task for the child than the establishment of causality in his or her physical world. As Piaget (1977) noted, factual knowledge is objective and testable, social knowledge is quite variable and often arbitrary.

Five and six year olds are quite able to make dispositional attributions, even though they do not use trait information in describing themselves and others. There is a fairly simple explanation for this apparent difference in what children can do and what they actually do. From a relatively early age children can appreciate the contribution of individual and situational factors to their attributions, but they weight the importance of these factors differently from older children and adults. Research by Rholes & Ruble (1984) found that children as young as five years are capable of making dispositional attributions for current behaviour, though they did not use this information to infer that the actor would behave in a consistent manner in other situations. Such consistency of attributions does not appear until about nine years of age.

Children may not use trait-like terms before the age of eight or nine years, not because they are unable to make internal attributions, but because they are uncertain about the stability of these traits or do not perceive this information as salient. There is a tendency for younger children to focus on the immediate situation and external attributes at the expense of dispositional assumptions. Clearly the young child's inability to use trait terms and concepts severely limits his or her ability to understand, predict and influence others systematically; knowledge is situation specific and so the behaviour of others will often seem puzzling to the young child unable to recognise the underlying common bases of apparently different behaviours. A six year old using a trait like "kind" is more likely to be using it to describe a cause for recent behaviour rather than a stable attribute with implications for future conduct. Trait-like terms are more salient to nine year olds who can use labels like "kind" as a shorthand for expressing an expected consistency.

The principle that effects covary with their causes has proved profoundly influential in the way causal attribution has been modelled by social psychologists. Indeed, until recently social psychologists made little attempt to investigate if other bases for attribution could and would be used if available. This was an unfortunate oversight as it seems perfectly sensible to suggest that what the individual can do and what the individual does do are not always the same thing. Even if an individual can use covariance information in attributing characteristics and intentions to others, this does not mean that she or he will ordinarily do so. It is important to understand under what conditions specific social inference processes are used. In the real world individuals often form hypotheses about events and actively seek specific information which would provide an inductive test of these (Lalljee, Watson & White, 1983). From this perspective, interest should focus on changes in the hypotheses children of different ages have about events rather than how they combine various types of information. The young child's assumptions about events are markedly different from those of older children or adults. The potential relevance of the background and cultural knowledge of the individual has been widely acknowledged, not least by Kelley (1973) himself, though as yet it has prompted only minimal research.

Subject, object and society

Before continuing further it is appropriate to note that the picture presented so far has been of the child almost as an objective, if sometimes limited, processor of information. To my mind, one of the most significant papers published which dispels this notion (it could be called a classic study, except that this is often used as a euphemism for "old and outdated") was conducted by Dornbusch et al. (1965). In this study children of 9–11 years of age attending a summer camp described their tent-mates. The content of their free descriptions was analysed and three major comparisons were made to determine the degree of overlap in descriptions. First, between one child's descriptions of two others ("1 on 2"). Second, two children describing the same other child ("2 on 1"). Third, two children each describing another child ("2 on 2"). These comparisons give an indication of what the perceiver, the perceived, and "culture" bring to the perception process, though the authors were cautious in using such labels because each description is based on a different target, or at least a unique interaction experience. The percentage of overlap for these three categories of comparison was 57%, 45% and 38% respectively. The important point made by this study is that all three factors affect the child's perception of others. The objective characteristics of the other child by no means swamped other factors. Indeed, these limited results indicate that the descriptive categories used by the perceiver are a more important determinant of person perception than the actual characteristics of the target.

The social context of attribution

Although attribution theory provides useful models of social inference processes, we must not lose sight of the fact that we are trying to understand what people actually do rather than what they can or should do. A number of potential sources of bias in the attribution process have been noted. For example, a study by Berndt & Das (1987) found that perceptions of a classmate's personality were affected by friendship with the classmate and by the classmate's popularity. But the biases originating in personal and social evaluations are far from uniform; they are also affected by the actual behaviour that is being judged. Whether a behaviour is positive or negative and whether the child performing the behaviour is liked or disliked are both likely to affect how an act is interpreted (Hymel, 1986). A child tripped by another child that has previously shown aggressive behaviour will react very differently than if tripped by a friend because of differences in the attribution of intent on the part of the other child (Waas & Honer, 1990). Positive behaviours are more likely to be seen as dispositional when caused by a liked peer than when performed by a disliked peer. In contrast, negative behaviours are more likely to be seen as dispositional when performed by disliked peers than when performed by liked peers; greater responsibility and blame is attributed to disliked peers than liked peers. It is easy to see how these patterns of attribution ultimately become the basis of self-sustaining reputations in the peer group and why so many social skills training programmes fail to produce long-term effects. Peers are likely to ignore the prosocial behaviour of problem children and to focus on their negative behaviours (Solomon & Wahler, 1973). The selective attention to negative behaviours is likely to produce a response which maintains the behaviour which resulted in the child being rejected in the first place. Further bolstering for this self-perpetuating system comes from the tendency for blame and dispositional attributions to be applied to the negative behaviour of rejected children (Waas & Honer, 1990). The overall conclusion that must be drawn is that the child's own cognitive processes, rather than the other child's characteristics, provide much of the consistency in a trait-based account of another's behaviour. The attribution of traits is a useful and economical way of achieving predictability in social interaction, though it can easily be biased and tells tell us as much about the perceiver as the perceived.

As well as the reputation of the other child, the social experiences and popularity of the perceiver both affect and are affected by their perception of a social situation. In studies by Sobol & Earn (1985a) and Earn & Sobol (1990) the social attributions of children differing in sociometric status was compared, i.e. the role ascribed to factors such as personality, mood, luck and others' motives. Popular fourth to sixth grade children were more aware of social cues and causes and were more likely than the other sociometric groups to see themselves as personally responsible for their social successes. Although all sociometric groups tended to externalise the causes for failure, this was accomplished in a more sophisticated manner by the popular children. Rather than simply putting failure down to luck they invoked explanations such as the motives of other people. This finding indicates that another's behaviour is interpreted differently by popular and unpopular children. Popular children are more accurate in perceiving the effects of their behaviour and regard their world as more controllable.

These patterns of attribution shown by popular children are an important ingredient underlying their social confidence and success. Rejected children overestimate their peers' evaluations of their social competence (Patterson, Kupersmidt & Griester, 1990), and where they do perceive social failure be less likely to externalise blame. It can be a useful defence for our self-esteem to be able to blame our social inadequacies on situational factors or to be able to blame rejection directly on another, and failure to do this has severe consequences for the child. The attribution of social failure to personal incompetence is associated with a greater deterioration in strategies for initiating relationships in comparison to children attributing rejection to the characteristics of the other child or simply interpersonal factors such as incompatibility. In a study of fourth and fifth graders Goetz & Dweck (1980) found that children of low sociometric status were more likely to make personal attributions of incompetence as explanations for their rejection and this could be an important factor pushing the unpopular child into a cycle of helpless non-avoidant self-blame.

The impact of cognitive factors on children's friendships is great. At present research is in its infancy but an encouraging sign is that its practical applications are already being explored. Cognitive approaches to therapy for children with relationship problems do already exist, and their research on their efficacy is likely to continue apace. This is examined further in Chapter 10.

3 Physical appearance and attractiveness

Regardless of context or age of participants, society tends to view the physically attractive as inherently better than those of less physical attractiveness.

(Patzer, 1985, p. 11)

Visit any art gallery or museum and it will rapidly become evident that beauty has long been celebrated within human culture. It will also be evident that cultural and historical definitions of beauty show great variety. Whatever the reigning standard, artists have and continue to produce great works in its praise and the layman may aspire to these ideals of perfection. But the influence of physical attractiveness extends beyond art. Even in everyday life we pay homage to this invidious master, evidenced by the lengths to which we will go to manage our appearance and create the desired impression. In all, physical attractiveness has been, is, and seems set to remain an important cultural influence upon each of us individually throughout our whole lives. And yet its major social significance comes from the fact that its influence extends considerably beyond its impact on us as individuals, because it affects our social interactions.

This chapter examines the influence that physical attractiveness has on the child's social and personal relationships. The first section of this chapter traces the roots of physical attractiveness effects through infancy. In particular it shows how attractiveness effects are not simply cultural artefacts, they have a biological foundation and function. Research suggests that even very young infants, well below the age at which they might be expected to have acquired social stereotypes, can discriminate and prefer physically attractive faces. The subsequent sections of the chapter examine the nature and impact of physical attractiveness stereotypes throughout childhood and adolescence. Physical appearance and attractiveness have considerably more significance than their idle curiosity value. They can and do affect the course of children's lives. A number of authors have delineated the conditions that must be met if physical attractiveness stereotypes are to have any major and long-term social and psychological effects. To test how adequately these conditions are met, we examine the content of physical attractiveness stereotypes, how these stereotypes are internalised, produce expectations, and ultimately provide the basis for a self-fulfilling prophecy. Although most research on attractiveness has focused on facial appearance, the final section attempts to put this literature in a more realistic context by examining the impact of contribution of physique to perceptions of attractiveness. This topic is of special developmental importance because of the great changes in physique that occur over childhood and adolescence.

Infancy

The physical attractiveness stereotype has typically been noted in children from about three years of age (Langlois & Stephan, 1981). Below this age, it seems to have been assumed that children will lack the social experience necessary to learn the beliefs comprising the stereotype. This does not, however, mean that the consequences of physical attractiveness do not affect the life of infants.

Even the youngest of babies exists in a social world and, on a daily basis, will interact with adults, and possibly older children, who possess physical attractiveness stereotypes. Their stereotypes concerning what constitutes a cute baby, and the expectations associated with this stereotype, are likely to have a considerable effect on the infant's interaction experiences, and have significant implications for the establishment of expectancies and patterns of behaviour which will influence the child's subsequent peer relationships.

This picture emphasises the distinctive way in which physical attractiveness stereotyping affects the infant. It is empirically well founded but does tend to portray the infant largely as a "victim" of physical attractiveness stereotyping. Research suggests that this view of the infant's abilities represents a considerable underestimation. Even young babies appear to respond to the physical appearance and attractiveness of their caregivers (Langlois et al., 1987). Unfortunately this does not mean that we can simply lower the age at which we acknowledge the impact of physical attractiveness stereotyping by infants. It is difficult to accommodate traditional models of the acquisition of social stereotypes to these findings. Instead it may be more appropriate to interpret infants' responses to physical appearance and attractiveness as a possible basis for the later development of social stereotypes. Despite the undeniable importance of physical attractiveness in the lives of infants, it is inappropriate to include them in many of the generalisations that can be made about physical attractiveness stereotypes in later childhood and adolescence. Alternative explanations need to be considered for the effects of physical attractiveness on children during infancy, they will consequently be considered separately in this section.

Two main issues will be addressed by this section. First, we will consider what characteristics make an infant attractive and the effects that a child's appearance has on his or her caregivers. Second, we will examine infants' responses to the physical appearance and attractiveness of adults.

Attractiveness of infants

From birth, physical attractiveness (though with babies researchers often prefer to use the term cuteness) plays an important role in children's lives. There is a substantial level of agreement between adult raters on evaluations of infant attractiveness (Hildebrandt, 1982). A great deal of recent research has been devoted to finding out what cues are used in such evaluations of attractiveness. The most obvious and important factor is the infant's actual physical appearance, some babies are simply perceived as more physically attractive than others, but other factors also have significant roles. For example, smiling babies, especially those of unexceptional levels of cuteness, are typically regarded as more attractive than their unsmiling counterparts (Hildebrandt & Fitzgerald, 1983), and even mere familiarity increases attractiveness evaluations (Hildebrandt & Fitzgerald, 1983).

Facial features account for about half the ratings of an infant's cuteness (Hildebrandt & Fitzgerald, 1983). Infants generally, and more so the cute infant, tend to have short and narrow features, large eyes and pupils, a round head, and a large forehead (Hildebrandt & Fitzgerald, 1979; Alley, 1981). These baby-like characteristics also evoke positive personality and behavioural expectancies. Attractive infants are expected to be likeable and not irritating, attractive, normal, cute, fun to be with, to eat well, and to cause their parents little worry and concern (Maier et al., 1984). The evaluative impact of cues which are regarded as prototypically babyish appears to increase through early infancy, until approximately 11 months of age (Hildebrandt & Fitzgerald, 1983).

From earliest infancy the differential ratings of attractiveness accorded to infants appear to affect the treatment and amount of attention a child receives. A study by Hildebrandt & Fitzgerald (1978) found that adults look at photographs of attractive infants for longer than their unattractive counterparts. As gaze is an important component and regulator of interaction, the authors of this study suggested that physical attractiveness is also indirectly important for the regulation of parent–infant interaction. This conclusion appears to be supported by Parke & Sawin (1975) who found that mothers and fathers of attractive infants showed different patterns of interaction with their child from parents of less attractive children. For example, mothers showed more eye contact, fathers showed more stimulation by touching and moving the child. Both parents kissed the child more. These differential behaviours represent an early manifestation of the interaction experiences underlying the socialisation of the physical attractiveness stereotype.

The differential treatment and preference for attractive children appears to be maintained throughout infancy. In a group care programme for children up to approximately three years of age, attractive children were found to receive more attention than unattractive children (Hildebrandt & Cannan, 1985).

Looked at from a converse perspective, the disadvantages of unattractive children are no less marked than the advantages of the attractive child. If a baby-like appearance is attractive and facilitates caregiving behaviour, then less attractive and prototypically babyish infants will elicit correspondingly less of this behaviour and possibly even negative responses from adults. Anecdotal evidence does indeed reveal that rejecting mothers often describe their infants as ugly and not cuddly (Hildebrandt & Fitzgerald, 1983). Though with this sort of evidence it is often difficult to be sure of the direction of cause and effect. Do parents reject their infants because they are ugly, or do they rationalise their rejection by labelling the child as ugly? Probably both effects are fairly common. Certainly there is evidence of children being rejected because they are physically unattractive. Parents often experience great problems in adjusting to infants with even fairly minor and non-disabling physical abnormalities, especially those that are most visible. The available evidence suggests that consequent patterns of caregiving and interaction (rather than the physical abnormality itself) are often the producer of any observed personality and adjustment problems encountered in later life (Bernstein, 1982).

An ethological explanation of the effects of baby-like characteristics on adult behaviour has been proposed by the ethologist Konrad Lorenz (1943). Lorenz argues that baby-like features act as releasers for caregiving patterns of behaviour. A releaser is essentially a cue which triggers innate, fixed patterns of behaviour. This deterministic perspective sees much caregiving behaviour as a relatively automatic and inevitable consequence of baby-like appearance cues. A model by Hildebrandt & Fitzgerald (1978) develops this idea further but builds in a greater element of cognitive and behavioural flexibility; they propose of a two-component theory of responses to physical attractiveness in infants. The first component represents a general positive response to baby-like appearance cues, a general characteristic of infants. All children would benefit from this component. The second component is the cognitive response to an individual child's cuteness or physical attractiveness. This may vary considerably from infant to infant and is an important factor determining the length of time, attention and contact with the infant that is maintained.

Baby-faced adults

From the general notion that baby-like features can act as relatively automatic triggers for positive evaluations and preference, it is a short step to infer that older children and adults possessing such characteristics will benefit from the generalisation of this effect. This does indeed seem to be the case. Children and adults appear to be differentially evaluated according to the extent to which they possess babyish features. For example, babies show low vertical placement of features, small chins, large round eyes, a small nose, and high eyebrows. These features also appear to be major factors in the evaluation of physical attractiveness in adults. This effect appears to have a greater impact on the evaluations of female rather than male attractiveness. This finding has been explained in terms of the social definition of sex roles, though this is difficult to reconcile with the notion that the responses to baby-like features are supposed to be innate and automatic. Often without realisation, adult and adolescent females often use cosmetics to enhance these baby-like characteristics, especially eye size and definition, and individuals with these qualities are perceived to be warmer, more honest, submissive, and naive (Berry & McArthur, 1986).

Infants' responses to faces

So far in this section, we have considered what makes a baby attractive, and noted the implications of this for the way the baby is treated, the child's future development and relationships. It is now necessary to consider the extent to which the child is able to discriminate physical appearance and attractiveness and the use which the child makes of such information. Most of the research on this topic has been concerned with the face and so this will be the focus of this discussion.

A substantial body of literature attests to the importance of the face as a stimulus (for a general review of this literature see Hopkins, 1980; or Bull & Rumsey, 1988). Early research appeared to show that neonates preferred pictures of faces over other stimuli (e.g. Fantz, 1963), leading to the suggestion that there was a innate preference for such stimuli. It did not take long for this conclusion to be cast into doubt. It appears that there is an innate ability or predisposition to recognise certain stimulus attributes and it is the fact that these characterise a face that is more important than the fact that what the infant is viewing is recognised as a face per se. For example, eyes seem to be an especially important cue. By about one month of age infants are starting to establish eye contact, and infants of under two months will not smile at a face with the eyes hidden – but even dots in place of eyes will elicit the response (Ahrens, 1954). Quite simply, it appears that the reason that the human face gets greater attention than many other stimuli presented to a young child is because it combines many important visual stimulus attributes, it is associated with vocalisations, is most likely to be present in the very young child's limited visual field (focal length being about eight inches in the newborn and remaining at roughly this level for the first few weeks of life), and is likely to be associated with rewards such as food or social stimulation.

Increases in attentional capacity mean that the number of aspects of the face that are required to elicit smiling increases with age (Bower, 1977). Young children appear to look for moderately complex patterns, contrast, curvilinear features, boundaries and contours, and movement. Children over about two months of age pay more attention to internal features such as the eyes, and by about three months the child is more interested in the internal features of the face than its edges. At this age the child can even discriminate between photographs of similar strangers; and photographs of the mother are recognised and preferred to those of strangers (Barrera & Maurer, 1981a, 1981b). This appears to be more properly a perception of faces. It is also at about this age that the child begins to show finer discrimination between faces in terms of facial expression and attractiveness. Children as young as two or three months show a preference and differential responses (e.g. smile more) to attractive rather than unattractive adult faces (Samuels & Ewy, 1985). Physical attractiveness also makes strangers less anxiety arousing to the infant. By one year of age, when there is typically attachment to the caregiver and a fear of strangers, infants show less withdrawal, more play involvement, and a more positive pattern of emotional expression with an attractive, rather than an unattractive, unknown woman (Langlois, Roggman & Rieser-Danner, 1990).

Combining the findings of the research cited above with the results from studies of adults' reactions to smiling infants, some interesting and as yet largely unrecognised inferences can be made. Research indicates that the infant with attractive caregivers will react accordingly, such as by smiling and behaving in a generally positive manner. Further research suggests that these positive behaviours will in turn be regarded as attractive by the caregiver and elicit positive, attentive responses. The end-product of this pattern of reciprocal influence is a better socialisation experience for the baby with an attractive caregiver than for than a comparable baby with a less attractive caregiver. In short, the attractiveness of adults can affect the perceived cuteness of an infant and hence the treatment that is meted out. This is a fascinating idea, but it must be kept in perspective. Even given that the pattern of effects is correct, caregiver attractiveness is but one factor among many affecting social interaction. The importance of this factor in comparison to other factors is unclear.

Research on the infant's use of physical attractiveness cues has important implications for the common assumption that attractiveness is simply a reflection of cultural values; infants as young as two months have had little opportunity to learn the ideals of attractiveness in adults. As Langlois et al. (1987) point out, these predispositions in facial pattern recognition and preference can be interpreted as representing the rudiments of a physical attractiveness stereotype. If this is the case, then the social biases deriving from the physical attractiveness stereotyping are likely to prove particularly difficult to eradicate. It is to a consideration of the nature and effects of later physical attractiveness stereotyping that we now turn.

Life after infancy

Physical attractiveness is an important influence on children's interpersonal relationships for at least two main reasons. First, as physical attractiveness is visible and extremes can be identified, it is consequently easy to stereotype. Patzer (1985) argues that only race and sex are equally visible characteristics and that discrimination from physical attractiveness is more marked (though less acknowledged) than from either of these factors! Second, because of its early manifestation, the child will usually be aware of a person's appearance and attractiveness long before the child hears the person speak or is able to make use of the finer aspects of non-verbal communication.

Physical attractiveness appears to have an implicit reward value. This is evident even in children of preschool age who, for example, prefer to look at photographs of attractive peers for longer than they look at photographs of unattractive peers (Dion, 1977). However, the significance of physical attractiveness extends considerably beyond this "pleasing to the eye" effect. Because information about physical appearance is so readily accessible, evident even before we are close enough to meet or converse, it has the potential to exert a substantial impact on the subsequent course of a relationship. A child's physical appearance can even determine whether his or her peers seek interaction with him or her. Rightly or wrongly, children do anticipate a peer's patterns of behaviour on the basis of physical appearance and level of attractiveness. Attractive individuals are attributed many desirable characteristics while the less attractive, disfigured, and handicapped go unnoticed, or are shunned and actively rejected.

When interaction does ensue, the effects of physical attractiveness are far from over. For some children this interaction is freely chosen, for others it is inescapable because of parental influences, or the structure of a preschool or school. Either way, the physical attractiveness stereotype will affect the salience of subsequent information (Fiske & Taylor, 1984). It will determine what information is sought, attended to, remembered, and the interpretation that is placed on this additional information. Research indicates a tendency for children to try to confirm initial expectations and impressions rather than properly testing them. Over and above this effect, the ultimate significance of differences in physical attractiveness lies in their long-term consequences. Childhood is a qualitatively different experience for individuals of different levels of attractiveness. The accumulation of differential expectations and treatment based on the physical attractiveness stereotype has important implications for the individual's future personality and behaviour (Adams, 1977). The child is, to a significant extent, the prisoner of his or her own appearance, and the sentence is usually for life.

The social context of physical attractiveness

It is the contention of this review that physical attractiveness is an important factor which must be considered in any attempt to understand socialisation and social interaction. This does not, of course, deny the impact of many other factors or that physical attractiveness must be viewed in the context and in relationship with these other influences. Certainly many studies have tended to examine physical attractiveness in isolation, though these provide a distorted and overly simple view of the importance and effects of the phenomenon. As the main or even sole independent variable in an experiment the impact of physical attractiveness is often substantially overestimated. As Hildebrandt (1982) noted, the attractiveness stereotype is likely to be most influential when other concrete information about the child is unavailable, in situations of ambiguity. In this context much of the existing research which has used unacquainted children or photographs as stimuli, and with minimal other information, must be regarded as a foundation for an understanding of the physical attractiveness phenomenon rather than a complete explanation. They *at best* tell us about initial impressions and initial attraction.

There is now a substantial and growing literature showing that the effects of physical attractiveness are pervasive, and possibly extend further than even the enthusiastic early researchers could have foreseen. Following on from Berscheid & Walster's (1974) review of the literature, which did a lot to open up the area and give respectability to research on physical attractiveness, the following decade saw a number of excellent reviews specifically examining or giving detailed attention to developmental aspects of the phenomenon (e.g. Langlois & Stephan, 1981; Hildebrandt, 1982).

Research on physical attractiveness has examined the impact of a number of characteristics, some of which are of significance only in specific racial and ethnic groups, cultures, or historical times. Despite differences and changes in the features that are considered attractive, the nature and mechanisms of physical attractiveness effects appear consistent (Patzer & Burke, 1988). Characteristics which have been examined include height, race, physique, dress, and facial attractiveness. The focus of research has been on this last characteristic, which has been revealed as a major determinant of attractiveness judgements. This reflects the importance of the face in communication which requires that it is attended to (Argyle, 1988). Following the major line of research, this chapter will also focus on facial attractiveness.

Though somewhat less extensively researched, some consideration must be also given to the effects of physique as a dimension of physical attractiveness. This is important and necessary on two counts. First, because many studies looking at physical attractiveness stereotypes have failed to distinguish these two factors. Often with little justification or explanation, many studies have used either full-length photographs or actual acquaintances as stimuli. In both instances the effects of facial attractiveness and physique are confounded and can best be understood from a background knowledge of each factor individually. Second, in the course of a child's development substantial and obvious changes in physique are found. These effect the impressions formed by others, and coming to terms with such changes in physical appearance and interpersonal evaluation are important developmental tasks, especially for the adolescent. From this perspective justification would be needed if these changes were not to be taken into consideration and examined.

The cognitive context of physical attractiveness

Research on the role of physical attractiveness stereotyping in children's peer relationships has spanned a wide age range, from at least three years of age through to adolescence. Before the results of this research can be meaningfully examined it is necessary to acknowledge that the child's use of physical attractiveness will vary according to the child's age or, more precisely, level of social cognitive development. At the risk of stating the obvious, it should be emphasised that physical attractiveness will have a different role and significance at different stages of social cognitive development.

Chapter 2 discussed the nature of developmental changes in children's social cognitive abilities and noted the corresponding changes in the significance of physical attractiveness in children's friendship concepts. In this chapter a more detailed consideration of the physical attractiveness phenomenon is given. The detailed analysis of social cognitive development will not be duplicated at this point, but should emphasise two major implications that it has for our current consideration of the effects of physical attractiveness on children's relationships: social cognitive development affects the stability and intimacy of relationships. Both of these factors impinge on the role of physical attractiveness in children's relationships and so each will be examined in turn.

The child's level of social cognitive development imposes limits on the stability of peer relationships. It is now well established that the general peer relationships of young children of preschool or elementary school age are less stable than those of older children or adults. This does not necessarily imply that stable, reciprocal relationships are not possible in young children (Gershman & Hays, 1983), merely that the pattern is for them to become increasingly stable with age either to an asymptote at about the age of 11 years (Busk, Ford & Schulman, 1973) or until adulthood (Lindzey & Borgatta, 1954). The limits of stability in a relationship in turn affect the patterns of interaction and levels of intimacy that can be developed in a relationship (Selman, 1981). Although not impossible, intimacy is less likely in very short-lived relationships.

The intimacy that can be developed in relationships is not only limited or determined by their stability. Although stability in relationships is a necessary condition for the development of intimacy in a relationship, it is not a sufficient condition. The child's level of social cognitive development will also impose direct limits on friendship expectations. There are marked differences from one stage of social cognitive development to the next in the quantity and types of social information that can be used by the child (see Chapter 2). It is now well established that as the individual progresses through childhood, peer relationships become increasingly important and can develop to greater levels of companionship and intimacy (Buhrmester & Furman, 1987). At all ages physical characteristics are frequently mentioned when describing others, but with increasing age its impact is moderated by an ability to also incorporate additional, more abstract information (Livesley & Bromley, 1973).

Building relationships

It is important to distinguish between the level of intimacy that currently exists in a relationship and that which is ultimately possible. The friendships of preschoolers, young children, adolescents and adults are all likely to begin as relatively superficial interactions. The result of the influence of differences in levels of social cognitive development and relationship stability on young children's friendships is that they are doomed to remain at this relatively superficial level while those of older children and adults can grow in intimacy (Buhrmester & Furman, 1987).

Several sequential models of relationship growth have been proposed for adults (e.g. Duck, 1977; Murstein, 1986), though there are few direct tests of the limits of the developmental applicability. These models argue that different characteristics are important at different stages in a relationship. For example, we may initially choose interaction partners on the basis of their physical appearance and attractiveness. From this "field of eligibles" we subsequently choose to become better acquainted with some individuals because of other characteristics, such as similarity of attitudes. To develop our relationships still further, yet other information is sought, such as similarity on some aspect of personality (Duck, 1973a). In the case of children, sequential development in relationships is likely to be directly affected and limited by the two factors that have already been examined, social cognitive development and relationship stability. For progress in relationships it is necessary that they are maintained and that the participants are able to process information at deeper, more intimate levels if and when it become available. The younger child has simpler friendship expectations and is unable to use the deeper, more abstract types of information such as aspects of psychological similarity (Bigelow, 1977, 1980). As a consequence, the child will also be unable to progress to the deeper levels of relationships.

Overall it seems that the limits set by cognitive development produce very different patterns in the progress of friendships and peer relationships at different stages of childhood. Because physical attractiveness is a very visible, concrete cue, even young children are able to use it and do use it. Egocentrism is evident in the descriptions of the young child of, say, seven years of age; physical characteristics and actions of personal relevance dominate their descriptions of peers. The relative importance of physical appearance (rather than more abstract traits) when describing others appears to decline with age, mirroring changes in social cognitive development and interpersonal orientation. Physical attractiveness then often serves as a cue to these abstract characteristics such as attitudinal similarity (this is discussed further at a later point in this chapter and also in Chapter 3). Children of nine or ten years of age are able to use more complex information and, most noticeably, considerably more sophisticated organisational strategies in their descriptions of peers than are their younger counterparts. Relationships not only possess but are explicitly recognised as involving reciprocity, they are seen as requiring give and take, as possessing both rights and obligations. With the advent of adolescence descriptions of peers start to show the complexity and characteristics redolent of adults' patterns of description. Adolescents are able to produce descriptions of their peers which are organised around a consistent theme and integrated with abstract information about traits and dispositions. Appearance is but a facet of a complex friendship concept and can act as a cue for more abstract psychological attributes. Overall, it is evident that in order to understand the effects of physical attractiveness on children's relationships it is necessary to take cognisance of the level of social cognitive development (roughly indicated by age) of the individuals under consideration.

Internalising stereotypes

The significance of physical attractiveness stereotyping in children lies in its implications for later life. In particular, because the physical attractiveness stereotype is internalised by the child. It is this theme that represents the focus of this chapter. It will be argued that the relationships between physical attractiveness, social behaviour, and personality constitutes a natural dialectic, a system of reciprocal and mutually transforming influences. The importance of a dialectic notion in explaining the effects of physical attractiveness is that it implies that socialisation is not the simple shaping of the child by outside forces; rather, the individual is seen as promoting and as being closely involved in determining his or her own development. From a dialectical perspective, the accumulation of feedback, of experiences, can lead to qualitative changes in the system of reciprocal influences and in the children themselves. This idea of children as active agents in their own socialisation can be made more explicit by outlining the paths of influence that have been proposed for physical attractiveness effects: an attractive child elicits different expectations and treatment from peers and adults than does an unattractive child. These produce differences in patterns of behaviour and ultimately in personality and self-concept. In subsequent interactions, the child will thus be changed and consequently evoke a different set of responses. These differences will feedback to further influence the expectations held for the child and the way the child is treated. Sounds fairly complex? It's not even this simple! Don't forget that influences will be reciprocal. Each child of a pair, or all members of a group, will be having these sorts of effects on each other. The overall pattern of mutual, interdependent influences is extremely complex. The evidence for the various links in the chain outlined above are examined in the later sections of this chapter.

Necessary conditions

As many authors have pointed out (e.g. Lerner, 1982), for physical attractiveness to have an impact on child development in the form of a natural dialectic of reciprocal influences, at least five conditions must be met. First, there must be some degree of agreement in the child's social network on what constitutes physical attractiveness. Inconsistency would imply that the effects of physical attractiveness would also be inconsistent and to all intents and purposes cancel each other out.

Second, not only must there be agreement on what constitutes physical attractiveness, but a given individual must have some developmental stability in his or her level of physical attractiveness. The rationale for this is exactly the same as for the first factor: instability would imply that the effects of attractiveness would be cancelled out in the course of normal developmental fluctuations in physical attractiveness. Taken together, these first two factors are concerned with the discrimination of attractiveness.

Third, specific stereotypical expectations must be associated with individuals differing in their levels of attractiveness.

Fourth, for the stereotype to become reality individuals must be treated differently because of their physical attractiveness and its associated expectations.

Fifth, and finally, for a dialectic to be upheld, differences in the way children of different levels of attractiveness are treated must come to result in such individuals showing psychological and behavioural differences consistent with the physical attractiveness stereotype.

As we shall see in the course of this chapter, there is ample evidence to support the notion that physically attractive individuals are treated differently and do grow to be different from their less attractive peers on a number of characteristics. This chapter examines the nature and some of the possible origins of the physical attractiveness stereotype in children, individual characteristics which affect the importance attached to physical attractiveness information, and the potentially stigmatising effects of an atypical physical appearance.

Cultural stereotypes

In terms of the model outlined above, if physical attractiveness stereotypes are to have any marked effect on the individual, it is essential that they elicit reasonably consistent responses from the individuals with whom the child comes into contact. This is only likely if these various adults and children hold the same, or at least similar, sets of stereotyped beliefs about physical attractiveness. To some authors this is implicit within the very definition of the term stereotype. The role of social consensus in stereotyping is emphasised by Mackie (1973, p. 435): "A stereotype refers to those folk beliefs about the attributes characterising a social category on which there is substantial agreement." Unfortunately other authors accept that stereotypes may be either personal or shared. Ashmore & Del Boca (1981, p. 19) define a stereotype as "the set of beliefs held by an individual regarding a social group . . . the term cultural stereotype [should] be used to describe shared or community-wide patterns of beliefs". In view of the disagreement over whether stereotypes by definition entail a cultural consensus, it is appropriate to briefly examine the level of agreement that exists in evaluations of physical attractiveness.

In research, physical attractiveness has often been treated as a dichotomous variable, pitting attractive against unattractive individuals as stimulus figures. This ignores possible effects due to gradations in levels of attractiveness. Treating physical attractiveness in this way not only goes against common experience but means that research findings based on this approach give considerably more potency to the variable than it ordinarily has in everyday life. In a study of children and adolescents, Cavior & Dokecki (1973) found that there was less agreement on the attractiveness ratings of individuals around the average mark than on their peers of more extreme appearance; their conclusion, echoed by Hildebrandt (1982), was that for the averagely attractive person personality and behaviour are more significant for interpersonal perception and attraction, though for the very attractive or unattractive individual appearance will have a much more significant and biasing effect.

The attractiveness judgements made by children also appear to show generally good levels of peer and developmental consistency. At any given age there is generally a good level of agreement among peers, and children of different ages also show similar patterns of judgement. For example, a study using subjects from age seven to adulthood revealed no significant age differences in the attractiveness ratings of a set of portrait photographs (Cross & Cross, 1971). Even children aged three to six years old show substantial agreement in their evaluations of physical attractiveness (Dion, 1973).

In contrast to the studies discussed above, a slightly discrepant but ultimately enlightening result (Cavior and Lombardi, 1973) has found that below the age of six children do not show significant levels of agreement in the evaluation of physical attractiveness. From six years of age children were found to show significant levels of agreement in their judgements of physical attractiveness but even here this continued to increase until, at about the age of eight, the evaluation of the stimulus photos and the levels of agreement of raters was on a par with a comparison group of 17 year olds. Differences between the findings of this study and the studies of Cross & Cross (1971) and Dion (1973) are probably due to differences in experimental procedures, stimuli (use of full-length photographs rather than facial photographs), and the age of the stimulus figures (considerably older than the subjects). What is perhaps most noteworthy in this study was that younger children were initially more consistent in their judgements of the attractiveness of the fifth-grade rather than the eleventh-grade stimulus figures – suggesting that the criteria for physical attractiveness are initially learned or at least applied in relation to one's own age group.

Stability of physical attractiveness

Most research has found a good deal of stability in an individual's level of attractiveness across a wide age range. For example, Adams (1977) showed that students' ratings of photographs of the same individuals while at kindergarten, elementary school, during adolescence, as young adults and as middle-aged adults showed a reasonable level of stability in their physical attractiveness over this long age range, and especially over adjacent age ranges. Subsequent research has provided support for these findings. Sussman et al. (1983) showed stability in the facial attractiveness ratings of a set of 13 girls over the periods from grade one to grade ten. Pittenger, Mark & Johnson (1989) found a moderate degree of stability in undergraduates' ratings of individuals at six ages ranging from early childhood to late teens. An interesting and noteworthy feature of this last study is that a few individuals did appear to show a progressive decline in their levels of physical attractiveness – evidently individual differences are potentially significant and must be taken into account.

Based on the studies examined in this section it appears that physical attractiveness does indeed possess the stability needed to produce different socialisation experiences for children differing in levels of physical attractiveness (Lerner, 1982). This does not imply, of course, that other factors such as race, sex, social class, and many others, are unimportant determinants of socialisation. Physical attractiveness is but one factor among many, but it is a very obvious, pervasive, and permanent factor.

Great expectations

Our cultural history attests to the fact that physical attractiveness has a strong association with various personal characteristics and values. The bad or evil characters in fairy stories, pantomimes, and comic books are often dressed in black and portrayed as ugly, malformed, and with warts. The hero is invariably charming, witty and good-looking. With the advent of television these stereotypes could then be directed into most households in a compelling and powerful way. Glossy TV shows and even glossier advertisements now repeatedly show us that the world is populated mainly with very attractive people and that physical attractiveness is closely associated with success, happiness and a luxurious life style. The positive personal characteristics and benefits supposedly associated with physical attractiveness appear to be both directly and indirectly taught to children during all their waking hours.

Physically attractive children appear to benefit from positive evaluations consistent across most of the significant figures in their social world, from teachers, parents, and peers (Byrnes, 1987). These differential evaluations cover both social, personal and academic attributes – in fact most attributes which are evaluated positively.

As children spend a substantial portion of their lives in school, and many peer relationships are established there, anything which affects their behaviour in that context must also have significant implications for the child's broader sphere of relationships. It is to the school that we will first go to examine the nature of the attractiveness stereotype. A number of studies demonstrate that teachers evaluate the school-work and adjustment of children differently depending on their level of attractiveness. These effects seem to occur both in relation to unknown children and to the teacher's own pupils. More attractive children are perceived as more intelligent and are expected to achieve better grades, show better academic adjustment, and be more popular than their less attractive counterparts. This finding appears relatively consistent across the whole of the primary and secondary school age range and has been observed in both the UK and the USA (e.g. Kenealy, Frude & Shaw, 1988). Even experienced teachers appear to show that their expectations of characteristics such as popularity, intelligence and academic potential are influenced by a pupil's physical attractiveness (Clifford & Walster, 1973). There seems, however, to be a flip-side to the beautiful is good stereotype. A study by Kehle, Bramble & Mason (1974) showed that attractive children were seen as more uncontrolled, impulsive, and unpredictable. Perhaps an element of the physical attractiveness stereotype is that attractive children are likely to be spoiled and indulged.

It is not, of course, only teachers that succumb to the influence of the attractiveness stereotype. Other adults also perceive attractive children to be more socially popular, active, assertive, and less likely to exhibit antisocial behaviour (Guise, Pollans & Turkat, 1982). Should serious antisocial behaviour occur it is likely to be evaluated less negatively in attractive children. In contrast, the transgressions and mistakes of unattractive children are more likely to be attributed to dispositional causes, to be seen as a personality trait of the child and as likely to be repeated (Dion, 1972, 1974).

Children's stereotypes

The stereotype associated with attractive children also seems to be held by the children themselves. In an early study, Dion (1973) showed that even preschoolers (aged 3–6 years) hold consistent stereotypes associated with the facial attractiveness. This is an important and much cited study and so it is worth outlining its methods and findings in some detail. In this study adult judges rated facial photographs of unknown children of approximately six years of age for attractiveness. A total of 12 photographs (three each of attractive and unattractive boys and girls) were then selected and presented to the preschool subjects – 31 girls and 34 boys between the ages of approximately three and six years. Each child was shown the photographs of the male and female stimulus figures separately and asked to indicate two children that she or he would like as friends and two that she or he would not like as friends. The child was then asked to indicate which of the targets would be most likely to exhibit various behaviours. The study ended with the child being presented with pairs of photographs and being asked which was prettier or cuter. Attractive children were seen as more prosocial, as more likely to be friendly to other children, and to dislike fighting and shouting.

Unattractive children were seen as more antisocial, more likely to hit others without good cause, to hurt them and to scare them. In view of these portraits it comes as little surprise that attractive children were also more likely to be picked as potential friends.

Of course, photographs of unknown children are likely to elicit different expectations from those held for acquaintances. To examine this possibility Dion & Berscheid (1974) used a similar technique to that outlined above except that the stimulus photographs were of the child's nursery school classmates. Similar results were found: unattractive classmates were less popular and were more often seen as scary, the boys were also perceived as more likely to show antisocial aggressive behaviour such as fighting, hitting and yelling at the teacher, or saying angry things. Unattractive girls were more often nominated as fearful. Attractive children were seen as more prosocial, independent, self-sufficient, and unafraid.

Research on older, school-age subjects shows that they hold similar physical attractiveness stereotypes to those possessed by adults and preschoolers (Dushenko et al., 1978). Research indicates that physical attractiveness has a greater impact on person perception than a variety of other factors which are also stereotyped. For example, physical attractiveness may have a greater impact on sociometric choice than ethnicity. In a study by Langlois & Stephan (1977) kindergarten and fourth-grade children (ages approximately six and ten years) evaluated unknown attractive second-grade children as more likeable and friendly, smarter, needing less help, and lower on meanness and hitting than their comparable unattractive children. Black, white, and Mexican-American children were used in this study, but the attractiveness effect outweighed the impact of any ethnic differences. This appears to support Patzer's (1985) assertion that "Discrimination based on physical attractiveness probably excels prejudicial discrimination based on sex, race, or religion" (p. 11). However, unlike these other forms of discrimination, society does not legislate against discrimination on the grounds of physical appearance. Given this condition and the subtle, pervasive nature of physical attractiveness effects, this form of prejudice is likely to be with us for some considerable time to come.

A pointer to the nature of the intergenerational transmission of physical attractiveness stereotypes is indicated by the work of Adams, Hicken & Salehi (1988). In this study of children ranging in age from preschoolers to the fifth grade, it was found that the extent to which parents expected their child to use physical attractiveness stereotypes correlated with their actual use by the child. This suggests that parental attitudes are an important influence in the socialisation of the physical attractiveness stereotype.

This section has shown that there exists a relatively clear and unambiguous physical attractiveness stereotype. The nature of this stereotype is succinctly summarised in the title of Dion, Berscheid & Walster's (1972) article, "What is beautiful is good''. We must not, however, forget that like much person perception research, the answers that have been found are a result of the questions that have been asked. Ask different questions and different answers will be found. Physically attractive individuals fare well in terms of one set of traits but in terms of a different set of they appear considerably less advantaged. For example, if traits such as "vain" and "spoilt" are used the attractive child is likely to score higher on these characteristics and so appear to be less positively evaluated than a less attractive peer (Kehle, Bramble & Mason, 1974).

Beautiful relationships

There is considerably less research on the behavioural consequences of physical attractiveness than on the nature of its stereotype and associated expectancies. There does appear to be significant agreement in the ratings of attractiveness given to photographs and live ratings (Lerner & Lerner, 1977). Most studies using children who are known to adults or acquainted peers show a similar pattern to the results of person perception studies that have already been examined.

Studies of teacher behaviour have found that teachers interacted more with attractive seventh graders than with their less attractive classmates, though this was not found to characterise their relationship with younger pupils (Adams & Cohen, 1974). None the less, even in grades two to six attractive pupils do benefit from a greater acceptance of their ideas by teachers (Martinek, 1981). Not only do more attractive pupils appear likely to get more attention, they are likely to be awarded better grades. A significant correlation has been found between a child's level of attractiveness and the grades awarded by elementary school teachers (Lerner & Lerner, 1977). The source of this effect is unclear, it could reflect teacher expectations, the child ability, or greater motivation on the part of the child.

Of course attractive children are not angels, like any child they sometimes break rules or even laws. Should attractive children be called to account for their transgressions they none the less still appear to reap the benefits of the physical attractiveness stereotype and fare better than their less attractive counterparts. Negative behaviour is likely to be less severely punished in attractive children, and evidence suggests that such effects are widespread and occur in the home, school and the wider social world of the child. For example, adult females role-playing the part of a child's parent give more severe punishments to unattractive children (Berkowitz & Frodi, 1979) and adult females monitoring a child's performance and giving penalties for incorrect responses are more lenient towards attractive children (Dion, 1974). An apparently contradictory result was Barocas & Black's (1974) finding that attractive third graders are more often referred for psychological or educational assessments than their less attractive counterparts. The authors themselves do not perceive this as a discrepant result and explain such referrals as helpful and advantageous as the child is being sent for remedial help rather than for the control of behavioural difficulties.

Peer relationships

An association between physical attractiveness and children's peer popularity is also evident. A substantial number of studies of both preschoolers and older children have found that attractive individuals have more positive, prosocial peer relations, are more influential and persuasive, and have fewer aggressive encounters (such as fighting) than their less attractive classmates (e.g. Spence, 1987; Weisfeld et al., 1987). In the case of adolescents, physically attractive individuals were also more likely to have a steady dating partner (Chess, Thomas & Cameron, 1976).

By early adolescence the impact of physical appearance on interpersonal attraction is marked (Freedman, 1984). One reason for this is the major physical changes which the child is experiencing but, paradoxically, it is also be due to the more sophisticated cognitive abilities of the adolescent. Elkind (1967) has argued that as the child enters adolescence and achieves the ability to think in more abstract, conceptual terms a second period of introspective egocentrism is common. The adolescent becomes primarily concerned with his or her own needs, attributes, social standing, and social relationships (Williamson & Campbell, 1985). If this scene is considered in conjunction with the physical changes that are starting to occur at this age, it should be of no surprise to note the concern of many adolescents with their physical appearance. As eminent theorists have noted, a major task of adolescence appears to be the coming to terms with one's body and appearance (Erikson, 1963; Havighurst, 1972).

Some studies have suggested that the consequences of attractiveness are greater for girls than boys (e.g. Krantz, 1987). There appears to be a greater association between physical attractiveness and self-concept for girls than for boys (Lerner & Karabenick, 1974). For girls especially, an attractive appearance is often an important component of the self-concept and feminine gender role in adolescence (Freedman, 1984). This may explain the heightened self-consciousness that is a common feature of the young teenager, especially girls (Simmons & Rosenberg, 1975). Determination of one's standing on attributes that are defined in terms of social evaluation and consensus is significantly affected by the reflected appraisal of peers (Felson, 1985), especially at this age when peers are starting to become the child's major reference group. To this extent the often noted closer relationships of girls represent an important factor in the adolescent girl's ability to evaluate her relative physical attractiveness. Perhaps this is one reason why physical attractiveness is able to be more significant for adolescent girls than for boys.

Continuities and differences

Some studies examining the social consequences of physical attractiveness have come up with results that conflict with the broad pattern outlined above, perhaps indicating that physical attractiveness does not have identical effects in all situations and circumstances. The results of studies of physical attractiveness in children are at least in part determined by the particular subjects and rating procedures employed (Smith & Krantz, 1986). Adams & La Voie (1974) found that teachers rated the work habits of attractive children lower than those of their less attractive peers. Research by Langlois & Styczynski (1979) has found that children view attractive peers with whom they are well acquainted in more negative terms than would be expected from the stereotype they hold and typically apply to unfamiliar targets – they were regarded as more inclined to tantrums and aggression. A possible explanation for these findings is that attractive children are more self-confident and assertive and that more attention is given to their behaviour (Hildebrandt, 1982); this could result in both more positive and more negative behaviour from attractive children and in this being more likely to be noticed. Whatever the explanation for these results, it certainly establishes that familiarity is an under-researched variable which may be a significant factor affecting the expectations associated with physical attractiveness.

The results of research on the effects of the attractiveness of young children on their expected social interaction shows continuity with the findings of research on babies. From this research some insight may be gleaned in to the intergenerational transmission and behavioural realisation of physical attractiveness stereotypes. A study by Adams & Crane (1980) found that parents and teachers expected their preschool children/students to see attractive children of elementary school age as nicer than unattractive figures and to prefer attractive boys over unattractive boys as potential playmates (the exception to this finding was parents seeing the lack of an attractiveness effect on social choice for girls; this may be due to the more general attribution of girls being generally more pleasant and prosocial). The children themselves also showed the observed attractiveness effect on evaluations of niceness but did not show any significant preferences for playmates based on levels of attractiveness. This evidence, that parents and teachers assume physical attractiveness will serve as a basis for social choice before it actually comes to have such an influence, suggests that many of the child's physical attractiveness stereotypes are acquired from significant adults during this early phase of childhood. This conclusion receives additional (and even more interesting) support from Adams & Crane's additional finding of a significant correlation between mother and teacher expectations and children's actual use of the physical attractiveness stereotype.

The matching hypothesis

In adults and adolescents there is ample evidence for a matching in levels of physical attractiveness between friends and between romantically involved couples (Cash & Derlega, 1978; Murstein, 1986), and for attractiveness being associated with deeper characteristics which have been shown to be important factors in attraction and friendship – such as perceived similarity of attitudes (Cavior, Miller & Cohen, 1975) or an aspect of personality, personal constructs (Erwin & Calev, 1984). There is considerably less evidence in younger age groups, and though similar results are being found in children, interpreting such findings is difficult as a child's perception of similarity is constrained by his or her role-taking ability, the ability to take the other child's perspective (Shantz, 1975). None the less, there is suggestive evidence for a matching effect even in very young children. In a study by Langlois & Downs (1979) the level of attractiveness of both members of pairs of same-sex preschoolers appeared to be important in determining behaviour. Higher levels of positive social behaviour characterised dyads matched in levels of physical attractiveness.

Beauty – more than skin deep?

As we have seen in the previous sections of this chapter, a child's level of physical attractiveness results in both adults and other children having fairly specific ideas about how she or he is likely to behave. The reflected appraisal of others also constitutes an important basis for the child's evaluation of his or her own level of physical attractiveness (Felson, 1985), which in turn facilitates the child being able to form expectations about personal abilities and behaviour. Research indicates that physical appearance and attractiveness are important components of the self-concept in both elementary school-children and adolescents (Lerner & Karabenick, 1974; Salvia, Algozzine & Sheare, 1977) and are associated with aspects of an individual's personality (Erwin & Calev, 1984). It appears that the differential expectations of others and our personal stereotypes come to affect our behaviour and ultimately turn into self-fulfilling prophecies. It is to this issue that this section is devoted.

Original research by Rosenthal & Jacobson (1968) appeared to clearly demonstrate an association between teacher expectations and a pupil's academic performance. Although a much criticised study (e.g. Thorndike, 1968), this research did provide this impetus for more systematic research on the nature of expectancy effects. Though subsequent research in this controversial area has been far from unanimous it has provided substantial support for the idea that one person's expectations may have the effect of a self-fulfilling prophecy on the behaviour of another person (R. Rosenthal, 1973). More directly relevant research has attempted to show that expectations originating in the physical attractiveness stereotype can also produce such expectancy effects.

A rather good demonstration of the behavioural consequences of expectations based on physical attractiveness was provided in an experimental study by Snyder, Tanke & Berscheid (1977). Although this study used adult subjects, the effects observed have a potentially far greater generality and significance. In this study men were shown a photograph of an attractive or an unattractive woman and were led to believe that this was a women with whom they would talk over the telephone. A ten-minute telephone conversation was then held with a female subject. Analysis of the conversations showed that the women portrayed as attractive had actually come to behave in a more friendly, outgoing, sociable manner than her supposedly less attractive counterparts.

Living the stereotype

There is not a vast amount of developmental research examining the self-fulfilling nature of expectancies based on physical attractiveness stereotypes, though what there is does seem to confirm at least the possible existence of the effect. Studies on individuals of high school age confirm the finding of a positive relationship between physical attractiveness and achievement in terms of school grades and, perhaps more objectively, scores on standardised achievement tests (Murphy, Nelson & Cheap, 1981). Langlois & Stephan (1981) report a study by Styczynski (1976) in which similar results were found with younger children. In this study a positive relationship was found between physical attractiveness and the scores fourth-grade children obtained on an achievement test. An interesting aspect of these results was that a comparison of the children's current and second-grade test performance appeared to show a growing divergence of the scores of attractive and unattractive individuals, possibly indicating the increasing influence of expectancy effects with age.

Research has also confirmed that expectations about social behaviour can become self-fulfilling prophecies and that attractive children may come to attribute more self-control over the outcomes of their interactions than their unattractive peers (McArthur, 1982). In a study of seven and eight year olds Rose (1991) found that during school playtimes attractive children showed more affiliative behaviour, were more likely to make approaches to peers, and were more likely to be involved in interactive play. In contrast, unattractive children were significantly more likely to be involved in solitary play activities.

A similar pattern of results has been found with preschoolers. A study by Trnavsky & Bakeman (1976) observed the behaviour of preschoolers in free play. The type of play exhibited and whether it was negative was recorded. In line with the expected effects of physical attractiveness on popularity, attractive children were found to spend less time playing by themselves – though there were no differences in the number of their social contacts or negative behaviour. In similar vein but using a more detailed coding system, Langlois & Downs (1979) found that acquainted preschoolers in same-sex dyads showed several behavioural differences depending on their level of attractiveness. Unattractive children were more active, preferred more masculine toys and, for five year olds but not three year olds, were more aggressive; attractive children were less active and preferred more feminine toys. These differences may come to have significant implications for a boy's evaluation and treatment by his peers as with increasing age large activity-based groups increasingly become the focus for boys' friendships (Douvan & Adelson, 1966).

An interesting and important qualifier to the findings on the consequence of expectancy effects due to physical attractiveness is made by Krantz, Friedberg & Andrews (1985). In third-grade and fifth-grade children these authors found the usual relationship between objective ratings of attractiveness and popularity. This study then took the analysis one step further and went on to examine how the child's subjective ratings of attractiveness were related to popularity. A significant relationship was found for the fifth graders only. The authors argue that this may be due to developmental differences in person perception. It certainly seems to imply that for young children many physical attractiveness effects originate in the expectations and behaviour of others rather than an anticipatory response of the child.

The above research seems to provide support for the idea that not only are a child's social and academic expectations likely to differ according to his or her level of attractiveness, but that these are likely to be translated into real-life experiences. Unattractive children carry with them their own micro-climate of lower expectations, severe verbal or physical punishment of mistakes and transgressions, and less peer popularity. In short, such children experience a considerably different and poorer pattern of socialisation than their more attractive peers (Berkowitz & Frodi, 1979).

Physique

So far this review has focused on facial attractiveness. It is important not to forget a lesser researched area – but one that cannot be discounted – the impact of physique on judgements of physical attractiveness. For example, in a study by Kleck, Richardson & Ronald (1974) over 50% of their subjects – 9–14-year-old boys – referred to posture, head shape and body size as important factors when explaining their attractiveness evaluations of photographs.

Fortunately, the literature in this area is fairly consistent and straightforward. Children are able to make stable and consistent attributions about another on the basis of body weight cues. From at least five years of age figures of average build are generally preferred and evaluated more positively than those that are thin or, especially negatively stereotyped, those that are obese. The strength of this stereotype appears to increase with age. An exception to these general principles appears to be the finding that some girls prefer the thin body-type, presumably because of its association with role models and stereotypes of female physical attractiveness.

Heavier physiques are rated more negatively in terms of physical attractiveness, a variety of personal attributes, and their social relations. They are seen as less popular than children of slimmer physiques and adjectives such as sloppy, lazy, mean, ugly, and stupid are attributed to them. In contrast the figure of average build is seen as honest, good-looking, happy, and as having lots of friends (Lerner & Korn, 1972; Brenner & Hinsdale, 1978).

Much of the research on the effects of body build has tended to use either simple line drawings or, somewhat less artificial, photographs. More realistic research suggests that caution should be exercised in generalising these results to the real world. Contextual factors and the mode of stimulus presentation have a significant effect on the results of research. To illustrate this point, a study by Young & Avdzej (1979) used videotapes of obese or normal-weight boys interacting with an adult in an obedient or disobedient way. Results showed the impact of physical appearance on social evaluation and preference was outweighed by the boys' behaviour during the interaction.

Obesity is a relatively common characteristic which influences the way in which an individual is perceived. A study by Counts et al. (1986) examined the stereotypes associated with obesity which were held by children in grades three to five. When only body-build information is available, an obese figure is rated significantly worse as a potential partner and leader, and is rated lower on a variety of negative traits, including being significantly more sad. Though a comparison of attractive and unattractive facial appearance was not made, the authors do note that a photograph of a facially attractive obese person was rated above average in terms of contact desired, attractiveness and competence. Apparently facial attractiveness can reduce the negative evaluations associated with obesity.

The body-build stereotypes noted above may possess or become a behavioural reality. Children with body characteristics which they and others see as less attractive (such as obesity) show lower levels of social acceptance and more negative self-concepts and lower self-esteem than their more attractive peers (Lerner & Karabcnick, 1974). Fortunately a study of children of approximately 12 years old and above has shown that for most children there is only a small degree of body-figure dissatisfaction relative to their ideal, and they did not perceive themselves to be significantly different from the size they considered most attractive to the opposite sex (Cohn et al., 1987).

Overall, the results of research on physique are consistent with those examining facial appearance. Some physiques are regarded as more attractive than others, and the consequences of stereotyping may ultimately become internalised by the child. Despite these similarities, physique and facial attractiveness are not perfectly correlated and so both must be taken into consideration when examining the consequences of stereotyping based on physical appearance. It is indeed unfortunate that most research has ignored the possible effects of physique.

4 Social skills

Children, like adults, need not be perfect. In the end, they will be judged not simply by their behavior but by their goals and values.
(Asher, 1983, p. 1432)

In Chapters 2 and 3 attention focused on children's social cognitive abilities and knowledge and how these can affect their friendship and peer relationships. In this chapter the focus moves to encompass overt behaviour. The main sections of this chapter trace the patterns and development of social skills throughout childhood and adolescence. An important early topic here is the the continuity of the young child's skills with the mother and peers. This literature has generally not taken the child's level of attachment into account but represents a complementary perspective to that discussed in the context of the maternal precursor hypothesis in Chapter 1. It provides important evidence that parents serve as important facilitators of their child's general sociability. Despite this, the evidence does not show children as dependent on their parents as the direct source of their specific peer relationship skills. Subsequent sections examine the social skills that children use with both familiar and unfamiliar peers across a wide age range. A knowledge of the characteristics of successful and unsuccessful relators provide important background for our understanding of children's friendships and, more importantly, open the possibility of social skills training to help isolated children. This is a topic explored further in Chapter 10. The final sections of the chapter examine the social skills and social cognitive abilities between children. Taken together these provide a more balanced, complete, and predictive analysis of children's relationships.

Clear evidence exists for a relationship between social cognitive variables – such as interpersonal understanding and social problem solving – and social competence (Mize & Cox, 1990), though as Gottman & Parkhurst (1980, p. 199) observed, "research on social cognition needs to be supplemented by an observational methodology". We need to know what children actually do in their relationships, not simply what they can do. Fortunately, since Gottman & Parkhurst made the above statement there have been a number of substantial studies on children's social behaviour with their peers and friends. As Rubin (1983, p. 1383) noted, "Research concerning peer relationships and social skills in childhood is booming". At the time he made this statement a very substantial 22% of manuscripts submitted to the journal *Child Development* were in this area. Unfortunately, as Burleson (1985) points out, this does not imply that this area of research has given many particularly clear-cut answers; it is beset by conceptual and methodological problems. Much of the research in the 1970s and 1980s, let alone before that time, was ahead of detailed theoretical analysis.

One thing is clear, the child needs not only the ability to take the role of another but, as Russell (1984) points out, role-making is also important. The child needs to be able to construct an appropriate complementary role if successful social interaction is to ensue. Effective role-taking and role-making limits and controls the roles constructed by others and hence their power to define the social situation and relationship. We need to know not just what children think about relationships and relating to others but also what they do in their relationships and how situational constraints may limit (or be defined by) the child's behavioural performance.

Basic considerations

Just as children learn behavioural skills to perform various physical tasks, so social skills represent the learned behaviours that they use in social interaction. Different authors have treated and conceptualised social skill and social competence in at least two fundamentally different ways, as a trait characterising the individual and as an ability in specific social situations (McFall, 1982).

A trait approach has been the most common level of analysis. It views social skills as a relatively enduring characteristic of the individual, rather like personality traits. Thus some children are labelled as more socially skilled than others and there would be an expectation of cross-situational consistency (Rathjen, 1980). This approach recognises that there are many equivalent and equally competent solutions to the problems encountered during social interaction. Social skills are often treated on a global level with little attempt to specify their components. For example, many studies simply categorise children's behaviour as friendly or hostile and do not specify what responses comprise these classifications.

In contrast, the molecular–behavioural approach sees the child's unique, situation-specific behaviour as representing his or her social skill. To be of use this approach requires some means of identifying and categorising units of behaviour. It is important to note that this does not imply that it is possible to compile a list of discrete behaviours which endow social competence. Indeed, Berndt (1983) cautions that social skills are but one contributor to a child's social status and popularity.

Whichever of the above approaches is adopted, they have often been used in a similar manner, based on a deficit model of social skills (Hymel & Rubin, 1985). Basically, this argues that if we compare the skills of socially popular children with other less popular or rejected children then we will find a number of behavioural differences and these are likely to be the reasons for the differences in popularity. If the deficit groups can subsequently have their sociometric status increased through being taught the social skills which have been identified as lacking then this is seen as additional proof.

Skills versus competence

Many authors appear to use the terms social skills and social competence almost interchangeably, and so it is important to make clear the distinction between them. Social skills represent the specific abilities required in order to perform competently. Social competence is a general evaluative term referring to an individual's adequacy on some task (McFall, 1982). This does, of course, pose the question as to what constitutes adequacy. The child's satisfaction with his or her performance? Success in meeting social demands? Determining the course and consequences of social events? There is plenty of room for value judgements here! Like social skills, competence has also been typically assessed in one of two major ways, representing different levels of analysis (Waters & Sroufe, 1983). First, it has been defined in terms of specific skills. Second, it has been defined and measured in more general terms such as "effectiveness". Each approach has its advantages and disadvantages. A global level of analysis does more justice to the complex, multi-faceted nature of children's social relationships but can appear vague and give little indication about what specific behaviours would be measured. The more analytic approach closely specifies what should be measured but at the risk of losing sight of the complex interrelationships and multiple external influences that also affect the impact of the behaviour.

Whatever way adequacy is defined, it is evident that competence is a function of both specific behavioural skills and situational or task demands. The implication of this is that with a change in task demands, or in an unfamiliar situation, there are consequential changes in a child's level of competence. This perspective is further complicated by various individual and reputational characteristics. For example, a child's physical attractiveness, peer reputation, and specific history of interaction with other children are all likely to be important. An identical behaviour performed by two different children may be labelled very differently in terms of the level of competence that it represents. Social competence is first and foremost a performance variable, not a specific behavioural trait.

Non-verbal behaviour

Social competence has both verbal and non-verbal components. Chapter 5 gives detailed consideration to one aspect of the verbal component, self-disclosure. The present section examines the contribution of non-verbal behaviour.

The ability to produce and recognise emotions in others, especially from facial expressions, is an important component of children's social competence and liking and peers (Walden & Field, 1990). The use of non-verbal behaviours, such as gaze, touch, and interpersonal distance, as a mechanism for regulating social involvement and control is also well established (Edinger & Patterson, 1983). Communication is an acquired aspect of non-verbal behaviour, possibly derived in the first instance from the mother behaving toward the child as if his or her behaviour has communication value (Hopkins, 1983).

Non-verbal behaviours combine to form an extremely complex system of communication whose relevance for children's peer relationships is only just beginning to unfold. For example, information from facial and body movements, proximity, and the physical characteristics of speech all influence the impressions that children form of their peers. Non-verbal communication is multi-channelled and encounters many barriers and obstacles. There are social and physical barriers to effective communication, such as membership of social groups and seating arrangements within a classroom, and the communication skills of the sender and receiver are also likely to be significant. Despite all these problems in using non-verbal communication, even young children can and do use it, and often very effectively.

Non-verbal communication is especially significant in communicating emotional information, and hence in children's friendships (Patterson, 1988). In personal relationships words are often inadequate or embarrassing. In these circumstances non-verbal communication becomes a potent channel of communication. A study of fifth- and sixth-grade children rated as unattractive by their peers characterised them as having greater non verbal hostility; popularity or rejected status was not correlated with verbal hostility (Nowicki & Oxenford, 1989). Differences in non-verbal communication parallel the differences in children's levels of involvement and intimacy in their peer relationships. For example, in a study of 6–18 year olds, Montemayor & Flannery (1989) found that expressive behaviour in mother–child dyads decreased between childhood and mid-adolescence, while that between male–female dyads increased.

The face has been regarded as one of the main sources of non-verbal information and the ability to interpret facial expressions accurately is an important factor in peer relationships. A study by Spence (1987) found a significant correlation between the ability to decode facial expression (labelling photographs) and positive peer nominations, and Vosk, Forehand & Figueroa (1983) showed that accepted children were significantly better at the identification of emotion in videotaped interaction sequences than were their rejected peers. This type of ability is crucial in children's judgements, for example, of aggressive intent by another (Schiff et al., 1980). This will in turn affect reactions to the other's behaviour and the likelihood of an aggressive, rejecting response or a positive, accepting response.

Proximity is another factor that has long been recognised as significant in social interaction and relationships. Proximity effects can be seen on at least three levels. First, in terms of physical and geographical limits it determines who is likely to meet whom. Functional proximity has been shown to be an important factor in interpersonal attraction in children (e.g. Byrne, 1961). Second, in terms of familiarity, the mere exposure hypothesis (Zajonc, 1968) argues that repeated exposure to people and objects leads to their being more positively evaluated. These two effects of proximity are considered in more detail elsewhere in this book. The third effect of proximity, is ongoing interaction.

Proximity both reflects and in part determines the positivity of an ongoing interaction. Even preschoolers appear to appreciate the role of proximity and gaze as cues to liking. By four years of age children can use proximity as a cue in judging the relationship between people (Post & Hetherington, 1974). It also reflects the status of their own peer relationships in the nursery school. A study by Shea (1981) found that as children settled into nursery school groups their frequency of adopting close interpersonal distances showed corresponding increases – with the largest increases being for children attending the groups most frequently. This pattern of more frequent close proximity was also accompanied by a general increase in interpersonal distances between peers, which the authors argue may reflect increased sociability producing higher activity levels and therefore necessary spacing. The changes in proximity noted in this study genuinely appear to be reflecting the changing character and status of children's peer relationships.

Popularity

The following sections look at popularity and differences in competence in social interaction. A number of authors have delineated the characteristics of popular and unpopular children (e.g. Cantrell & Prinz, 1985; Putallaz, 1987). A number of these characteristics are physical (see Chapter 3), cognitive (see Chapter 2), or reflect relative maturity (see Chapter 6). In any event, these various characteristics receive their expression through behaviour and it to this aspect that we now turn. For orientation, this section gives a brief general description of the behavioural profiles of children of different social status. In subsequent sections these descriptions will be examined in more specific developmental terms.

A number of positive adjectives have been used to describe the behaviour of the popular child, these include outgoing, gregarious, helpful, co-operative, supportive, enthusiastic, and kind. The behaviour of popular, well-liked children is generally friendly towards others, relatively non-aggressive, rewarding, and supportive. Such children often also have specific skills which are deemed attractive, such as at sports and games, and tend to be successful at school.

The picture of the neglected child is only marginally different from that of the popular child. They do tend to perceive themselves as less socially competent than their peers, are often less talkative, and receive fewer nominations as being helpful and nice. There is little difference from the popular child in terms of assertiveness, or self-rated shyness, unhappiness, or feelings of acceptance.

The behavioural characteristics of the unpopular or rejected child are almost the opposite of those of the popular child. Negative, problem behaviour is a major correlate of negative peer status (Spence, 1987). In comparison to the accepted child the rejected or disliked child is likely to be disruptive, short-tempered, argumentative and aggressive, critical, disruptive, inattentive, and generally less friendly, supportive or mature. The child is also likely to overestimate his or her competence as rated by peers (Patterson, Kupersmidt & Griester, 1990).

Of course, outlining the characteristics of popular and unpopular children does not tell us whether these characteristics cause the observed popularity or were developed as a consequence of living a popular life style. It seems that both of these factors are often involved. If unacquainted children are observed during their initial interactions, those which display the most consistently positive, supportive behaviour are likely to end up as leaders and social stars, those consistently in conflict are more likely to be rejected (Dodge, 1983; Shantz, 1986).

The behaviours that contribute to sociometric status show marked changes developmentally. With age the skills required to establish and maintain social status become increasing complex and subtle (Asher & Hymel, 1981). To facilitate the further examination of these skills the following discussion is thus divided up into a number of convenient, if rather arbitrary, developmental blocks.

The first year

Unless the child has brothers or sisters, regular interaction with peers may not occur unless and until the child is enrolled in some alternative care setting, such as a kindergarten or preschool (Lamb, 1988). The incidence of such arrangements has increased dramatically in recent years. In one relatively early study, Lewis et al. (1975) found that only 22% of one year olds and 28% of 18 month olds attended playgroups. In a second study they reported that only 15–20% of one year olds had a regular playmate. Many parents in this study indicated they did not feel the need to encourage peer contact for their infants. More recent statistics show considerably more than a doubling in the numbers of registered child minders and nurseries in Britain between 1976 and 1989 (*Social Trends*, 1991) and the significance and potential consequences of early peer relationships are becoming increasingly acknowledged (see Chapter 9).

Given the opportunity, social awareness and attempts at peer interaction are evident from an early age. The first positive interest in other children occurs at approximately six months of age (Hay, Nash & Pedersen, 1983). With an observer and the child's mother present, Becker (1977) notes that nine-month-old infants directed more behaviour to a peer than to any other available target (adults, toys, or surroundings); this constituted 33% of their behaviour per play session. Non-social activity occupies much more time than social behaviour in children of this age, the young infant lacks the social skills to sustain the attempted social interactions (Hartup, 1983). In children 6–12 months of age, approximately 47% of the child's attempts at peer interaction were successful in achieving co-ordinated social behaviour, though most of these successes consisted of a single action–response sequence (Vandell, Wilson & Buchanan, 1980).

Children at this age will look at each other, touch and imitate each other's actions, vocalise, and smile at each other (Vandell, Wilson & Buchanan, 1980). Those infants with more extensive turn-taking experience with skilled partners such as mothers or older siblings tend to show more extensive skill with peers (Vandell & Wilson, 1987). As well as representing a continuity of other social interactions, these early social contacts appear to be useful foundations for future peer interaction. In a naturalistic observation of nine-month-old infants over a period of ten play sessions, Becker (1977) found an increase in the level of complexity and social involvement in their behaviour toward peers. More interestingly, these changes appeared to generalise to a new playmate in an eleventh play session. A comparable group of infants that experienced only two play sessions showed no such increase in peer-directed behaviour. Ensuring that the child has plenty of opportunities to play with other children and providing toys and materials fostering interaction is an important contribution that parents can make to their child's social development (Asher, Renshaw & Hymel, 1982).

Despite the very evident social abilities of infants, we must, none the less, not lose sight of the fact that their social skills are still quite basic (Lamb, 1988). Many of the social overtures by a very young child are brief, lasting only a few seconds or a minute, and often go unrecognised by the other child (Vandell, Wilson & Buchanan, 1980). In the words of two important contributors to our knowledge of such relationships, "It would be a mistake, however, to over-estimate the skills one sees in these twelve-month-olds. During the first year many of the social behaviours appear isolated social behaviours" (Vandell & Mueller, 1980, p. 184).

Skills with mothers and peers

The preceding section mentions that children with turn-taking experience with more skilled partners, such as their mother, tended to be more skilled in their peer interactions. This observation necessitates a review of the nature of the mother's contribution to her child's peer interaction skills. To what extent are the skills used in the child's peer relationships the same as those used in a child's relationship with a mother? And, more importantly, are the skills initially developed to interact with the mother and then simply generalised to peer interactions?

Observations of 5–14-week-old infants' behaviour to their mothers and strange peers have shown even at this age there are distinct differences in behaviour to each of these figures (Fogel, 1979). The infant's behaviour to the mother was relaxed, varied and finely detailed; in contrast, behaviour to a strange peer generally involved gross movements of the arms and body. Despite these differences it does also appear that some behavioural characteristics of the infant's interactions with the mother are also used with peers of the same age. Disagreeable and demanding behaviour in a mother's interaction with her child is associated with the child reciprocating disagreeable and demanding behaviour toward the mother and peers (Putallaz, 1987). It seems reasonable to conclude that the child's general level of sociability is affected by his or her maternal interactions.

A study by Vandell & Wilson (1987) showed that infants spending more time interacting with their mothers at six months of age interacted more with peers some three months later. Similar results have been obtained with children in their second year. Vandell & Mueller (1980) report a study by Vandell (1977) in which children were observed with their mothers and peers on three occasions, at 16, 19, and 22 months of age. Mother–child interaction at 16 and 19 months was predictive of the child's level of peer interaction at 22 months.

The parent as a social skills coach plays a significant role affecting the young child's social competence and peer popularity. The play of young preschoolers with an unfamiliar peer seems to benefit from parental assistance more than older preschoolers (Bhavnagri & Parke, 1991). But the way in which the parent fulfils the role of social skills coach is very variable. Research suggests that one important influence on the way this role is fulfilled is the parent's recollection of her or his own childhood peer relationships; these memories are related to how active a role they take in their child's social relationships, and ultimately the level of social competence displayed by the child (Putallaz, Costanzo & Smith, 1991). The parents of preschool and first-grade children of high sociometric status appear to interact in a more sensitive and positive manner with their children than do the parents of less popular children, who appear to be more controlling, directive and intrusive in their interactions (Austin & Lindauer, 1990). These patterns of interaction do not only characterise the adult–child relationship, they also reflect the characteristic way in which parents manage their child's peer interactions. A study by Russell & Finnie (1990) examined the guidance given by mothers to their four- and five-year-old children for joining an existing unknown pair of peers at play. The mothers of popular children were more likely to suggest a group orientated strategy (such as how to integrate with the ongoing strategy) while the mothers of neglected children were more likely to draw attention to play materials. The mothers of less popular children also show more negative and controlling behaviours toward their children. The mother's pattern of behaviour toward her child appears to be duly reciprocated by the child. First-grade children of high sociometric status speak more and have more influence during their interactions with their mothers (Putallaz, 1987).

In general terms, the social orientations implicit within caregiver–child and child–peer interactions do appear to be related. Caregivers regularly offering toys to their child produce children who in turn are more likely to offer toys to their peers – though all children do show some prosocial behaviour at this age (Zahn-Waxler & Radke-Yarrow, 1982). In similar vein, aggressive children are often reflecting their learning experiences, in the family or wider social world. Rejecting parents using frequent prohibitions and controlling behaviour have been consistently associated with aggressiveness in their children, as has high levels of physical punishment. Clearly parents are, wittingly or unwittingly, acting as models for their child. Observing successful or rewarded aggression, or being actually involved in successful or rewarded aggression serves to promote the behaviour. Conversely, other relationships, with a second parent, a sibling or peer, can provide a buffer and moderate the psychological impact of family violence on children (Moore et al., 1990).

Emphasising the role of social cognition and communication skills, a significant body of research is beginning to clarify the relationships between maternal and child characteristics. Suffice it to say at this point that a child's level of person-centred communication (which predicted peer acceptance) was found to be a function of the child's social cognitive skills, which were in turn a product of maternal communication styles – being positively related to the use of reflection enhancing modes of control and comfort (Delia &

Applegate, 1990). The interrelation of these maternal and child characteristics are dealt with in more detail in Chapter 2.

It is often assumed without question that interaction with the mother is a training ground preparing the child for future peer interaction. Although this sequential order is suggestive of the mother's role in the child's acquisition of peer relationship skills, it is not sufficient on its own. Lamb & Nash (1989) point out a number of methodological and conceptual factors that at the current time prevent such a conclusion being sustained. For example, studies often confound a number of variables such as age, familiarity (no peer can be as familiar to the child as the mother), and the social skill of the partner (mothers tend to be more socially skilful than peers, and even peers vary markedly in their levels of competence). Studies on peer interaction in young children have also varied in whether they have allowed the parent to be present with the child during experimental observations, the instructions given to the parents on the limits of their interaction with the child, and whether the child's response to the parent are recorded or not. Lamb & Nash (1989) conclude that "there is currently little support for the belief that peer skills are ontogenetic derivatives of infant–mother skills" (p. 231). In other words, skills do not appear first in interaction with parents and only later in interaction with peers.

Two to five years

Throughout this age range, and continuing through to adolescence, there is an increasing shift to more interaction with peers and less with parents (Ellis, Rogoff & Cromer, 1981). In the patterns of young children's play we can also begin to see the origins of closer peer relationships and true friendships. Evidence suggests that perhaps more than half of all preschoolers establish relatively stable reciprocal friendships (Gershman & Hayes, 1983). In these relationships they try to be understood by friends and to respond to the needs of friends in a manner appropriate to the regulation of the encounter; friends engage in more connected discourse and speech relevant to fantasy and role-play activities than do strangers (Gottman & Parkhurst, 1980).

Studies by Hartup, Glazer & Charlesworth (1967) and Masters & Furman (1981) have outlined the major characteristics underlying peer preference and popularity at this age. Sociometric status (popularity) in nursery school children of four to five years of age is associated with overall levels of giving and receiving positive, reinforcing behaviour (e.g. giving or gifts, attention, or acceptance); negative behaviour (e.g. aggression, rejection, and non-compliance) is associated with sociometric rejection. As Masters & Furman (1981) point out, popularity is not synonymous with specific personal relationships and so comparisons must also be made at this level. Children of this age showed more positive behaviour to and from friends than non-friends. There was not a higher level of negative reinforcements from disliked children at this specific, individual level of analysis. Not being a given child's friend does not imply that the other child has the characteristics of the sociometric rejectee.

A requirement for maintaining a relationship is consistency in evaluations (which, of course, is not necessarily the same thing as an actual stability in the other's behaviour). Preschoolers' perceptions of aggressive and co-operative behaviour in others is relatively salient and stable, showing low to moderate correlations over a three-week period (Ladd & Mars, 1986). These perceptions of peers also reflected actual behaviour and sociometric status. Peer rejection has been regularly reported as related to aggressive, hostile forms of behaviour, lower levels of interaction, and generally less mature forms of play (e.g. Rubin & Hayvren, 1981; Rubin, Daniels-Beirness & Hayvren, 1982).

It is worthy of note that the above descriptions do not necessarily portray the rejected child as an isolated child, in the sense of being alone and devoid of interaction experience. Foster & Ritchey (1985) observed no difference in the rates of positive and negative initiations of interaction by rejected and accepted children. The rejected children did, however, receive fewer positive responses to their overtures. Rejected children show the same levels of interaction as their more popular counterparts, but the nature of these interactions is crucially different (Gottman, 1977a). The overall picture is, unfortunately, complicated and made more difficult to interpret by some authors not distinguishing between neglected, rejected and withdrawn children when making comparisons with popular peers.

Predicting school social adjustment

The behavioural patterns discussed in the preceding section set the stage for the child's entry to grade school. But to what extent are they predictive of social status in grade school? This question has been addressed in an interesting study by Putallaz (1983).

In a highly structured, experimental study of young boys, in the summer before entering the school first grade, Putallaz (1983) examined children's entry tactics when joining an existing group of two unfamiliar experimental confederates, boys already in the first or second grade. The behaviour of the confederates was scripted and centred around the playing of a series of games. During the games the preschool subject was provided with the opportunity to respond to several problematic social situations. For example, at one point a confederate would say that he needed help in the course of a game and the second confederate would respond by saying that he would like to help but wasn't able to. Both confederates would then look at the subject. These experimental sessions were videotape recorded. After the experimental session the videotape was played back to the child and he was questioned about the behaviour of the confederates and his own intentions. Analysis consisted of coding the recorded verbal behaviour according to a content coding scheme devised by Putallaz & Gottman (1981) which had been found to discriminate between popular and unpopular children. Sociometric status was evaluated four months later. In other words, this study allowed a test of the prediction of future social status based on current verbal behaviour strategies used in entering ongoing peer interactions. This represented a considerable step forward from the many previous studies which had simply noted social skills correlates of sociometric choice. The ambiguity implicit in correlational studies meant that there could be no assurance that the apparent association wasn't due to some third factor exerting an equal influence on the two observed factors. This study allowed a predictive test and as such enabled more confidence in assuming a direct link between the two observed variables. The results showed that children attempting to enter groups by using *relevant* conversation were subsequently more likely to have high sociometric status than were less skilled peers. This relationship was even more marked for those children that also accurately perceived the ongoing behaviour of the group. Children making irrelevant statements or tending to be disruptive were more likely to be subsequently rejected by peers.

School age

Friends come to play a considerably greater role in the life of the school-age child than is the case for younger children. In this era there are evident increases in the effectiveness of interpersonal communication, mirroring developments in social cognitive abilities such as role-taking. There is also an increase in displays of prosocial and co-operative behaviour, such as sharing, and a reduction in aggression. All of these factors are closely related to children's sociometric and friendship status.

A study by Dodge (1983) examined the development of sociometric status in unacquainted second-grade boys that met in groups of eight for a series of eight one-hour sessions. Boys that were to go on to become identified as rejected or neglected engaged in more inappropriate social behaviours. In particular, the rejected boys showed more physically aggressive behaviours than any other group; the popular children refrained from aggression. The rejected and neglected children showed no shortage of attempts to initiate social contacts but they were frequently rebuffed, the approaches of popular children were generally positively received. An interesting meld of these two profiles occurs in the controversial child, the child with both positive and negative sociometric choices. Controversial children showed both high levels of prosocial and antisocial behaviour. The overall pattern shows that approach patterns and peer directed aggression are crucial determinants of peer status.

Similar results have been obtained in an experimental study of children with familiar peers. In a study of second- and third-grade children, Putallaz & Gottman (1981) found that the unpopular child appeared to show more social disagreements and friction while playing a game with a classmate. They were less likely to provide a general reason or rule for their disagreement or to suggest constructive alternatives when criticising a peer. Unpopular children were less likely to be accepted and more likely to be ignored when attempting to join dyads; these entry attempts are characterised by children being disagreeable, calling attention to themselves, freely giving of their own opinions and feelings, talking about themselves, and asking informational questions. These strategies were more likely to lead to being ignored or rejected than to being accepted.

The above pattern of results also holds true for older children and in more naturalistic settings. Gresham (1982) reported a significant correlation between behaviour and sociometric status in third- and fourth-grade children. A naturalistic study by Dodge, Coie & Brakke (1982) observed third- and fifth-grade children in the school classroom and playground. Rejected children showed fewer task appropriate behaviours and more task-inappropriate and aggressive behaviours than their popular counterparts. A comparable number of prosocial approaches (physically approaching and attempting to verbally initiate an activity) were made by both types of child, though responses to rejected children were more likely to be negative. Neglected children showed few task-inappropriate and aggressive behaviours; they made few social approaches to peers and these tended to be rebuffed.

The negative characteristics associated with poor sociometric status are well recognised by the children themselves. In a study by Carlson, Lahey & Neeper (1984), second- and fifth-grade children were asked to indicate which of a series of 19 statements describing patterns of social behaviour were characteristic of specified popular, neglected or rejected classmates. In comparison to their popular peers, rejected children were perceived as possessing a number of behaviours likely to have negative repercussions for peers, they were seen as more irritable, aggressive, complaining, bossy, likely to violate rules of games or try to change the game being played, and to bother others while trying to work. Neglected children differed from their popular peers only in being less likely to brag about their ability to beat everybody up! Although this study deals with children's perceptions of the behaviour of their peers (and limits the range of description possible by supplying evaluative statements rather than eliciting them), it none the less points us in the direction of social behaviours and skills that have been found to be important bases of children's social relationships.

A word of caution is in order before leaving the apparently straightforward issue of the relationship of aggression to social popularity. In an observational study of first and second graders Shantz (1986) found that when the effects of aggression and conflict were examined separately, with the other factor held constant statistically, aggression showed a much lower correlation with social rejection than conflict. This shows that conflict is much more directly related to peer rejection than is simple physical aggression. It is also interesting to note that being liked by peers was *not* related to rates of conflict or aggression; apparently the characteristics are not in themselves a sufficient reason for rejection; the perceived justification for such behaviours is crucial.

The distinction between friends and non-friends is clearly reflected in the behaviour of children when dealing with familiar peers and grows more marked with age. In a study of first and fourth graders Berndt (1981a) found more compromise, mutual accommodation, and prosocial intentions and behaviour in the older age group. Learning to handle conflict in relationships is a natural part of the child's learning to relate to others, and it is to this that we now turn.

Handling conflict

Older children are able to tolerate and resolve conflict within their relationships better than their younger counterparts. Disagreements are seen as a natural part of relationships and need not necessarily lead to its collapse (Parker & Gottman, 1989). A study by Berndt & Perry (1986) found that support and conflict were seen as being part of the same dimension of a relationship in 7–10 year olds but were differentiated and constituted separate concerns for young adolescents. Conflict, it appears, is a more isolated and independent aspect of relationships for older individuals. Indeed, Nelson & Aboud (1985) propose that learning to manage interpersonal conflicts is an important skill developed in the atmosphere of open, honest relationships between equals. Their experiment on eight to ten year olds showed that friends were more critical of others, but were also more likely to explain the bases of their disagreements. In a study of children in kindergarten, and school grades two and four Berndt (1981b) found that for some boys of elementary school age this frankness and tolerance takes the paradoxical form of friends behaving more competitively, being less willing to share a crayon with a friend than with an acquaintance. A subsequent study by Berndt (1985), showed that by the eighth grade children were more likely to show generosity and help to a friend than a neutral classmate. Children of grades four and six treated friends and classmates similarly. For the older children seeking equality of rewards appeared to be important and there was an increased sensitivity to the other person's individual needs. Competitiveness declines as middle childhood gives way to early adolescence and equal sharing becomes an ideal and norm (Berndt, Hawkins & Hoyle, 1986)

Pecking orders

A pecking order or dominance hierarchy is a social structure reflecting the social status of the individual, it predicts which child will be successful in the event of competition over a toy or play area. Differences in levels of competence and social skills of individual children mean that by two to five years some members can be seen to play more central and influential roles in the group than others (Strayer, 1980). In these young children the pecking order does not seem to reflect popularity or positive interaction (Vaughn & Waters, 1981), though there is evidence for their linkage in children of elementary school age. In five and six year olds in a playgroup, dominance is closely associated with popularity.

The relevance of dominance hierarchies for children's friendships is that children of different social status appear to form distinct interactional groups (Ladd, 1983). Ladd's findings about the behaviour of popular and rejected third- and fourth-grade children broadly confirmed the portrait already painted of these individuals – popular children showing more prosocial behaviour and rejected children showing more aggressive and solitary behaviour. More interesting than these findings was the revelation that popular and unpopular children appear to form sub-systems that differ substantially in their patterns and quality of interaction. Rejected children experienced a larger proportion of their interactions in small groups and to younger or other unpopular children. The popular children were more likely to be named as friends by their frequent playground companions and also were more likely to be part of networks that were cliquish or comprised mutual friends. These findings perhaps explain, along with an undoubted number of other possible factors, the failure of many social skills training studies to produce improvements in a child's sociometric status. Not only must skill be improved but the child (or other agency) must also change the social network to which she or he belongs.

Indeed, popularity at least partly reflects a child's status in the dominance hierarchy. Past the age of four or five years socially competent children falling mid to high in the dominance hierarchy tend to interact in groups which show more affiliative and altruistic gestures, seldom resort to overt physical aggression, and more frequently initiate or co-ordinate social activity.

In a study of a group of familiar five year olds Haslett & Bowen (1989), in common with the observations of the many other researchers, noted individual differences in social skills. They go one step further and suggest that these differences fall in three broad levels. Level 1, the most skilful children, are labelled as agenda setters. These are the children that commonly initiate and dominate play. They are likely to show an overall high level of talk, to be physically active and interactive, to play over a large area and to be persistent with attempts at interaction even if initially unsuccessful in attempts to initiate play. The second level of skill Haslett & Bowen term responders. These children react appropriately to play bids and can maintain interaction but do not establish the agenda or initiate change. Children with the lowest level of skill are termed isolates. They show poor recognition of opportunities for interaction, are unable to respond appropriately, are insufficiently persistent, or respond in too weak a manner and are often overlooked. These children frequently appear to be in parallel play.

Familiarity and social responsiveness

In a study of the expressive and communicative components of social interaction, it has been found that there is a higher level of affective and reciprocal communication exchange between friends rather than other peers. This holds true for children across a wide age range, both in structured or unstructured task situations (e.g. Newcomb & Brady, 1982; Brachfeld-Child & Schiavo, 1990) and social activities such as watching cartoons (Foot, Chapman & Smith, 1977), or in free play (e.g. Lewis et al., 1975).

Preschoolers

A number of studies have reported findings on the interaction patterns of unacquainted versus acquainted preschoolers. Prior experience and familiarity with other children appear to be crucial factors in the levels of sociability and social skill that are observed in preschoolers. Peer social interactions appear to become more frequent, sustained, and mature as newcomers become acquainted (e.g. Doyle, Connolly & Rivest, 1980; Feldbaum, Christenson & O'Neal, 1980; Doyle, 1982). A study by Roopnarine (1985) showed that exposure to peers on a daily basis in preschool increases the rate of dispensing positive behaviour (such as giving help, showing affection, and inviting others to join in play), and neutral behaviours (such as watching and engaging in general conversation with other children). Children of three to four years of age that have had prior experience with peers show higher levels of preference for interacting with peers rather than adults and for engaging in social play rather than spending time alone (Harper & Huie, 1985).

In a study of preschoolers aged approximately 3–5 years, Black & Hazen (1990) found that children sociometrically identified as rejected were less responsive to and more likely to make irrelevant comments to both known and unknown peers than were their popular counterparts. In addition, with acquainted peers they were less likely to direct communication at a specific individual. The authors suggest that sensitivity and conversational responsiveness are important in establishing and maintaining social status whereas directed communication is the result of a negative reputation and contribute only to maintaining social status.

In a programme of research by Gottman (1983), similar to that of Dodge (1983) that has already been outlined, two studies were conducted to examine the conversational behaviour of 3–9-year-old children. Some observations were of pairs of strangers, some studied over three sessions as they became better acquainted, and some were of established friendship dyads. In the case of those unacquainted dyads that met over several occasions, the mothers were asked two months later to complete a 21-item questionnaire to indicate the children's subsequent progress towards friendship (e.g. asking if the child spoke to her about the other child or asked to see the other child again).

An observational coding system was used to note a number of communication variables. These were communication clarity and connectedness; information exchange; establishing common ground activity; exploration of similarities and differences; conflict resolution; positive reciprocity; self-disclosure. These variables were predictive of a behavioural measure of how well the children got on together (which had been validated by comparing it with information about actual friendship status and the mother's responses to the questionnaire about her child's progress toward friendship). Gottman found that these variables could account for over 80% of the variability in the behavioural criterion for how well the children hit it off in a first meeting, and over 90% of the variation in second and third meetings. Initial encounters were significantly affected by information exchange, conflict resolution, and reciprocity. In other words, it appeared that there was a striving for a co-ordinated, low conflict exchange of information. There was also a marginal effect for the establishment of common ground activity suggesting that this getting-to-know-you phase was occurring in this context. Those children that met for a further two sessions showed an increase in the importance of all the process variables except for reciprocity (which actually declined); there was an increasing emphasis on communication clarity, information exchange, developing common ground activities, conflict resolution and self-disclosure. The relationships were apparently becoming more complex and more involved.

Entering the preschool group

Beginning preschool is a momentous occasion in the life of young children and their parents. A number of studies have examined the social assimilation of the young child to the preschool group and the subsequent effects that it has on the child's social behaviour (e.g. McGrew, 1972b; Shea, 1981; Roopnarine, 1985). Rather than examining separate groups of familiar and unfamiliar peers, or relatively short-term experimental groups which manipulate the level of contact between children, this approach allows a naturalistic and relatively long-term examination of changes in patterns of sociability with growing familiarity. This is, of course, at the sacrifice of some control over potential extraneous variables which could bias the results. Despite the potential for problems, naturalistic studies have been remarkably consistent in their results. As examples of the genre, we will examine two of the major studies of children starting preschool.

An early and notable study on children starting preschool was conducted by McGrew (1972b). This study followed the introduction of new 3–4-year-old children to an existing playgroup consisting of peers of approximately the same age. The initial reaction of the existing members was characterised as neutral curiosity and ranged from indifference to friendliness. The incoming child was subdued, spoke little or quietly, and showed signs of ambivalence on the first day; the surroundings and other children were inconspicuously investigated; competitive and quarrelsome situations were avoided. Within a matter of days "nervous exploration" decreased and more social approaches were being made. These trends continued and by about 65 days the behaviour of the new children was indistinguishable from the earlier group members.

The study by Shea (1981) confirmed and extended McGrew's earlier findings. Shea observed four year olds entering nursery school. Their playground behaviour was recorded over a ten-week period. As with McGrew's study, Shea found that all measures of social behaviour excepting aggression increased with preschool experience. Aggression declined with opportunities to interact with peers in a nursery school. Those children attending the nursery school most often showed the most marked changes in their behaviour. Verbal aggression, such as name calling, is rare in two year olds, reflecting their limited verbal ability, but subsequently increases. The aggression of two year olds is largely instrumental, aimed at obtaining or damaging an object rather than hurting another; it is most common after conflict with parents. The aggression of four year olds is, by contrast, a hostile aggression which does aim to hurt someone or their feelings. This is most common after peer conflict. At this age the child is relatively unskilled at alternative methods of resolving conflict; this is a notable development of later childhood.

The social benefits of good preschool experience for the young child seem clear and are carried forward to later adjustment at kindergarten and beyond (Ironsmith & Poteat, 1990). This suggests the obvious possibility of compensatory education programmes, though the picture is a little more complicated. We must be wary of assuming that children are passive recipients of the nursery school experience. A study by Pennebaker et al. (1981) shows this to be far from the case. The evidence that they present indicates that relatively less sociable children miss more nursery school due to illness than their more sociable counterparts – though health records were similar before beginning school. Those shy, withdrawn children which would benefit most from the nursery school experience also find it most difficult to cope with, and hence have a higher rate of absenteeism and ultimately benefit less from the experience than their more outgoing peers.

School-age children

Although less socially naive, studies of school-age children also reveal important familiarity effects on social interaction. In a study of 6–7 year olds, Jormakka (1976) noted the behaviour of pairs of acquainted and unacquainted peers. Choice of content and play activity was determined mostly by a child's sex, though non-verbal behaviour and speech did show differences between acquainted and unacquainted peers. The unacquainted children usually began with gazing at the other's face (in 86% of cases). In 79% of acquainted children the initial reaction was, by contrast, to look around; the peer was familiar, the observation room was not. Where avoidance or displacement activities occurred (e.g. gaze avoidance, immobility and automanipulation) these were always from unacquainted children and presumably reflected the high levels of anxiety aroused by an initial meeting in a strange situation. The unacquainted children showed a longer initial silence, though when interaction was established the early lack of talking was followed by levels of talk greater than those for the acquainted children. Personal talk, about oneself or asking about the other, was more common among unacquainted children getting to know each other, especially girls. The total verbal output was none the less lower than for acquainted pairs. At the initial stage of meeting, unacquainted children were less likely than acquainted children to give suggestions, orders, or negative reactions. The overall picture is one of qualitatively different forms of interaction between acquainted and unacquainted groups. Initiating relationships requires a different set of skills to maintaining relationships.

Studies of older children have also demonstrated the significance of the familiarity variable. In second-grade boys meeting over a number of sessions, Dodge (1983) found that the number of social approaches tended to increase over the first two or three sessions but then declined subsequently, presumably as social networks were established. An interesting point to note here is that these friendship networks are likely to reflect the children's pre-existing social status, whether or not the children were previously acquainted.

In a study by Coie & Kupersmidt (1983) fourth-grade boys of known sociometric status (popular, average, rejected, or neglected) were formed into four-person groups which met weekly for six weeks; half the groups were comprised of classmates and half of unfamiliar peers. Observations showed different and distinctive patterns of interaction associated with the different types of social status. Rejected boys showed higher levels of aggressive and inappropriate behaviour than their popular or neglected peers; the popular boys used more prosocial behaviour and seldom resorted to aggressive tactics. Within three sessions social status was correlated with the child's school-based status for both familiar and unfamiliar groups. Rejected boys were extremely active and aversive, but not more physically aversive than average boys – though group members perceived the rejected boys as starting fights. Popular boys engaged in more norm setting and were more prosocial in the unfamiliar group. Neglected boys showed the lowest level of interaction and aversive behaviour; they were more visible and active in the unfamiliar group and seemed most affected by the new social context. This is perhaps the most interesting finding of this study. It makes the important point that, unlike the rejected child, the status of the neglected child is relatively changeable with a change in circumstances.

Knowledge of friendship-making skills

Relating to another requires an ability to transmit and receive information. As there are considerable developmental and individual differences in children's communication knowledge and ability (e.g. Ellis & Beattie, 1986; Crick & Ladd, 1990), it is not surprising that this has been given substantial attention as a factor in establishing and maintaining peer relationships. A study by Rubin (1972) on children from kindergarten through to sixth grade found that scores for communicative egocentrism and popularity as a companion at playtime were related for the two younger groups of children but not for the older groups. The ability to adopt another's point of view is important in younger but not older children. This is particularly surprising as most older children should have at least a basic level of this ability. In a study of fourth- to seventh-grade children intraindividual variability in friendship reasoning was a major social cognitive basis for disruptive peer reputations (Pellegrini, 1986).

The results of Rubin's (1972) study were confirmed and extended in a similar study by Gottman, Gonso & Rasmussen (1975). These authors argued that the popular child should be more knowledgeable about how to make friends. In this study of third and fourth graders, popular children were found to be more knowledgeable of how to make friends and more skilled on a referential communication task (implying a better ability to accommodate to the other's perspective in communication). Naturalistic observation of social interaction in the classroom also showed that popular children distributed and received more positive reinforcements than unpopular children. Interestingly, the form that these social reinforcements take is affected by socioeconomic considerations. Verbal reinforcement being more significant for children in the middle-income school and non-verbal reinforcements for children in the low-income school. Even more interesting was the finding that in the middle-income children positive non-verbal behaviour was actually negatively related to liking! Inappropriate modes of communicating friendship overtures are not only ineffective, they can backfire. This again emphasises the context specificity of many social skills. As the authors observe, this has significant implications for any intervention programme aimed at improving social skills. Social competence is determined in the context of specific situational demands (Russell, 1984).

Norms, scripts and goals

Social scripts are mental representations of the structure and sequence of events and appropriate behaviour that constitute an activity or situation (e.g. playing a game). Scripts enable relatively automatic, predictable behaviour. The existence of shared scripts smooth the to-and-fro flow of interaction, they reduce the number of topic violations, and mean that the likelihood of failed communication is less (Furman & Walden, 1990). Although a study of children aged 3–8 years has shown that scripts grow in detail with age (Nelson & Gruendel, 1979), the benefits that they confer in terms of ability to sustain communication are most marked in the difficult early interactions and with younger, less socially adept children (Furman & Walden, 1990).

Where there is no shared script, for example about appropriate behaviour to initiate interaction, there is likely to be less effective communication and difficulties in establishing a common frame of reference. Many social problems have a complex or contradictory structure and before any appropriate behaviour is possible the demands of the situation and appropriate goals must be established. A study by Ladd & Oden (1979) has examined the importance of normative behaviour in sociometric choice. Third- and fifth-grade children were interviewed in response to three cartoon themes (a child being teased by peers, yelled at by a peer, and having a school work problem). They were asked to suggest helpful behaviour from the perspective of the giver of help and the person receiving the help. The uniqueness of responses (unique being non-normative) was found to be an important predictor of low sociometric standing. It accounted for 15% of the variability in the popularity of girls as play partners and 7% for males. This seems to indicate that for both groups norms are important, but that the closer, more personal relationships of girls at this age make these norms even more significant. For both groups, inadequate social knowledge often underlies inappropriate or inadequate goals, expectations, and behaviour in at least some aspects of their interpersonal relationships (Renshaw & Asher, 1982).

Individual differences in social goals were directly examined in a study by Renshaw & Asher (1983). Children aged eight to almost 13 years of age were interviewed about their goals and strategies in four hypothetical social situations. These situations dealt with peer contact, group entry, friendship and conflict. For example, the contact vignette gave the following information: "Your parents have moved to a new town. This is your first day at a new school. As recess begins, the children go out to play." There was a general recognition of the appropriateness of various goals, though significant individual differences were found in the sophistication of strategies proposed to achieve these goals. Older and higher status children gave more sophisticated, friendly responses to achieve prosocial goals. Similar conclusions, but with children of kindergarten age, were reached in a study reported by Asher & Renshaw (1981).

Social problem-solving

Social problem-solving has been defined as the process of influencing others to attain personal goals. The effectiveness of this activity, the success of achieving these goals, has been considered a central feature of social competence by many authors (Krasnor, 1982). Social problem-solving ability has been linked with superior scores on positive items on a checklist of interpersonal behaviour, such as making friends easily and having many friends, and inversely related to negative items on the checklist, especially items related to aggression, such as arguing or fighting with teachers or other children (Marsh, Serafica & Barenboim, 1981).

The solutions proposed by children to a set of hypothetical peer conflict situations were examined in a study by Rubin & Daniels-Beirness (1983). In this study the children were initially tested when in kindergarten, and then again one year later when they were in the first grade at school. The number of prosocial solutions proposed was positively associated with peer acceptance while the number of agonistic solutions was negatively associated with peer acceptance. More importantly, the proportion of agonistic strategies proposed by the kindergarteners was negatively related to their future sociometric status in the first grade one year later; the number of relevant social problem-solving strategies positively predicted future sociometric status. Once again this result confirms the importance of conflict and aggression as a factor in peer rejection, and once again it emphasises that such behaviour reflects different interpretations of social situations and different interactional goals. We must, however, remember that the interplay between cognition and behaviour at any given point in time means that the prediction of future sociometric status cannot really be attributed to any single factor. If social problem-solving affects current behaviour and patterns of current interaction then it is this general milieu that predicts future status rather than any single component.

A cognitive model of social competence

Dodge et al. (1986) have proposed a social information processing model of social competence. This model sees competent behaviour as fundamentally dependent on the individual's processing of environmental cues. Each individual comes to a situation with a unique set of experiences and goals. Identical social cues may consequently be interpreted in different ways and lead to different responses. The processing sequence has been divided into five broad steps, though as Dodge et al. (1986) have noted, "Relatively little work has examined processes within each of the gross steps postulated here" (p. 60).

Stage 1   This consists of finding and encoding the available cues. Here social cues are identified and received through sensory processes. This is essentially the reception phase.

Stage 2   The cues identified in Stage 1 are mentally represented. This perception phase is an interpretive or evaluative rather than an objective process and includes a consideration of desired goals and existing knowledge or memories.

Stage 3   The search for an appropriate response. The represented cues can act a stimulus to generate a set of potential behavioural responses from memory.

Stage 4   Evaluate and decide among alternative responses. This is based on such factors as their adequacy and probable consequences.

Stage 5   This final stage requires the encoding and enacting of a response. Children must find appropriate behaviours within their repertoire and produce these. This is not always straightforward! Verbal ability, for example, sets severe limits on the interaction of young children.

It must be immediately obvious that this plan sounds too mechanically perfect to be true! And, of course, in the simplistic form in which it has so far been presented, it is. Biases and cognitive heuristics do abbreviate and can distort the information processing at each stage (Price & Dodge, 1989).

Dodge et al. (1986) hypothesised that successful social information processing would contribute to evaluations of competence by peers, and the peers' behaviour toward the child. Two studies were conducted to test these hypotheses. In the first study children from kindergarten through second grade were rated for competence at peer group entry and identified as competent or non-competent by their peers and teachers. Based on these scores the most and least competent individuals were chosen for further study. The children were shown a videotaped film showing two same-sex peers sitting at a table playing a board game. They were asked how much they thought each of the children in the film would like the child to play with them. They were then asked to explain their answer and to indicate as many strategies as possible that could be used so that they would be allowed to join in. They were then shown the original scene again but with the arrival of a third child using various entry strategies. They were then questioned on these. Finally, the children each participated in an actual peer group entry task with two classmates.

Results showed that measures of each of the five processing steps in Dodge et al.'s model predicted both competence and success in the behavioural task and that variables from several processing steps were unique contributors to the model's predictive power. Performance at the peer group entry task predicted peer judgements of the child and behaviour toward the child.

A second study generalised these findings to children in grades two to four. This second study also examined the application of the model to the situation of peer provocation, and showed that domain specific models are required. Processing variables predicting competence at peer group entry did not predict responses to provocation, and processing variables predicting responses to provocation did not predict competence at peer group entry. Overall, competence in peer relations is a broad and complex multi-domain phenomenon. An important message for clinicians, therapists and trainers.

Social cognition, social skills, and popularity

Biases impinge at all stages of social information processing. For example, children that have experienced different social outcomes in the past will expect different social experiences in the present and future, attend to different cues within the social milieu, and interpret these cues differently. An interesting approach to explaining why some children respond to a situation in an aggressive manner while other children do not has examined children's ideas about their relationships. Sobol & Earn (1985a) showed that popular children pay more attention to situational cues when making social attributions than do their less popular counterparts. A more general illustration of the role of social cognitive biases on our interpersonal behaviour is evident in the study of aggressiveness, a characteristic of unpopular, rejected children. As children are more likely to show aggression in response to aggression from another, it seems likely that, especially in ambiguous situations, aggressive children are actually interpreting the intentions underlying the behaviour of their peers in a different way from their less aggressive counterparts (Dodge & Frame, 1982). This aggressive behaviour is then likely to become self-sustaining in that their expectations about the other's aggressive intentions will be confirmed by the child's response to the retaliation.

The predisposition to define situations in certain ways has the potential to disrupt the smooth flow of interaction in more general ways than illustrated by the simple example of responsiveness to aggression (Russell, 1984). There is a tendency for popular and unpopular children to interpret social situations in fundamentally different ways and produce a bias that essentially confirms their expectations about what their world has in store for them. Regular recipients of prosocial behaviour have readily available schemata (organised memories) of these experiences and so expect such behaviour and interpret ambiguous cues in a positive way. On the other hand, the regular recipient of rejection and aggression will tend to interpret ambiguous cues as a part of this pattern. The ready availability in memory of specific types of social experience serve as a cognitive heuristic (Tversky & Kahneman, 1974), a short-cut in information processing. The child's reaction to these social cues then follows relatively automatically from the social scripts which have been defined over innumerable prior experiences of the predisposed cues (Nelson, 1981).

Overall, the greater responsibility and blame for negative behaviours that is attributed to disliked peers is likely to maintain their outcast status. Once a child's status as a popular or rejected individual has been established it seems, unfortunately, that this is then likely to become a self-fulfilling prophecy as evidence to confirm existing beliefs is sought (Snyder & Uranowitz, 1978). In ambiguous circumstances aggressive intent is likely to be attributed to the rejected child (Dodge, 1980). Observations of classroom interaction indicate that the prosocial behaviour of problem children is largely ignored by their peers, while their deviant actions are focused upon (Solomon & Wahler, 1973). This is an unfortunate state of affairs as peer rejection is one of the few aspects of early childhood functioning that is consistently associated with behavioural problems and emotional disturbance in adolescence and adulthood (Hartup, 1984). Fortunately, as shown in Chapter 10, peer acceptability can be improved through various forms of social skills training.

5 Self-disclosure

*. . . there is evidence that much of what friends do together, especially
as they get older, is talk.*
(Parker & Gottman, 1989, p. 98)

By definition a relationship involves connectedness between people, a sharing
of themselves. To this extent the ability to communicate is important in any
intimate relationship (Derlega, 1988). From the pre-verbal communication
of the infant evolves a sophisticated system of language and verbal
communication through which the development and maintenance of
relationships is facilitated. Verbal communication is an important factor in
peer interaction and friendships throughout childhood and adolescence
(Johnson & Aries, 1983; Crockett, Losoff & Petersen, 1984). This chapter
is concerned with how verbal communication is used to make ourselves known
to others in order to build our relationships. Self-disclosure of private
thoughts and feelings is both an important factor in the development
of relationships and a vital indicator of relationship status (Derlega, 1988).
These considerations alone would make the phenomenon interesting and
worthy of attention and careful research, but its significance extends much
further.

The potential psychological importance of self-disclosure was implicitly
recognised at least as long ago as 1936, when Lewin published his paper on
"Some socio-psychological differences between the United States and
Germany". Since its early recognition the significance of self-disclosure
has been continually re-affirmed by psychologists interested in personality
and social processes (e.g. Allport, 1961), and clinical and counselling
psychologists have long regarded it as a topic of central importance (e.g.
Jourard, 1958). Unfortunately for a considerable period of time it has, to
a large extent, remained on the periphery of interest to social and
developmental psychologists (Derlega, 1988). Current trends do show an
increasing recognition of its general relevance for social behaviour and
development.

In line with a growing interest in self-disclosure, since the late 1950s there
has been an increasing amount of research activity which has seen many

foundation stones laid for a systematic understanding of the phenomenon. This optimistic pattern is, unfortunately, limited to the literature on adults and, to a lesser extent, adolescents. There is still considerable research to be undertaken to provide even a half-way complete picture of the phenomenon in children, though recent research seems to show that significant attention is beginning to be paid to developmental considerations. For example, it is now recognised that a great deal of self-disclosure occurs in the course of children's games and play (Gottman, 1986b). This growth of interest in developmental aspects of self-disclosure looks set to continue for at least the foreseeable future and should lead to a rapid development of the area. This chapter presents a broad picture of self-disclosure but with a specific focus on children and its implications for their relationships. The patchy literature on self-disclosure in children means that, for completeness, it will sometimes be necessary to extrapolate and incorporate material from relevant research on adults.

Available evidence indicates that patterns of self-disclosure undergo substantial changes as the child grows toward adulthood, though there is still much research to be conducted in this area if we are to fully understand the role and functions of self-disclosure in children's friendships (Parker & Gottman, 1989). At present there is noticeable lack of substantive research in this area. This has been excused on the grounds that children below the age of about eight years have difficulties with the instructions or procedures of some experimental paradigms (Cohn & Strassberg, 1983). Fortunately some researchers have been inventive in overcoming these obstacles. In an early study, Skypeck (1967) demonstrated that with appropriately adapted methods research with groups at least as young as six years of age is possible.

Even if methodological ingenuity eventually gives us a clear picture of patterns of self-disclosure in children's relationships, it is important not to see this in itself as the ultimate goal. Equally important and worthy of consideration are factors which predispose these given patterns of disclosing. Without taking these into account the phenomenon cannot be fully understood, and intervention to improve dysfunctional patterns of disclosing would be rash. In discussing factors affecting an individual's patterns of self-disclosure, Norrell (1984) implicates the home environment, family relations, and an individual's prior pattern of disclosing (especially to a given recipient). All of these issues must be considered to gain a balanced view of children's self-disclosure.

So far, this discussion has left its central term undefined. As some very different definitions of self-disclosure have been proposed, it is necessary to discuss and clarify these. This is an important task as different definitions have led researchers to collect different types of data, interpret them differently, and come to very different conclusions.

Defining self-disclosure

Before getting too involved in the intricacies of research findings on self-disclosure it is important to be absolutely clear about exactly what falls within the limits of the term. There have been many definitions of self-disclosure placing different emphases on many and varied aspects of the phenomenon. These various definitions have produced a wide variety of ideas about what should be measured and how one should go about measuring it. This at least partially explains some of the contradictory research findings in the area, it also makes it very difficult to compare or combine the results of studies by different researchers. For the purposes of deriving a characterisation of self-disclosure to guide us through this chapter, this section has tried to emphasise some of the threads of consistency which run through the various definitions.

The concept of self-disclosure received its first major, systematic analysis from Jourard (1958). Self-disclosure was seen as the honest revelation of thoughts and feelings to another. Jourard (1971a) succinctly summarised his position in his book *The Transparent Self*: "To disclose means to unveil, to manifest, or to show. *Self*-disclosure is the act of making yourself manifest, showing yourself so others can perceive you" (p. 19). Such an ability to self-disclose, in conjunction with the feedback it prompts, was seen as facilitating an accurate and broad self-knowledge. As such Jourard regarded it as a sign of a healthy personality. Although clearly expressed, Jourard's definition is not unambiguous, it can be subject to different interpretations and so more precise working definitions are required for research. There has been no shortage of alternative definitions rendered by other authors.

One of the best-known and most commonly cited reviews of the literature on self-disclosure is that of Cozby (1973) – highly recommended for the literature up to its date of publication. Cozby defined self-disclosure as "any information about himself which person A communicates verbally to person B" (p. 73). Although non-verbal behaviour can undoubtedly convey a great deal of personal information, this definition emphasises that self-disclosure is verbal. Explicitly or implicitly this emphasis characterises most definitions of self-disclosure. Perhaps Cozby's (1973) definition of self-disclosure has proved popular because it is a very basic definition, and as such it can encompass a very broad range of phenomena. A number of other authors have suggested definitions which are somewhat less all-encompassing.

The concept of self-disclosure has been further refined by Allen (1974) who defined it as the "uncoerced exchanging of personal information in a positive relationship" (p. 198). This certainly overcomes any concern about the role of volition in self-disclosure, though purists may care to debate the nature of freedom of action further. Disclosure is seen as voluntary, suggesting that much of it is intentional, and as an exchange, implying some form of reciprocity. But this definition also has other virtues. First, it stresses the social relationship within which self-disclosures are exchanged; disclosure is seen as an integral part of that relationship rather than simply a characteristic of the individual. This coincidentally also satisfies the emphasis by some researchers that the information must not otherwise be readily accessible to the recipient. Second, the emphasis that the term self-disclosure should be used to refer only to the exchange of personal information eliminates many technical or purely informational communications.

Whereas Cozby's definition can be criticised for being too general, we have the opposite problem with Allen's definition. Although it is admirably specific, this limits its developmental applicability. Allen's definition was intended to apply to adult friendships, though there seems little problem in also accepting it for adolescents. More caution must be exercised in applying it to younger age groups. The main potential problem in applying it to children is the idea that self-disclosure must entail an exchange. As outlined in Chapter 2, when discussing social cognition, below about six to eight years of age children's role-taking abilities and friendship expectations limit the extent to which they perceive friendship as entailing reciprocal demands and obligations. Consequently the idea of a norm of reciprocity in self-disclosure, if it exists, is likely to be rudimentary. This idea is discussed in a later section of this chapter. As a working definition we can regard self-disclosure as the child's voluntary revelation of personal information in the course of a relationship. This definition is sufficiently general to be used in the context of children's friendships across a wide age range and yet is still sufficiently specific to provide a useful frame of reference for evaluating research findings.

Having established what self-disclosure is, we will now examine how it is measured. An awareness of measurement issues is an essential prerequisite appreciating typical research practices and their implications for the results that they ultimately produce.

Measuring self-disclosure

A long-running debate in self-disclosure research has concerned the issue of what should be measured and how it should be measured. These are the issues that will be examined in turn in this section.

A given self-disclosure can be characterised in terms of a number of parameters, all of which have featured as research variables. Cozby (1973) mentions the significance of the amount (breadth) of information disclosed, the intimacy (depth) of information disclosed and the duration (time) spent on a given disclosure – he also presents evidence of some interrelationship between these factors. Chelune (1979) adds two further factors to this list: the affective (emotional) manner of presentation and flexibility (across recipients and situations).

The above parameters of self-disclosure have been assessed using a wide variety of methods. Chelune (1979) places these in three broad categories: observational methods, objective methods, and the ubiquitous self-report inventories and questionnaires. Each of these will be examined in turn below.

Observational methods

The observational approach often consists of observing, recording, or collecting samples of actual self-disclosure. These will commonly be disclosures made in the context of an actual interaction, though written sources such as essays or letters could also be included in this category. To simplify matters, and control or eliminate extraneous variables, the situation in which such disclosures are made is often standardised (e.g. an observation room), and the recipient (target) typically occupies a specific social role in relation to the child (e.g. friend).

The data collected by observational methods will usually require some form of processing or content analysis before appropriate comparisons in terms of the experimental variables can be attempted. This is typically achieved by evaluating it according to a set of criteria determined by the researcher's hypotheses. For example, Cohn & Strassberg (1983) led children between the ages of approximately eight and thirteen years of age to believe that they were participating in a study on "how kids get to know each other" (p. 99). After listening to an initial disclosure by an unknown child, they were given a relatively free choice in what they revealed about themselves. The revealed information was then rated for intimacy.

Observational methods are relatively time-consuming but do not require self-insight by respondents, which would be a potential artifact, or at least a disadvantage, when dealing with young children. A major point in their favour is that they give an indication of actual and current self-disclosure – albeit limited to the experimental situation. It might be argued that using independent raters in observational studies of self-disclosure bypasses the most insightful of all judges – the discloser himself. Some studies do indeed use participant observers, and a number of other studies have examined the potential biases of judges with different characteristics. Arguably it is only through a dual perspective that we will come fully to understand the phenomenon (McCarthy, 1981).

Objective methods

Objective methods of assessing self-disclosure are superficially attractive tools for research, but in practice they are difficult tools to use. To use an objective measure you must be very precisely sure of what exactly it is that you wish to measure and how you can measure it. Some measures are relatively obvious and straightforward, for example the amount of time spent in speech (Vondracek, 1969). But what does this actually mean? Is the amount of speech the same as the amount of self-disclosure? It is difficult to see the relationship of some supposedly objective measures to conceptual definitions of the phenomenon.

Self-report measures

This section examines questionnaires that have been developed to measure self-disclosure. More importantly, it considers the extent to which they actually achieve this. The scales that follow have been devised for, or at least used in, research with adolescents. Modified versions have sometimes been used with even younger children, though at present there is a lack of specialised research instruments for use with these age groups.

The next few paragraphs refer to modified versions of the original Jourard Self-Disclosure Questionnaire (JSDQ) and so it is appropriate to briefly draw attention to the implications of the practice of making ad hoc adaptations to scales. It is very noteworthy that many researchers seem to totally ignore the psychometric implications of their actions when it comes to creating such modified scales. The various modified scales are often treated as equivalent to the original (and presumably each other) and yet seldom is evidence presented to support this assumption. In similar vein, any reliability or validity data pertaining to the original form of the scale would be of doubtful applicability to the modified version. If we can't be sure that the various modified scales are consistently measuring the same thing how can we meaningfully compare or combine their findings?

The best-known and most commonly used self-disclosure questionnaire is that of Jourard & Lasakow (1958). The JSDQ consists of 60 statements in six categories (attitudes and opinions; tastes and interests; work or studies; money; personality; body). Respondents are required to indicate the extent to which they have talked about each item to specified target figures (mother, father, male friend, and female friend). This scale was originally devised for use with adults, though with modifications it has also found use with adolescents (e.g. Dimond & Hellkamp, 1969) and occasionally even with children (e.g. Rivenbark, 1971).

Jourard (1971b) has marshalled the evidence in support of the validity of his self-disclosure questionnaires, though this issue is still far from settled. The statistical procedures used by Jourard in the original evaluation of his questionnaire have been severely criticised. For example, Davidson, Balswick & Halverson (1980) note "various peculiarities in his procedure" (p. 948). To remedy this situation they investigated the structure of a modified JSDQ for a sample of adolescents. Statistical analysis showed the questionnaire to be composed of four general dimensions of self-disclosure: revealing general information, revealing sexuality to parents, revealing personal information, and revealing sexuality to peers. This does seem to provide some support for Jourard's findings. It also helps to generalise his results and the use of a modified version of his scale to an adolescent age group. Above all, the important point to be derived from the combined results of Jourard (1971b) and Davidson, Balswick & Halverson (1980) is that self-disclosure is composed of specific dimensions of revealingness rather than a general motivation to disclose.

Other authors have also proposed self-disclosure inventories for adolescents and have attempted to provide some basic evidence for their validity. For example, a self-disclosure inventory by West & Zingle (1969) yields a grand score plus six target scores (for self-disclosure to the mother, father, male friend, female friend, teacher, and counsellor) and six aspect sub-scores (health, personal concerns, boy–girl relations, home and family, school concerns, money and status). West (1971) provided a realistic examination of the validity of his self-disclosure questionnaire for 80 Canadian adolescents by comparing the discloser's self-reported revealingness with reports obtained from targets. Statistical measures of the scale's validity varied across topics and targets and ranged from low to moderately high. The overall validity coefficient was low but acceptable, though when split into male and female components it became apparent that this average level hid a substantially higher coefficient for females and a poor coefficient for males. West & Altman (1987) have more recently presented a revised edition of this inventory.

In his 1971 article West made some important points concerning the apparent contradictions in the results of self-disclosure research, and failures of attempts to validate self-disclosure inventories. He argued that many contradictory or inconclusive results are due to the use of restricted subject samples and the misuse of the disclosure questionnaires. The use of college samples is especially criticised; generalising to adolescent samples can be hazardous to the health of any conclusions drawn!

Questioning the use of questionnaires

Up to this point we have managed to avoid a rather thorny question – how valid is the questionnaire approach to measuring self-disclosure? However good a picture such scales produce of what a person says is their characteristic pattern of self-disclosure, they lose a lot of their usefulness if they do not reflect children's and adolescents' real-life disclosure patterns within relationships. Questionnaires are short-cut ways of gathering information but this must not be at the expense of accuracy.

Implicit in the questionnaire approach to measuring self-disclosure is the notion that self-disclosure is a relatively stable aspect of personality, though substantial research does attest to the fact that it is significantly affected by the social context within which it occurs. Chelune (1979) points to a number of implicit sources of variation within the self-report questionnaire approach to measuring self-disclosure (e.g. the circumstances in which a given self-disclosure might occur or be appropriate), though arguably many of these are or can be assessed and controlled.

The relative ease of the interview/questionnaire methods of measuring self-disclosure have made them extremely popular, though many authors have criticised the use of these approaches to gathering information on self-disclosure and relationships (e.g. Parker & Gottman, 1989). With questionnaire studies there is always the nagging doubt or question as to whether individual respondents are fully aware of their behaviour, its intentions, and its consequences. Berg & Derlega (1987) come to the rather pessimistic conclusion that research has shown "relatively few consistent relationships between JSDQ scores and other variables . . . the ability of the JSDQ to predict respondents' self-disclosing behavior was found to be quite weak" (p. 2–3). The problems of the questionnaire method have led Klos & Loomis (1978) to go so far as to state that "we question the validity of any study which employs self-ratings of intimate disclosure" (p. 819). How a person says they behave is often not consistent with how they do behave, how they say they have behaved in the past, or how they say they will behave in the future. Add on to this developmental differences in role-taking abilities and it is evident that there is a great deal of room for problems in self-report measures of self-disclosure. If the use of self-disclosure questionnaires is questionable in adolescents, it is doubly so in younger children.

Overall, questionnaire methods of measuring self-disclosure have important limitations, and must be used with due circumspection. None the less they have and will continue to represent an important and popular research tool. No doubt they will continue to feature prominently in future research on self-disclosure. As consumers of this research our task is to welcome it, but also to evaluate its procedures and instruments carefully.

Nature and effects of self-disclosure

So far we have looked at ways in which self-disclosure has been defined and measured. Although these have been suggestive of the sorts of theoretical accounts which have been proposed to explain the phenomenon, they have not directly addressed the questions of why we self-disclose and what are the interpersonal consequences of self-disclosure. It is to these issues that we now turn.

The self concept

Possibly the earliest recognition of the importance of self-disclosure came from psychotherapy, long before Jourard (1958) actually coined the term. To many therapists and counsellors it still maintains a position of central importance for the explanation and treatment of psychological disorders (Derlega, 1988). To quote Jourard & Lasakow (1958), "accurate portrayal of the self to others is an identifying criterion of healthy personality, while neurosis is related to inability to know one's 'real self' and to make it known to others" (p. 91). From this perspective successful treatment is treatment that increases a client's self-awareness and ability to acquire and use feedback.

The importance of social interaction in the formation of the self-concept has been analysed in detail by the symbolic interactionists (e.g. Cooley, 1912; Mead, 1934). This school of social psychology emphasises that social meaning is a product of individual interpretation and social negotiation. The idea that the self-concept is constructed, at least in part from the perceived evaluations of others – Cooley's "the looking-glass self" – has a venerable history. To the extent that self-disclosure is an important component of interaction it is not surprising that it came to be seen as vital for our own self-concept and the understanding of others (Sullivan, 1953).

From its inception, and over the whole lifespan, the self-concept is in a constant state of development. From at least four or five years of age children are aware of their standing in terms of a number of social categories, such as age, sex, and size (Lewis & Brooks, 1978). It then becomes important for the child to evaluate his or her standing on these attributes. Self-disclosure is an important basis for the social comparison processes which provide the consensual validation of the child's social reality; to this extent it has been viewed as an important factor in the establishment of children's relationships and their subsequent ability to form and maintain close relationships in adult life. These early chum relationships have been portrayed as the foundation on which subsequent relationships are built (Sullivan, 1953). Despite their very different natures a wide variety of adult relations, such as parent, friend, and romantic partner were seen as building on this base. The still influential implication highlighted by Sullivan's clinical perspective is that inadequate chumship relationships create problems for relationships in later childhood and adulthood.

As with other concepts, the self-concept of children between the ages of about five and twelve years undergoes substantial elaboration. It become more complex and more concerned with internal rather than external qualities (Montemayor & Eisen, 1977). As part of the process of socialisation, mutual self-disclosure supplies the reflected appraisal which allows children to reduce egocentric distortions in their interpersonal perceptions. This enables them more accurately to understand and test the reality of how they are perceived by others, and the similarities and differences between self and others (Piaget, 1959). Self-disclosure is greater to friends and to others perceived as similar (Skoe & Ksionzky, 1985), the shared perspective founded on similarity serves to clarify and confirm for the child the reality within which the self exists.

The Johari window

The Johari window (see Figure 5.1), a name derived from the joint names of its originators – Joe Luft and Harry Ingham – is a graphic representation of the areas of the self and its accessibility to the individual and others (Luft, 1970). This diagram highlights the structural limits of self-disclosure. It also shows that these limits are changeable. Social interaction and communication can affect the relative sizes of the four rectangles comprising the Johari window and consequently play an important role in personal insight and adjustment. The main points to note in the diagram are that an area of the self is freely revealed and is known by ourselves and others, a further area is known by ourselves but hidden from others, an area is known by others but hidden from our own consciousness, and the final area is unknown by both ourselves and others. The course of self-disclosure, whether in the normal course of a personal relationship, child development, or the therapeutic situation, alters the relative size of these areas. Through self-disclosure the open area is enlarged and, in the course of feedback, the other areas are reduced as self-awareness and psychological adaptation is facilitated.

	Known to self	Unknown to self
Known to others	Open	Blind
Unknown to others	Hidden	Unknown

Figure 5.1:   The Johari window
Source: Adapted from Luft (1984) by permission of Mayfield Publishing Company

Fulfilling relationships become more likely as they become increasingly based on a greater awareness and ability to share information about the self.

At this point a word of caution is appropriate to avoid an over-simplistic interpretation of the benefits of self-disclosure. As Kempler (1987) points out, there are also risks and potentially negative consequences of uncritical self-disclosure, which is why as a children develop they learn to protect important aspects of the self from both others and their own self-consciousness. Uncritical self-disclosure to inappropriate others will simply leave the child vulnerable. A simple and crude increase in self-disclosure is not a laudable end in itself; increasing an ability to freely self-disclose in an appropriate fashion is.

Cognitive elaboration

The benefits of a readiness to self-disclose extend considerably beyond the development of the self-concept. Halverson & Shore (1969) have noted that adults ready to confide personal information to others tended to be more integratively complex, i.e. possess a more complex interpersonal cognitive system. Social experience and interpersonal communication have been shown to have similar cognitive benefits for children (see Chapter 2). The nature of causality in these observations is unclear: Do cognitively complex people recognise the utility and reward value of greater self-disclosure, or is it that high disclosing facilitates development and elaboration of the interpersonal cognitive system?

It is possible that both factors are important and effective simultaneously. The results of research on the general relationship between social and cognitive development would certainly suggest such a reciprocal pattern of influence. Self-disclosure rewards through the confirmation (consensual validation) of the existing interpersonal cognitive system and because of the better adaptation resulting from elaboration of the system. Elaboration of the interpersonal cognitive system is based on information and so, for this aspect, disclosure must be seen as crucial. More general explanations of relationships also suggest that both aspects are important. Perhaps this is not too surprising if one remembers that much self-disclosure will be of attitudinal information. Some research has attempted to delineate the descriptive (revelation of intimate facts) and evaluative (expression of judgements or affect) components of self-disclosure, though these are usually confounded in research (Morton, 1978).

Self-disclosure and relationship development

Having examined the self-disclosure at a global level of analysis, it is now appropriate to consider the more immediate factors affecting self-disclosure within social interaction and, more specifically, its effects on the progress of relationships. Again, in this area there is a paucity of research on children. What research there is does indicate a broad continuity with findings on adults and adolescents, though within limits which are predictable from a knowledge of children's social cognitive development. The disparity between the wealth of information on adults and the minimal amount on children is also useful in highlighting research issues which need to be clarified developmentally.

The Social Penetration Theory of Altman & Taylor (1973) conceptualises development in relationships in terms of mutual self-disclosure. The revelation of personal information to others is to reward them. The more intimate the information, the greater the reward. Self-disclosure of intimate information indicates trust, and tells the recipient the level of intimacy at which interaction is sought or seen as appropriate, it also creates an obligation to return rewards of equal value. Progress in relationships is seen as determined by past and potential rewards. This theory sees self-disclosure as both a cause and measure of relationship development. Relationships are seen as following an orderly progress from less to more intimate stages, and levels of self-disclosure correspondingly increase with time and development within the relationship. Self-disclosure to strangers is typically rather bland; little is revealed about personal feelings and opinions (evaluative information) or private facts (descriptive information). Acquaintances are allowed access to evaluative information, but it is only with the trust shared by friends that both descriptive and evaluative information are revealed (Hornstein & Truesdell, 1988).

Although the child's social cognitive abilities limit his or her use of self-disclosure, with appropriately adapted research methods even children of kindergarten age have been shown to use different patterns of self-disclosure to friends and non-friends. In accord with Altman & Taylor (1973), personal information is mainly revealed to friends. Less personal information is equally likely to be disclosed to friends and non-friends. Even children of kindergarten age recognise the role self-disclosure in relationships, though the pattern of restrictive self-disclosure to friends becomes increasingly distinct with age (Rotenberg & Sliz, 1988). It is not until middle childhood, with improvements in the child's social cognitive abilities, that the meaning of self-disclosure is fully understood and patterns of reciprocity begin to resemble those of adolescents and adults (Rotenberg & Mann, 1986), an issue discussed later in this chapter.

In the course of interaction the rewards provided by self-disclosure also serve important tactical functions, they can be used as an approach/avoidance strategy and co-ordinated with other non-verbal sources of information in indicating and regulating intimacy (e.g. Wada, 1986). The young child's limited role-taking abilities limit this use of self-disclosure, though by middle childhood it becomes important. This is the era of the all-important chum relationships, the foundation on which future intimacy and trust in relationships is built (Sullivan, 1953). The friendships of middle childhood are marked by their emphasis on sharing, values, and obligations. These relationships offer a consensual validation of the child's feelings, interests, and opinions, and contribute to his or her feelings of efficacy and self-esteem; they provide an arena for the development of sensitivity, intimacy and trust. Sharing a secret is often a major test and indicator of friendship, supporting the contention of Wheeless & Grotz (1977) that self-disclosure is both based on and produces trust.

To the extent that self-disclosure functions as an instrumental behaviour, predictably it has a number of effects. Research suggests that adolescents and children willing to confide information to others are better liked. Even in children as young as three, more communicatively skilled, self-disclosing individuals are likely to fare better in establishing peer relationships, and self-disclosure is an increasingly important aspect in developing the relationship (Gottman, 1983).

Topics and targets

One of the first systematic attempts to examine differences in self-disclosure devised a questionnaire and presented it to a large and heterogeneous sample of young adults (Jourard & Lasakow, 1958). Six aspects of self-disclosure to various targets were examined. They found, not too unexpectedly, that some topics, such as attitudes and opinions, tastes and interests, and work (or studies), were more commonly disclosed than were other topics, such as money, personality, and the body. A number of characteristics of the respondents to the questionnaire were also related to patterns of disclosure. Several of these findings have been followed up by subsequent research: choice of person to disclose to, target figure, sex differences, cultural/ethnic differences, and differences in disclosure according to the perceived nurturance of parents.

Various studies, as highlighted in the section on measurement issues, have shown that self-disclosure is not a simple, unidimensional or general motivation to self-disclose, it is a complex and multi-faceted phenomenon. It has been argued that self-disclosure is composed of specific dimensions of revealingness (Davidson, Balswick & Halverson, 1980). On this basis, it is hardly surprising to find that some types of self-disclosure are more likely to one target rather than another.

Developmental patterns

A number of studies have examined developmental patterns in topics of self-disclosure and the choice of recipients. Selective disclosure of personal information to friends is evident in children at least as young as kindergarten age (Rotenberg & Sliz, 1988). Skypeck (1967) found a linear increase in self-disclosure to peers between the ages of six and twelve, though she did not collect information relating to other target figures such as parents.

Other research shows that in middle childhood self-disclosure to parents is still greater than that to peers. A common finding is for the mother to be the most important recipient of self-disclosure, though that directed to peers continues to increase with age while that to parents, especially for boys, declines (Rivenbark, 1971; Buhrmester & Furman, 1987). Changes in choice of targets for self-disclosure are a reflection of changes in the child's reference groups and a desire for social comparison with peers. Friendship and peer relationships become increasingly stable and important as children grow older (Buhrmester & Furman, 1987). Friendship preferences are mainly for same-sex peers (LaFreniere, Strayer & Gauthier, 1984) and sentimentality and anything to do with the opposite sex is avoided, especially by boys, who believe that it will lead to embarrassment and rejection by peers (Fine, 1987).

A child's customary response to disclosure by another child is the expression of solidarity or an affirmation of similar experience (Parker & Gottman, 1989). These characteristic patterns are borne of increasingly sophisticated cognitive abilities and a desire by children to establish the concrete principles and rules of their social world (Piaget, 1977). As the child moves into early adolescence there are dramatic changes in the intimacy of relationships and these are mirrored by changes in patterns of self-disclosure (Sullivan, 1953).

At least for younger adolescents, the mother is still the most popular target for self-disclosure, there is more self-disclosure to same-sex peers, and the father is typically the least favoured target figure for all groups (Garcia & Geisler, 1988). As in earlier years, throughout adolescence self-disclosure to parents continues to decline and there is a corresponding increase in the levels of disclosure directed to peers, especially those of the same sex with whom there is a close relationship (Brooks-Gunn et al., 1986; Buhrmester & Furman, 1987; Papini et al., 1990).

Adolescents are able to perceive their relationships as complex and multi-faceted. Self-disclosure assumes a central role in their relationships, it becomes more abstract as emphasis is placed on openness, honesty, and commitment in relationships. These become important topics of discussion and analysis – and a common basis for conflict (Parker & Gottman, 1989). Self-disclosure even achieves the paradoxical status of becoming an important topic of self-disclosure in its own right as adolescents discuss the intimacy, possibilities, and obligations of their relationships.

Patterns of disclosure in adolescence are prime indicators of the new status of their relationships. In general, these show not only an increase in the quantity of self-disclosure but also qualitative differences. This mirrors the findings of a large amount of empirical research on the development of children's friendship, which shows an increase in references to intimacy with age (e.g. Berndt & Perry, 1986; Buhrmester & Furman, 1987). Some young adolescents experience a period where this pattern is distorted. With the advent of an ability to think in complex, abstract ways, some early adolescents go through a period of high self-consciousness concerning the opinions and reactions of others (Elkind & Bowen, 1979). The occurrence of this distinctive form of egocentrism has been linked with a temporary reduction in characteristic levels of self-disclosure (Sinha, 1972).

The child's perception of the quality of his or her relationships is an important factor underlying some of the individual differences in levels of self-disclosure (Vondracek, 1969). As one might expect, children from homes of high perceived nurturance disclose more to parents than friends, the reverse pattern being shown for children from less nurturant homes. Somewhat more surprising, children and adolescents from homes they perceive as affectionate and nurturant also show higher levels of self-disclosure to people outside of the home, to friends and strangers (Doster & Strickland, 1969; Snoek & Rothblum, 1979). As modelling can alter an individual's characteristic level of self-disclosure (Fantasia, Lombardo & Wolf, 1976), this suggests that parents are playing an important role in their child's learning of appropriate patterns of self-disclosure. It also reflects the greater trust which children from nurturant homes have in their relationships.

Within the broad patterns outlined above, self-disclosure is also crucially determined by the personality of the target figure. A study by Skoe & Ksionzky (1985) provided a personality portrait of targets that facilitate self-disclosure. The overall picture is of an intelligent, caring extravert. The sort of person that is generally very easy to like. A similar, though less benign, personality portrait can be sketched of targets less likely to be the recipients of self-disclosure. Such targets can be characterised as either too critical, perfect and self-involved, or else defensive and dependent.

Cross-cultural patterns

Although one might expect that selectivity in topics and targets of self-disclosure would be a phenomenon crossing cultural and national boundaries, it seems equally sensible that precisely what it is permissible to reveal, and to whom, might be expected to vary according to culture. Research confirms that such differences do exist, though there are also a great many similarities. There is no systematic developmental research on self-disclosure incorporating a cross-cultural emphasis. The research discussed in this section must be treated with caution in its implications for children below the age of adolescence.

Jourard (1961) found that British and American students differed in their levels of self-disclosure but agreed on choice of targets and items which were readily disclosed and those which were withheld. In a study of Indian males in four groups aged 12–21 years, Sinha (1969) found a pattern of results similar to those in European and American adolescents. Melikian (1962) examined the self-disclosure patterns of male students of nine nationalities at university in Lebanon. Some overall differences in levels of disclosure of various topics and to various targets were noted, and these did show differences from the data discussed above. For example, there was no significant difference in levels of disclosure to mothers and fathers. The national groupings also showed differences in choice of targets for self-disclosure and in topics of information revealed; unfortunately, the precise nature of these differences was not made clear in the published article.

Within the limited range of cultures examined, the evidence seems fairly straightforward. Some cultures do show differences in what is disclosed and to whom, but there are also a great many similarities. This mirrors the fact that there are also a great many similarities between the various cultures and the specific groups tested. Differences due to religion, family structure, and sex roles are all likely to be factors which should be taken into account when assessing cultural effects. Comparisons with markedly different and more isolated cultures could be instructive.

It is worthy of note that topics and targets also have profound implication for the "norm of reciprocity" in self-disclosure. This important area is discussed in more detail next.

The norm of reciprocity

An important debate in the self-disclosure literature has concerned the extent to which disclosure by person A to person B will elicit a reciprocal level of disclosure from B to A. The norm of reciprocity makes a great deal of sense if, as argued previously, disclosure has reward value and participants in relationships are attempting to derive equitable levels of reward. Such a pattern of reciprocal self-disclosure would constitute a pattern of reciprocal reward at an appropriate level. Sounds logical and straightforward? Unfortunately, as Hill & Stull (1982) have noted, research in this area has been plagued by conceptual and measurement issues. They point out that reciprocity can take at least three forms. First, as an exchange which shows reciprocity but not necessarily at an identical level. A change in person A's level of disclosure results in a change in person B's level, though not necessarily of an identical amount. This is a covariant exchange, possibly the most common form of reciprocity assessed by research (e.g. Cozby, 1972). A second form of reciprocity, a sub-set of the first, is an equivalent exchange – an exact reciprocity of intimacy or amount. Finally, the simple act of turn-taking in self-disclosure also represents a basic form of reciprocity. Comparing across studies which have used differing notions of reciprocity is at the very least a difficult task, though there are discernible patterns in the literature.

Two main models of reciprocity have been proposed. The linear model, based on equivalent exchange, argues that the greater person A's self-disclosure, the greater will be person B's reciprocal disclosure and liking. The curvilinear model, based on covariant exchange, argues that high self-disclosure can actually result in a reduction in the amount or intimacy of the reciprocated information (e.g. Cozby, 1972). Here it is important to take into account the nature of the relationship between the discloser and the recipient. A decline in the need for reciprocity, or at least immediate reciprocity, of intimate information is a normal characteristic of long-term, well-established relationships (Altman, 1973). On the other hand, most research is short term and conducted in a laboratory and a curvilinear effect in this situation could partly reflect high levels of self-disclosure producing anxiety in the recipient.

Initial research strongly supported a simple linear model of reciprocity in self-disclosure (Jourard & Landsman, 1960). The more we are disclosed to, the more we are likely to disclose in return. This reciprocity held for both quantity and intimacy of information (Jourard, 1959).

Developmental skills

Implicit within the ability to reciprocate self-disclosure are certain expectations and skills which are dependent on the child's social cognitive abilities, such as seeking intimacy exchange in relationships and possessing an ability to discriminate the level of self and other's intimacy of disclosure. This analysis suggests that as reciprocity of self-disclosure is built on basic role-taking abilities, and true, non-egocentric role-taking is unlikely below school age (Selman, 1981). The meaning of reciprocity in self-disclosure is not fully appreciated until middle childhood. At this age the child's relationships will be sociocentric and emphasise rules, obligations, and reciprocity in general. Some support for this analysis was provided by Cohn & Strassberg's (1983) findings on children in the third grade at school, and by Rotenberg & Mann (1986), though these latter authors did not find reciprocity in children below the sixth grade. The difference in these findings probably reflect differences in research methods. Rotenberg & Mann's (1986) study was based on children's evaluations of a videotaped interaction sequence while Cohn & Strassberg (1983) measured children's actual self-disclosures. Indeed, with appropriate methods even children as young as about six years can be shown to prefer and disclose more to those peers who disclose more to them (e.g. Skypeck, 1967). This reciprocity effect in self-disclosure is unlikely to be evident in children much below school age.

Although ample research on older age groups does show an association between reciprocity and liking, one cannot assume this in younger children. They learn to use reciprocal patterns of self-disclosure before they fully appreciate their significance. There is little relationship between a child's perception of the intimacy of his or her relationship and rates of self-disclosure (Parker & Gottman, 1989). Also supporting this conclusion, Rotenberg & Mann's (1986) study did not find reciprocity of self-disclosure in kindergarten to fourth-grade children. Reciprocity, and corresponding attraction to reciprocal disclosers, was only evident in sixth graders. This study must be treated with caution, however, as its methodology probably underestimates children's abilities. The subjects in this study were evaluating videotaped scenes of two children conversing rather than actually being involved themselves. It is conceivable that young children evaluate videotaped scenes differently from personal experiences. The role-taking involved in evaluating the videotape makes it a considerably more complex task than simply responding to a direct, concrete cue.

As attitude theorists have recognised for many years (e.g. Fishbein & Ajzen, 1975), and developmental psychologists have recently been arguing (e.g. Furman, 1984a), knowledge and expectations have a complex relationship to actual behaviour. A number of additional factors, such as motivation, social norms and constraints, also intervene to determine what behaviour will occur and what form it will take.

Alternative explanations

The observed reciprocity of self-disclosure (let alone the function it is serving) has not gone without question. Disputes concerning the norm of reciprocity have taken two main lines. Some authors have tried to modify and explore the limits of the phenomenon. Other authors have argued that it is largely illusory, a product of research methodologies.

Two major paradigms are especially common in self-disclosure research. In the first, a subject is simply required to self-disclose or indicate a willingness to self-disclose at a given level. In the second, subjects are required to evaluate two disclosers on the basis of a vignette presented by a researcher. Both of these approaches are rather limited and limiting. In a study by Brewer & Mittelman (1980) the reciprocity effect was eliminated if the demands of the experimental situation (i.e. the topics to be discussed) implied a given level of intimacy. Initial and reciprocal self-disclosures matched the normative cue for intimacy rather than the other's self-disclosure. At the very least this indicates that reciprocity of self-disclosure is not automatic, it is influenced by a variety of contextual factors.

Although interpersonal costs incurred by self-disclosure are often balanced against the rewards gained from the reciprocal self-disclosure by the other partner in the relationship, this need not always be the case. Other behaviours and sources of reward are substitutable (Foa & Foa, 1971). For example, in adults disclosure is greater to attractive others and from less attractive others (Pellegrini, Hicks & Meyers-Winton, 1979), possibly to equalise the relative reward each gets from the association. Although there is no comparable study on children, circumstantial evidence suggests that such a relationship exists. Self-disclosure is greater to more popular individuals, and more popular individuals also tend to be more physically attractive (see Chapter 3).

Berg & Archer (1980) suggest a flexible interpretation of the norm of reciprocity. They showed that an appropriate expression of interest and concern can be adequate reciprocation and create a more positive impression than even a reciprocal disclosure at an appropriate level. This provides support for Davis & Perkowitz's (1979) contention that appropriate responsiveness is more important than simple reciprocity. This also provides at least a partial explanation for the apparent decline in reciprocity in long-term relationships. The observed reciprocity effect often represents the only way open to a person, especially in a psychological experiment, to indicate responsiveness; it doesn't mean that responsiveness cannot be indicated by other means. This importance of responsiveness has long been recognised by counsellors (albeit in terms of different jargon) – here the client should do most of the talking and yet the counsellor must be able to facilitate and make acceptable this state of affairs.

Characteristics of self-disclosers

There has been no shortage of research looking at the association of various individual characteristics with patterns of self-disclosure in adults and adolescents, but there has been very little on children. None the less, this area of research is worth examining for the indications that it provides concerning the basis for individual differences in levels of self-disclosure.

Despite the undoubted importance of research into this area, there are very few conclusions that can be drawn. One major conclusion that a cynic might draw is that the prevalence of studies on the characteristics of self-disclosers is due to the fact that they are very quick and easy to do rather than because of deep theoretical concerns. A self-disclosure questionnaire and a personality questionnaire or two distributed to fairly large groups of subjects is a relatively effortless procedure. What the results of some studies of this ilk actually mean is another matter – and one sometimes passed over when such research is reported.

This aspect of the self-disclosure literature has been divided into three categories by Altman & Taylor (1973): personality characteristics, demographic and biographical characteristics, and sociocultural characteristics. The following discussion will be based on this taxonomy.

Personality characteristics

With few exceptions, the correlations between personality and self-disclosure are confused and contradictory. Many assertions are made of the basis of relatively weak statistical relationships (e.g. Pedersen & Higbee, 1969). The results of different studies – even involving the same authors – can produce inconsistent results (e.g. studies of adolescents by Sinha & Tripathi, 1975; Tripathi, 1979) and hence are difficult to interpret or have confidence in. Even if these were consistent, they show personality factors to account for only a small percentage of the variations in self-disclosure and, being correlations, they provide no indication of the direction of causality. Does possessing a given personality trait promote a given level of self-disclosure, or is it that a willingness to reveal personal information provides feedback and experiences which promote the development of the personality trait?

The apparent inconsistencies in the literature are due, at least in part, to the way self-disclosure is conceptualised and measured. In terms of conceptualisation, many authors have attempted to view self-disclosure as a relatively permanent and invariant personality trait. This has been criticised as underrating the effects of specific situational influences (e.g. Cozby, 1973). Greater consistency will be obtained when self-disclosure is recognised as a characteristic of specific interactions and relationships (Altman & Taylor, 1973). In terms of measurement, many studies have relied on self-disclosure questionnaires, which have been much criticised as being better as a description of past behaviour rather than a prediction of future behaviour patterns (Cozby, 1973).

So, with all the above reservations and problems, what can be said about self-disclosure and personality? Not a lot. Despite the intuitive appeal of such a link, the existing research on adults and adolescents has patently failed to reveal a consistent relationship between self-disclosure and a number of personality dimensions, including supposedly obvious traits such as neuroticism and anxiety. The main (relatively) consistent finding is of a correlation between self-disclosure and extraversion or sociability (e.g. Pratap & Bhargava, 1982). In support of Jourard's conceptualisation of self-disclosure, the literature is also suggestive of a positive association between self-disclosure and self-concept (Agrawal, 1983); studies show that more self-aware adolescents are more willing to self-disclose (Davis & Franzoi, 1986).

Demographic and biographical characteristics

The relationship between self-disclosure and various demographic and biographical factors has also produced a wealth of results – though once again the usefulness of these descriptions needs to be considered. As descriptions of a specific culture at a specific time in history they are interesting, but surely there should be more? The significant question is what creates these individual and cultural differences? And what are the implications of these differences for relationships between children of different backgrounds? These questions have received considerably less research attention.

The typical methodology of demographic/biographical studies is to correlate various subject characteristics with a self-disclosure questionnaire – often the JSDQ. Factors of interest have ranged from family structure and socioeconomic status, sex differences, birth order, age, and ethnic group. Several of these factors are dealt with elsewhere in this book. To give a flavour of the research in this area we will briefly examine birth order at this point.

Birth order is an interesting and well-researched factor affecting self-disclosure. In studies of adolescents, Dimond & Munz (1967) and Dimond & Hellkamp (1969) found that later-born children scored higher on a self-disclosure questionnaire, arguably because being born into an existing family system enabled them to become more socially adept. However, data from Snoek & Rothblum (1979) suggests that birth order effects are complexly related to patterns of parental control. First-born children from families exercising a democratic style of parental control showed higher levels of self-disclosure than children from permissive or autocratic homes. This pattern was reversed for the later-born children; possibly rivalling an older sibling is more difficult in a democratic structure than in a permissive family, where roles are less clearly defined, or an autocratic family, where roles are clearly and inflexibly defined.

Sociocultural characteristics

Based on Lewin's (1936) original speculation of differences in the openness of Americans and Germans, a number of cross-cultural studies have been conducted. Studies have found that Americans reported more self-disclosure than either the Germans (Plog, 1965), or the British (Jourard, 1961). Within the American population research has found that self-disclosure was greater for white adolescents than for their black counterparts (Dimond & Hellkamp, 1969; Jourard & Lasakow, 1958), who in turn disclosed more than comparable Mexican-American groups (Littlefield, 1974). In accord with Lewin's (1936) original speculations, one may question if these differences reflect corresponding differences in the ease with which relationships are formed and in their level of involvement.

Sex differences

The question of sex differences in self-disclosure is directly related to sex roles and the existence of sex differences in patterns of relationships (see also Chapter 7). A number of authors have suggested that boys tend to form large, activity-based groups whereas girls' relationships are more likely to be one-to-one and intimate (e.g. Douvan & Adelson, 1966). This pattern of relationships is underpinned by patterns of communication which have been seen as characteristic of male and female sex roles in our society. Restricted levels of self-disclosure are often seen as characteristic of the traditional masculine sex role, while more extensive communication are regarded as typical of the feminine sex role.

The question of whether there are sex differences in self-disclosure is, superficially, quite simple to test. You simply measure self-disclosure in males and females and compare. Certainly some researchers have adopted this approach. Many studies have simply summed disclosure scores across all ages, targets, and topics. Unfortunately, as the previous sections should have alerted you, things are seldom this simple!

A frequently found sex difference is that self-disclosure is greater by females. Cozby (1973) states that no study finds that males disclose more. I know of only one study since Cozby's review which has found significantly greater overall self-disclosure by males – Kobocow, McGuire & Blau's (1983) study of seventh- and eighth-grade adolescents. Within the broad pattern of a sex difference there is considerable variation, though cross-comparison is often difficult as many studies have confounded amount and intimacy of self-disclosure.

Studies of adolescents sometimes report greater self-disclosure by girls (e.g. Papini et al., 1990). A similar pattern of results is also shown in some of the more limited research on younger children. O'Neill et al. (1976) report that preadolescent girls between the ages of approximately seven and thirteen years report more frequent and more intimate self-disclosure to significant targets than do boys. Behavioural confirmation of this pattern of self-disclosure to peers was subsequently provided Cohn & Strassberg's (1983) study of children in grades three and six (approximately nine and twelve years of age). Girls spent more time in total self-disclosure and intimate self-disclosure to peers than did boys. In a study spanning a wide age range, approximately 10–18 years of age, Rivenbark (1971) also showed greater levels of self-disclosure by females. These and more recent studies suggest that throughout childhood girls are more likely to be willing to confide personal feelings and experiences to their friends and because of this are also more likely to possess an intimate knowledge of their friends, especially in adolescence (Bryant, 1985; Belle, 1989).

Differences in disclosing what, to whom?

In apparent direct opposition to the above findings, at times research has not revealed a sex difference in adolescent self-disclosure. For example, Skypeck's (1967) study of self-disclosure to same-sex peers by 6–12-year-old pre-adolescents found no significant sex differences. One must be cautious in interpreting these sorts of negative result. As Belle (1989) points out, equal levels of self-disclosure do not necessarily imply that the goals and expectations that the child holds for the disclosure and relationship are also identical. An interesting study by Belle, Burr & Cooney (1987) suggested that girls disclose in order to elicit social support and practical help with a problem. Boys on the other hand disclose in order to comply with external expectations, to convey factual information or because the other ought to be told something or would be likely to find out anyway. This confirms West's (1970) study of the disclosure of biographical information by Canadian ninth graders (approximately 15 years of age) – boys tended to be more selective in terms of disclosure content and girls were more selective in terms of confidants (targets).

Several explanations have been proposed to account for the grave inconsistency in research findings on sex differences in self-disclosure. A relatively straightforward explanation is that this lack of a consistent sex differences is due to a variety of uncontrolled variables masking any differences. Such factors might include age differences in subject groups, differences in target figures, and the geographical locale in which the research was conducted (Mulcahy, 1973). If self-disclosure is examined in more specific terms it becomes apparent that any sex differences are likely to depend on the content of the information (topics) being revealed and the targets to whom the revelations are directed. If children are rewarded for sex-typed behaviour (for example with approval), and disclosure of the behaviour to another is considered an extension of that behaviour, then one might well expect sex-appropriate disclosure to also be rewarded (O'Neill et al., 1976).

Children's own reports of their patterns of self-disclosure to peers provide support for the idea that the sexes differ in the content as well as the levels of their self-disclosure. A study by O'Neill et al. (1976) found that pre-adolescents' self-disclosures tended to be of sex-appropriate information. Females more readily revealed intimate information on topics associated with emotionality, anxiety and dependence. Arguably these were more readily communicated precisely because they are acceptable to females. A similar pattern of results is evident in adolescents. Mulcahy (1973) found that females disclosed more on tastes and interests, and personality. Males showed a cluster of topics including tastes and interests, work and studies, and attitudes and opinions.

Broadening the range of targets considered, Davidson, Balswick & Halverson's (1980) study found four basic dimensions of adolescent self-disclosure. Adolescent females disclosed more in terms of general information and personal information dimensions, males were more disclosing in terms of revealing sexuality to parents and (non-significantly) revealing sexuality to peers dimensions.

Sex-roles

As an alternative explanation, it has been argued (Chelune, 1979) that many of the conflicting results on sex differences in self-disclosure are due to differences in masculinity–femininity. Here again the evidence is contradictory. There are certainly studies which examine this possibility and do not find a masculinity–femininity effect (e.g. Pedersen & Higbee, 1969) and so do not support this interpretation. But the sex-role explanation of differences in self-disclosure should not be abandoned with undue haste; there is a feasible explanation for the inconsistency of evidence relating to sex roles and self-disclosure.

It has been argued that sex roles do not represent a simple dichotomy. A more complex interpretation may be appropriate to our modern society and to interpreting the results of masculinity–femininity studies. Rather than masculinity and femininity representing the two poles of a single dimension they can be regarded as two independent dimensions (Bem, 1974). From this stance people do not simply have to fall on a masculine–feminine continuum, they may also be either androgynous or undifferentiated in terms of sex roles. The androgynous person would show a high level of both traits that are typically labelled masculine (e.g. assertive) and traits that are typically labelled feminine (e.g. nurturant). The undifferentiated person would show low levels of masculine and feminine traits. In support of this explanation Lavine & Lombardo (1984) found that self-disclosure was related to sex roles but not gender; results from androgynous and undifferentiated individuals obscured any simple sex difference.

Conclusions about sex differences

The available evidence does, on balance, seem to weigh in favour of the conclusion that there is a genuine sex difference in self-disclosure. What the evidence does not yet do adequately is to provide an explanation for this sex difference or reasons why some research has failed to find it. In line with research observing sex differences in levels of disclosure, a number of studies (of adults) have empirically examined the consequences of maintaining or violating these norms.

In accordance with the sex differences discussed above, high disclosing females express more satisfaction with their interpersonal relationships than do high disclosing males; low disclosing males are more satisfied with their relationships than are low disclosing females (Lombardo & Wood, 1979). It is a common finding that high disclosing males are less liked than their lower disclosing counterparts, though preferences for high disclosing females depend on what she is disclosing – disclosure seen as aggressive or threatening does not produce such preferences (Kleinke & Kahn, 1980). Similarly, the sex composition of dyads is likely to play an important role.

At least part of the explanation for the discrepancy in the levels of self-disclosure of males and females is probably due to males actually encouraging self-disclosure in females. Davis (1978) showed that no matter who started in a male–female self-disclosure exercise, males took the lead and proceeded independently in choice of topics. Females matched the pace. A possible explanation for this effect is that the females altered their characteristic disclosing behaviour to accommodate that of the male, a modelling effect (Fantasia, Lombardo & Wolf, 1976). Of course it is possible to go yet one step further back in the analysis and ask why males should wish to encourage self-disclosure in females. One explanation is simply in terms of patterns of socialisation. Boys being taught the stereotype of the "strong silent male" (Balswick & Peek, 1971), or to withhold self-disclosure in order to take and maintain control in a relationship (Rosenfeld, 1979).

Some final thoughts about self-disclosure

This chapter began by pointing out that self-disclosure was achieving increasing recognition as an area of central importance to social and developmental psychologists. This chapter has tried to show the broad scope of what has already been achieved by the many dedicated researchers in the area – though there were many contradictions, gaps, and weaknesses evident in the theorising and research in the area. This is an unfortunate characteristic of a young, inter-disciplinary area of study; in the longer term this broad background to the area is likely to prove a vital strength. Much has been achieved and recent research is setting new and more ambitious goals and standards.

6 Similarity and social comparison

It is fair to say that every friendship must be built at least in part on a base of similarity, but there is more to it than that.
(Rubin, 1980, p. 72)

Similarity was one of the earliest antecedents of friendship to be noted, being discussed even as far back into history as the ancient Greek philosophers (e.g. Aristotle, 1953). It now stands as one of the most systematically researched aspects of interpersonal attraction and friendship in adults. Both behavioural and cognitive psychologists have stressed the importance and relevance of similarity as a basis for relationships. And, despite their differences in theoretical orientation, both behavioural *and* cognitive researchers have gone one step further and stressed the importance of social comparison as a basis for similarity effects in relationship. Children's relationships provide a context for social comparisons and similarity is functional, at least in part, because of its role in such comparison processes. Together similarity and social comparison processes in relationships validate the child's attitudes and personality and provide a basis for the child's sense of individual identity, a notion evident in a great deal of psychological and psychiatric theorising (Rubin, 1980).

This chapter starts by examining the motivation underlying social comparison processes, and the mechanisms by which social comparisons are made. There has been substantial controversy concerning developmental changes in patterns of social comparison. Inevitably simple models have been forced to take account of a variety of background factors to explain why children's abilities are often greater than is shown in their everyday behaviour. From this background, more focused attention is devoted to examining the role of similarity in social comparison. This constitutes an area of continuing debate as researchers attempt to clarify the functional nature of similarity effects in social comparison. The main body of the chapter moves the focus of analysis from social comparison in its own right to an examination of its role, directly and in terms of similarity, in children's relationships. There is a substantial body of research in this area. Models of the changing role of similarity in children's friendships are relatively recent but serve as useful and important bridges between cognitive developmental theory and social psychological research on relationships. The final topic examined in this chapter is the continuing debate concerning sex differences in similarity effects. This debate is likely to run for some considerable time, and even established conclusions are likely to need reviewing as sex roles change.

The effectance motive

The effectance motive was originally proposed by White (1959). In a wide-ranging literature review, covering Freudian, ethological, and child development literatures, White argued that a basic, innate striving for competence and autonomy has been widely recognised. A motivation to be successful in mastering one's environment was seen as adaptive in evolutionary terms and as producing positive feelings of efficacy. This efficacy derived from mastering one's environment does not only apply to the physical world. As Dunn (1988) notes, children also derive pleasure from efficacy in social relationships. Social comparison is an important means of by which the child gathers social information and evaluates his or her competence. The effectance motive and social comparison have been used to explain the much vaunted similarity–attraction effect (e.g. Byrne, 1971).

Social comparison

For several decades social comparison has been a major area of study by social scientists interested in the self-concept and by educationalists interested in children's achievement motivation. Symbolic interactionists, a school of sociology, were among the earliest social scientists to give systematic attention to social comparison processes. Symbolic interactionism is not a single theory but rather a broad school. The common emphasis of social interactionist theories (e.g. Cooley, 1912; Mead, 1934) is that meaning is not inherent within the objects and so human behaviour cannot be regarded as consisting of inevitable responses to stimuli with immutable meanings. This approach is important in highlighting the dynamic and socially situated nature of social comparison process. It emphasises that the self is a social construct. Identity is seen as being actively constructed out of the individual's social interactions. We act toward others, and others act toward us, on the basis of the meanings that we hold for each other. These interactions with others then essentially serve as a "looking glass" in which the self is reflected (Cooley, 1912). From this perspective, the ability to compare oneself with others is a basic requirement if the self is to be differentiated from the general social milieu. Interestingly, a similar point has more recently been made by attachment theorists who see the history of an attachment relationship as being reflected in the personality structure and self-concept of the child. For example, rejected children often see themselves as unworthy of love and attention (Bretherton, 1985).

Social comparison is a phenomenon often mentioned in the literature on personal relationships but it is rarely given detailed attention (Dakin & Arrowood, 1981). Because of this imbalance in research on social comparison a great deal of the evidence reviewed here is based on studies of achievement comparison in children. While this is far from ideal, Ruble (1983) has argued that the developmental patterns revealed by this research do have implications for the way the process is seen as operating within other domains of social development, such as friendship. Unfortunately, she also argues that differences between areas of study account for some of the apparently contradictory results in social comparison research. She is undoubtedly correct, but it does mean that we must be careful not to over-generalise from existing research in other domains.

Background to social comparison in children

The child is born into the social world of a family and is immediately surrounded by individuals showing sophisticated levels of social analysis. These sophisticated social beings are discussing and drawing inferences about others, making evaluations of the abilities and actions of others and, most importantly, comparing themselves with these other people. The child is a natural part of this ongoing activity; even young children appear to show an interest in comparing themselves to others. The word "appear" is used to draw attention to the fact that the age of onset of social comparison is an issue of considerable debate. In the fullness of time these disagreements over the age of onset of social comparison will more than likely come to be shown to be largely illusory. As with disagreements over children's social cognitive abilities, polarised positions are more a reflection of the way the process is defined by the researcher than what the researcher is observing in children.

Though the frequency of social comparisons does change developmentally, one needs only to watch children for a short period of time to be made aware that even preschoolers are without doubt making simple comparisons between themselves and their peers (Ruble, Feldman & Boggiano, 1976). They show clear interest and concern with matters such as who is the biggest, who has the most presents, and how to co-ordinate play.

A number of studies have illustrated the nature of social comparison processes in young children. In a naturalistic study of 3–5-year-old preschoolers in free play, Judith Chafel (1984a, 1986) found social comparisons were actively and freely used in their interactions. In their verbal statements young children regularly and spontaneously made comparisons of similarities and differences, attempted to resolve cognitive uncertainties (such as approaches to solving some problem during play), and evaluated their relative standing on a number of basic attributes. The specific forms of comparison used depend on the activities in which the child is engaged. For example, there are more competitive and "besting" comparisons during constructive play than during dramatic play (Wallace, 1991). An example from Chafel (1984a, p. 118) will serve to illustrate a typical social comparison involving a "besting" statement; the children, "A." and "S.", are four and five years old, respectively:

> S. Asks A.: "How old are you?"
> A. replies: "Four and a half"
> S. explains: "I'm five and a half"

In addition to age and differences due to settings and activities, a great deal of attention has been devoted to examining possible sex differences in social comparison. Although differences are fairly regularly reported, the pattern is not consistent and the picture remains far from clear at the present time (Chafel, 1988a, b).

Competitiveness

Social comparison is needed if a child is to achieve a realistic estimate of his or her own capabilities. Often social comparisons are the child's only source of information about the social desirability and social adequacy of his or her behaviour (Santrock & Ross, 1975). These self-estimates of appropriateness and adequacy are, Suls & Sanders (1979) argue, very important in young children as early feelings of mastery are necessary for a sense of personal competence. They also imply a hierarchical distinction between self and others, a notion that is consistent with the finding that even young children, from just over three years of age, form dominance hierarchies and well-ordered affiliation networks in the nursery school (e.g. Strayer, 1980).

In older children, social comparison theory provides an explanation for the findings of studies which have reported competitiveness in children's friendships. By middle childhood, at least for some boys, an exception to the general picture of mutual co-operation and consideration underlying friendship has been highlighted in a study by Berndt (1981b). In this study, some boys in grades two and four showed a friendly rivalry or competitiveness with their friends. On a series of tasks in which sharing with or helping the partner was likely to result in fewer rewards for the child himself, boys appeared to behave less prosocially to their friends than to acquaintances. The use of the word "appeared" is because presumably the greatest compliment to the friend is recognition that he is valued, a person worthy of the child's informality and involvement. Previous research has shown the importance of shared interests and activities in children's friendships, especially in this middle childhood and especially for boys (this is discussed in more detail later in this chapter). Competitive activities consequently provide a means and opportunity for the child to compare himself on salient attributes with another child that he regards as similar and equal. This competitiveness declines as the child enters adolescence. The adolescent has considerably more sophisticated friendship concepts and equal sharing becomes an idealised norm (Berndt, 1985).

A study by Tesser, Campbell & Smith (1984) helps to put the competitiveness of boys in perspective, and relate it to the similarity effects that form the basis for children's relationships. In this study of fifth and sixth graders it was found that children generally preferred to be friends with classmates that were similar in terms of their overall level of performance on relevant interests and activities. But within this general pattern there was an interesting twist: the children preferred others whose performance was inferior to their own on certain specific, highly valued activities, and better than their own on other less personally significant activities. This highlights a second role of social comparison: self-enhancement (Goethals & Darley, 1977). If friends have similar overall preferences but rate the importance of specific activities differently this is an elegant solution to the impossible dilemma of both children seeking superiority on relevant attributes; it is essentially a form of complementarity within the overall pattern of similarity.

Explaining social comparison

The early contribution of sociology to an understanding of social comparison processes in the form of theories of symbolic interactionism has already been mentioned. The first and most significant contribution to a psychological understanding of the social comparison process was made by Leon Festinger (1954). In this seminal paper Festinger argued that there exists a universal drive for individuals to evaluate the status of their opinions and abilities, the basic information necessary to construct social reality (Olson & Hazlewood, 1986). The significance of the concept of a drive for social comparison is that it implies a variable motivation. The need to compare may be higher at one time than at another, in one situation rather than another, or in one person rather than another. Other factors affecting this drive might be expected to include things such as the individual's level of certainty of personal opinion or ability, the importance of the attribute for the individual, and the prior opportunities for comparison.

According to Festinger, the preferred means of comparison are non-social (i.e. objective physical reality) but, of course, much social interaction cannot be readily subject to such measures. Where non-social means are not available the comparison is likely to take the form of a social comparison with other appropriate social figures, i.e. the comparison will be based on consensual validation of opinions and abilities. This could have distinct advantages – far better to evaluate a potential danger through comparison with others than risking life and limb on a trial and error test!

Festinger continues his analysis by noting that in the absence of an opportunity for comparison the individual's subjective evaluations of personal opinions and abilities will be unstable. This has important implications for children's friendships. The rejected child is likely to remain so as he or she lacks the opportunities for social comparison, to establish appropriate norms. As shown in later chapters, rejected children tend to overestimate their level of social competence; opportunities to interact with peers can be a useful means of improving children's social skills and the accuracy of their self-perception.

Importantly for our consideration of the role of social comparison in children's friendships and peer relationships, Festinger argues that when choosing social comparison figures the tendency is generally toward others similar in opinions and abilities. In other words, if children wish to evaluate their peer interaction skills they should compare themselves against others of similar levels of skill. The comparison against similar others is supposed to allow more accurate evaluations of the individual's relative standing on the attributes assessed. It also seems to imply, however, that the drive is for the individual to have confirmation of the adequacy of personal opinions and abilities rather than a real test of their truth or relative competence (Goethals & Darley, 1977). The consequence of this utility of similar others for comparison purposes is an attraction toward these individuals. Indeed, Festinger noted that the pressures for social comparison are so great that they are not just based on similarities but are likely to result in moves to greater uniformity.

Relevant comparison figures are of, as theorised by Festinger, usually similar others – similarity here referring to the opinions and abilities being compared. Subsequent writers have questioned this interpretation of similarity. As shown later in this chapter, the debate over precisely what constitutes similarity has been a major theoretical problem for researchers interested in social comparison processes. First, it is necessary to examine more specifically the nature of social comparison in children.

Development of social comparison ability

The age of onset of social comparisons is unclear. This picture is due at least in part to the methodological and conceptual limitations of existing research in the area. On a conceptual level the situation is not dissimilar to the debate over the development of empathic understanding. Depending on how tightly the concept is defined it can be observed in three year olds or not until eight or nine. Very young children *do* compare their activity with others, but they are not able to make sophisticated inferential judgements about ability as a personal trait on the basis of their observations.

In addition to the conceptual cross-talk noted above, methodological issues have served to multiply the difficulties of reconciling and interpreting the results from different researchers. Much of the existing research has tended to focus on achievement comparisons and the child's verbalisations; it has also tended to be highly experimental, though the emphasis does appear to be changing and a number of recent studies have examined social comparison in naturalistic situations (e.g. Chafel & Bahr, 1988). The literature on role-taking, must alert us to the sorts of problems that these different theoretical and methodological perspectives can produce.

Veroff's developmental model

A three-stage model of the development of social comparison has been proposed by Veroff (1969). This has a number of similarities to the models of children's friendship expectations outlined in Chapter 2, emphasising their common social cognitive bases. According to Veroff's (1969) model, below the age of about five years the child does not show *spontaneous* social comparisons with others. In this first stage of the development of comparison processes, the stage of autonomous competence, internal, personal norms dominate. The child's concern is to establish personal competence and mastery over his or her world. The second stage is that of social comparisons and begins at about the time of first entry to school; here the child is orientated by social norms. The emphasis is on comparisons, especially with similar others. The final stage is one of integration. About the age of ten to twelve years old social and personal norms are integrated and reconciled. Which of these is salient will vary according to their appropriateness in different situations. An important point to note about this approach is that it sees Festinger's theory as inapplicable to young children, below the age of about five years, as such children are egocentric and lack the background of rewards which promote comparison behaviour.

A substantial body of research has examined Veroff's hypothesis. It has generally received a good deal of support but does appear in need of some refinements and modifications. A study by Ruble, Feldman & Boggiano (1976) showed that with age increasing numbers of social comparisons were made by children between the age of five and seven years, though there were no differences in the proportion of children using social comparison as an explanation for their behaviour. These authors also reported that the younger children did not appear to translate the comparison information that they gathered into changes in their behaviour, such as greater task-directed effort if they were performing poorly on a task. In short, although there does appear to be a developmental progression in levels of social comparison, even children as young as five seemed to be interested in comparison information.

Further evidence suggests that even five years old is a conservative estimate of the age at which children are interested in making social comparisons in one form or another (Chafel, 1985). Masters (1971) reported that four year olds compare the rewards they receive with those received by others. A study by Mosatche & Bragonier (1981) showed that even children as young as three can and do spontaneously make social comparisons in the naturalistic environment of free play at preschool. Preschoolers are interested in establishing similarities and differences between themselves and others, especially in concrete areas such as possessions and activities. Status and attitudes were used less frequently, confirming previous research on the cognitive developmental limitations on children's friendship concepts (e.g. Barenboim, 1981).

As with role-taking ability, characterising the young child as egocentric in any absolute way is far from the whole truth (Chafel, 1984b). In naturalistic situations preschoolers are more likely to make concrete comparisons (e.g. about possessions, activities) rather than comparisons on abstract categories such as attitudes and personality. By the first grade children can and are keen to use social comparison to evaluate their performance in relation to similar others. Note, however, that these first graders are still using comparisons on a simple, physical level, to equalise rewards, for example, and not to make self-evaluations or to infer the level of their own or another child's ability (Ruble et al., 1980). These developments in social comparison ability have been linked with corresponding changes in children's attributional abilities, in particular, with children's ability to apply the covariation and discounting principles (Aboud, 1985). Older children are able to moderate their evaluations to take account of additional factors. For example, performance on a test is judged in the light of the time taken to complete the test. This sort of inferential ability does not appear until about the age of eight or nine – the age at which children are starting to pay attention to behavioural consistencies as representing personal traits (Barenboim, 1981; Rholes & Ruble, 1984)

If social comparisons are to be found even in children as young as three years of age, previously postulated developmental changes in the phenomenon will need to be reconsidered. The results of study by Morris & Nemcek (1982) led them to suggest a "stepwise" developmental progression in social comparison. Children of three could produce a hierarchy of ability, though this bore little relation to an actual hierarchy of ability. At about four years of age the children were showing general accuracy in the construction of their hierarchy, though still distorting their self-rating. By five this distortion disappeared and accuracy was high, and by six the developmental progression culminated in the familiar adult-like selective preference for similar but slightly better comparison with others.

Social comparison in context

In an excellent and balanced review of the social comparison literature, Ruble (1983) attempted to reconcile the contradictions and inconsistencies in the extant literature by suggesting that social comparison is a multi-step process involving three main elements, set background factors, inferences based on comparison information, and behavioural consequences. Developmental differences in social comparison ability can originate from any of these sources.

The background factors include a basic set of cognitive capacities, interest and motivation to make social comparisons, and a knowledge of appropriate strategies (such as comparing with similar others). Even relatively young children have the basic cognitive capacities required to make simple social comparison judgements (see Chapter 2), they do show an interest and motivation in making such comparisons, and they are able to appreciate the utility of similarity and of a standard-setter (a comparison figure excelling on the dimension compared). In short, by school age children appear to possess the necessary background factors to enable them to make social comparisons. Indeed, they can and do make social comparisons, but these do still show developmental trends. Interest in making social comparisons does appear to increase with age. More marked developmental differences appear to result from the uses made of the social comparison information that is gathered, the inference stage of social comparison.

In accordance with the findings of research on the development of social cognition and attribution processes, there is a developmental trend for social comparison to move from the concrete to the abstract. Three to four year olds can and do make comparisons at an overt level (e.g. sharing rewards) and for concrete characteristics such as strength or possessions, rather than unobservable characteristics such as attitudes and abilities. Most comparisons of young children do not entail unobservable inferences of stable attributes such as competence, traits, and dispositions removed from concrete differences. As Turiel (1983) points out, if the child lacks a stable concept of internal psychological processes in others, what is there to compare other than observable characteristics?

The use of social comparison for self-evaluations comes later in the developmental sequence as the child becomes increasingly self-reflective and evaluates his or her performance relative to others rather than in terms of personal outcomes in isolation. For young children, relative performance evaluations are meaningless as they are still concerned with self-mastery and identity. They are concerned with questions of similarity and consensus rather than evaluation (Mosatche & Bragonier, 1981). In contrast, older children, of, say, six years of age show an emphasis on establishing individuality and contrast through their friendships (Gottman & Parkhurst, 1980).

Similarity as a basis for social comparison

In his original theory of social comparison processes, Festinger (1954) emphasised the role of similar others as appropriate figures for social comparison. Although this seems logical, there is, as Olson & Hazlewood (1986) note, a basic paradox in a simple interpretation of this hypothesis. If the other is known to be similar, why bother comparing with him or her? What further information about similarity would be gained by this? Of course, we are seldom that accurate or certain about our social judgements and, as we shall see in due course, we often make comparisons on several levels. In this context the apparent paradox is more illusory than real.

An initial attempt to clarify the role of similarity in social comparison was made by Goethals & Darley (1977). These authors pointed out that social comparison is inferential and must take into account a number of attributional considerations. A given opinion or level of ability can be due to a number of extraneous factors (e.g. age, sex, prior experience) and so direct social comparisons with similar others is relatively uninformative. The factors that give rise to similarities and differences are likely to be more informative and significant. In other words, information from others that are similar not on the focal opinion or ability but on related attributes is likely to be more useful than information about direct similarity. This is the related attributes hypothesis (Wheeler & Zuckerman, 1977). For example, a boy wishing to evaluate his sporting ability will probably wish to compare himself against another boy of approximately the same age if he believes that age and sex are dimensions relevant to evaluating his sporting performance. Comparing himself with someone of a different age and sex, even if they perform equally well at sports, is relatively less informative. Standards for the appropriateness of behaviour show very definite age and sex differences (Masters, 1971).

In a clarification of the related attributes hypothesis, Miller (1984) suggested that because of an individual's self-schema (a self-concept that guides information processing about the self), unrelated attributes are sometimes important determinants of the choice of comparison figure. It is common for school-children to show a preference for comparisons with peers of the same race and gender (Meisel & Blumberg, 1990). If gender is schematic for a girl then comparisons are aimed not so much at ascertaining her absolute standing on some ability but rather how consistent her performance is in relation to her conceptualisation of herself as feminine – even though gender is an irrelevant dimension. An example will clarify this point. For a number of years schools have been concerned with encouraging more girls to study science and engineering subjects, with varying degrees of success. At least a part of the problem of the under-achievement of girls in these subjects can be attributed to a self-schema which is gender schematic and does not recognise the study of engineering and technical subjects as consistent with the female sex-role stereotype. When girls are evaluating their performance in these subjects a level of ability lower than that of their male peers may be regarded as normal and consistent. Fortunately, these cultural stereotypes appear to be declining. This explanation emphasises the importance of knowing not only the dimensions on which a person is similar or dissimilar, but the dimensions on which a person is schematic or aschematic. Only then can the individual's choice of comparison figures be predicted and understood. This interpretation of the related attributes hypothesis explains the inconsistent findings of much previous research which has attempted to determine universal characteristics that make other people appropriate comparison figures. The characteristics of the perceiver and the perceived must both be taken into account; it is important to recognise children as active contributors to their own socialisation (Ruble, 1983).

Although the related attributes hypothesis explains the nature of social comparison with similar others, there is also evidence that people sometimes prefer to compare with dissimilar others. Presumably social reality can be constructed by finding out what you are not, as well as what you are. The search for an element of dissimilarity is a natural part of the process of relationship development. Once the security of an initial level of similarity has been established it is functional to compare oneself with others that are not totally identical. This process would both confirm the individual's identity and facilitate further differentiation of the interpersonal cognitive system. There will be more on this in due course.

So far this discussion has presented social comparison almost as an inevitable component of social interaction. In fact it is sometimes threatening or involves personal costs to the individual. For example, social comparisons showing the child in a poor light can threaten his or her self-esteem. Under these circumstances social comparison is likely to be avoided. A classic study by Sarnoff & Zimbardo (1961) showed avoidance of social comparison by subjects (adults) anticipating a potentially embarrassing event. The utility and potential destructiveness of social comparisons are essentially two sides of the same coin.

Developmental changes

A number of developmental changes have been noted on the role of similarity information in social comparison processes. Suls (1986) proposes a five-stage process in the development of social comparison and preference for similar comparison figures. As the last two stages relate to adults, just the first three stages will be outlined at this point. In accord with Veroff's (1969) general model of the development of social comparison processes, Suls sees little evidence of social comparison ability before the age of about five. The typical 3–5-year-old child is seen as lacking a social orientation. This early era is seen as emphasising temporal comparisons of outcomes, of past and present performance. In early grade school social comparison emerges. Suls argues that in this second stage of the development of social comparison the choice of comparison figure is relatively indiscriminate, using similar and dissimilar others. Although indiscriminate patterns of comparison may produce disadvantageous results, because these occur before the results of such comparisons are able to be related to the individual's concept of ability they are not likely to produce lasting effects on the child's self-concept.

Research by other authors suggests that Suls (1986) is overly conservative in his estimate of the age when children can and do use social comparisons with similar other. By six years old children already prefer similar others as comparison figures for their abilities (Morris & Nemcek, 1982). A study of first- and fourth-grade children has shown this similarity preference continues into middle childhood, but it does not indicate a developmental increase in levels of similarity preference (France-Kaatrude & Smith, 1985). These findings are consistent with Festinger's (1954) original theoretical analysis of the phenomenon but appear to conflict with Suls' (1986) developmental analysis. Suls argues that cognitive limitations and limits on the child's ability to make social attributions prevent a consistent preference for similar others as comparison figures until middle childhood, the age of at least eight or nine years. This disagreement is more apparent than real, essentially a disagreement over what constitutes similarity. Similarity in young children may occur but be due to temporal comparisons and the implicit rewards of similar others rather than true social comparison. Social comparison in its more restrictive guise can then be used to account for similarity effects in later childhood, perhaps from about nine or ten years of age.

Social relationships and social comparison

An interesting study by Gottman & Parkhurst (1980) has included a direct examination of social comparison in the conversations of children aged 3–6 years old. In this study three types of social comparison were coded, those aimed at establishing solidarity or similarity (e.g. "I'm doing mine green", "Me too"), contrasts or differences (e.g. "I'm doing mine green", "I'm doing mine yellow"), and exploring the other's feelings ("Do you like coffee?"). The authors found that young children of less than five years engaged in all three social comparison activities with their friends. Older children (more than five years of age) did not engage in as much social comparison activity, and when such processes were evident they focused on contrast or difference comparisons. With strangers all the children tended to use contrast comparisons, though older children did show some evidence of exploratory comparisons also. The authors hypothesised that the poorer performance of the young children with strangers could be either a reflection of their greater shyness or a genuinely lower level of skill with strangers.

Based on the results of their study, Gottman & Parkhurst drew parallels with the literature on models of sequential development within relationships. These models are examined in the next section of this chapter. They note that the emphasis on similarity and common ground found in the social comparisons of young children is also characteristic of the early stages of adult friendships. Older children, on the other hand, appeared to be less concerned with social comparisons, supporting research on differences in similarity between younger and older children (discussed later in this chapter). The older children appeared more concerned with the other person as an individual, a different and distinct person. Where comparisons did occur in the older children these were largely concerned with contrasts or differences. This was seen as paralleling the second stage of a sequential model of relationship development in which dissimilarity is important. Once the security of major similarity has been established, personal and relationship growth may be fostered by an element or dissimilarity. A friend possessing characteristics lacked by the individual can serve as a model for their acquisition (White, 1972).

Similarity as a basis for friendship

Similarity, of various sorts, has proved to be an extremely popular variable with researchers into children's relationships. Early studies on popularity and friendship were largely correlational in nature. They often consisted of identifying sets of friends and then comparing them with other nominal or random pairs of subjects. If these studies had a developmental component, comparisons were usually made on a cross-sectional sample rather than by following one set of individuals over an extended time period.

An alternative and very productive methodology used to examine the attraction stage of relationships adopted an impression formation approach. This was the overwhelmingly dominant approach to research on attraction in the 1960s and 1970s. It was largely laboratory-based and aimed to test specific theoretical propositions. The typical approach of these studies was to present subjects with various pieces of information about a real or imagined stimulus figure (e.g. information on similarity of attitudes) and require them to give their evaluation of the person. Although allowing more control than the correlational approach, this experimental paradigm has been criticised as artificial, and as distorting and over-simplifying the normal attraction process. Despite these limitations this era did see the laying down of foundations for a systematic understanding of children's friendships. Subsequent research has attempted to provide more naturalistic and genuinely longitudinal data.

In the preceding chapters great emphasis has been given to developmental processes, and in particular how basic aspects of relationships are influenced by these considerations. Such developmental processes are no less significant when considering the role of similarity in children's friendships. We have reviewed evidence that children's expectations of their friendships show relatively consistent developmental trends. Young children appear to emphasise an apparently egocentric, simple reward-based approach to their relationships, older children emphasise norms of sharing, and adolescents emphasise individual identity and commitment. If these considerations are borne in mind it is evident that some types of similarity are likely to be significant across the life course, while other types of similarity are likely to show developmental changes in pattern and form. So, for example, age is an almost universal type of similarity characterising friendships, while certain types of personality similarity appear to change developmentally. Similarity for a young child is rewarding because it involves a shared activity whereas it is rewarding for an older child or adolescent because it implies other deeper, more abstract characteristics of the person.

Sequential models of friendship formation

In addition to developmental changes in the bases of friendship, it is important to be aware of sequential changes within a relationship as it grows. These changes influence and are influenced by a number of factors which change developmentally, such as the stability of relationships and levels of social cognitive development.

A sequential model of friendship formation in adults has been proposed and extensively tested by Duck (1973a). The potential developmental applicability and limits of the model were subsequently discussed by Duck, Miell & Gaebler (1980), though it has, unfortunately, been the subject of relatively little developmental research. None the less, Duck's predictive filter model of friendship provides useful insights into relationship development and dynamics across the lifespan. The model, based on Kelly's (1955) Personal Construct Theory, emphasises the role of the interpersonal cognitive system in attraction and friendship, rather than simply the characteristics of the other person. To be used as a basis for friendship, information about another person must be within the "range of convenience" of the individual's construct system, i.e. it must be seen as relevant and applicable. This forms a basis for describing relationship development: as information is assimilated and integrated into the cognitive system it alters the system such that the relevance and ability to use other types of information is altered (i.e. the range of convenience is changed). Thus relationship development is be seen in terms of a hierarchical and constructive use of interpersonal information. To the extent that the child's model of the other person provides consensual validation (the other being seen as a valid comparison figure and as confirming the individual's own cognitions) the other is liked and the relationship continues. Now here is the important point – at each stage of a relationship the information that is salient and that can or will be used in making comparisons with others differs and is determined by the information already acquired. Note that in this context stage does not refer to a discrete phase in a relationship; it is intended to indicate that certain types of information are sought, preferred, and given greater weight than other types of information at specific sequential points in a relationship. This pattern must also slot into general patterns of social cognitive development (see Chapter 2): as children become cognitively more sophisticated they are able to progress their relationships to increasingly sophisticated, deep levels; for younger children the sequence of stages in a relationship is truncated.

This model explains discrepant results from many previous studies which have failed to take into account the stage of development of relationships. Simple, concrete information characterises younger children's relationships and the earlier stages of relationship development in older children. But unlike their young counterparts, the relationships of older children and adults do not stop at this superficial level of relating, they become increasingly sophisticated; increasingly abstract qualities assume a greater importance in the later stages of their relationships.

Also worthy of note is Duck's (1973a, b) observation that there are stages where less similarity (dissimilarity) is sought. With an effectance notion it is conceivable that the developmental ideal is to maximally exercise and elaborate the cognitive system and hence within limits conflict will increase the differentiation and scope of the system and thus be functional. These ideas can be derived from Kelly's (1955) choice corollary.

Overall, a developmental model of friendship that stresses a dynamic, hierarchical equilibrium in cognitive structures, rather than a static cognitive base, seems to be a more adequate conceptualisation of children's friendships.

Social and cultural determinants of similarity effects

The importance of similarity depends at least in part on cultural and environmental circumstances (Rubin, 1980). Our society is structured hierarchically and actively pushes children and adults towards forming relationships with similar others. Living in the same neighbourhood, attending the same school, being in the same class, and even seating position in the classroom serve as important limits on who a child meets. These factors also serve to emphasise and draw attention to some of the characteristics of others and hence determine who the child is likely to become friends with. Even the grouping practices within a classroom create similar, shared experiences which affect friendship patterns. These factors appear to account for at least some of the observed similarities between friends in terms of age, socioeconomic, and demographic backgrounds.

The influence of social groups on similarity effects extends considerably beyond the simple setting of limits. Group dynamics create pressures to be similar, to conform to group norms. Part of the often observed increase in conformity in elementary school children is due to the need to compare favourably with similar others and gain their approval. The ability to make such comparisons is considerably less well developed in younger children and hence the observed levels of conformity are, at least in part, reflecting this (Aboud, 1981). Informal groups often exclude individuals that are deviant from their prevailing standards and norms, whether this be in terms of social values, appearance, race, intelligence, or whatever. Even deviance less than that warranting exclusion engenders pressures to change, to conformity and solidarity with the group ethos (Schachter, 1951). Dissimilarity is likely to lead to less acceptance by the group and, from the individual's point of view, makes the group less appropriate as a basis for one of the main functions that it is supposed to serve: social comparison.

Because of many pre-existing and group generated similarities the search for yet further similarity really does highlight the importance of the phenomenon – but it also explains why on some characteristics it is also sometimes elusive. Even within Western culture researchers have tended to ignore sub-cultural and individual differences in the significance of similarity for relationships. In a somewhat different context, though no less applicable, Kerckhoff (1974) goes so far as to argue that the similarity–attraction effect is largely a middle-class phenomenon. Much research on adults has really been research on students, a very select population, and so we must be wary in generalising to other adults, let alone to children.

Functions of similarity

Hallinan (1981a, b) delineates three reasons for the importance of similarity in relationships. First, similarity provides a basis for evaluating and validating one's social identity (Schachter, 1959). This is a commonly emphasised function of similarity which links in directly with Festinger's (1954) theory of social comparison processes, which stresses the universal need for individuals to compare and evaluate their opinions and abilities. This in turn has been associated with a proposed drive for the individuals to feel effective in their social worlds (e.g. Byrne, 1971), based on the effectance motive proposed by White (1959). Both these theories have already been discussed in this chapter.

Second, similarity increases each person's approval of the other. As Aronson (1988) notes, we both infer other characteristics in the other on the basis of the information that we already possess, and we derive expectations about whether the other person might like us. This implied evaluation and reciprocity of liking phenomenon is a potent determination of interpersonal attraction (Insko et al., 1973).

Third, and finally, similarity reduces the areas of conflict between people. The trust and shared meanings implied by similarity increases the effectiveness of communication and thus minimises the likelihood of misunderstandings; it also biases the perception of other individuals and other groups such that dissimilar others are held more responsible for negative interactions and outcomes and less responsible for positive effects (Sherif et al., 1961; Deutsch, 1973). In this context it is worthy of note that forming children into groups which then share a common experience is in itself creating new dimensions of similarity.

Similarity of what?

Similarity has been found to be one of the most consistent predictors of interpersonal attraction. Even in toddlers similarity plays a crucial role. As Zick Rubin (1980) points out in his extremely readable and perceptive book, "The most central basis for toddlers' friendships, however, is probably the existence of similarities between their level of development, their temperament and their styles of behaviour" (p. 33). Familiarity and interaction also lay a foundation for young children to grow to be more similar in their patterns of responding (Lewis et al., 1975). Playgroup experience will tend to produce similar social repertoires and consequently help promote and maintain further social contacts among infants (Foot, Chapman & Smith, 1977), thus strengthening the similarity effect further.

Social–demographic similarities

Similarity has been examined along many dimensions; probably almost any characteristic you can think of has been examined at one time or another. Hartup (1970) notes a variety of physical factors, ranging from physical attractiveness, body build, strength and athletic build, and maturation. Friends tend to be of similar age and levels of general popularity (Clark & Drewry, 1985), perhaps not surprising considering Ladd's (1983) finding that children tend to form sub-groups depending on levels of popularity; dominance rankings (Savin-Williams, 1980); socio-demographic and behavioural characteristics (Kandel, 1978b); social skills (Burleson & Lucchetti, 1990); perceived self-competence (Kurdek & Krile, 1982); ability in relevant activities (Tesser, Campbell & Smith, 1984); scholastic standing (Mohan, Sehgal & Bhandari, 1982) and aspirations to attend college (Duncan, Featherman, & Duncan, 1972). Two especially well-researched areas in the similarity–attraction hunt, especially in adults but with some overspill into the developmental literature, have been attitudes and personality and these will be considered in detail in later sections of this chapter.

In a study of nearly 2000 adolescents between the ages of 13 and 18, Kandel (1978b) noted that similarities between friends appeared to be highest on social-demographic characteristics (such as school grade, sex, race, and age), show good levels of concordance for some behaviours, especially the use of illicit drugs, and were actually lowest on psychological dimensions such as attitudinal similarity. Interestingly, attitudes to drugs did show good levels of similarity between friends, confirming what has been known for a very long time: important attitudes are a better basis for similarity effects in relationships than are attitudes perceived as irrelevant or of little significance (Byrne, 1971).

Similarity of race and sex appear to be particularly important limiting factors in children's friendship choices, with the latter characteristic apparently the more influential (Hallinan & Williams, 1989). Studies typically report more same-sex and same-race preferences and relationships throughout childhood (e.g. Kandel, 1978b; Maccoby, 1990). Same-sex relationships are more stable and consequently are more likely to show increasing friendliness over time, i.e. to change from non-friend to friend, and from friend to best friend (Tuma & Hallinan, 1979). Even preschoolers show a great deal of sex segregation in the activities, and by grade three the preference for same sex associates (especially for boys) is well established, and almost total. These same-sex preferences then appear relatively consistent until junior high school from when they show a gradual decline (with girls then coming to show greater same-sex preferences from about the seventh grade onwards). In contrast, racial segregation was at a minimum in elementary school and increased rapidly through to grade seven (Shrum, Cheek & Hunter, 1988). These descriptions do not, of course, capture the potentially vast differences which exist in different groups of children from different backgrounds and in different social contexts.

Beyond the superficial level of appearance similarity can still be seen to be important in children. Reciprocity of self-disclosure and behaviour generally is an important determinant of interpersonal attraction (Skypeck, 1967; Newcomb, Brady & Hartup, 1979).

Similarity of attitudes

A vast amount of research effort has been devoted to examining the role of attitudinal similarity in adult interpersonal attraction. Considerably less attention has been devoted to generalising findings to younger populations.

A study by Byrne & Griffitt (1966) suggested that attitudinal similarity is an important determinant of attraction from middle childhood onwards. In this study children in grades four through twelve completed an attitude scale, examined a scale supposedly filled out by another school pupil, and indicated their attraction toward the stranger. There was a significant association between the proportion of similar attitudes and level of attraction by a child for the bogus stranger. This finding appeared to show continuity of an attitudinal similarity–attraction effect that Byrne and his associates had extensively documented in adult samples (see Byrne, 1971).

Byrne's research on children must be evaluated on the same basis as his general work on adults, within his much criticised bogus stranger paradigm. Many authors have reviewed the strengths and weaknesses of this paradigm (e.g. Duck, 1977). For our purposes it is sufficient to note that this extremely sensitive research method typically tests attraction as a response to very limited amounts of information (e.g. often attitudes only) presented in a rather unusual manner, and possibly short-circuiting the processes of relating (a great deal of other information about a person is usually collected before we get to the stage of sharing attitudes, especially personally significant attitudes). These problems do not mean that the results of studies using the bogus stranger paradigm should be dismissed; far from it. There are answers to some of these criticisms, and many of the others represent limitations on the extent to which the results can be generalised rather than methodological flaws. In the end, what these criticisms are telling us is that we must be careful in how we interpret and use the results of these studies. This, of course, should be a guiding principle for the use of any psychological research.

One additional word of caution is in order, though. We must be especially cautious on data gathered from children by this method; biases may be exacerbated by developmental factors.

Similarity of personality

In the young child the styles of interaction with friends appear paramount, but by 12 years old friends are recognised as unique individuals. The person and not just his or her actions are important for the early adolescent. Similarity of personality is sought but differences are tolerated (Smollar & Youniss, 1982). Indeed, differences can be an important factor in building a relationship if it is to succeed in the longer term. Once a basic background of similarity provides the security for more detailed comparisons, some degree of difference can be stimulating, and the literature on social comparison also suggests that it is at the same time functional.

Despite several decades of research, similarity as measured by various standardised personality tests has been inconsistent, and consequently inconclusive, as a predictor of attraction and friendship. Similarity of personality has regularly been found to be associated with liking and friendship (e.g. Mohan, Sehgal & Bhandari, 1982; Clark & Drewry, 1985). Unfortunately, similarity of personality has also been found not to be associated with interpersonal attraction (e.g. Hoffman & Maier, 1966), or to be associated with interpersonal attraction only under limited conditions or with specific subject groups (e.g. Rosenfeld & Jackson, 1965). Many different types of standardised personality test have been used in the similarity–attraction equation but the sought-after similarity effect has remained elusive. Part of the reason for this apparent inconsistency is because as relationships develop the important aspects of similarity change (Duck, 1973b). The apparently contradictory results of some studies are probably due to relationships being examined at different stages in their development.

A new approach to the search for personality similarity in friendship was pioneered by Steve Duck in the 1970s (e.g. Duck, 1973a) and this seemed to provide a way of obtaining the sought-after consistency. The novel aspect of Duck's approach was the conceptualisation of personality not in terms of some standardised instrument but in terms of the individual's own perceptions of his or her social world. This approach was based on George Kelly's (1955) theory of personality, his Personal Construct Theory. Kelly's theory adopts a highly structured approach to measurement, the repertory grid, which has proved to be an extremely useful research tool (Fransella & Bannister, 1977). It can be used to elicit the individual's perceptions of similarities and differences in his or her social world, his or her system of personal constructs. Personal constructs constituted the basic units of comparison for assessing similarity in Duck's research.

In a developmental study of adolescents, ranging from about 12 to 15 years of age, Duck (1975) showed higher levels of construct similarity in friends rather than nominal pairs of group members. The types of similarity that were important showed both sex differences and developmental differences. Young adolescents showed similarity in terms of constructs emphasising factual descriptions, and in the case of girls physical descriptions also. Older adolescent boys and girls showed a divergence in the types of similarity that were important: from mid-adolescence girls begin show an emphasis on similarity in psychological constructs and in late adolescence this is joined by an emphasis on physical constructs. The adolescent boys showed a move to emphasising similarity of interaction constructs in mid-adolescence and, in the oldest group, physical constructs. These changes appear to reflect the increasing use of abstract interpersonal descriptions (Barenboim, 1981), sex differences in patterns of relating (Douvan & Adelson, 1966), and the process of coming to terms with physical maturation (Erikson, 1968).

Many studies have developed Duck's original research on construct similarity to take account of, for example, different types or levels of relating and different types of similarity. In a study of young adults, Lea (1979) showed that similarity of personal constructs is greater between mutual friends than unreciprocated friendship nominations which in turn was greater than levels of similarity between nominal pairings of subjects. Not only were levels of similarity greater, but the similarity effect was most marked in terms of the use of deeper, psychological constructs.

Although Duck's research provided new and useful insights into the personality similarity debate, its developmental relevance largely relies on the parallels that Duck, Miell & Gaebler (1980) and Duck (1989) have noted in the factors which are important in the acquaintance process in children and adults. A similar approach, but deriving from developmental theory and research, has been proposed by Brian Bigelow, based on his research into children's friendship expectations.

Similarity of friendship values does appear to be an important and predictive factor for children's friendships (Bigelow & La Gaipa, 1980), though current evidence suggests that children ideally prefer others at a conceptual level one above their own (Bigelow, 1980). This preferred discrepancy in social–cognitive abilities is in accord with Festinger's (1954) theory of social comparison processes which states that there is a unidirectional drive upward in terms of abilities but not opinions. A friend just one level more advanced than the child is similar in the way he or she construes the world and yet sufficiently more advanced to facilitate this drive upwards. Of course, not all children can be paired with a slightly more cognitively advanced peer and the ultimate compromise is a matching in terms of level of friendship expectations. It is also unclear if this preference for more advanced peers is characteristic of all children's friendships or only at certain stages. The frequently noted relative instability of younger children's friendships (Bigelow & La Gaipa, 1980) might be interpreted as indicating that progress beyond an attitudinal level of similarity, or similarity of simple behavioural concepts, is unlikely.

Perceived similarity

Not only do similarity effects operate in actuality, they also operate in the eye of the beholder. In an early study of children at a summer camp, Davitz (1955) found that perceived similarity in preferences for camp activities predicted sociometric status; actual similarity did not. The children thought their friends were more similar to them in their activity preferences than were non-friends, but this was largely illusory.

Perceived similarity can be an important determinant and *consequence* of attraction. In a study of eight and eleven year olds, Boulton & Smith (1990) found that children ranked their classmates in terms perceived liking and strength. Children tend to overestimate their own and liked peers' standing in the hierarchy and to underestimate the standing of disliked peers. The end consequence of this is a perceived similarity in the physical attribute of strength. In similar vein, Cavior & Dokecki (1973) found a positive correlation between physical attractiveness and perceived attitude similarity for fifth and eleventh graders, both factors also being correlated with interpersonal attraction. In a study of black five, seven, and nine year olds, Reaves & Friedman (1982) found that physical attractiveness and perceived similarity were again both related to affiliation preferences.

Similarity as cause or consequence

A great deal of research has identified similarity as an a priori basis for relationships. There is an active selection and preference for getting to know and forming relationships with similar others. Similarity on various dimensions can apparently predict liking rather than simply being the product of liking (Byrne, 1971; Duck & Spencer, 1972), and dissimilarity on other, deeper dimensions can even predict dissolution of relationships (Duck & Allison, 1978). None the less, in a study of early adolescents Berndt (1982) showed that in addition to selecting friends on the basis of similar orientations to school and peer culture (such as music and fashion), there is also an element of social influence. This finding was supported in Kandel's (1978a) large-scale, longitudinal study of adolescents (of unspecified age). In this study, which tested 957 best-schoolfriend dyads at the beginning and end of a school year, it was found that friendships which survived the year were more similar than those which collapsed and, more interesting, those relationships that survived appeared to show increased levels of similarity at the end of the session than at the beginning. Similarly, friendships which formed in the course of the year appeared to show the participants adopting some of the existing characteristics of the friend. These results are predictable (but none the less provide welcome corroboration) on the basis of a fundamental corollary of Festinger's (1954) theory of social comparison – if membership of a group is important to the individual then the pressures to uniformity in opinions and abilities is correspondingly greater. These pressures are generally applicable, though the peer group assumes critical importance for the adolescent and hence the pressures to concordance are correspondingly greater.

Sex differences

The idea that the peer relationships of boys and girls differ in form and function has a long history and is reviewed in detail in Chapter 7. At this point it is, however, appropriate to consider whether any potential sex differences in the nature of relationships are reflected in the types of similarity information that are sought. The issue of sex differences in the cognitive bases of boys' and girls' friendships was directly examined in a study by Erwin (1985). In this study two groups of children, aged approximately between seven and ten years old, completed a sociometric questionnaire, an attitude questionnaire, and a construct rating questionnaire (a series of statements describing friends). Similarity effects were found mainly in the younger children. Boys were more similar to each other in attitudes than were girls, and girls were more similar to each other in construct ratings; levels of similarity were greater for friends than between pairs of non-friends. We have previously discussed evidence which suggests that constructs often characterise the deeper levels of relationships, though the constructs of these children were quite simple and concrete. The children's sociometric choices had also been ascertained six months earlier and showed no sex differences in the stability of relationships. In short, it appeared that for these young children the more personal information contained in the construct rating questionnaire was more relevant for girls while attitudinal information was more relevant for boys. These similarity effects were most marked in the younger children and led to the conclusion that other factors assume greater influence in middle childhood, such as normative comparisons. This explanation is given an element of support by Clark & Drewry's (1985) study in which sixth graders were found to be characterised by higher levels of social self-concept but lower levels of personal self-concept than their younger, third-grade counterparts. A study of first and fourth graders by Ladd & Emerson (1984) also suggested a decline in partner similarity with age and an increase in awareness of differences; they also found that mutual friends had higher levels of similarity than unilateral friendship nominations.

Research on pre-adolescent and older populations shows a reasonable level of consistency in indicating that similarity is an important basis for children's peer relationships, although this again shows sex differences and patterns of change as relationships develop. Bukowski & Kramer (1986) gave fourth and seventh graders descriptions of hypothetical pairs of boys and girls to rate for probability of their being friends. Characters described as similar (or not), helpful (or not) and intimate (or not) with each other. The target dyads were differentiated on the basis of these three factors. There were stronger effects for intimacy among older students and for girl characters; there were stronger similarity effects for the boy dyads among older students.

For adolescents the best friend is seen a constant companion and a relatively irreplaceable confidant. This relationship again emphasises the role of similarity, but also mirrors the results of research on young children in showing a sex difference in the types of similarity that are important. Richey & Richey (1980) review research showing female adolescent relationship to be nurturant and based on the principle of friend as confidant, while those of males give more emphasis to companionship and similarity of attitudes.

7 Gender and sex differences

Any differences that exist in the sociability of the two sexes are more of a kind than of degree. Boys are highly oriented toward a peer group and congregate in larger groups; girls associate in pairs or small groups of agemates.

(Maccoby & Jacklin, 1974, p. 349)

Sex differences and sex segregation are regularly noted as characteristic of children's friendships and peer relationships. This chapter examines these sex differences. To what extent are sex differences in social functioning inevitable? And, what are the origins of these observed sex differences?

Sex differences in psychological functioning have, in general, proved a controversial area of research. It has been argued by Grady (1979) that given the same social situations, reinforcement contingencies, and expectations both sexes will react similarly. But females and males do typically encounter different types of situation and different social standards for appropriate or effective behaviour. Arguing from a slightly different tack, Unger (1979, p. 168) notes that "Differences tend to be exaggerated and similarities ignored, with little theoretical attention to the integration of similarity and difference". Research on sex differences often ignores individual variation within the pattern of means (e.g. not all boys are aggressive) and influences due to situational factors, race, social class, religion and other sub-cultural factors. In reality, sex segregation is dynamic, far from complete, and less central to the organisation and meaning of some social situations rather than others.

Sex differences in social behaviour originate from two main sources. First, the child. Quite simply, boys and girls bring different patterns of behaviour to their social encounters. Second, in the ways others treat the child. Boys and girls are typically treated differently by other people and this also affects their behaviour. In discussing adult friendships, Wright (1982, 1988) makes some points that are equally relevant to sex differences in children's relationships. Wright argues that sex-differences in friendships are readily interpretable in terms of traditional sex roles and socialisation practices. When differences are found they are seldom large and provide no basis for predicting the character of any specific friendship.

In the light of the above comments, the first section of this chapter will briefly review the development of gender identity and gender specific behaviour, acting as a background to a detailed review of sex differences in children's social relationships. The topic of sex differences in the styles of children's social relationships is dominated by two main topics. First, the extent to which this produces a sex segregation in friendship and peer relations. Such a phenomenon is well established, but it is also equally clear that there are definite developmental changes. These sex differences in patterns of relating have been associated with corresponding differences in patterns of intimacy. This is the second major topic that has concerned researchers. Within the broad patterns in the topics listed above, there are also a number of qualifiers that need to be made. Although children's cross-sex relationships are less common than same-sex relationships, they do none the less exist. Similarly, there are also cross-cultural variations in the extent of sex segregation in children's peer relationships. These topics are examined in the final sections of the chapter and serve to end our consideration of the controversial topic of sex differences in relationships on a moderate, balanced note.

Development of gender identity

For the young child gender is an over-generalised concept that is gradually refined. The child increasingly recognises that many characteristics are associated with but not necessarily defining of gender. Gender concepts develop in an invariant sequence. Gender identity (emotional and intellectual awareness of being male or female) is apparent in children by about 15–18 months of age (Bee, 1989). By two years old the child can distinguish and identify males from females, though they have more difficulty applying gender labels to themselves (Thompson, 1975). Between two and three years old children can correctly label the sex of others, their own sex, and are starting to show an awareness of sex stereotypes (Cowan & Hoffman, 1986). Young children often manifest a same sex bias, classifying positive attributes as appropriate to their gender. Gender constancy continues to undergo further developments and the child comes to understand that gender is stable over time. Between four and eight years old the child understands that gender is constant despite superficial transformations (e.g. of appearance). From five years old there are also the beginnings of sex stereotypes about personality and this increases throughout childhood.

Only rudimentary gender understanding is needed before children begin to acquire sex stereotypes and to show sex-typed behaviour and preferences for peers and toys (Martin & Little, 1990). Sex segregation has been recorded in children only 33 months of age (Jacklin & Maccoby, 1978). Later developments in gender concepts are paralleled by an increasing preference for same-sex peers (Huston, 1983), and an increase in the proportion of appropriate sex-typed activities during same-sex interactive play (Smetana & Letourneau, 1984).

Gender specific behaviour

The term "sex role" refers to those personality characteristics, attitudes, and behaviours society ascribes to a particular sex. These show considerable variation cross-culturally. Norms of sex appropriateness are often important to sex differences in behaviour (Shaklee, 1983). In general, as children grow from infancy to early and middle childhood the number and degree of sex differences in behaviour increases – especially those related to sex-role appropriate activities (Weinraub & Brown, 1983). With decreasing levels of sex-role differentiation in our society it will be interesting to note the extent to which this gap narrows.

Family influences

A number of studies have noted differences in the socialisation of males and females from an early age. There are clear though small differences in treatment of babies in the early months of life (Moss, 1967). Mothers look, smile and vocalise more to girls, and touch and hold boys more frequently in the first six months of life. After six months girls are touched more and encouraged to stay closer to the mother than are boys. Girls are encouraged to show more dependency, affectionate behaviour, and expression of tender emotions while boys are encouraged in more active play often involving gross motor activities.

Even before entry to nursery school, parents seek same-sex playmates for toddlers and encourage sex-appropriate activities. Parents begin this process at home by supplying different toys for boys and girls. Dolls are almost exclusively provided for girls (Rheingold & Cook, 1975). Throughout childhood, there is an increasing emphasis from parents, schools, and the various media on the sex appropriateness of children's behaviour and interests (DiLeo, Moely & Sulzer, 1979). In older children household chores are often allocated according to sex, and more physical punishment is used with boys (Newson & Newson, 1976); girls spend more of their leisure time with families, boys with friends (Coates, 1987). Boys are given more opportunity to play away from home and independent of adult supervision – possibly an important factor in learning independence.

Group dynamics

A major contributor to the sex segregation of children's friendships are the pressures to belong to peer groups. In developmental terms, groups based on relatively superficial characteristics, whether they be appearance, temperament, or skills, seem almost inevitable, though not necessarily enduring (Aboud, 1988). These categorisations provide meaning to the world and identity to the individual. To prevent them we would need to prevent children from categorising others on the basis of these superficial attributes. And yet for the child between the ages of, say, six and twelve years, social cognitive limitations preclude more sophisticated forms of categorisations (see Chapter 2). What this means in terms of gender is that young children are likely to use these labels as a basis for social grouping regardless of the existence of adult pressures to do so.

The child's recognition that she or he belongs to the group of males or females is an important step in the development of identity, though belonging to a group will have important costs and benefits in terms of the child's subsequent social development and behaviour. Group membership is associated with attraction to in-group members, preferential treatment of them, and beliefs that the out-group is more homogeneous and less valued than the in-group (Tajfel, 1982).

Group members tend to interpret the social world so that the beliefs of their group are confirmed, and their own group is made distinct from other groups. In terms of gender, differences between the sexes are exaggerated and attributes irrelevant to the initial distinction are assimilated to the stereotype; male and female are viewed as opposites (Deux, 1985). The members of the out-group, the other sex, are treated on the basis of the membership of their gender group. Denigrating out-group members enhances the group's identity and consequently improves the child's status within his or her own group, especially if the two groups are in conflict/competition (Hogg & Abrams, 1988). This makes movement between the groups difficult (Brown, 1988).

Group membership is rewarding because of the opportunities that it provides for social comparison (see Chapter 6). Similarity between group members is seen as providing a consensual validation of the child's thoughts, feelings, and behaviour. But groups do not only validate the individual's identity, they actually tend to make their members more similar to each other and different from the out-group. There is pressure to conform to group expectations and standards because of concerns over group acceptance (Sherif & Sherif, 1953). Members deviating from group norm are reprimanded or severely sanctioned by their being excluded from group activities or relationships with group members. Experimental studies have clearly demonstrated how the attention of peers can change the frequency of several of the child's social behaviours (Wahler, 1967). Observations of children's everyday interactions also show the power of social influence, though in these circumstances the effects are often more subtle, unintentional and even contradictory. In a study by Fagot (1981), the male peer group was an effective shaper of sex-typical behaviour in boys even when they initially entered the playgroup with other styles of play. It seems that parental ideas about sex roles are no guarantee about the child's attitudes and values. Pressures to conform to group norms and beliefs increases with age, possibly peaking at about 12 years of age (Hartup, 1970).

Patterns of behaviour

The sex-role stereotype is most accurate in relation to aggressive, assertive behaviour. In accord with the stereotype, ten-year-old boys expect less guilt and less parental disapproval for aggression, especially for provoked aggression towards another boy (Perry, Perry & Weiss, 1989). There is a greater compatibility of behavioural styles between same-sex peers. In a naturalistic observation of nursery school children, Smith & Connolly (1972) report that talking to another child was more common in girls' play; boys showed overall higher levels of physical activity and more frequent noisy, rough and tumble play. Girls actively avoid contact with boys because of their roughness (Haskett, 1971).

Some authors have concluded that there is a biological basis for these sex differences in aggression (Maccoby & Jacklin, 1974, 1980), which suggests that sex segregation is an inevitable and immutable aspect of children's early friendships. Other authors have disputed this (e.g. Tieger, 1980). On balance it would seem difficult to deny the impact and interrelatedness of both social and biological influences on aggression (Parke & Slaby, 1983). Hinde (1987, p. 60) concludes that "In humans it seems that the prenatal and hormonal influences on gender role differences are of lesser importance compared with the experiential effects of the treatment received from others and the self-image acquired as a result of that treatment". In the next paragraphs we will look at the role of aggression in children's relationships, and how this also affects the treatment the child receives from others.

In a study of preschoolers, McGuire (1973) found that boys, overall, were considerably more aggressive than girls. The study then focused on children above average in aggressiveness for their sex. Highly aggressive males tended to be unpopular while highly aggressive females tended to be popular. Higher levels of assertiveness was beneficial for the girl among her less active peers, while for boys an increase in assertiveness beyond the already relatively high levels of his peer group was aversive. Although there must be high and low limits for acceptability of aggression in both sexes, sex norms make exceeding the lower limit relatively uncommon in males and exceeding the upper limit relatively uncommon in females.

These findings are supported and extended by Ladd's (1983) study of third- and fourth-grade school children. This study found that unpopular girls, in comparison to popular girls, were less likely to be involved in social conversations and spent more time in parallel play. Unpopular boys were less likely than more popular boys to be involved in co-operative play activities and spent more time in rough and tumble play. This emphasises the role of sharing, co-operation and communication in positive relationships, and the role of aggression in rejection, especially for boys.

Sex differences in social interaction

A common emphasis in the literature on children's friendship is that girls have more intimate and exclusive friendships than boys (Berndt, 1982). In fact, this is only half of the story. The other half is that boys tend to play in larger groups. Developmentally, the overall pattern of sex differences is fairly complex. In terms of sociability and interest in others, boys seem more peer-oriented than girls in the preschool. In elementary school boys have more friends and play in larger groups and girls have fewer but stronger friends. In adolescence, there is no marked difference in the number of friends had by boys and girls, though female friendships are more intimate.

A fairly consistent research finding is that boys show more rough and tumble play in early childhood and more aggression and competitiveness at virtually all ages. Fagot & Hagan (1985) observed playgroups of 18–36-months-old toddlers. Young toddlers showed more aggression than their older counterparts, though these were briefer incidents. Assertive behaviours were more common in boys than in girls. The most common assertive act was to a grab for a toy, followed by hitting and then verbal assault. Girls' assertive acts were more commonly ignored – especially by boys. The authors note that responses to aggressive acts affect their continuation and consequently are likely to strengthen emergent sex differences.

Some authors stress the social influences which foster these patterns of aggression (Brooks-Gunn & Matthews, 1979). For example, Snow, Jacklin & Maccoby (1983) found that with children as young as one year old fathers were more punishing and prohibiting of behaviour in sons than daughters. There is pressure from parents (especially the father) for 4–5-year-old boys to adopt more "boyish" behaviour and attitudes (e.g. to play physical games and to be assertive). Parents' responses to their children's aggression is important in shaping the behaviour.

In many areas children's social behaviour does not match the sex-role stereotypes. Girls are not more dependent, nurturant, or socially oriented.

Most studies show no significant differences, though if a difference is found, girls are usually higher. Anecdotal evidence abounds of nurturant young girls. A touching account is given in a study by McGrew (1972b). Older preschoolers, especially females showed more nurturance to their younger classmates. Observations of children's entry to nursery school showed that four-year-old girls were more likely to attend to new three year olds than were boys. Several showed maternal attentiveness and verbal and non-verbal comforting, often in response to the newcomers' specifically expressed fears. For example, in response to a young boy's question "When's my mummy coming back" a young girl answered "All the mummies come back after milk. When the bell rings" (p. 139). Females also made use of physical comfort – holding the newcomer's hands, patting their backs, and gently hugging their shoulders. Boys could be friendly to newcomers but mostly showed indifference. Newcomers did not participate in predominantly male activities on the first day.

Overall, there are a great many similarities in the function and content of boys' and girls' social behaviour, though there are also some consistent and notable sex differences.

Play activities

A substantial amount of research has examined sex differences in children's patterns of play. As much of children's social interaction revolves around play activities, this is an important area for us to consider.

A sex cleavage in patterns of play and friendship is evident even in toddler groups and continues throughout childhood. A study by Howes (1988) examined the free play of toddlers in day-care centres. There was a preference for same-sex playmates, strongest in the oldest girls. Boys tended to refuse or ignore girls' initiations when these took the form of specific requests to play a game, though they were more amenable to a more general friendly approach. Friendships tended to be formed with members of the same sex. A second study used children ranging in age from early toddlers through to preschoolers. Some children had cross-sex friends, but the number of these decreased with age. Children with cross-sex friends did appear to be more socially skilful.

In young children there is a close relationship between choice of play patterns and toy usage. Pairs of 4–7-year-old boys and girls differ in the content of their interactions. The interaction of young boys typically centre on toys and manipulative tasks; they will often be located in the block and woodworking areas of nursery schools. In contrast, the play of girls often centres on dramatic play, art, and table activities and games; they will often be found in the book, doll, and housekeeping areas of the classroom (Shure, 1963; Quay, Weaver & Neel, 1986).

Eisenberg, Tryon & Cameron, (1984) observed four year olds during free play in preschool classes over a nine-week period. There was a relationship between preference for same-sex peer interaction and preference for playing with same-sex toys. The type of toys being played with determined who the child was likely to approach and who was likely to approach the child. Boys engaged in masculine or neutral play were likely to approach and be approached by other boys rather than girls. Girls involved in feminine play were also more likely to be approached by other girls rather than boys, though they did not show any sex preference in the contacts they themselves initiated. These results support the idea that play preferences structure interaction in such a way as to reinforce sex segregation in children's peer relationships.

The role of different types of play in structuring children's peer interaction was further explored in a study by Carpenter & Huston-Stein (1980). In this study preschoolers aged 2½–5 years old were observed in their classrooms. Girls spent more time than boys in preschool activities that were highly structured by teacher feedback or the availability of an adult model. Boys spent more time than girls in low structure activities. This showed a tendency for boys and girls to engage in different sorts of play activity, but more important was the finding that *when engaged in the same activities they showed similar patterns of behaviour*. In other words, play activities were a major determinant of the observed patterns of behaviour, regardless of sex. Both sexes showed less novel behaviour and more compliance in high structured activities, and more initiative, leadership, and aggression, when on low structured activities. For example, playing with blocks or rough and tumble play, preferred by boys, are usually more aggressive and involve interpersonal conflict in preschoolers. Art and playing house, typically preferred by girls, are characterised by low conflict and social interchange. As there are sex differences in play preferences, the play is reinforcing the sex differences in behaviour patterns. This is yet another example of children as active contributors to their own socialisation, though the pattern of activities did vary between classes, suggesting that adult influences can modify these tendencies.

Overall, the general pattern of results indicates that adult feedback produces differences in children's social behaviour, and that boys and girls select activities with different levels of adult involvement.

Patterns of sex segregation

Using evidence from a variety of sources, Dweck (1981) constructed a picture of the beginnings of sex segregation. Preschool girls show more prosocial behaviour and compliance in their social relationships, though this is done in a rigid, absolute manner. Interaction in boys is likely to be more boisterous and involve rough and tumble play (DiPietro, 1981). As boys do not conform to the obedience and order desired by girls, cross-sex associations are unpleasant for the girls and they are likely to reject the approaches of the boys. In a study by LaFreniere, Strayer & Gauthier (1984), 1–6 year olds in a Canadian day-care centre were observed over a three-year period. Rates of affiliative activity increased as a linear function of age. From about two years old girls began to address more social approaches to other girls. Boys were gender neutral a little longer but by three years old also contributed to the segregation, and by five years of age showed a stronger same-sex preference than girls. This initial segregation provides the opportunity for the sexes to evolve different patterns of play, patterns which make cross-sex interactions increasingly problematic over the course of childhood.

Girls play mainly with close friends in pairs or small, intimate groups and often in private places (Gilligan, 1982). This allows the direct practice and refinement of social rules and roles. They are learning to relate to others on an individual basis and to recognise and respond to subtle cues within the context of socially prescribed rules which are often implicit and difficult to articulate. Boys' play becomes more complex than that of girls. Boys form larger groups and are likely to play team games, are more physically active, wide ranging, and tend to have an explicit set of rules, explicitly defined goals, and are competitive. In their play boys are learning the organising skills necessary for co-ordinating activity within a larger system, to articulate long-term goals and to work actively and independently to achieve them. Boys pay less attention to giving and receiving subtle personal cues and information. This provides a climate with little tolerance for the more relaxed and informal style of relating shown by girls. Boys are now more likely to be the ones rejecting contact with the girls rather than the other way round. As this pattern illustrates, and is supported in a study by Maccoby & Jacklin (1987), sex segregation is more a matter of group dynamics than sex roles. "It appears, then, that the frequency with which a child plays with same-sex or cross-sex others may not be part of the within-sex masculinity and femininity personality clusters . . . It is as though *any* boy can, and does, interact with girls under some conditions, and no boy will do so under others" (Maccoby, 1988, p. 760).

Sex differences in children's patterns of play lay the foundation for differences in peer relationships. In a study of ten and eleven year olds, Lever (1976) noted six differences between the play of boys and girls, though these are closely related and do not represent six independent characteristics. For example, it seems fairly reasonable that children engaging in team sports are more likely to be found in large groups and are more likely to be found playing outdoors. The six characteristics noted by Lever were:

1. Boys played outdoors more than girls.
2. The social play of boys was based in larger groups than that of girls.
3. The social groups of boys were more diverse in ages than those of girls.
4. Girls were more likely to play predominantly male games than boys were to play in girls' games.
5. Boys played competitive games more often than girls and tended to control the large fixed spaces designated for such activities. Teams, or "gangs", and competitiveness are common even when not in engaged in sporting activities. The play of girls was more co-operative and involved more turn-taking. They more often played close to buildings, doing tricks on monkey bars (which became areas for sitting and talking in the sixth grade) and using cement areas for games such as skipping or hopscotch.
6. Boys' games lasted longer than girls' games (72% of all boys' activities lasted longer than one hour, compared with 43% for girls). Lever argues that part of the reason for this difference is the lower levels of skill that are required for many of the games that are played by girls. This results in girls' games being completed or becoming boring quicker than boys' games.

The significance of these sex differences in play is potentially great. Dweck (1981) argues that early differences in values and interests produce different experiences which produce different world-views and areas of competence. They make it increasingly difficult for boys and girls to bridge the gender divide. A boy and a girl with the same level of cognitive sophistication, socially skilled and adept at perspective taking within their own groups, may none the less not be able to take each other's perspective and relate to each other successfully.

Situational factors

This chapter has so far focused on sex differences in rather abstract terms. But these differences are likely to vary in magnitude in different situations. "Any individual varies greatly, from one situation to another with respect to how gender linked his or her behavior is" (Maccoby, 1988, p. 755). It is to this topic that we now turn.

It is very easy to assume that much sex segregation is the result of adult influences on children's social interaction. But in fact there is considerable variation in the extent to which sex segregation in children's relationships is encouraged or inhibited by adult pressure or social structures. Segregation is often greatest in situations not structured by adults. For example, in school refectories rather than classrooms (Lockheed & Klein, 1985).

Early learning of sex roles is typically reinforced in the nursery school. A study by Bianchi & Bakeman (1978) compared children in a traditional preschool and an open nursery school which consciously attempted to avoid sex-typing in its expectations regarding children's interests and personality. In both schools, children spent over 80% of their free-play time with other children, though children at the traditional school were more likely to play in same-sex groups while children in the open school were more often in mixed-sex groups. Apparently schools strengthen patterns of sex segregation, though the effects due to the school ethos are usually confounded with other social variables, such as parents choosing a particular school because of its philosophy.

The role of the teacher is also crucial. Appropriate encouragement and reinforcement of preschoolers' co-operative cross-sex play will dramatically increase its frequency. In a study by Serbin, Tonick & Sternglanz (1977), rate of cross-sex play increased from approximately 5% to almost 30% of the children's time, though not at the expense of same-sex play.

In many schools gender is used as a visible marker in the adult organisation of the school day (e.g. staff often use gender terms), and sometimes to sort or organise children or activities. This imposed social organisation may destroy the natural spontaneity and creativity of children's play and make it an institutionalised and impoverished arena for learning about relationships.

Sex roles and intimacy

Traditional ideas about sex differences in children's patterns of relating are based on a view of male and female sex roles as representing two poles of a single dimension. But this unidimensional view of sex roles has not gone unchallenged. An alternative formulation does not necessarily see male and female sex roles as exclusive, but rather as independent dimensions (e.g. Bem, 1974). From this perspective it is possible for an individual to have stereotypically male and female qualities (e.g. competence, assertiveness, leadership, independence, self-reliance *and* nurturance, warmth, sympathy, kindness, gentleness, cheerfulness). Such a person would be androgynous. The person low on both dimensions is termed undifferentiated. Because androgynous individuals are more likely to engage in cross-sex behaviour, they are more effective in some social situations. It has been argued that some androgynous behaviour is generally desirable and facilitative in social relationships (Ickes & Barnes, 1978).

A study by Jones & Dembo (1989), examined the levels of intimacy in the relationships of children between the ages of eight and fifteen years. As would be expected, best-friend intimacy was relatively low at eight years of age but increased in late childhood. The interesting slant of this study, however, was that traditional sex differences, with females higher than males in intimacy, were better explained as a sex-role difference in which females and androgynous males form a homogeneous high intimacy group, whereas sex-typed males scored significantly lower. This study is a warning against making over-general statements about simple sex differences in children's friendships.

Friendship: the early years

Observations of children from 1–12 years of age, at home and outdoors, show a significant trend for same sex companionship to increase with age (Ellis, Rogoff & Cromer, 1981). In the first two years, if toddlers interact at all it is in pairs. Groups are seldom formed. There is little evidence of any same-sex preference in children's peer preferences (Hay, Pedersen & Nash, 1982), though there is some evidence of parents tending to seek same-sex playmates for their toddlers (Lewis et al., 1975).

By three to four years of age there are notable changes in the size and sex composition of groups. Children still spend much of their time in pairs but are also starting to play and become concerned with belonging to larger groups. There is also an increasing preference for same-sex playmates and friends. In a classic study by Jacklin & Maccoby (1978), 90 previously unacquainted 33-month-old children, most without nursery school experience, were brought together in pairs in a laboratory playroom. The room contained two chairs for the mothers plus two chairs and a table for the children. Several toys were presented to the children in a series. Mothers were present throughout the session but spent most of the time filling in questionnaires and so interacted little with the children. This study found that a preference for same-sex friends even in these young children.

From about three years of age, same-sex choices are evident in parallel play, and same-sex co-operative interaction is approximately four times as frequent as similar opposite-sex interactions (Serbin, Tonick & Sternglanz, 1977). Reinforcement for interaction is more common from same-sex others (Charlesworth & Hartup, 1967). Children are also more responsive to reinforcements from their own sex and relatively indifferent to the reactions of opposite-sex children (Fagot, 1985). At this time boys are also starting to become more assertive and influential in group decisions than are girls (Lockheed, 1985).

By nursery school age there is already much sex segregation in children's playmate and friendship choices, and this increases with age (Hayden-Thomson, Rubin & Hymel, 1987). In a study by Gottman (1986a), 35% of the friendships of preschoolers were cross-sex, but by 7–8 years old almost none were. A characteristic of friendships of middle childhood is their almost total exclusivity in terms of gender. Possibly in recognition of this many activity groups also segregate at this age.

A longitudinal study by Feiring and Lewis (1989) has tracked the development of this growing sex segregation in children's friendships. Children were tested at three, six, and nine years old. The youngest children had the largest number of cross-sex friendships. With age they gained more same-sex friends but lost cross-sex friends. Interestingly, a few girls at six years old showed almost as many male as female friends; no boys showed this pattern. Teachers saw these girls as more independent and aggressive than other girls, though it is unclear whether this judgement is based on the girls' actual behaviour or simply labelling due to their association with boys. Perhaps we see here the young girls who will later come to be called tomboys?

Patterns of relating

In the study by Jacklin & Maccoby (1978), referred to in the previous section, children of less than three years of age showed more social acts toward same-sex peers than opposite-sex peers, but there were few differences in the overall levels of social behaviour of boys and girls. This applied to both neutral and positive behaviours, such as imitation, reducing interpersonal distance, and touching but not attempting to take the other's toy, and negative behaviours, such as withdrawing from the other's reach, attempting to take the other's toy, or resisting such an attempt with vocal prohibitions. Children, both boys and girls, were more likely to show social withdrawal, crying, and remaining close to the mother when partnered with a boy. This effect was especially marked for girls, who, when paired with boys were also more likely to passively watch their partner play or sometimes simply hold a toy but not play with it. In same-sex pairs the partner would usually back off in response to vocal prohibition. In mixed-sex pairs a prohibition from the boy usually had an effect, though one issued by a girl did not appear to influence the boy.

In comparison to three year olds, four and five year olds show an increased number of attempts to initiate social contact with their peers, especially those of the same sex. Approximately equal numbers of contact attempts are made by preschool boys and girls. Strategies for initiating contact differ between the sexes and produce more success with same-sex peers. Phinney (1979) observed the strategies used by 3–5 year olds in order to initiate social contact with peers. Girls were twice as likely as boys to use requests and questions (including those for permission and information) and made fewer suggestions and bids for attention. Most successful contacts involved showing or offering an object or joining in an ongoing activity. Cross-sex attempts at contact appeared to be less successful than same-sex contacts – apparently because of the use of these differing strategies. Phinney & Rotheram (1980) report that girls were more successful with approaches to other girls if they used polite, mature strategies but were more successful with approaches to boys if they used a more direct, assertive strategy. Boys tended to use a higher proportion of commands, especially to girls, made more non-verbal overtures, especially aggressive approaches to boys and joining in with girls. The aggressive strategies of boys were only partially successful with other boys and totally unsuccessful with girls. Boys rarely made information statements and offers to girls, but when they did these were invariably successful. These differences, and the problems of adapting to same and opposite sex peers, explain why even at this early age there are significantly more approaches to same-sex rather than opposite sex peers. Children of this age do not appear to select strategies which are successful in preference to those which are less successful.

Over this period from about three to five years old there are also marked developments in children's influence attempts in the course of their social interactions. For both sexes there is an increase in influence attempts over this period (Serbin et al., 1984). In girls this was due almost entirely to a growing use of polite suggestions. In boys it took the form of increasing numbers of direct demands. Boys also became increasingly less responsive to polite suggestions. Thus the girls' style of influence was becoming progressively less effective with boys. Using pairs of three- and five-year-old acquainted children, Langlois, Gottfried & Seay (1973) report a similar pattern of same-sex behavioural compatibility in five year olds but not three year olds. Five year olds showed more smiling talking, non-word vocalisations and body contact in same-sex pairs than opposite-sex pairs. In the younger children interactions involving boys were generally less positive, most markedly when both partners were male.

These sex differences in preschoolers' patterns of relating and social influence were clearly brought out in a fascinating and extremely creative experiment by Charlesworth & Dzur (1987). In this study, same-sex quartets of 4–5-year-old children were given access to a movie viewer with an eyepiece which enabled only one child at a time to view a cartoon – and then only with the assistance of two other group members, one to turn a crank and one to push a light button. A dominant child tended to emerge. Dominant boys often attained extra time at the viewer by pushing others out of the way. Girls gained greater time by the greater use of verbal persuasion, consistent with the results of Savin-William's (1979) study of older children. This does not mean that the boys' groups were brutish and unfair. Quite the contrary. More positive affect was shown in the boys' groups than in the girls' groups, and their physical style did not usually involve hostility – they appeared to be having fun. In an earlier study, Charlesworth & LaFreniere (1983) had also used the movie viewing procedure but with mixed-sex groups of preschoolers. This study again highlighted the problems of cross-sex behavioural compatibility in young children's peer relationships. Boys generally achieved the dominant position. The influence techniques used by dominant girls when in all-girl groups did not work well with boys.

Overall, behavioural differences in the social behaviour of boys and girls are evident from an early age, and with increasing social interest and activity these become increasingly marked. By the time the child is approaching the age of school entry, these contribute to a substantial sex segregation in play and friendships.

Sex segregation in school-age children

Sex segregation is immediately evident in the elementary school, for example in classroom and refectory seating, in playground areas, and in queues. "Sex segregation is so common in elementary schools that it is meaningful to speak of separate boys' and girls' worlds" (Thorne, 1986). This segregation carries across to the children's friendships. A large number of studies suggest that this holds true regardless of grade or whether liking is reciprocated (Hartup, 1983). Sex segregation in children's friendships is virtually complete from about grade three. From about grade six it shows a relatively consistent and gradual decline. Cross-sex relationships become increasingly common during high school years (Shrum, Cheek & Hunter, 1988).

In adolescence a sex cleavage in relationships is still marked (Douvan & Adelson, 1966; Savin-Williams, 1980), though whether it serves the same functions or has the same origins that it had in younger children is open to question. Boys and girls have grown up with different models of relationships. Douvan & Adelson (1966) argue that differences in the form of adolescent relationships reflect traditional sex-role stereotypes and different needs in the transition to adulthood.

The female experience of intimate, dyadic play produces a style of moral reasoning emphasising empathy and sensitivity and "knowing the other as different from the self" (p. 11). The group involvements of boys lead to a style of moral reasoning emphasising respect for rules and relying on a more abstract view of relationships (Gilligan, 1982). Girls have learnt nurturance and emotional expression – social skills most relevant to the family. In their larger groups boys have learned to operate within a larger system of rules and with others that are not especially liked – arguably relevant to modern organisational life (Douvan & Adelson, 1966).

Douvan & Adelson argue that peer-group pressure is especially important for boys, influential because of group norms and claims on loyalty. The friendship group supports the adolescent males in their move toward autonomy, and provides peers for them to identify with in their rebellion against authority. They depend on the group as a source of strength and reciprocate with loyalty. Girls do not defy authority as openly and do not need or seek such group solidarity. Females are more concerned with close ties and emotional intimacy to one or a few best friends. They see the group as a network of intimate friendships, a place to find a friend, or as a source of support and confidences. Among adolescents, females are more likely to turn to peers for support (Burke & Weir, 1978), "But they do not generally value the authority or solidarity of the group qua group the way boys often do" (Douvan & Adelson, 1966, p. 201).

Among girls, the 14–16-year-age range is a particularly crucial period for same-sex friendships. Girls of this age are distinctive in demanding loyalty and absolute security in friendship, in the strength of their need for similarity (or identity) and reciprocity between friends (Douvan & Adelson, 1966). And yet despite their intensity, or possibly because of it, the social relationships of adolescent girls are also less permanent than those of their male counterparts. The girls' intense need for intimate sharing can produce more misunderstandings and conflict than are evident in restrained male relationships (Kon & Losenkov, 1978). "Since it is considerably less demanding to maintain casual relationships than an intimate friendship, the sex differences in stability may simply be an artifact of boys' less intense friendships" (Douvan & Gold, 1966, p. 494).

Modes of interaction

Boys' friendships are commonly experienced within the context of a larger group; they are often to be found in groups of three or more. These groups are often relatively heterogeneous in age and become a centre for elaborate games and team sports.

In contrast, girls prefer dyadic interaction with its opportunity for emotional intimacy (Waldrop & Halverson, 1975). These friendships are more exclusive than those of boys (Eder & Hallinan, 1978). Girls value intimate conversation and knowledge of friends more than boys (Berndt, 1982), and are more likely to engage in intimate talks with peers – and even with adults and pets (Bryant, 1985). In adolescence girls report more intimacy than do boys (Youniss & Smollar, 1985).

The two classic studies on sex segregation and social interaction in children's friendship will now be outlined. In a study of 7½ year olds Waldrop & Halverson (1975) collected data on 62 children. The mothers of these children kept diaries of their child's social activity over a one-week period to assess the amount of time their child spent with one peer (an intensive pattern of relating) and the time their child spent with a group of peers (an extensive pattern of relating). A particular note was made of the child's activities with peers, e.g. who the child played with, who initiated contact, and what they played. Based on this data, the researchers calculated the number of hours the child spent with one peer, the number of peers seen, and number of times the child initiated peer contact or determined what game was played.

The peer relationships of highly sociable girls were typified as intensive, centred a single best friend, while those of boys were typified as extensive, centred on a group of peers. Social maturity and success had different correlates for boys and girls. Girls who were highly intensive in their relationships were more socially competent than were girls with less intensive relationships. In contrast, boys with extensive relationships were more socially at ease than boys with less extensive relationships. The socially adept child is the individual who can most successfully accommodate to peer gender expectations. Fortunately, with increasing age the child becomes less myopically reliant on gender stereotypes. The child is increasingly able to moderate his or her expectations of others in accordance with the extent to which their previous behaviour was gender stereotypic (Berndt & Heller, 1986).

Similar-sex differences in patterns of relating have also been shown in preadolescents. Eder & Hallinan (1978) found that the proportion of exclusive friendship dyads was greater for females than for males in four out of five classrooms examined. Participation in non-exclusive friendships was more common among boys, as were non-mutual choices. The results of seven sociometric tests over the course of the school year showed that initially non-exclusive choices of girls were highly likely to become exclusive as the year progressed. Those of boys either became more non-exclusive or showed no change. Over time, girls tended to return to isolated dyads while boys tended to expand their dyadic friendships to include a third person.

Different interaction styles with network members produce different coping strategies and benefits for males and females. Divorce and its impact on children is a good example of this. The overall quality of children's relationships are likely to greatly affect their adjustment to their parents' divorce and living in a one-parent family (Huntley & Phelps, 1990). But the relationship styles of boys and girls produce different patterns of coping. In the transitional period following divorce, more girls than boys have friends and use them as a support system (Wallerstein & Kelly, 1980). The supportiveness of girls' peer relationships is related both to the simple number of friends that they have and to reciprocity in these relationships (Frankel, 1990). However, during the initial crisis of divorce, during which children often seem unable to get comfort from friends or family, boys are able to make more use of peers for distraction (Wallerstein & Kelly (1980). The introspective style of female relationships underlie the preponderance of females who are depressed, whereas men seem more likely to seek distraction when distressed (Nolen-Hoeksema, 1987).

Intimacy

The overwhelming weight of evidence indicates that female friendships tend to be intimate and usually with a small number of select others. Boys, in contrast, are commonly found to form large, activity-oriented groups.

Research reviews have concluded that females tend to be more empathic than males, though not necessarily more adept at assessing another's affective, cognitive or spatial perspective (Feshbach, 1978). This empathy in females is part of a general prosocial affective orientation. As Feshbach points out, girls are less inhibited in expressing feelings, especially negative ones such as fear. Females have a greater tendency to imagine themselves in the other's place, whereas males are more inclined to instrumental action to remedy problematic situations.

This does not, of course, deny an empathic ability in males. Studies of empathy support sex-typed perspective of relationships. Children are more sensitive to the feelings and relationships of same-sex others in situations with which they are familiar or in which they can imagine themselves (Feshbach, 1978). In a study of children in grades two and four, Rotenberg (1984) showed that they trusted their own sex more than the opposite sex and that levels of trust were higher for pairs of girls than pairs of boys. This pattern of trust was not evident in kindergarten children, presumably because of their poorer social cognitive abilities. In similar vein, Rotenberg (1986) found fourth-grade children perceive that opposite-sex peers break secrets more frequently than same-sex peers. These studies suggest that patterns of trust reinforce sex segregation in friendship.

The more personal nature of female friendships was examined in Bigelow & La Gaipa's (1980) study of children's friendship expectations (see Chapter 2 for a more general consideration of this study). Sex differences in the reported significance of "intimate" information were not as dramatic as expected. In middle childhood the only sex difference was due to girls describing their friends in more global, affective terms (68% versus 48%). In early and late adolescence females emphasised intimacy more than males (23% versus 9% and 60% versus 40%). In late adolescence females also placed more value on loyalty and commitment (75% versus 52%); much of this related to maintaining confidentiality, i.e. intimacy of information (55% vs 35%). Loyalty and commitment were also critical in friendship terminations. Females cite disloyalty more in early (47% versus 21%) and late adolescence (47% versus 32%).

Despite their interest and relevance, these results constitute only limited support for Douvan & Adelson's (1966) argument that boys are less concerned with the affective aspects of friendship. First, because the differences that have been noted suggest a considerable degree of overlap between the sexes. Second, because Bigelow & La Gaipa found little difference between the sexes in the value placed on emotional support and helping, ego reinforcement, acceptance, and genuineness as aspects of friendship.

The research of Bigelow & La Gaipa has been criticised by Bukowski & Kramer (1986) as dealing only with same-sex conceptions of friendship. These authors examined possible gender effects in fourth and seventh graders. Children read descriptions of hypothetical pairs of boys and girls and rated them for the likelihood that they were friends. The descriptions indicated the sex of the characters, levels of similarity, helpfulness/support, and intimacy. There were no gender effects, i.e. boys and girls evaluated the hypothetical pairs similarly. All the experimental factors affected ratings. There were stronger effects for intimacy among older subjects, stronger effects for intimacy in the stories about girls' characters, and stronger similarity effects for boys' characters among older subjects. The boys and girls were themselves aware of sex differences in the intimacy of children's peer relationships.

Research is consistent in finding both a sex difference and a developmental trend in the intimacy of relationships (e.g. Blyth & Traeger, 1988). Changes in the intimacy of children's relationships were examined in a systematic study by Sharabany, Gershoni & Hoffman (1981). These authors examined the same-sex and opposite-sex best friendships of children over a wide age range. Subjects were drawn from school grades five, seven, nine, and eleven. Girls' same-sex friendships showed greater intimacy in terms of attachment, giving and sharing, and trust and loyalty. Whereas same-sex friendships were already quite intimate in even the youngest children, opposite sex relationships showed, as one might expect, dramatic increases in intimacy with age. This reflects trends in the establishment of dating relationships. Again, however, the basic pattern of females showing higher levels of intimacy than males was evident in ninth and eleventh graders.

Adolescence is a time of great change in children's relationships. The peer group becomes increasingly significant and cross-sex relationships are beginning to appear. This has made adolescence a time of great interest for researchers interested in the development of intimacy. A number of studies have reported sex differences in patterns of intimacy in adolescence.

Adolescent female friendships are typically described as more intense, demonstrative, exclusive, and nurturant. Females are in more frequent contact with their friends than are boys (Blyth & Traeger, 1988), and depend heavily on friend as confidant with whom they could come to understand and develop their own personalities (Richey & Richey, 1980). Their intimacy with same-sex peers exceeds that with parents at an earlier age than is the case for adolescent boys (Blythe & Foster-Clark, 1987; Buhrmester & Furman, 1987). In adolescence girls self-disclose more than boys (Youniss & Smollar, 1985). Although males also confide at an intimate level, their relationships are more likely to be based on enjoyable companionship and similarity of attitudes, with less emphasis on the continual analysis of experience (Richey & Richey, 1980). The functions of self-disclosure are also different between the sexes, even if the levels are identical (Belle, Burr & Cooney, 1987).

Cultural considerations

This section examines the extent of sex segregation in children's play and relationships in different cultural contexts. Cultural influences have a central role in shaping and maintaining sex segregation. Gender is a significant component of identity and, hence, children are motivated to demonstrate their mastery of sex-appropriate behaviour however this is defined by their culture. Sex segregation supports the child's emerging gender identity. Because mothers are often the primary caregivers, the sex segregation in children's relationships is especially important for boys, who have less access to routinely available same-sex adult models.

Children in many Western countries, such as the UK, Germany, the USA, and the Russian Federation, show a high degree of sex segregation in children's friendships (Kon, 1981). Non-Western societies also show a sex cleavage in children's play and patterns of relating, though the extent and expression of this varies with the sex roles that are being taught; it is most marked in primitive cultures hunting large animals (Barry, Bacon & Child, 1957).

Sex-typed activities provide an environmental context for learning personal and social behaviour such as independence or dependence. Sex differences in social behaviour across cultures is consequently learned through differences in exposure to particular social contexts and tasks (Whiting and Edwards, 1973, 1988).

Examining data from a number of cultures, Whiting & Edwards (1973, 1988) found that about two-thirds of 4–5 year olds' interactions and more than three-quarters of 6–10 year olds' interactions with non-sibling children were same-sex. They conclude that the emergence of a same-sex preference in childhood is a "cross cultural universal and robust phenomenon". Segregation is least marked in societies which do not venture far from a settled home, and consequently provide the child with only a limited choice of companions. Segregation is most pronounced where children have more peers of the same age available as possible playmates in public places. As with Western cultures, boys tended to range further from home, on errands and at play. Where the culture gives the female more contact with infants than males, they show more nurturant behaviour; there is no difference where the amount of contact does not differ. Children that have been caretakers of very young children also behaved in a more nurturant way to peers more often. Girls tended to be given such responsibility, perhaps as a preparation for their later adult roles.

Although Harkness & Super (1985) also acknowledge the effect of cultural demands on patterns of sex segregation in children's peer groups, they note that these do not necessarily become the children's preferred patterns of association. In an observational study of the Kipsigis of Western Kenya, Harkness & Super (1985) found that children's peer groups were not segregated below the age of about six years old. At about this age changes in settings, parental expectations, and customary duties result in a substantial increase in the proportion of same-sex peers. Patterns of sex segregation were related to parental expectations and children's duties around the homestead. The authors also note that children over six years old spent more time with same-sex peers but did not choose them differentially as targets of social interaction – suggesting segregation is as much a product of parental authority and routine duties as the child's personal preferences.

Cross-sex interaction

Despite the widespread acceptance that throughout much of childhood there is a widespread sex segregation in children's friendships, it is also undeniable that under some circumstances there is deliberate cross-sex interaction and in other circumstances there are inadvertent violations of the boundaries of sex segregation. Both these situations need to be considered to gain a full picture of the role of gender in children's peer relationships.

Cross-sex play can expose boys and girls to a wider range of behavioural styles and activities, expand the pool of potential friends, and help develop an appreciation of the qualities shared by the sexes. Cross-sex friendships in childhood are considerably less stable than same-sex relationships (Tuma & Hallinan, 1979), though the experience of cross-sex interaction is likely to improve the child's ability to sustain fulfilling relationships in later life (Rubin, 1980). Up to the fourth and fifth grades a prime insult is to say that a boy likes girls' games or that a girl likes boys' games. A number of ritualised mechanisms exist for dealing with the boundary violations which occur in these patterns of sex segregated play (Gottman, 1986a). By about the fifth or sixth grade this sex segregation in children's play and relationships starts to break down, though there is still a good deal of teasing initially. Thorne (1986) describes a number of characteristic forms of cross-sex participation in the games of boys and girls as detailed below.

Borderwork

Borderwork is interaction across, but based on, strengthening gender boundaries. For example, contests and chasing games. Boys also commonly invade the games of girls. A nice example of this that I have observed was of boys playing dive bombers on the play houses being constructed by girls out of piles of fallen leaves. If girls seek access to boys' games it is usually to join in rather than to disrupt.

Interactions infused with heterosexual meaning

Children's knowledge of sex-role stereotypes makes them intensely aware of each other as potential romantic partners, but they none the less follow a pattern of avoiding cross-sex contact. Even during the sex segregation of late childhood a number of children express interest in others of the opposite sex. This interest is not necessarily known to the other child, but it does represent a foundation for the emergence of full sexual interest in early adolescence (Broderick, 1966). Male–female interaction in late childhood is usually strained and often involves indirect or overheard indications of attraction, teasing, and "fooling around". Sexual concerns are often aired in sessions often filled with loud, giggly laughter, insults, and bravado (Fine, 1980). Group discussion can arouse anxiety, but also give support and reassurance. Schofield (1981) notes they do not allow relaxed, extended interaction necessary for friendship. From about 14 years of age choices are more realistic and involve expectations of reciprocity (Broderick, 1966).

As Thorne notes, in school heterosexual and romantic meanings can be the basis for some ritualised interactions (e.g. teasing when cross-sex interest or associations occur). Possibly because of this, early cross-sex friendships tend to be quite unstable (Gronlund, 1955). Through elementary school and increasing with age, cross-sex interaction is risky in school. Interestingly, Thorne notes that some cross-sex interaction does occur under other circumstances, such as in the home neighbourhood or at church, but this is often hidden at school.

By grade five a few individuals begin to affirm rather than avoid charges of cross-sex friendships and there is even often a gain in status by publicly choosing a companion of the opposite sex. The same-sex cliques in early adolescence give way to heterosexual cliques in mid-to-late adolescence, generally later for boys than girls (Dunphy, 1972).

Crossing the gender boundary

The extent to which gender boundaries are crossed is variable. Some children have little or no cross-sex interactions and some participate in specific activities or sports. Only a relative few fully cross the gender divide and spend most of their time with the other sex. This is mostly represented by females becoming tomboys. These girls fully participate in the play of boys, and even join in the fighting and teasing typical of boys' groups.

Crossing the gender divide is by no means easy. Even in young children there are important sanctions to encourage conformity to gender norms for behaviour. In a study by Lamb, Easterbrooks & Holden (1980), the reactions of 3–5 year olds to playmates engaged in sex-appropriate or sex-inappropriate (cross-sex) activity was observed. Children generally reinforced sex-appropriate play and this then tended to continue. Peers were quick to criticise or disrupt a companion's sex-inappropriate play and the activity usually ended in less than a minute. This effect is especially marked for boys (Huston, 1983). Boys more feminine in games preference and gender presentation tend to be less socially successful (Klein & Bates, 1980), and a young boy engaging in doll play or dressing up is likely to be teased or ignored by both boys and girls (Fagot, 1977a). In contrast, girls are given more leeway in their violations of sex roles (Feiring & Lewis, 1989). Fagot & Littman (1975) suggest that in part this is because play is irrelevant to society's definition of femininity. In the light of these studies it is hardly surprising that children are less likely to play with sex-inappropriate toys if peers are present (Serbin et al., 1979).

Relaxed cross sex interaction

This tends to occur when children are involved in an absorbing task or when children are not responsible for the formation of groups, such as when activities are structured by adults. Uncontrolled cross-sex interaction is often abrasive and simply reinforces sex-role stereotypes. Co-operative interactions, such as in small, mixed-sex instruction groups help to reduce stereotyping and produce an increase in integration (Lockheed, 1986). Sex segregation in activities is also less when there are other overriding factors to consider (e.g. interests), and where there are few alternative playmates or witnesses to the boundary violation.

Overall, this section provides an appropriate end to the chapter as a whole. For while one cannot deny the sex segregation in children's friendships, this section highlights that it is far from complete and provides a view of the child in a world of more balanced social experiences.

8 Social structure and context

We should not attempt to measure "general" tendencies to affiliate, but rather the extent of such tendencies in different types of situations.
(Fox, 1980, p. 306)

No relationship is an island; it has a history and a context. The history of a relationship, its development, has already been examined in considerable detail in the earlier chapters of this book. Contextual influences have been given considerably less attention – until now. In this chapter two main issues are examined. First, the extent to which a wide variety of factors serve to limit or structure children's interactions and peer relationships. These factors range from the simple physical characteristics of the environment through to the social context within which the interaction occurs. Second, it is important to bear in mind a complementary perspective, the extent to which relationships affect the child's choice of situations or how situations are structured to meet the requirements of the relationship. For example, the friendships of boys and girls centre around different types of activity which require different resources.

Environmental and situational influences on various aspects of children's behaviour are evident from an early age and have received a great deal of research attention. The social behaviour and response patterns of preschoolers show a high level of consistency across time providing the situational context of the observations remains the same (Russell, 1984). There are only poor levels of consistency for behaviour across different classroom situations (Rose, Blank & Spalter, 1975). Although the preschool group and the grade school classroom have been particularly fruitful sources of research, a substantial amount of research has also been devoted to other environments, such as the home neighbourhood. Based on their study of four different neighbourhoods, Berg & Medrich (1980, p. 341) concluded that "the act of play itself was partly a product of social interaction patterns which, to an extent, were related to the land use configuration and nature of the built environment". As Eggert & Parks (1987, p. 284) emphasised, there is a need to consider not just dyadic relationships but "dyadic relationships and their embeddedness in social contexts".

Gestalt psychology represents an important perspective that emphasises the holistic nature of social and psychological processes – summed up in the saying that the whole is more than the sum of the parts. Representing this perspective, Lewin (1931) argued that behaviour is a function of the person and environment or situation, summarised in his famous equation $B = f(P,E)$. More importantly, this mutual connectedness was seen as influencing future as well as current behaviour. Effects are cumulative and hierarchical. Experiences are carried over from one situation to the next and affect the way in which these are interpreted, and the consequent responses that they elicit. Taking this idea of the interconnectedness of the person and his or her environment a step further leads one to the ecological psychologist's concept of synomorphy, the idea that behaviour and environment become similar in form or shape (Gump, 1978). This is a plausible end point of a dynamic process of environment and behaviour being mutually adapted or changed until some point of equilibrium is reached between the two forces.

Generalising the basic ideas of the ecological psychologists, it becomes evident that complex patterns of relating emerge when environmental context is taken into account. For example, a study by Durrant & Henggeler (1986) found that children's sociometric standing tended to be similar in school-based groups and outside groups. This does not, however, necessarily imply that patterns of interaction and relating in these two situations are identical, or even similar. A study by Montemayor & Van Komen (1985) found that as adolescence progressed groups observed out of school became smaller and more mixed-sex while those in school remained relatively large and homogeneous with regard to sex.

There is little doubt that different children interact with their environments in different ways. Different types of environment suit different types of children, though it is equally clear that there are some environments which are generally dysfunctional. The clear evidence indicating the importance of environmental influences on children's health and behaviour, including their social behaviour, is such that some authors have been prompted to advocate the need for more explicit environmental policies for children (e.g. Van Vliet, 1986).

Most research on the influence of contextual factors on children's peer relationships has focused on the preschool and elementary school years. The extracurricular activities of adolescents are likely to be of greater significance in their lives, but they are also more complex and wide ranging, and have proved considerably more difficult to investigate – especially using an experimental approach. Because of these considerations the main material covered in this chapter will refer to early and middle childhood, though some enlightening studies on infants and on adolescents and college students are also included.

Family organisation

Parents are widely acknowledged as playing an important role in "setting the stage" upon which children's friendships are to be played out (Rubin & Sloman, 1984). Whilst the influence of parental controls is a factor in all children's relationships, and a potential area of dispute, especially with adolescents, it is most significant as a limiting factor for the preschooler. In this age group especially, parents are often responsible for initiating, structuring, and almost totally controlling the frequency of their child's peer contacts (Parke & Bhavnagri, 1989). This has significant implications for the child's social experience and future peer competence. In a study of preschool and kindergarten children, Ladd & Golter (1988) found that parents initiating higher proportions of peer contacts tended to have children with a large number of different play partners, more consistent companions outside of school, and, for boys, greater peer acceptance.

Social class

A major characteristic that affects children's peer relationships is social class. This will directly affect the socialisation practices of parents, and ultimately children's relationship expectations. Social class has a direct effect on relationship values and style, and an indirect effect due to its impact on other factors, such as the child's use of publicly available social facilities. Each of these influences will be examined.

In a study of third- and fourth-grade children, Gottman, Gonso & Rasmussen (1975) found that popular children were more knowledgeable about how to make friends and more skilled on a referential communication task (implying a better ability to accommodate to the other's perspective in communication). Popular children also distributed and received more positive reinforcements than unpopular children. These findings are typical of those reported in the literature on the antecedents of children's peer popularity. A more novel finding of this study was that the form that these social reinforcements took was affected by social class. Verbal reinforcements were more significant in children attending the middle-income school and non-verbal reinforcements were more important in children attending the low-income school. Even more interesting than this, and indicating that the social skills underlying popularity are not universal, was the finding that positive non-verbal behaviour was actually negatively related to liking in the children attending the middle-income school. Inappropriate modes of communicating friendship overtures are not only ineffective, they can seriously backfire. This emphasises the context specificity of many social skills. As the authors note, this has important implications for any intervention programme aimed at improving social skills. It would certainly be unwise for middle-class psychologists to give children from other socioeconomic classes social skills training without first being sure that appropriate skills are being taught. Social competence is determined by the appropriate application of social skills in specific situations (Foster, DeLawler & Guevremont, 1986).

In a less direct manner, social class affects children's relationships through its impact on their involvement in community organisations such as youth clubs. Involvement in community organisations increases with age until about adolescence and is associated with definite social benefits: they provide an approved meeting ground, a place to make friends, and the opportunity to acquire and test new social skills (Bryant, 1985). Children of more educated and economically advantaged parents receive more encouragement to participate in community organisations and, in comparison with children of lower social class, they are more than twice as likely to do so. They are also more likely to participate on a regular basis and, supporting the activity, their mothers often become involved. In contrast, children from working-class backgrounds are more likely to use facilities on an ad hoc basis or to use only those facilities specifically targeted at low-income groups (O'Donnell & Stueve, 1983).

Poverty and socialisation in the family

Far from supporting positive social interaction, the enforced presence of others can actually promote withdrawal or aggressive behaviour. The freedom to choose to be alone or in company is a crucial determinant of whether the presence of others is perceived as pleasant or aversive (Wolfe, 1978). Crowded living conditions limit the child's opportunities for privacy. A high within-household density for fourth- and fifth-grade children (measured in terms of the number of people per room and/or high numbers of people) is associated with peer nominations of aggressiveness at school (Murray, 1974). Of course, it is sometimes difficult to separate simple density effects from other causal or possibly mediating factors. Poor families are likely to be larger and occupy less adequate housing (Broman, Nichols & Kennedy, 1976). Families of low socioeconomic status are also more likely to use more restrictive, authoritarian, and punitive strategies of child control, which increases the likelihood of aggression due to the disinhibition, reinforcement, and modelling of aggressive behaviour (Maccoby, 1980; Parke & Slaby, 1983). Murray (1974) suggests that the higher use of punitive child-rearing practices simply reflects the greater levels of contact between the family members.

Physical environment, proximity and interaction

Proximity has been one of the most researched aspects of environmental influences on peer relationships. The physical characteristics of an environment affect the opportunities for interpersonal contact that it provides. It also determines the character of interactions and patterns of relating that occur.

In a study by Berg & Medrich (1980), 11 and 12 year olds from four neighbourhoods in Oakland, California were interviewed about their patterns of play and the physical settings of their neighbourhoods. These neighbourhoods differed in status, terrain, and the amenities that they offered. The physical environment had a significant effect on the children's relationships in many interesting ways. A difficult, hilly terrain, for example, made it more difficult for children to casually visit a friend's house on their own and is an obstacle to many common children's games. Simple safety considerations have been highlighted as the major environmental influence on how far afield children range and their patterns of play (Moore & Young, 1978). Children will typically treat roads and sidewalks (pavements) as important play areas that are literally on their doorstep. If there are no sidewalks or the road is busy then safety reasons make this facility less available to the child. Even worse, a busy road can prevent the child from using other neighbourhood facilities. For example, when it obstructs access to public areas such as parks. The lack of feelings of autonomy that result from constraining neighbourhood characteristics, and possibly a dependency on adults for supervision or transport, are major concerns of preadolescents who "by and large, seemed to view themselves as captives in their own neighbourhood" (Berg & Medrich, 1980, p. 343).

Proximity as a facilitator of social interaction

Contact is a self-evident prerequisite for forming relationships. In its absence there is no possibility of a relationship. If it occurs, even if it is enforced, then at least it provides the possibility of the development or modification of initial attitudes, including interpersonal attitudes. One of the most famous studies which shows this was conducted by Festinger, Schachter & Back (1950). This study was of a student housing community. This is a rather older age group than is the concern of this chapter, but it highlights some points of general applicability. From the point of view of this book, the important finding of the 1950's study was that the spatial location of accommodation had a marked impact on friendships and group membership. The siting of accommodation determined, at least in part, contact with neighbours. For example, having an end apartment rather than an apartment with neighbours on either side is likely to lead to less accidental or casual contact. People are more likely to become friends with others on the same floor than with those on other floors or in other buildings. These are effects due to the sheer physical structure of the environment, though the functional characteristics of the environment are also important. An example will clarify this point: accommodation located in busy thoroughfares (e.g. by the stairwells in an accommodation block) facilitated casual contact and resulted in the individuals in these accommodations receiving more sociometric nominations. Of course people often recognise the social restrictions imposed on them by their environments and take appropriate compensatory action. Individuals in quiet locations can spend more time in communal areas, if they exist. People in busy locations can spend less time in these areas and more time in their rooms if they feel a social overload and desire privacy and time alone.

The results of the Festinger, Schachter & Back (1950) study highlight the potential importance of proximity for social relationships, and especially how the physical structure of an environment affects functional proximity and interpersonal contact. An interesting study by Van Vliet (1981), on 14–16 year olds, showed how this basic principle is also applicable on a larger geographic scale and to a younger age group. This study found that adolescents living in neighbourhoods with relatively large numbers of children were less likely to complain about a lack of friends that lived in the neighbourhood, actually had more friends that lived in the neighbourhood, and shared more activities with these friends.

The opportunities for social interaction that are provided by physical proximity are crucial in facilitating friendship formation and in maintaining established friendships. In a study of 8–15-year-old children attending a children's camp, Shapiro (1977) found that low-attraction and more recent friendships are more likely to dissolve if participants are separated than are high-attraction friendships (which actually become stronger). The friendships of females were also more likely to dissolve than were those of males. Overall, it appears that causal friendships are more substitutable, but also that the more personal and intimate friendships of girls are more prone to collapse following separation. This again shows the importance of physical proximity as an important factor in establishing and maintaining satisfying social relationships. It is comforting to know that apparently contradictory proverbs, our gems of cultural wisdom, can both contain a grain of truth under appropriate conditions: absence can make the heart grow fonder in close relationships, though for girls' relationships and superficial relationships it may also be a case of out of sight, out of mind.

The field of eligibles

So, as we have seen, at its most basic the field of eligibles, those others that are available as possible friends, is limited to those individuals with whom the child comes into contact. This in itself operates on several levels. First, it operates in terms of simple geographic proximity. At a very simplistic level, a child or youth is simply more likely to meet someone in the same town than someone living on a different continent. Systematic research has examined the impact of different neighbourhoods on children, including their friendship patterns (e.g. Berg & Medrich, 1980; Medrich et al., 1982). A number of physical characteristics of neighbourhood environments were found to affect children's relationships. A neighbourhood with a high social density was likely to facilitate large group play and spontaneity in play and team sports. In comparison to children from neighbourhoods with little distance or barriers between houses, pre-adolescents from neighbourhoods where houses were widely separated and with fewer sidewalks reported travelling further distances to be with friends. This is relatively obvious; more interesting is the finding that they also tended to have fewer friends and that their friendships were more formal and rigid. A visit to a friend some distance away became a special trip rather than a casual encounter with someone who might be bumped into in the street or called on during brief free periods. Availability of facilities such as parks and playgrounds also promoted a larger circle of friends and more spontaneous and large group play – though undeveloped, unplanned play areas which children discovered for themselves and which were private from adults were often better appreciated!

Even within a restricted geographic area there are factors limiting the amount of contact that is likely between peers. There is often a limited set of eligibles, and encounters with these children vary considerably in the extent to which they are prestructured. Murstein (1977) has used the terms open field and closed field to delineate different types of encounter. An open field encounter refers to a situation in which interaction between individuals is not based on a prior relationship; they do not hold predefined roles in relation to each other. This description would obviously apply to individuals that are spatially proximate yet do not interact. Children beginning school for the first time are entering a new and open field of peers. In a closed field reciprocal roles have been defined and interaction is limited. It is possible for the members of a closed field to occupy many different roles in relation to the child. They may be friends, acquaintances, or even individuals rejected because of their aggressiveness. Whatever the relation between the individuals, it is likely to colour their further interaction. Either way, interaction has occurred. For example, children in the same class, especially if it is small, are likely to be forced to interact.

A nice example of how the field of eligibles affects children's relationships is evident in the patterns of group formation in preschoolers. With smaller groups of preschool children every child is inevitably brought into contact with every other child; subgroups are larger (if they occur at all) and splitting off into exclusive friendship pairs or becoming a social isolate is less likely (Rubin, 1980). In a study by Smith & Connolly (1980) group size was varied, though the ratio of space and equipment was maintained (as the number of children increased, so proportionately did the amount of space and equipment). Same-sex pairs of children playing together were more common in the larger classes. Children in the smaller classes all knew each other well and formed a close social network with large subgroups, more cross-sex interaction, and more fantasy play. Presumably the sub-dividing of a large group enables a manageable friendship network to be maintained and overcomes the problem encountered in initiating new contacts and gaining entry to existing groups. A small group produces a closed field situation and reduces the possibility of forming independent subgroups.

The extent to which the field of eligibles is open or closed is determined by a variety of situational factors. The patterns of interaction of school pupils will be partly determined by the school structure and the way in which teachers organise their classrooms. Groups are likely to provide yet further restrictions. Similarity of values or socioeconomic and religious background is likely to close the field of eligibles. Friendships are likely to be formed from within these groups.

Although forced encounters usually result in positive liking, this is not invariably so. Proximity can also be an important factor in negative social choice (Warr, 1965). Obliging children to interact with someone they actively dislike can help them to change their opinion about the person or it can provide the confirmation that they were right in the first place – and possibly even that their initial evaluation was excessively mild (Sherif et al., 1961). They may stop disliking the other child in order to begin hating him or her!

At least one further effect of proximity can be identified and is worthy of detailed consideration. The increased level of contact promoted by proximity means that children will be exposed to, and so become more familiar with, some individuals rather than others. Over and above any more complex effects, simple familiarity is likely to have a direct effect on levels of interpersonal attraction.

Familiarity and liking

The opportunity for contact produces a direct effect on liking through simple familiarity (Saegert, Swap & Zajonc, 1973). The familiarity effect is a pervasive phenomenon not confined to interpersonal attraction. It was originally argued that there is a monotonic relationship between familiarity and liking for stimuli, the "mere exposure" hypothesis (Zajonc, 1968). More recent research suggests a more complex analysis of the mere exposure effect. Although liking does initially increase with repeated exposures to a stimulus, in many cases high levels of exposure produce satiation and boredom and liking for the stimulus declines. This inverted-U relationship between exposure and liking is affected by the complexity of a stimulus, with its peak occurring at extremely low levels for simple stimuli and at relatively high levels for more complex stimuli (Sluckin, Colman & Hargreaves, 1980). The inverted-U relationship between stimulus familiarity and liking has been noted in children at least as young as ten years (Sluckin, Miller & Franklin, 1973). People are relatively complex stimuli and to this extent repeated exposure is likely to increase liking over a substantial period. Of course, in the real world, as opposed to the experimental laboratory, an individual has some degree of control over exposure to certain classes of stimuli but relatively little control over others. If a child dislikes someone then he or she will tend to avoid that person, whereas getting to know a friend will often take a very long time and involve a substantial amount of contact. The implication here is that even simple familiarity effects have a differential impact on relationships of different types or closeness.

Group size and density

Density is a concept closely allied to the notion of proximity, but it recognises that number as well as the closeness of others is important. McGrew (1972a) makes the useful distinction between social density, the number of people present in an area, and spatial density, the area available to a given number of people. It is unfortunate that social density is probably the more influential form of crowding but research has concentrated on spatial density. Even within this analysis there remains room to recognise that the subjective experience of crowding is likely to represent yet a further factor worthy of consideration (Stokols, 1972). Situational and personal factors can mean that a given level of density is experienced as crowded under one set of conditions but pleasant under another. A full analysis of the consequences of crowding requires that consideration is given to the joint effect of both social and spatial density, to small and large environments with differing numbers of people, while also paying heed to children's subjective experiences. As McCarthy (1981) points out, it is appropriate for a science of personal relationships to pay heed to both objective factors and subjective perceptions as the determinants of relationships.

The importance of distinguishing between different types of density or crowding lies in the fact they produce very different consequences (McGrew,

1972a). They also interact differently with a number of additional factors, such as the use of partitions to divide rooms and play areas, and whether other resources and opportunities are maintained. All these factors will be considered in more detail in subsequent sections of this chapter.

Social density and crowding

The sheer number of potential friends available to the child, the size of the field of eligibles, is important in determining his friendship networks. Hallinan's (1979) study of children in school grades four to eight suggested that the greater social opportunities of larger classes facilitate friendship formation – children in larger classes generally indicate a greater number of friends than their counterparts in smaller classes. This does not necessarily mean that social relations are improved by squashing as many children as possible into each class! Studies on social density (which is dealt with later in this chapter) indicate that overcrowding leads to more aggression and *less* social interaction. Other researchers have argued that partitioned play areas in day-care classrooms facilitate children's interaction and fantasy play (Field, 1980). Presumably these provide zones of high spatial density but low social density (i.e. relatively small spatial amounts of space per child but with relatively few children in each area). There is undoubtedly a fine line to be drawn when considering the relationship of social and spatial density to crowding effects, and one which is likely to be affected by a host of other factors, such as age, social class, school ethos, and the physical organisation of the classroom. The multitude of variables which influence the pattern of density effects on social interaction has produced a complex literature. A clear picture has only recently started to emerge.

Social and spatial density

Beyond the limits imposed by the availability of friendship partners, the number of others present in a situation affects relationships due to the effects of crowding. There is accumulating evidence of the adverse effects of crowding on social interaction. Crowding produces decreased levels of general social interaction, increased aggression, and decreased opportunities for a child to be the sole user of an object (e.g. Weinstein, 1979; Li, 1984). Unfortunately, the pattern of results is not totally consistent. Some authors actually report that crowding produces an increase in interaction and a lack of notable negative consequences (e.g. Fagot, 1977b). As is often the case in psychology, part of the problem is due to differing ways of defining the behaviours of interest. Is rough and tumble play included in an index of aggression? Is aggression recorded separately from overall levels of interaction? As long as different researchers use different operational definitions of crucial variables there are likely to be continuing difficulties in comparing the results from different studies. Even if these conceptual problems are resolved, a host of other issues await consideration. A substantial degree of theoretical refinement is necessary to account for potential differences due to cultural and sub-cultural factors, and to explain the role of resources such as toys and equipment in the experience of crowding.

An example of the difficulties in interpreting much of the research in this area can be gleaned by considering a short-term study by Loo (1972). The results of this study are at variance with the findings of much of the other research in the area and it is instructive to examine the possible reasons for this. Loo (1972) compared spatial densities of 44 square feet and 15 square feet per 4–5-year-old child in groups of six. Though rather unnaturally perhaps, it appears that unacquainted children were put together for the experimental sessions. The movable object resources were kept constant across the different conditions. The results showed less social interaction and aggression and more interruption of activity in the higher spatial density condition. Loo explained her findings in attributional terms: increasing social density is likely to result in the additional children being seen as responsible for the crowding. In contrast, an increase in spatial density makes a group more cohesive as the children come to see themselves as the common victims of someone else's actions. In these circumstances a decrease in within-group conflict and aggression is understandable. Loo concluded that if interaction normally facilitates mature social behaviour then the effect of crowding will be to retard it. Unfortunately, Loo's results are notably different from those of a number of other studies. Alternative explanations to the one given by Loo provide a better account for these differences. A couple of points which bear on this unusual pattern of results are particularly worthy of note. First, the results relating to aggression are difficult to interpret as, like many studies in this area, rough and tumble play is inadequately distinguished. As rough and tumble play normally declines under conditions of high spatial density this could account for the apparent decrease in aggression (Smith & Green, 1975). Second, children going from low to high density groups showed more negative effects associated with crowding than the reverse situation, supporting Smith & Connolly's (1980) speculation that experimental artifacts contributed to the unusual results of this study.

Many studies of social density have been potentially confounded because of the effect of changes in spatial density. A child that has known only a high level of density is likely to behave very differently from a child initially playing quite happily in a room at a low level of density which is then suddenly and dramatically increased. This problem was avoided by Fagot (1977b) who made naturalistic observations of four year olds in three high-density Dutch and one medium and one low-density American nursery schools. The average levels of spatial density were, respectively, approximately one, two, and ten square meters of space per child. Fagot did find some significant social consequences of density, in terms of rates of playing alone and positive interaction, though she did not, unfortunately, report the mean scores. She reported that the Dutch children did spend almost twice as much time in positive social interaction (50% versus 27%). The direction of the difference for rates of playing alone is not specified, though Fagot concluded that her findings did not support the notion that density relates directly to detrimental behavioural consequences. Over and above the density of the schools, Fagot noted that teachers in the crowded schools appeared to show more planning and a more directive style of classroom management with, for example, the Dutch children being assigned to room areas. Large motor activities were limited due to space constraints, though outdoor activity was provided. Although this study suggests that children adapt readily to crowding, care must be taken in interpreting the results due to the possible confounding of social and spatial density and classroom organisation. The use of classrooms in different countries also makes comparisons between the low and medium-density groups and the high density groups difficult. As Li (1984) points out, comparisons within cultures are probably more appropriate.

The equipment factor

Many density findings are more easily explained in terms of experimental artifacts than genuine effects. For example, manipulating social and spatial density may disrupt groups. Many studies using higher densities also tend to be of relatively short duration and so introduce this factor, and the effect of novelty, as potential artifacts. Studies also vary in the pre-existing relationships between the children. Some studies use strangers, some use familiar others. A major factor that has been highlighted as a frequent artifact when manipulating social and spatial density is the relative availability of toys and equipment (Fagot, 1977b). Changes in amounts of playground toys and equipment produce corresponding changes in patterns of interaction. A reduction in the resources available to children is associated with increased levels of social contact and conflicts such as teasing and quarrelling (Johnson, 1935). Gump (1978) goes so far as to argue that spatial density is simply a specific instance of a more basic form of density–population size relative to the available resources (materials and apparatus). Changes in the availability of toys and apparatus are accompanied by changes in social behaviour. A decrease in resources typically produces an increase in social interaction, fewer social isolates, more large groups, aggression, and stress behaviours.

In their review of factors that have been manipulated in crowding studies, Smith & Connolly (1980) conclude that the major studies of crowding have manipulated different factors (e.g. social density, spatial density, and equipment) and this accounts for the many apparently divergent results. Also, these studies have often failed to distinguish aggression from rough and tumble play and have insufficiently controlled the effects of novelty in restricted space conditions. To remedy some of these shortcoming in the research literature Smith & Connolly (1980) conducted a number of naturalistic studies in a nursery school established especially for their research programme. This permitted a systematic manipulation of highly controlled variables.

In one study, Smith & Connolly varied spatial density and group resources independently. Group sizes were held constant at 24 children. Between one and three sets of basic play equipment were provided to the children at different times during each spatial density condition of 25, 50, or 75 square feet per child. The main consequences of the experimental manipulations were on children's choice of activities. In larger spaces there were often more large-scale activities, such as running about, and the active use of apparatus. In smaller spaces there was more use of the climbing frame and slide (an outlet for otherwise restricted gross motor activity), and more enforced physical contact between children. Despite this, there were no significant differences in levels of social or aggressive behaviour.

In a further study Smith & Connolly varied spatial and social density independently. Spatial density was 15 square feet or 60 square feet per child. Two levels of social density were examined by forming two groups of different sizes. One group consisted of ten children and the other of 30 children. Equipment density was maintained at one play set per ten children. The results of this study showed a tendency for less group play in the higher spatial density condition (though this was not statistically significant), and more aggression in the small space condition. Rough and tumble play decreased significantly as space decreased. The authors suggest a possible threshold effect of 25 square feet per child for aggressive behaviour. Increasing density to 15 square feet per child produces more aggression. These findings are contrary to the results of Loo (1972), which have already been discussed and examined in detail and criticised.

Although it is still difficult to make broad generalisations about space, one thing is becoming clear: social density and competition for resources are at least as important as spatial density in determining children's social behaviour.

Types of materials and apparatus

Not only the quantity but the specific types of play resources available to the child have been found to produce differential behavioural effects.

Kritchevsky & Prescott (1969) argued that materials that differ in their complexity, variety, and amount to do per child, relates to behaviour such as attention and social participation. Some toys and materials are also designed to be played with in specific ways and limit the number of users that can be accommodated simultaneously. For example, blocks are typically an extremely popular material that is often played with co-operatively, but they are also associated with higher levels of conflict as participants disagree (Phyfe-Perkins, 1980). The high usage of a classroom or play area need not necessarily result in high levels of social interaction. The quantity and type of material resources in an area is a crucial consideration.

An experiment by Quilitch & Risley (1973) examined the effects of changes in play materials on the patterns of interaction of seven year olds. The children were given a free choice from six social toys (e.g. checkers, playing cards, and pick-up stix) or six isolate toys (e.g. play-doh, jigsaw puzzles, and crayons) in a free-play situation. With group size constant, there were large differences in the amount of time the children played together (social play) or alone (isolate play) in the two conditions. Social play occupied 16% of the time if the children were given isolate toys, 78% of the time with social toys. If toys are removed but furniture and apparatus remain then the behaviour of children actually becomes more creative as they find novel uses for these objects in their play activities (Smith, 1974). A table may become a house, and a chair may become a car or an aeroplane.

A series of studies by Smith & Connolly (1980) varied the types and number of toys and equipment available to the child under differing levels of spatial density. If provided only with apparatus (tables, chairs, toy chests and lids, climbing frames and slides, Wendy houses, a pram, a tricycle, and a rocking boat) there was a significant increase in the observed levels of verbal and physical interaction, group play and object exchange. One of the most noticeable changes in the apparatus-only condition – the authors described it as startling – was the increased unusual use of equipment (e.g. sitting on a line of chairs or tables as an imaginary train or bus). The behavioural changes in a toys-only condition were less marked than for the apparatus-only condition. In the toys-only condition there was more table play and fine manipulation of objects, but also more automanipulation. There was less kicking, throwing, hitting, and open smiling than in the apparatus-only condition. The control condition (providing both apparatus and toys) showed lower levels of aggressive and agonistic behaviour than either experimental condition, though this was not statistically significant. Earlier studies by the authors, involving less severe equipment manipulations, showed that a decrease in amount of equipment produced more sharing of equipment but also more competition over popular items and a consequent increase in aggression and agonistic behaviour (similar to Johnson, 1935), and no major differences in level of social contact.

Thus reducing number of toys per child can lead to aggression, and variations in equipment can affect social interaction. Increases in density do not necessarily lead to an increase in aggression, though the type, amount, and availability of equipment is a crucial determining factor. Most conflict in preschoolers occurs in relation to materials (Smith and Green, 1975) and so it should come as no surprise that a reduction in these resources produces aggression in free play situations – where the most frequent activities involve the use of toys and equipment.

Toys as mediators of social interaction

This section examines children's uses of toys and equipment. More specifically, the extent to which they promote children's interaction and direct their patterns of play.

In a three-month study of children of approximately one year of age in a playgroup situation, Mueller & Lucas (1975) described a series of stages in the development of the infants' peer relationships. An important component of the model was the emphasis given to the mediating role of interaction with objects. This model will be briefly outlined as a basis for evaluating the role of toys in children's early social interactions.

The first stage in Mueller & Lucas's (1975) model occurs late in the first year of life and is object-centred. Infants will often gather around a single toy, but they pay more attention to the toy than to each other. Gradually children begin to show simultaneous attention to the same object, obvious reactions to peers, and contingent interaction sequences, marking the transition to stage two, the stage of contingency interchanges. In stage three, the stage of complementary interchanges, the child is able to interact directly with other children in a flexible, complementary fashion. The child shows deliberate attempts to influence his or her peers and a primitive reciprocity in play. This study found complex patterns of interaction to be relatively rare until the child was well into his or her second year. All these interactions were based on dyads, the authors noting that larger groups were not observed until the playgroup was reconvened after the children's second birthdays.

More recent research on infants as young as six months old casts considerable doubt on the notion that peer interaction derives from interaction with objects. In reviewing the relevant literature Hay, Pedersen & Nash (1982) conclude that infants will be most influenced by the presence of peers where there is an absence of other distractions, such as mothers or toys. A study by Vandell, Wilson & Buchanan (1980) showed that infants of 6–12 months showed more frequent and longer interaction sequences in the absence of toys. The social interaction of young infants is less reliant on object mediation than those of toddlers (Hay, Pedersen & Nash, 1982). This empirical research gives considerable credence to Lamb's (1988) argument that the stages proposed by Mueller & Lucas (1975) are probably an experimental artifact, a reflection of the way in which they coded their behavioural observations and which may have missed some subtle aspects of the interaction.

Though children of ten months to two years of age do show a basic social awareness, up to about one year of age infants with an unfamiliar peer show more interaction with another if toys are not available. Though putting this in perspective, these early interactions usually rapidly end in distressed behaviour. With toys, the interaction that does occur represents a synchronous contact with the same play material. Children will often show and exchange toys. The other child is recognised as a person and not simply another toy (Eckerman & Whatley, 1977). From about one-year to eighteen-months of age children are often found playing with toys in parallel with other children (i.e. playing near each other but not together) though sometimes co-operatively. Genuine peer interaction and cooperative play increase markedly as children enter their second year of life (Jacobson, 1981), and continues to increase in frequency through the early years of childhood. Some authors have viewed parallel play as a bridging stage between solitary and interactive play (Mueller & Brenner, 1977; Bakeman & Brownlee, 1980), though this is more important for younger children. Smith (1978) found that parallel play was a necessary intermediate stage for many 28 and 33 month olds but not for older preschoolers. The type of parallel play shown by the child is also a crucial determinant of its significance and evaluation. K. H. Rubin (1982) found that constructive parallel play (such as doing artwork at the same table) did correlate with sociometric status and social competence in terms of problem-solving ability. Conversely, parallel functional (repetitive motor activity in close proximity to other) and solitary dramatic forms of play were actually negatively associated with measures of competence and sociometric status – they appear to lead to conflict or at best lower levels of positive interaction.

Activity structure

In play, there is a commonly noted sex difference in children's choices of activity, place and objects (e.g. Harper & Sanders, 1975). Boys tend to play outside, and to be involved in active pursuits which use large amounts of space; they are more likely than girls to use sand, tractors, and climbing structures in their play. Girls were more likely to play indoors in craft and kitchen activities. Sanders & Harper (1976) further report that patterns of fantasy play appear to relate to these characteristic sex differences in places of play. Boys showed more fantasy play than girls when outdoors but girls showed more fantasy play than boys when indoors.

If boys and girls tend to prefer different types of play, it is hardly surprising that different play centres also differ in their frequency of use by boys and girls. Shure (1963) classified and recorded behaviour in five nursery school settings: art, books, games, dolls and blocks. The block areas were more likely to attract boys and produced a moderate level of social interaction. Social interchanges were also common in the doll area but relatively infrequent in art.

Although children generally show more positive behaviour and social play than negative behaviour or non-social play, their patterns of interaction appear to be determined at least in part by the play centre or activity in which they find themselves, and how they are conceptualised within the context of the classroom structure (Emihovich, 1986; Quay, Weaver & Neel, 1986). More negative social behaviour occurs when children are involved in woodwork, with blocks, dolls, and doll's houses. Art centres are relatively tranquil areas.

Because certain types of activity appear to be associated in children's preferences, their common properties have been the subject of investigation. In a study by Carpenter & Huston-Stein (1980), 30–60-month-old preschoolers were observed in free play in their classrooms. The children's activities were classified on the basis of their structure. Girls spent more time than boys in preschool activities that were highly structured by teacher feedback or the availability of adult models, and hence this was a major determinant of dependence. Boys spent more time than girls in low structure activities. This does show a basic sex difference in activity preferences, though the levels of participation in various types of activity did also vary between classes. This suggests that adults as well as the characteristics of activities are affecting children's play preferences. Comparisons across classrooms showed that children from classrooms with high rates of teacher feedback (high structure) spent more time in organised activities, were more compliant, and showed less novel behaviour. Both sexes showed less novel behaviour and more compliance in high structure activities. An important point to note about the findings of this study is that within a given activity there were no sex differences in behaviour. Specific play activities were associated with specific behaviour patterns, independent of sex. Children of both sexes showed more compliance and bids for recognition in highly structured activities and more initiative, leadership, and aggression when on low structured activities. For example, playing with blocks, or rough and tumble play, preferred by boys, is usually more aggressive and involves more interpersonal conflict in preschoolers. Art and playing house, activities typically attracting girls, are characterised by low conflict and social interchange. As there are sex differences in children's play preferences, these play activities reinforce sex-role differences in behaviour patterns. This constitutes an aspect of the child's self-socialisation.

Overall, it has been suggested that lower teacher pupil ratios or rates of teacher pupil interaction are likely to facilitate peer interaction (Field, 1980; Innocenti et al., 1986). Adult feedback produces differences in children's social behaviour, and boys and girls select activities with different levels of adult involvement. The formation of peer relationships is facilitated by ensuring that the child has plenty of opportunities to play with other children and providing toys and materials fostering appropriate interaction.

Physical environment of the classroom

Having considered the effects of other children, space, and equipment on patterns of play, it now remains to examine the physical environment of the classroom: the impact of classroom structure and facilities on patterns of interaction. The physical design of a school building or a classroom communicates expectations and has definite functional consequences not only for the children's academic performances but for their communication, play and relationships. Hall (1966) categorised space as fixed or semi-fixed. Fixed spaces would include aspects of the building such as doors, windows, and room size. Semi-fixed spaces would include items such as furniture. It is difficult to alter fixed spaces, but semi-fixed spaces are amenable to easy modification in order to maximise children's opportunities for positive interaction. The characteristics of the classroom environment interact with task and equipment characteristics to encourage co-operation, competition, or co-action. For example, seating arranged in small groups rather than rows and columns substantially changes the social climate of the classroom.

As well as providing opportunities for interaction, some educationalists also argue that there is a need for classrooms to make provision for privacy (e.g. Prescott, 1978). This would ameliorate some of the affects of crowding, examined earlier. Sheehan & Day (1975) noticed that children tended to wander, were more irritable and showed more aggressive moods in day-care centres with no private areas. They added tall dividers and low shelves for frequently used materials to a large, open classroom known for its noisy, boisterous character. There was a drop in frantic behaviour and increase in co-operation. Similar results have been reported by subsequent studies (e.g. Weinstein, 1977). As Phyfe-Perkins (1980) notes, "It seems self-evident that young children may need a chance to rest and to control or to limit their interaction with the world when they feel the need" (p. 101). The systematic, naturalistic observation of child-care centres by other authors (e.g. Moore, 1986) have similarly noted more exploratory behaviour, social interaction, and co-operation in spatially well-defined behaviour settings than in moderately or poorly defined settings.

Clearly, adult-designed classrooms are not always optimal from the child's point of view. An interesting insight into what a child-centred classroom would look like was provided by Pfluger & Zola (1974). In this study of nursery school children, their classroom was emptied and they were free to return equipment and position it as they needed it. It took on a very different appearance than previously. The piano and chairs were not returned. Semi-fixed features were arranged against the walls leaving a large, open play area.

School organisation

The effects of classroom structure and organisation has proved to be an understandably popular area of interest for educationalists and psychologists. On the one hand it is appropriate to consider the most effective classroom organisation for instructional purposes. On the other hand, one must also give regard to the social climate of the school and the opportunities for interaction that such organisation is likely to produce. A rigid organisational structure destroys the essential spontaneity and creativity of play, it becomes institutionalised (Mand, 1974). Programmes devised by adults often segregate children by age and foster skill elitism, sex discrimination, and competition rather than co-operation, participation and sharing. The result is an impoverished learning environment for what Mand (1974) termed the fourth R: relationships.

A number of studies have examined how school children across a wide age range benefit from teaching strategies based on open classroom structures and small group problem solving. In these contexts pupils come to appreciate their interpersonal connectedness and the value of co-operative interdependence (Dlugokinski, 1984). Pupils from classrooms emphasising co-operation and interdependence perceive their peers and teachers as more positive, friendly and supportive (Johnson & Johnson, 1983). Classroom organisation and social climate are, of course, interdependent factors, but they do not exist in isolation. Social and spatial density are likely to be important factors affecting the implementation of different forms of classroom organisation.

The preschool classroom

The topic of school organisation has been the subject of a great deal of research by educationalists. It is now well established that classroom organisation affects friendship choices. A popular comparison used to highlight this fact has been between traditional, highly structured classroom formats and open, less structured formats. The major criterion often used for distinguishing between these formats is whether the child's activity is determined by the teacher or the child's own choice. An open classroom structure allows the child a greater degree of self-determination and exploration. Open tasks include block and doll play. The closed classroom structure tends to discourage exploration and be more directive toward the child. There is typically more involvement in less mobile activities such as copying tasks or puzzles. Friendship occurs when interaction contexts overlay one another (Button, 1979) and so the open classroom typically provides a greater functional availability of partners.

The school environment shapes children's behaviour from a relatively early age. Its effect on sex segregation in children's play and friendships was shown in a study by Bianchi & Bakeman (1978). This study examined children in traditional and open nursery schools. In both types of school the children typically spent over 80% of their time in free play with other children. But in the traditional school, which emphasises the active socialisation of the child and conventional standards of behaviour, this was more often in same-sex groups. Although the organisation of the school was probably confounded with other factors (such as the social attitudes and educational preferences of parents), this study none the less shows the potential importance of the school as part of the child's broader socialisation.

The influence of the preschool has also been revealed in children's patterns of helping behaviour (Simmons & Sands-Dudelczyk, 1983). High rates of helping responses are common among preschoolers, though different preschool environments appear to emphasise and produce different behaviours in reacting to another child's need for help. In a transactional analysis preschool children were likely to offer comfort and assistance. Montessori preschoolers provided compliant help. Only in the traditional preschool programme did the children offer to get adult help.

An important point to bear in mind is that the organisation of a school is at least partly determined by its size. Gump (1978) cites a study by Prescott (1973) showing that large day-care centres were likely to have more formal, closed structures whereas open structures were associated with smaller schools. Presumably a larger institution requires formalised structures to maintain effective organisation. This creates one effect due to social density that occurs before the child even arrives at the school. Presumably changing the organisation of these schools to produce a more open system would necessitate reducing their size, though the benefits of this should not be overestimated. A positive school ethos or climate should be a more important first consideration (Rutter, 1979).

The school classroom

The social impact of classroom organisation is likely to be even more marked in the grade school than the preschool because of the greater emphasis on academic achievements. It is important to recognise the significance of the context of classroom interaction for children's social relationships (Button, 1979). Co-operative interactions tend to produce positive peer attitudes while competitive interactions may produce quite the opposite effect. A study by Zahn, Kagan & Widaman (1986) compared the use of co-operative learning techniques and traditional whole-class methods of instruction with groups of second to sixth graders. Co-operative techniques produced a more favourable climate for social relations and better schoolwork attitudes. Classroom structure can be an important determinant of classroom climate and the child's social experience of school.

An illuminating study by Maureen Hallinan (1979) examined the effects of classroom organisation on the friendship choices of children in grades four to eight. The major interest of this study was a comparison of traditional classrooms (where there is often minimal peer interaction; students are often assigned to seats and instruction groups by the teacher) with open classrooms (where children choose their own seating and grouping arrangements and there is greater freedom for peer interaction). This analysis came up with the surprising finding that more best friend nominations were made in the traditional classrooms than in the open classrooms. The author suggested that this effect was a function of the traditional classroom providing less opportunity for such assertions of friendship to be disconfirmed! Supporting this, friendship networks are generally more integrated in open classrooms and there are fewer unilateral choices (Hallinan, 1976). The general pattern of variation in popularity also appeared to be greater in the setting of the traditional classroom. They contained both more popular and more unpopular children. The smaller classes did tend to produce more social isolates, possibly because of the lesser opportunities to find a compatible partner. Open classes also tended to produce more social isolates, suggesting that the skills and demands of friendships in these circumstances produce more social casualties.

Within the broad pattern outlined above, the social climate of the formal classroom is experienced as different according to the child's location within it. The best seating positions are much-prized possessions. In a study of ninth graders, MacPherson (1984) found that the front of row and column classrooms was associated with attention to academic matters and dependence on teachers. The back had fewer opportunities for attention to academic matters but greater freedom for peer interaction. Pupil's seating choices reflected the individual's weighting of academic and social opportunities.

Some of the mechanisms through which classroom organisation achieves its effects on children's peer relationships were examined in a useful longitudinal study by Hallinan & Tuma (1978). These authors argued that the way pupils were grouped, and teaching techniques, affected children's proximity and similarity in the classroom, and these in turn affect relationships. In a study of fourth, fifth and sixth graders the authors found that classroom variables did indeed have an impact on the stability of existing friendships and on the probability that children would become more friendly. Children experiencing greater proximity and opportunities for interaction, as indicated by having the same reading teacher and the percentage of reading time in which the class is organised in small groups, showed an increased likelihood of choosing each other as friends. The authors summarise the observed similarity effects by stating that "The overall results suggest that in classrooms where different groups work on the same topic and/or on the same materials, students are more likely to form close friendships" (p. 279). The impact of classroom variables is greater on weak rather than strong friendships.

The primary concern of most parents is that the school that their child attends provides them with a sound academic experience. This does not conflict with an emphasis that schools and classrooms should be organised to give the child a stimulating social experience. Far from it. Classroom structures facilitating good social relations in children do not detract from their academic attitudes or performance. Quite the contrary, they often prove beneficial. As Root (1977) notes, peer groups are important in everyday classroom functioning. Pupils' attitudes to school and academic work are affected by their peer group relationships, which in turn affect the whole social climate and atmosphere of the class.

9 Relationship problems and collapse

A review and analysis of the literature indicates general support for the hypothesis that children with poor peer adjustment are at risk for later life difficulties.

(Parker & Asher, 1987, p. 357)

From the earliest days of research on personal relationships there has been a concern over the importance of childhood relationships for later social and psychological adjustment, including the capacity for intimacy in later adolescent and adult relationships. This has resulted in considerable attention being devoted to relationship problems and methods of intervention.

Many problems associated with forming and maintaining relationships have, by default, already been discussed in the process of considering the factors which contribute to successful relating. For example, the differences in social skills between successful and unsuccessful relators (examined in Chapter 4) show both what the socially competent child is doing right and what the less competent child is doing wrong. These factors have been covered in the preceding chapters. In this section attention will be more specifically directed to the problems encountered within relationships themselves and the problems of relating experienced by children with specific problems and handicaps. It is important to note at this point that there is no agreed taxonomy of children's relationship problems (Gottman, 1991). A word of caution is appropriate: It is too easy to think of children's friendships as homogenous. Even a cursory observation will reveal this not to be the case. Thus an adequate approach must explain both the broad pattern of problems that generally characterise the course of relationship development and the differences between individuals in their patterns of relating (Tesch, 1983). Unfortunately most of the literature on differences in patterns of relating implies that some styles are good and some others are bad and must be "cured" or improved. This chapter examines some of the major problems that children experience with their relationships. Certain types or levels of relationships are not in themselves problematic: if a child is happy to play alone then that child does not have a relationship problem. If that child is alone because she or he wants to form friendships but lacks the skills necessary to initiate or maintain them, then it is appropriate to regard this as a problem.

Several factors can be pinpointed as important in children's relationship problems. First, relationships have history and so previous relationships and patterns of care will influence current patterns of relating. This has been touched on at several points in this book – most notably in Chapter 1, when considering the impact of attachment and styles of parenting on later peer relationships – and so will not be considered further in this chapter. A second major source of problems in relationships derives from the characteristics of the participants. Some of these characteristics of individuals are significant in their own right, some have an adverse effect simply because of the way they relate to the characteristics of the other person. Characteristics such as physical handicaps, mental handicaps, and problems of personal adjustment are likely to make relationships generally more difficult to initiate and maintain. On the other hand, some characteristics, values, and patterns of behaviour are problematic only because of the other person's values, attitudes, and behaviour.

As outlined earlier in this book, different characteristics are important at different points in relationships. The implication here is that different types of incompatibility will be significant at different points in relationships. The disadvantage of a visible handicap, for example, is likely to be greatest in the early stages of a relationship; it will put others off making social approaches to the child. If this can be overcome then, all else being equal, a normal relationship will ensue. A third broad group of factors affecting the course of relationships derive from the dynamics of the relationships themselves. Some aspects of a relationship will be unique and not predicted from the behaviour that the partners give and receive in other social contexts (Ross & Lollis, 1989). Obviously these three broad groups of factors, the characteristics of the relators and the history and dynamics of the relationship, are interrelated. Relationship problems can both cause and result from broader psychological problems. For example, handicap often leads to problems of attachment and poor attachment is predictive of poor patterns of peer relationships. The prognosis for these problems of relating to others is also affected by the relationships that the child is able to establish, and both these factors are also undoubtedly related to other social and biological influences. All in all this produces a very complicated picture. For the sake of simplicity each of the broad groups of individual and relationship factors will be examined in turn. First, individual problems and their impact on social relationships.

Individual psychopathology

A number of detailed reviews have examined the impact of various disorders on relationships. These have included developmental disabilities such as mental retardation, learning disabilities, and attention deficit disorder (Wallander & Hubert, 1987; Wiener, 1987; Klein & Mannuzza, 1991). Clinical texts have also recorded the social deficits found in more severely disordered individuals (e.g. Herbert, 1991), though there remains an urgent need to further integrate clinical, social and developmental perspectives within the study of personal relationships. Too often the literature in these different areas is all too obviously limited by a self-imposed restricted perspective. The literature is vast and so this review must necessarily be selective in its focus. We will examine two main types of psychological disorder and their implications for relationships: pervasive developmental disorders and mental retardation.

Pervasive developmental disorders

Psychol.
emotion associated or
with an idea or
set of ideas

Along with schizophrenia these constitute the most severe of childhood disorders. Cognition, affect, behaviour, personality and social relationships are all disturbed. Autism is typically evident before 30 months of age, though other forms of pervasive developmental disorder occur after a period of normal development, between three and twelve years of age. Estimates of the incidence of autism have typically been about four or five children in 10 000 (Wing et al., 1976), though some estimates have doubled this figure (Bryson, Clark & Smith, 1988). This probably reflects the strictness of the diagnostic criteria that are applied. For detailed descriptions, see textbooks on clinical child psychology (e.g. Frith, 1989), this brief discussion will focus on the impact of these disorders on the child's social relationships.

Autism derives its very name from its defining feature, autistic aloneness (Kanner, 1943). Autistic children vary considerably in their level of adaptation, though diagnostic schemes such as the DSM–III–R (American Psychiatric Association, 1987) do indicate a distinct diagnostic profile. Kanner (1943) argues that there are two necessary and sufficient features: autistic aloneness and an obsessive insistence on sameness.

Autistic aloneness represents an inability to relate to others in an ordinary way from the beginning of life. The child's social deficits are evident from the earliest time when attachment to the caregiver would be expected (Rutter, 1978), though the portrayal of the autistic child as totally lacking in social interest and responsiveness is an overly bleak picture. Some autistic children even show apparently normal attachment behaviours toward the mother initially. Indeed, the portrayal of autistic children as unresponsive is doing them a grave disservice. Impressive work by Sigman and her associates has begun to reveal more precisely the nature of the autistic child's deficits. In a study by Sigman et al. (1986) the social interaction of 3–6-year-old autistic children with their caregivers was compared with the behaviour of normal children and mentally retarded non-autistic children of the same mental age. Autistic children showed lower frequency of attention sharing (such as pointing or showing objects to the mother). They did not, however, show deficits in looking, vocalising and proximity behaviour. Where gestures are used by autistic children they are more likely to be simple, instrumental communication (e.g. come here) rather than an attempt to share attention or feelings. Thus although the autistic children did show a definite social deficit they were far from unresponsive.

As Volkmar et al. (1987) point out, the autistic child is not devoid of social interest and responsiveness at any age. Indeed, many of the autistic child's problems are simply due to mental retardation, though many other social deficits are also distinct from those shown by mentally retarded non-autistic children. In many skills the autistic child is able to cope rather well, with simple self-care for example, though in interpersonal skills the handicap is severe. The autistic child is poor at interpersonal communication and co-ordination (evident in activities such as sharing, co-operation etc.). Levels of socially directed and symbolic (meaningful) communication are directly related to the autistic child's level of social and cognitive functioning (McHale et al., 1980).

Social interaction and relationships

The social isolation of the autistic child is most marked between about three and five years of age. The social skills of the child improve with age, though socialisation is a long, slow process, impeded by the deficits in language and general communication skills. Learning the appropriateness of behaviour is especially difficult and this often makes it easier for the child to interact with teachers and caregivers than peers (McHale et al., 1980). Adults will often make allowances for the autistic child's difficulties. While relations with adults show improvement with age, social impairments in peer relations become increasingly clear after the age of about five years. Most autistic children and adolescents do not show an ability to work or play co-operatively and do not form friendships. And yet this, at least in part, reflects the social consequences of deficits rather than a lack of potential. Autistic children have difficulties forming and maintaining friendships with each other because they have similar social deficits and the combined obstacle this presents is usually insurmountable. In contrast, non-autistic children are better able to compensate for an autistic peer's social deficits, but they also tend to find the relationships demanding, difficult, and unrewarding. The autistic child does not represent an attractive playmate. Where opportunities for autistic children to interact with normal peers are manipulated, corresponding improvements in their levels of participation in peer interaction and relationships are noted (Lord, 1984). These improvements represent genuine qualitative advances. As Lord (1984, p. 222) notes, "Many of the autistic subjects in these studies gave clear indications that they did care about their partners (as did *some* of the non-handicapped children), for example by asking for them, looking for them, or crying when there was no play session". Unfortunately, this places great demands and requires great effort from the normal child, which is often not forthcoming in the normal classroom situation. The autistic child is consequently often isolated and handicapped both by original deficits and by social opportunities.

Autistic children are often happiest when left to their own devices. They appear bright and alert but aloof, just beyond the reach of communication. They are often described as being apparently on a different wavelength, as if they are cut off by an invisible wall or barrier. Wanlass & Prinz (1982) recognise autism as the extreme case of social withdrawal. A colleague of mine sums up this feature succinctly as a "black hole" for relationships. The child appears aloof and unresponsive, not anticipating or responding positively to attempts to initiate social interaction or physical contact, detached and looking through rather than at social figures. Emotions, moods and social responsiveness are evident, though these are often idiosyncratic and inappropriate to the prevailing social conditions (Ricks & Wing, 1976). In comparison to other children of the same mental age, both normal and mentally retarded but non-autistic, the autistic child is also likely to have more difficulties in correctly identifying emotions in others (Hobson, 1986a, b). The autistic child also invariably shows gross language disturbance and insistence on maintaining the existing order in objects and routine. Together these characteristics differentiate the autistic child from mental retarded non-autistic children.

Mental retardation and Down's syndrome

Mental retardation refers not only to low measured IQ (below about 70) but has as part of its necessary diagnostic profile impairments in adaptive behaviour, which includes social interaction skills. About 3% of the population show these characteristics. There are many possible causes for mental retardation: biological, social, and psychological. See specialised texts on child psychopathology (e.g. Schwartz & Johnson, 1985) for a more detailed discussion of these factors.

There is no known organic basis for most cases of mental retardation. This psychosocial retardation accounts for about 85% of diagnosed cases. The commonest single factor cause of mental retardation, possibly accounting for up to 20% of severely retarded children, is Down's syndrome. The incidence of Down's syndrome is about one in 600. The syndrome is due to a genetic condition (an extra chromosome) which produces several distinct physical abnormalities and characteristics (such as the eye shape which led to the syndrome originally being called mongolism) as well as mental retardation which is apparent during the first year. Down's syndrome children typically have IQs between 20 and 50, though they occasionally achieve an IQ of up to 60. There is considerable variability in their actual level of retardation and personality development. The cognitive and social development of mentally retarded children is similar to that of normal children, though slower and perhaps less even. Levels of affiliation and social status correlate with IQ and academic ability (MacMillan & Morrison, 1980).

In a study of moderately retarded adolescents, with IQs of around 50, Siperstein & Bak (1989) found similar social structures to those found in classrooms for pupils without mental retardation. There were differences in popularity, in acceptance and rejection, the students were selective in choosing friends and playmates, and there was reciprocity in friendship choices. Perhaps more so than adolescents without mental retardation, these individuals also nominated as friends peers from other classes, opposite sex peers and adults in the special school and community. The nomination of adults and peers from other classes probably reflects the unusual circumstances of the special school environment, and the special attention these children received from adults. The relative lack of sex segregation in relationships is comparable with findings on early elementary school-age children (with whom these adolescents are comparable in terms of mental age), though it does seem to raise the question as to whether these adolescents will ever progress to a stage where sex segregation is the norm.

Attempts to foster the integration of retarded children in the main school system have met with only limited success from a social relations point of view. Elementary school-children often indicate less liking for mentally retarded children and increased contact through integrated classrooms or open plan schools often increases their level of rejection as friends (Gottlieb & Leyser, 1981a). This reflects their perceived lesser competence in the classroom. Children have more positive attitudes towards playing with retarded children than working with them (Gottlieb, 1971). Perhaps a more co-operative rather than competitive approach is necessary to ameliorate these problems (Gottlieb & Leyser, 1981b). At present, even effective interventions produce only small improvements in the retarded child's social status and do not bring it on a par with that of non-retarded peers (Ballard et al., 1977). Though mainstreaming is commonly regarded as an essential prerequisite for promoting social competence in handicapped children (Guralnick, 1990), Gottlieb & Leyser (1981a, p. 163) have concluded that "there is little evidence that mainstreaming operates to the social or academic advantage of retarded children. The friendships with non-retarded children that were supposed to result from mainstreaming have, for the most part, not developed". None the less these authors do point out that appropriate intervention should still be sought in order to maximise the child's social potential.

Physical handicap and stigma

The literature on physical handicap, disfigurement and stigma provides a great deal of support for the notion that physical appearance can be an important determinant of a child's experiences and behaviour. The Greeks originally used the term stigma to refer to a sign cut or burnt on to the body to indicate a person's moral status, perhaps as a criminal or slave (Goffman, 1963). Modern usage retains some points of similarity but usually refers to negative physical or mental characteristics, "to an attribute that is deeply discrediting" (Goffman, 1963, p. 13). Disfigured individuals are often aware of the negative attitude toward them and anticipate and experience discrimination in a number of realms.

In terms of children it is sometimes difficult to separate the consequences resulting from abnormalities of physical appearance from effects due to the functional limitations of a disability – though visibility is a crucial factor in the stigmatising of handicap (Goffman, 1963). Problems of appearance (and especially facial disfigurement) are sometimes more stigmatising than a physical disability. For example, vitiligo, a disfiguring skin disorder involving patchy depigmentation of the skin, is often a traumatic and isolating condition for the sufferer but involves no functional disability (Hill-Beuf & Porter, 1984).

The more visible a handicap the more it disrupts the smooth flow of interaction. As the face is one of the most significant sources of non-verbal and verbal communication (Argyle, 1988) it requires attention and consequently disfigurement here is the most noticed, distracting and stigmatised. In an influential early study by Richardson et al. (1961) children were shown a standard set of drawings of children differing in physical characteristics and appearance. As predicted by the authors, there was consistency in the children's perceptions and evaluations of the stimulus figures. The most visible and stigmatised form of physical appearance was obesity, followed by facial disfigurement, and limb abnormalities. The authors concluded that liking is greater for individuals whose disability is more distant from his face. These results have been confirmed by more recent research (Giancoli & Neimeyer, 1983).

A number of possible reasons why disfigurement and physical handicaps affect social interaction have been suggested. Included in these is the notion that many people are unsure how to behave toward the disfigured individual (Hastorf, Wildfogel and Cassman, 1979). This problem is exacerbated in relation to the face because of its visibility and communicative significance.

People often find gaze and eye contact difficult with a facially disfigured individual because of their concern that normal gaze patterns will be interpreted as staring and lead to embarrassment. But the catch-22 is that successful communication and social interaction is considerably more difficult without facial non-verbal communication.

Developmental patterns

In children the earliest form of stigmatisation is a general bias against anyone physically deviant or different. In general, handicapped children are perceived as less attractive than their able-bodied peers. This early prejudice is largely due to the normal cognitive processes of the child. In young children categorisations are likely to be based on the physical and behavioural characteristics of other people (rather than more abstract attributions) and tend to be simple, superficial and exclusive (Piaget, 1970; Livesley & Bromley, 1973). Studies have suggested that children of nursery school to third-grade age show a preference for non-disabled peers of the same race and sex as themselves (Sigelman, Miller & Whitworth, 1986). An interesting finding of this study was that attraction to a wheelchair-bound individual increased with age while liking for obese and facially disfigured individuals decreased with age. There was also a tendency for girls to be more positive toward the wheelchair-bound child while boys were more positive toward the children with visual defects (obesity and facial disfigurement). This again seems to confirm the sex differences in the physical attractiveness phenomenon that have been previously noted – the greater importance of physical appearance for girls and the importance of physical abilities in boys' relationships.

Sociometric studies of children across a wide age range have shown that children with obvious physical handicaps, such as physical deformity, are perceived as less attractive, are less likely to be chosen as friends, and are less likely to have their choice of best friend reciprocated (Kleck & De Jong, 1983). Children with amputations are more likely to be nominated by their peers as saddest, least liked, least nice looking, and the least fun in class – though they may, of course, actually be different from their peers in behavioural terms (Centers & Centers, 1963). Simple exposure to handicapped individuals does not affect evaluations of handicap (Richardson, 1971), possibly because of peer group stereotypes and values (Rumsey, Bull & Gahagan, 1986), though it can ameliorate the way in which individuals are evaluated and treated because of their appearance (Richardson, Ronald & Kleck, 1974).

As we have already noted that physical attractiveness is often more significant for girls than boys, it is not surprising that Kleck & De Jong (1983) also found that the association between perceived attractiveness and sociometric rank was most marked for girls. More interesting was the finding that the physically disabled children had a lesser knowledge of the strategies for making friends. This social skills deficit is an area where immediate help could be given.

The implications of physical handicap and disfigurement for the individual depends on a number of factors, including the type of disorder, personality, age and situational influences. Problems with physical appearance are important factors predisposing expectancies and behaviour toward the individual, even to very young infants. Prematurity or physical abnormalities results in biological cues to cuteness and attractiveness being absent or distorted (Hildebrandt & Fitzgerald, 1983). Research has found a strong negative correlation between children's perceived attractiveness and predictions of abuse (Roscoe, Callahan & Peterson (1985). The possibility that this stereotype is a factor in child abuse is important and is certainly worthy of further research.

The junior high school years are especially traumatic for children with a disfigured appearance. This is an age when peer relationships are assuming increasing importance (Buhrmester & Furman, 1987) and there is a great concern over physical appearance and attractiveness (Freedman, 1984). But it is often also a time of stress because of changing school. Added together, these two factors result in a great deal of distress for the disfigured adolescent. Fortunately this situation can be alleviated by other interests and abilities that provide self-esteem (Hill-Beuf & Porter, 1984).

To the extent that an attractive appearance is essential to feminine gender role, striving to achieve this can cause adjustment problems even for many adolescent girls without abnormalities. They may suffer from a negative body image, eating disorders, self-consciousness, feelings of low self-esteem, and withdrawal (Freedman, 1984). Perhaps contrary to what one might intuitively expect, these problems of adjustment are often greater for attractive young adolescent girls than for their less attractive counterparts as their appearance is a more significant component of their self-esteem (Zakin, Blyth & Simmons, 1984).

Patterns of intervention

Not only is physical appearance associated with social adjustment and achievement, it also affects any remedial treatment which is recommended. Ross & Salvia (1975) found that elementary school teachers were more willing to recommend special class placement for unattractive children. In a further study Elovitz & Salvia (1982) presented a fictitious case report of a third-grade pupil to a large number of school psychologists. This report included a photograph of an attractive or unattractive child. The recommendations of the psychologists were commonly that the attractive child should be placed in programmes concerned with learning disability or socioemotional problems, or even in regular classes. The unattractive children were more likely to be placed in more stigmatising mental retardation classes and were expected to experience greater difficulties in peer relationships and future psychological evaluations.

Despite the many sad consequences of physical handicap and deformity it is still possible to end on a happy note. Many children do emerge from their battles against handicap, stigma, and possible social isolation and confound the predictions of many theorists that they should be maladjusted or develop deviant personality styles. Often such is not the case, especially with early treatment. With further research and understanding of the role of physical appearance in social interaction, perhaps in the future yet more children will be helped to find this happy ending.

Individual–situational problems

This is still a rather vague area, though it is possible to delineate (rather arbitrarily) some problems which are the product both of an individual's characteristics and the situation in which she or he finds him or herself. Two most popular topics to be addressed by the literature on personal relationships have been shyness and loneliness. The major literature on these topics refers to adults, though with a growing interest in children's relationships the last decade or so has seen a dramatic increase in developmental research in these areas. Each of these topics will be examined in turn.

Shyness

Extreme social withdrawal and isolation resulting from severe shyness and introversion have been acknowledged as significant disorders of childhood (American Psychiatric Association, 1987). But neither social withdrawal nor shyness are solely characteristic of clinical populations, they also represent considerable if less severe problems for many other children. This is a relatively under-researched developmental phenomenon, though Zimbardo & Radl (1981) have published a "parents' guide" to the shy child. Shy children and adolescents are likely to have fewer and less satisfying peer relationships (Richmond, 1984). "Children who cannot ask for themselves will often begin to shrink from the world, feeling that others do not give to them because they are not worth caring for" (Rotheram, 1980, p. 69). "Rather than acting so as to gain approval, the shy person acts so as to minimise disapproval" (Zimbardo & Radl, 1981, p. 81). These isolated children are likely to report and to be perceived as more lonely than their more outgoing counterparts (e.g. Rubin & Mills, 1988). Unlike loneliness, however, a degree of shyness has been seen as having a functional basis. A degree of shyness is normal and adaptive to the extent that it allows situations to be assessed before the child ventures forth and commits him or herself to a course of action (Zimbardo & Radl, 1981).

Most people can recall periods in their life when they have been shy (Zimbardo, Pilkonis & Norwood, 1974). In a German study preschool-teachers classified 16.8% of children as shy-inhibited (Asendorpf, 1986). Zimbaro & Radl (1981) report a survey of parents and teachers which found that more than 30% of preschoolers showed shyness. The authors argue that the problem gets worse with age, especially as the child's social world widens in adolescence. In an older sample, Lazarus (1982) found 38% of fifth graders rated themselves as shy. Adults typically report about a 40% incidence, though 54% of seventh and eighth graders report themselves as shy (Zimbardo, 1977). This indicates that early adolescence is a crucial time for the experience of shyness. Shy stages and shy feelings are normal aspect of many people's lives.

Evidence also suggests that shyness and passive isolation become increasingly stable characteristics of the individual with age (Rubin & Mills, 1988). This conclusion must be advanced with caution. The strongest evidence for the increasing developmental stability of shyness comes from peer ratings rather than systematic observation. These ratings could consequently reflect improvements in the social cognitive abilities of the peer group rather than genuine changes in the stability of the child's personal characteristics (Younger, Schwartzman & Ledingham, 1986; Rubin, Hymel & Mills, 1989).

Shyness has been defined as "the tendency to be tense, worried, and awkward during social interactions with strangers, casual acquaintances, and persons in positions of authority" (Cheek et al., 1986, p. 105). It is probably, however, also worth including the commonly mentioned notion that shyness is "an ambivalent affective state" (Asendorpf, 1986, p. 93), it represents attraction to interaction partners and yet a wariness of them. This is perhaps typically shown in the behaviour of children anxiously "hovering" on the periphery of a peer group (Gottman, 1977a). Shyness has cognitive, affective and, usually, behavioural components. This distinguishes it from forms of rejection where the child wishes to participate but is prevented, and social withdrawal or disinterest, which is simply an unconflicted avoidance of social contact. There has, unfortunately, been relatively little direct research on shyness in childhood, and what there has been has seldom adequately distinguished it from simple social withdrawal, isolation and introversion. Failure to make this distinction has profound implications for the child: labelling a quiet, reserved child as shy may come to produce a self-fulfilling prophecy (Zimbardo & Radl, 1981).

Situational and dispositional shyness

As with loneliness, shyness as has been conceptualised as having both dispositional (trait) and situational (state) components. This acknowledges that aspects of a situation can elicit shyness but also that some children show more consistent shyness across a broad range of situations and over an extended period of time (Asendorpf, 1986). Situational shyness is a transient state aroused in specific social situations. For example, some children show stable shy-withdrawn behaviour at kindergarten but do do not behave in the same way at home (Chamberlin, 1977). Specific characteristics of situations have been noted as making them more likely to elicit shy behaviour. The novelty of a situation, the presence of others, and the actions of others (e.g. their attention) can all serve to elicit shyness (Buss, 1980). School-children often feel particularly shy among strangers and when they are the focus of attention (Zimbardo & Radl, 1981). Dispositional shyness represents a tendency to react with shyness with a degree of temporal consistency and in a broad range of situations. It is important to note that these dimensions are inextricably linked; it is impossible to conceive of one without the other. Shyness is the result of the interplay between the individual's characteristics and the cues provided by the social situation.

Fearful and self-conscious shyness

A further distinction between different types of shyness has been made on the basis of their origins within child development (Buss, 1986). These have been termed fearful and self-conscious or early and late appearing forms of shyness. Children differ markedly in their temperamental fearfulness, and research shows a strong genetic component in this trait (Buss & Plomin, 1984). Because fearful shyness has a genetic basis it is relatively more enduring than self-conscious shyness (Plomin & Daniels, 1986). Fearful shyness is characterised by a sensitivity to novelty, intrusion and, in older children, social evaluation.

The early expression of fearful shyness is seen in the stranger anxiety that becomes evident during the child's first year of life – a common indicator of attachment. This response to unfamiliar people (adults initially and children later) usually elicits wariness and the child seeking the security of contact with the mother. It can also provoke more intense reactions such as crying. This stranger anxiety is normal and obviously adaptive for the young child, though it tends to wane as children mature and develop more sophisticated means of coping, of maintaining contact with the parents, and are more secure in their relationship with the parent. None the less a continuity of stranger anxiety is shown even in the third and fourth years of life. A majority of children still show some degree of ambivalence (a mix of wary and sociable behaviour) and act shy at least briefly in response to the approach of strange adults while they are in the presence of their mothers (Greenberg & Marvin, 1982). In novel social situations infants and young children often show hesitancy, gaze aversion, and automanipulation. It is interesting to note that because of cognitive limitations stranger anxiety towards peers usually develops later than that towards adults. The child only shows stranger anxiety once she or he has established a stable schema for the faces of her or his regular companions (Kagan, Kearsley & Zelazo, 1975). Shyness towards peers thus occurs later than towards adults because of the lesser contact with peers making the establishment of such schemata more problematic.

Developments in social perspective-taking mean that at about the age of four or five years the child becomes aware of the self as a social object and understands that some feelings or thoughts should not be revealed. Buss (1986) sees late developing or self-conscious shyness as the result of the development of this state of public self-awareness. Individual differences in this self-awareness constitute the trait of public self-consciousness. Children high in public self-consciousness are (according to Buss) more sensitive to the impact of their own behaviour and personality on others and this makes them prone to shyness. With these new-found abilities comes the capacity to feel embarrassed. Three years of age is about the earliest at which most mothers report their children as showing embarrassment or blushing. The incidence gradually increases over the next two years and peaks in five year olds from whence it remains in a steady majority of children (Buss, Iscoe & Buss, 1979). Self-conscious shyness is characterised by a sensitivity to criticism, breaches of privacy, being uniquely different, and formal situations.

Studies suggest that the larger number of young adolescents, relative to the number of younger children or older adolescents, that label themselves as shy reflects their greater self-consciousness. Just as Zimbardo (1977) noted shyness peaking in early adolescence, Simmons, Rosenberg & Rosenberg (1973) also noted that self-consciousness peaks in this age group. This increased self-consciousness of the young adolescent has its roots in social and cognitive changes that are occurring at this age.

In terms of cognitive developments in adolescence, Elkind (1978) noted that for some adolescents the onset of abstract, formal operational thinking promotes a period of egocentrism. The young egocentric adolescent perceives him or herself to be the centre of attention and evaluation and is immensely concerned with the reactions of others. This self-preoccupation produces an anxious shyness (Crozier, 1979). In a study by Elkind & Bowen (1979), spanning grades four to twelve, self-consciousness was found to peak in early adolescence (approximately 12–14 years of age) and then decline somewhat. This mirrors the previously noted pattern of adolescent shyness and suggests that the increase in shyness is due to this factor (i.e. it is an increase in self-conscious shyness).

The multi-determination of shyness

It is again appropriate at this point to emphasise the interrelationship of personal and situational determinants of shyness. Situational factors are a major component in the early adolescent upsurge in shyness. In particular, Buss (1980) notes that the major cause of shyness is novelty. And there is an awful lot of it around at various points in the child's life. As an infant and toddler the child is constantly encountering new and strange figures – most of a rather large size in comparison to the child him or herself. Isolation means that the child does not have the opportunity to develop strategies to cope with these strangers and to learn how to relate to them. "With younger children, shyness seems more related to a lack of appropriate social skills than to the overwhelming social anxiety that gets built up in older people over years" (Zimbardo & Radl, 1981, p. 90). As the child enters adolescence novelty again rears its head and is associated with feelings of conspicuousness. Hence self-conscious shyness is especially crucial at this time. The child is changing physically with the advent of puberty, psychologically with the advent of formal operational thinking, and socially in terms of new roles and relationships (Cheek et al., 1986). From this perspective it is not surprising that adolescence is a time when shyness increases markedly (Zimbardo, 1977).

The interaction between social personal factors is nicely shown in the study by Simmons, Rosenberg & Rosenberg (1973), which has already been mentioned. This study showed a peak in shyness in early adolescence but, more interestingly, the self-consciousness of 12 year olds starting junior high school was greater than those remaining in elementary school. Just as this transition is a major intensifier of age trends in shyness, so are other social, physical, and psychological changes that are occurring at this time.

Sex differences in shyness

Before leaving the topic of shyness it is appropriate to consider the extent to which the broad pattern outlined above is complicated by possible sex differences in the incidence or experience of shyness. Girls typically report greater increases in self-consciousness after the age of 11 than do boys (Simmons & Rosenberg, 1975). The increased prevalence of children labelling themselves as shy in junior high school is largely accounted for by girls (Elkind & Bowen, 1979). This is in accord with social stereotypes which portray shyness as more appropriate and acceptable in girls than boys (Bronson,

1966). Elementary school-teachers are considerably more likely to nominate girls than boys as being among the most shy youngsters in their classes (Lazarus, 1982).

Despite the above considerations, boys and girls are equally concerned with attracting the opposite sex. Boys often regard their shyness as a greater personal problem than do girls. The demands of the male sex role, with its emphasis on leadership, interpersonal confidence and assertiveness, means that boys are more likely to experience distress and behavioural problems associated with shyness than are girls. Girls report being more concerned about physical appearance than shyness (Porteus, 1979).

Loneliness

Loneliness is a topic closely related to shyness – shy children, children who do not take the initiative in social relationships, are also more likely to be lonely children. The topic of loneliness has received considerable attention from psychologists interested in personal relationships. Unfortunately, most interest and research has focused on adult populations (Asher et al., 1990). However, in the study of loneliness this is not simply an oversight. Part of the explanation for the relative paucity of developmental research is due to the perception by many authors that true loneliness cannot be experienced until adolescence, with the advent of more sophisticated cognitive abilities and greater peer-directed intimacy needs (Sullivan, 1953; Weiss, 1973). Loneliness peaks in adolescence and is among the most frequent problems mentioned by the adolescent (Brennan, 1982). But this in itself does not mean that loneliness is not experienced by children. Around 10% of elementary school-children are not named as a friend by anyone in their class and 10–20% are actively rejected by their classmates (Burleson, 1985). In similar vein, Asher, Hymel & Renshaw (1984) found that more than 10% of third- through sixth-grade children reported feelings of loneliness and social dissatisfaction. Contrary to some opinion, children do have well-developed notions of loneliness (Asher & Parker, 1989). As is evident in even the most casual observation of children, and as Z. Rubin (1982) points out, children do experience the pain of social isolation. This is evident in children at least as young as three, and while it "may differ in its details from the loneliness of adolescents or adults, I believe that we are talking about the same basic experience". (Z. Rubin, 1982, p. 266).

Paralleling earlier developments with adults, several authors have constructed reliable scales to measure loneliness in children across a wide age range (Asher & Parker, 1989). These show a modest correlation with sociometric status. Unpopular children show higher levels of loneliness than their popular counterparts (Asher, Hymel & Renshaw, 1984). However, closer examination shows that most of this effect is due to children that are actively rejected. Children simply neglected by their peers do not show any significant differences from their popular counterparts (Asher & Wheeler, 1985). This association is not surprising, indeed it would have been worrying if it had not been found, as the scale measures *loneliness and social dissatisfaction* and contains items relating to social isolation, such as "It's hard for me to make friends", "I am well liked by the kids in my class", and "I have nobody to talk to". It is hoped that the development of instruments to reliably measure loneliness in children will mark the advent of more extensive research activity in this area.

Defining loneliness

Many and varied definitions of loneliness have been proposed. A common agreement amongst them is that loneliness is a negative affective state based on the child's perception of inadequacy (in number or quality) of his or her social relationships (Peplau & Perlman, 1982). Note the word perception – lonely children do not necessarily have fewer or worse relationships than other people, but they do see them as inadequate. They associate loneliness with specific situations and the experience of a sense of marginalisation, distress, which is ultimately reflected in a sense of worthlessness, a feeling that they are not worth liking and that there must be something wrong with them.

The distinction is sometimes made between two types of loneliness termed trait and state loneliness (Jones, 1989) or emotional and social loneliness (Weiss, 1989). Trait loneliness is seen as dispositional, an enduring personal characteristic. Although this distinction has been examined in adults (e.g. Russell et al., 1984), there has been little research on this distinction in children. Some evidence for this view of loneliness comes from the finding that children's level of loneliness possesses a moderate degree of stability over the course of a year (Asher & Wheeler, 1985), though situational factors may also have been relatively stable over this period of time, of course. Psychodynamic theorists were among the first people to recognise the importance of early childhood in creating this form of loneliness. The infant's problems in establishing or maintaining intimacy with parents were seen as the root of loneliness in later life (Fromm-Reichmann, 1959). Following Bowlby's (1958, 1980) analysis of attachment, systematic attempts have also been made to understand the impact of attachment patterns in creating later relationship problems and predispositions to this form of loneliness (Weiss, 1989).

In contrast to trait loneliness, state loneliness reflects current circumstances. It is produced by a lack involvement and acceptance by others. All children feel lonely sometimes, such as when they change school or the family moves house and the current friendship network is left behind. This experience of loneliness is usually a transient condition. The distinction between trait and state loneliness highlights that both situational determinants and individual differences must be taken into account in explaining loneliness.

The role of parents and peers

As peers become increasingly significant in the lives of children and adolescents, satisfaction with peer relationships becomes increasingly important as a determinant of loneliness and the influence of parents declines (Schultz & Moore, 1989). Failure of the pre-adolescent to establish a satisfying intimate relationship with a chum in pre-adolescence is an especially significant cause of later chronic loneliness (Sullivan, 1953).

Despite the increasing significance of peers, the impact of parental relationships on feelings of loneliness is not eliminated as the child grows older and enters adolescence. First, because current parental relationships find their reflection in the degree of autonomy the child or adolescent experiences in his peer relationships (Steinberg & Silverberg, 1986). Close parental relationships are associated with less conforming and greater self-reliance in peer relationships. Second, because loneliness also reflects attachment histories and patterns of parenting. A background of secure attachment is associated with less frequent and less severe loneliness in later life than is evident in comparable insecurely attached individuals (Shaver & Hazan, 1989). Poor attachment histories and the experience of parental divorce, especially early in the child's life, is associated with the experience of loneliness later in life (Shaver & Rubenstein, 1980). Later patterns of low acceptance and high permissiveness in parent–child relationships are also associated with higher levels of loneliness in adolescence and later life (Schultz & Moore, 1986). These early influences impact on the child's internal models of relationships, and the ability to form relationships in later life. Early relationships have both a direct and an indirect impact on patterns of loneliness in later life.

Consequences of loneliness

Research has shown an association between sociometric status and children's self-ratings of loneliness. Ratings of loneliness are higher in rejected children than in their popular or neglected counterparts (Asher & Wheeler, 1985). Indeed, despite the difference in popularity, most studies do not find that loneliness in neglected children is significantly different from averagely popular children (Asher et al., 1990). This suggests the possible significance of three factors. First, that feelings of loneliness are in part derived from the feelings of exclusion (Asher & Parker, 1989). Second, that the greater temporal and situational stability of rejected rather than neglected status exacerbates feelings of loneliness in the former group (Asher, 1990). Third, though neglected children receive fewer best friend (reciprocal) nominations, if children are asked to rate the likeability of peers then the neglected children tend to be as well liked as their averagely popular peers (Asher & Wheeler, 1985); they are far from isolated.

Included in the complex, interrelated set of social factors associated with high levels of loneliness are a variety of social cognitive and social skills deficits. Loneliness is associated with negative patterns of self-perception and low self-esteem, a self-blaming attributional style, lower expectations for social outcomes, social skills deficits such as inappropriate self-disclosure, excessive self-attention (and inappropriate attention to communication partners), an inability to establish comfortable intimacy, and a tendency to make negative judgements of self and others (Shaver & Hazan, 1989). Together these form the basis for a self-fulfilling prophecy and help to make loneliness self-perpetuating even into adolescence and adulthood (Hymel & Franke, 1985).

Problems with relationships

As our knowledge of how personal relationships are formed and grow has improved it has also become apparent that they can only be fully understood in the context of how they fail. No matter how socially skilled and popular a child is, she or he will have experienced the collapse of a relationship. It is an inevitable and normal, perhaps even necessary, part of social development and growth. Levinger (1983) hypothesised a five-stage sequence in relationships: acquaintance; build-up; continuation and consolidation; deterioration or decline; endings (voluntary or involuntary). This section focuses on problems within relationships, situational and inter-individual factors which contribute to their deterioration and ending. First, a few words about the problems of research in this area.

Approaches to research

Problems within relationships are often difficult to study. In an ideal world one would start with a relationship and follow it through to the point of collapse. But, of course, one cannot be sure if or when the relationship will hit problems and collapse. Even if it does, the participants may not want to talk to researchers about their experiences. To get around these problems one potentially needs very large initial samples and plenty of time. This approach does seem to be becoming increasingly common, though it still leaves many other methodological and ethical problems unresolved. Does the fact of observing relationships affect whether they are likely to progress or decline? Does it affect the pattern of any progress or decline? Can one justify observing and recording rather than helping? There are lots of difficult questions but, unfortunately, few easy answers. An alternative approach has been to study relationships that are already in decline or that have collapsed.

Many analyses of relationship problems and collapse have been based on personal, retrospective accounts, with all their attendant problems. Although a child's explanation of his or her relationship problems is of interest, and indeed must be taken into account in any counselling, it is not necessarily the same as the actual causes. All such accounts are interpreted explanation of what has happened and, in young children especially, they are limited by the child's cognitive and verbal abilities. Add to this the distortions of memory which accrue over time and it can be seen that these are far from reliable sources of evidence. As Bigelow (1982) noted, ''the danger to our field of study is that the list of variables gleaned through interviews and the like will vary directly with the literary talent of the investigator and objectivity may well then be sacrificed'' (p. 3). Descriptive analysis and classification should only be the first stage of understanding a phenomenon, enabling subsequent systematic and directed research (Hinde, 1979). Much research on relationship decline and dissolution, especially on children, is currently still at this descriptive stage with no agreed organisational structure.

Natural endings

The occurrence of special "best friends" first appears at about the age of four (Gesell & Ilg, 1949), though the meaning of the term is quite flexible: throughout middle childhood best friends are chosen according to the demands of specific situations or occasions (Gesell, Ilg & Ames, 1965). Changes in the cognitive abilities and interests of the young child are a natural part of development and friends often develop in different directions or at different rates (McCall, 1982). Where there is a discrepancy in the expectations and friendship skills of the participants the younger child will be unable to progress to the deeper level of relationship sought by his or her partner, a state of affairs that is especially frustrating for the older child.

Children's friendships increase in stability with age, partly reflecting more stable interests, superior cognitive abilities, and better skills at constructive conflict resolution (Hartup et al., 1988). The relationships of older children are also more likely to be reciprocal, and consequently closer and more intimate (Drewry & Clark, 1985). Despite the lesser stability of their relationships, younger children actually make more friends than they lose. In contrast, older children become increasingly more involved in their relationships with peers than with parents (Ellis, Rogoff & Cromer, 1981). Older children seek and possess more intimacy in their peer relationships, but if they collapse this makes the loss correspondingly more painful. These relationships are considerably less easy to replace than those of younger children (Buhrmester & Furman, 1987). These older children lose more friends than they gain (Berndt & Hoyle, 1985). Learning how to cope with losing and changing friends is a normal part of growing up, it is complimentary to the process of learning how to make and keep friends.

As adolescence approaches, children undergo dramatic physical and psychological changes which are reflected in their social relationships. This is a paradoxical time in that intimacy is a considerable preoccupation of the adolescent and yet this is also an age at which it is difficult to achieve intimacy, and many relationships are maintained at a functional level. Thus the adolescent often relates well to peers and is part of a larger group but has problems in narrowing this down to form close personal relationships (Button, 1979). These problems are often most noticeable in the adolescent's cross-sex peer contacts. These can initially be quite uncomfortable or even antagonistic.

Just as models have been proposed to explain development in relationships, theorists have also attempted to chart the course of relationship dissolution. Early models of relationship collapse and dissolution were fairly general and largely descriptive (e.g. Duck, 1982), though these provided the impetus for later more detailed models and empirical research (e.g. Lee, 1984; Baxter, 1984). To date the focus of these theories has been adult relationships. The Lee (1984) and Baxter (1984) studies focused on romantic relationships. To cope with the very different patterns of relating found in children, more attention to same-sex friendships and cognitive developmental considerations is urgently needed.

Children's accounts of friendship termination are considerably less differentiated than their accounts of friendship formation (Bigelow, 1982). Although these become more complex as the child becomes more cognitively sophisticated, so do accounts of friendship formation. Quite simply, the lesser contact with ex-friends than friends, and the typically shorter process of friendship dissolution than build-up, means that there are fewer opportunities to develop finely detailed accounts of the deterioration and ending of friendship. Some relationships are reported as simply drifting apart as the participants find alternative attractions. Other relationships are disrupted by a single major disagreement, though attributional factors are likely to buffer potentially negative interpretations of the behaviour of friends (Hymel, 1986).

One thing is clear: the reason for friendship termination is not only an inability to satisfy the requirements for friendship formation. Bigelow (1982) argues that friendships often collapse because of the violation of general rules of good conduct, applicable to all social relationships, rather than specific friendship inadequacies. Research by Bigelow & LaGaipa (1980) has highlighted some of the explanations which 9–15-year-old school-children give for the collapse of their relationships. In middle childhood the major themes of explanations revolve around conflict and ego-degrading experiences. By adolescence the emphasis has moved to disloyalty (befriending others and betraying trust) and lack or loss of admiration (low moral character), which are evident in almost two-thirds of explanations. If continuing references to ego-degrading experiences are included, 82% of responses are accounted for. Adolescents share their feelings and secrets more, and are more knowledgeable about their friends' feelings. Consequently trustworthiness and being someone who could be confided in are important qualities in adolescent friendships and important reasons for relationship disputes (Konopka, 1983).

Precipitating factors

Events which precipitate the end of a relationship have been given relatively little empirical attention despite their undoubted significance. It is readily acknowledged, for example, that the characteristics of schools and classrooms affect the number and stability of children's friendships (Hallinan & Tuma, 1978), as do major social and academic dislocations such as moving house or going to a new school (Bogat, Jones & Jason, 1980). These events disrupt relationships and can be traumatic experiences for children (Hirsch & Rapkin, 1987; Asher & Coie, 1990).

   In young children especially, social contact is determined or limited by parents (Brown, 1981), and even older children have less control than adults over important factors which affect their relationships, such as geographic changes. This lack of control over extraneous factors which affect their relationships is an important factor in children's experience of the loss of their relationships. These sorts of disruptions are likely to play a more significant role in the lives of children than adults. Children find it more difficult than adults to overcome the obstacle of separation and maintain their relationship through letters, telephone calls and occasional visits (Levinger & Levinger, 1986). Some relationships are strong enough to survive these barriers, but for most they are destined merely to represent a transitional stage, cushioning the eventual decay of the relationship and acting as support while new friendships are formed.

   The transition from elementary to high school is probably the most common social dislocation experienced by children. Most children welcome the transition as an opportunity to have new experiences, to make new friends, and to gain in status. But they are also anxious about the move. From being the senior students in a small elementary school they are about to become the newcomers in the much larger world of the high school. Many children will hope to make the move with their friends, an important source of social support, though many friendships will not long survive the transition. Changing school is a common cause of relationships ending and a common opportunity for new relationships to form.

Changing school other than in the company of friends and peers is a considerably more traumatic prospect for the child, though this is a common experience when a family geographically relocates. The dual stress of relocation and school transfer can represent a major trauma in the child's life. Both the home and school peer networks are lost. Separation from friends can produce a grief reaction due to loss of companionship and support. The child feels angry, alone and depressed. Friends are sometimes remembered and missed for a considerable period of time. Younger children sometimes even incorporate them into their fantasy play. The major potential harm of these dislocations is not that they cause a brief period of pain, though this will seem to be the major drawback to the child at the time, but rather that they affect the child's working model for relationships. Frequent moves can be disastrous, and any move disrupting early close relationships may cause a permanent social handicap (Sullivan, 1953). Fortunately the trauma of these transitions can be considerably eased with a little forethought and an appropriate induction programme (Bogat, Jones & Jason, 1980).

Despite the potentially severe consequences, most children adapt reasonably well to the dislocation in their social network that results from a move of house. The major problem that is experienced is often with the forming of relationships in the new, established peer group. This is considerably more difficult than would have been the case in the old peer network. Friends engaged in an activity often protect it from outsiders and skill; subtlety and persistence are important if a newcomer is to gain acceptance. This situation is especially significant for older children where established and stable cliques are likely to exist. Many children that have moved from an established peer network are perfectly competent in responding to peer approaches but have problems in initiating contacts with strangers – they have had little experience of this. When the onus is on them to establish effective contact with unknown peers, once-popular children may become short of friends (Button, 1979). At this stage secure and supportive family relations are important to cushion and help minimise these effects, and to facilitate the child's social initiatives. Recent research has provided important insights into the way in which families increase or buffer a child's vulnerability to peer rejection. For isolated and aggressive children, the stress and consequences of unsatisfying school friendships are reduced if there is a good relationship with a brother or sister (East & Rook, 1992). Families can also produce or exacerbate stressful life experiences. Children from families under chronic stress, from factors such as low incomes, or experiencing acute stress, such as from parental divorce, are more likely to be rejected by their peers. Children experiencing both chronic and acute family stresses are potentially the most vulnerable of all (Patterson, Vaden & Kupersmidt, 1991). Though these findings open new questions as to how these consequences are brought about, some of their wide-ranging implications are obvious. In terms of the disruption resulting from moving house, it is evident that the child's relationships are doubly disrupted. Moving house is likely both to directly disrupt the child's relationships and to place stress on the family as a whole. Extra sensitivity and support are likely to be significant determinants of the speed and success of a child's adjustments to his or her new social environment.

The experience of relationship collapse

Despite the inevitability of development and change in friendships, the child's experience of relationship dissolution and collapse can be extremely traumatic. Separation from friends may produce feelings of depression, loneliness, irritability, guilt, resentment, and anger (Rubin, 1980). When a friendship collapses the child naturally seeks to explain the event. Children may be left wondering if the failure of a relationship was due to their personal characteristics and doubting their self-worth. This is especially likely to be the case when an older child perceives that he or she was abandoned by a friend who preferred a new companion. These self-attributions can fundamentally undermine the child's self-esteem and colour future relationships. If the child himself feels unworthy then what trust is to be placed in a friend who espouses a contrary view?

Because children's early relationships are relatively transient, the significance of the end of children's friendships is often unrecognised by parents. Both leaving and being left by a friend are potentially traumatic events and each entails its own problems. These problems differ considerably according to the age of the child and his or her interpretation of the causes of the relationship's collapse (Dweck & Goetz, 1979). At this point it is useful to recall Bigelow's (1982) words of warning: such accounts may take the form of personal philosophies about the nature of interpersonal relations rather than a record of the actual precipitating events leading up to a relationship collapsing. What children think they respond to and what they actually respond to in others are neither directly or necessarily related.

For the young child much of the pain when a relationship collapses comes from the incomprehensibility of rejection by a supposed friend. For the older child, improvements in understanding often underlie many of the pains and problems resulting from the collapse of a friendship. Self-blame for the collapse of a friendship creates difficulties for the child's future relationships. Personal attributions of incompetence as the reason for rejection in attempts to initiate relationships will result in less adaptive reactions to rejection, possibly resulting in more disruptive behaviour, withdrawal, or simply repeating the ineffective behaviour (Goetz & Dweck, 1980).

With the approach of adolescence the child often becomes very preoccupied with relationships and with the possibility of peer rejection. Greater attributional skills and role-taking abilities dramatically increase the brooding attention that the adolescent can devote to analysing why a relationship went wrong (Harvey et al., 1982). Relationship collapse is especially painful to the adolescent because of the feelings of insecurity which characterise this time of important changes in the individual's social relationships. The seriousness of breaking up at this age is exacerbated by the fact that the availability of alternative relationships is limited due to most others already being in established relationships. The death of a close relationship often leads the adolescent to develop negative self-evaluations (Coleman, 1980). For the sensitive adolescent even being the one to end a relationship is difficult because of the appreciation of the hurt feelings that this will cause the other person.

Consequences of children's relationship problems

This is an important topic because of its implications for therapy. If the social and psychological consequences of children's peer relationship problems are minimal then the justification for expensive and uncertain interventions is weak. If, on the other hand, the potential consequences are long lasting and severe then not only are interventions justified, their research and application becomes a matter of some urgency.

Many studies have attempted to clarify the effects of children's peer relationship problems on later social and psychological functioning. On a cursory inspection the range of outcomes is startling and impressive evidence for the importance of early peer relationships for later adjustment. Quality of earlier peer experience has been associated with the capacity for the development of intimacy in adult relationships (Crockett, 1984), school achievement and drop-out (Gronlund & Holmlund, 1958), antisocial behaviour and delinquency, which includes bad conduct while in military service (Roff, 1961), law breaking, arrests, and court appearances (Roff, Sells & Golden, 1972; Janes et al., 1979; Roff & Wirt, 1984), psychological problems and disorders, including alcoholism (Robins, 1966), suicide (Stengel, 1971), and even psychosis (Roff, 1963; Cowen et al., 1973).

Unfortunately, though the volume of evidence for an association between early relationship problems and later adjustment is impressive, the quality of the evidence is extremely variable. It is not sufficient to assume because rejection precedes later maladjustment that it necessarily caused it. Research designs are often weak. They are often based on the retrospective accounts of involved parties, anecdotal evidence, or use multiple sources whose comparability is unclear. The designs also tend to be correlational, and often based on unrepresentative groups such as clinic populations. As Parker & Asher (1987) note, it is possible to interpret at least some of the evidence as showing that the early forms of a disorder, which is not apparent and recognised till later in life, are affecting the child's pattern of relating rather than early patterns of relating causing the disorder. It has been argued that any patterns of cause are largely assumed rather than proven (Kupersmidt, Coie & Dodge, 1990). A review by Parker & Asher (1987) concludes that the evidence for a causal link between childhood relationships and later problems of adjustment is weakest in relation to predicting adult psychopathology. It is strongest in the association of early aggression with later juvenile or adult criminality and the association of low acceptance in the elementary school with later drop-out. Whatever the causal pathways, the evidence clearly does demonstrate that poor early relationships are a useful indicator of *some* aspects of later adjustment.

Conclusion

This chapter has merely touched on the broad array of factors that affect children's abilities to initiate and maintain satisfying peer relationships. Many of the factors, such as the constitutional characteristics of the individual, can never be eliminated, though other factors, such as the structure of social organisations, can easily be changed once their significance is acknowledged. Whatever the origins of children's problems with their peer relationships, their implications for the child's happiness and later adjustment has produced in many researchers a determination that they should be challenged. With appropriate education and intervention many characteristics of relators and relationships need not be regarded as problems. It is to approaches to intervention that we turn in the next chapter.

10 Improving peer relationships

The human relationship is the most powerful psychological behavior modifier known to man.

(Patterson, 1974, p. xi)

The array of approaches to resolving relationship problems is almost as diverse as the variety of problems themselves. As a systematic understanding of children's relationships and relationship problems has progressed over the last 20 years or so, so has the interest in intervention and the sophistication of these attempts (see Schneider, Rubin & Ledingham, 1985; Asher & Coie, 1990). Three main groups of theories have received substantial attention as approaches to improving children's social skills with peers. The emphases of the theories reflect where the locus of the relationship problems are perceived to lie and the researcher or therapist's theoretical orientation. At this point we will outline the different emphases of these approaches. Detailed consideration of specific programmes and their effectiveness is reserved till later in the chapter.

The first set of theories emphasises the learning and modification of children's behaviour or social knowledge. This approach is useful for teaching the basic skills, especially specific new skills or knowledge, required for social interaction. The second group of theories are concerned with teaching children new and more adaptive ways of thinking about people and social situations. This approach represents a complex and sophisticated analysis. It assumes that overt behaviour is mediated by cognitive processes (essentially covert behaviour) and that changing the pattern of these processes will lead to improvement in the child's social abilities. This is potentially a powerful approach because it operates at a more general level than the simple teaching of specific skills. The skills learning and cognitive approaches are complementary in that the former is essentially a "bottom up" strategy, teaching simple skills and assuming cognitive processes (if they are given consideration at all) will change correspondingly, the latter is essentially "top down", teaching general ways of social information processing which in turn should allow the child to understand and use those behaviours which are more appropriate and adaptive. Together these approaches provide both specific and general skills and are likely to produce more marked and stable improvements in behaviour.

The third approach to improving children's peer relationships aims to change the peer group structures that produce and/or maintain maladaptive patterns of behaviour. Previous approaches firmly emphasised the role of the individual in behaviour problems, the group approach recognises that social behaviour is meaningless outside of its social context. Many apparently successful training studies have ultimately foundered on the final test of their success – the stable use of the newly learned skills in the child's everyday social interactions. The peer socialisation approach addresses this problem directly and so can be an important addition to other skills training approaches. A supportive peer context provides an important aid to the development, maintenance, and generalisation of newly learned skills.

The above three approaches to improving children's peer relationship skills are not exclusive but represent differences in emphasis. It is possible, even desirable, to establish programmes with elements from all three approaches. Before giving more detailed consideration to the nature and effectiveness of each of these approaches, it is appropriate to consider some of the problems and issues which are relevant to deciding if children need help with their relationships and the choice of an appropriate mode of intervention.

The social context of relationship problems and interventions

Psychological interventions with children are complicated because several professional groups and agencies are often involved, sometimes with conflicting goals and approaches (Murgatroyd, 1980). A study by Takac & Benyamini (1989) showed relatively little overlap in the factors affecting the child's perceived adjustment in different circumstances. For example, in the school context the quiet, obedient child is often regarded as well adjusted because he or she does not interfere with the smooth running of the class. These characteristics are little recommendation for the peer group. Different figures elicit different behaviours and evaluate behaviour differently. It is important to recognise the role of the person who is deciding whether a child needs help or not. Different judges and measures of social competence often differ markedly in their evaluations. These differences occur both within groups of judges (e.g. teachers often differ in their evaluation of a child's behaviour) and between groups of judges (e.g. different evaluations are often given by parents, peers, teachers and sociometric measures). Age is a particularly important influence on peer evaluations. Preschoolers are less accurate at identifying their popular and socially competent peers than is the class teacher (Connolly & Doyle, 1981). Disagreements are especially marked for the more subtle aspects of behaviour (Ledingham & Younger, 1985).

Children's own reports of their peer interactions should not be discounted as potentially useful measures of their social adjustment (Bierman & McCauley, 1987). These can give a useful insight into how satisfied the child is with the current status of his or her relationships. These self reports do correlate with parent, teacher, and sociometric ratings, though further research is required to explore the utility of this criterion and how it is affected by individual differences such as age and verbal ability. Relationships are complex phenomena and each mode of assessment has its virtues and advocates, and also its disadvantages. The use of multiple criteria is most likely to provide a broad, balanced picture and avoid bias.

Other than for maintaining order to facilitate more formal teaching, peer relationships have not traditionally been the concern of the education system. Happily the system seems to be gradually changing as early peer relationships are recognised as significant for current and future psychological adjustment and academic performance (Cox & Gunn, 1980). For example, within the classroom the aggressive child is of concern because he or she is disruptive, yet this is also significant for peer relationships and later adjustment. Maladaptive behaviours can have many possible causes and many interrelated consequences. With changes in society, such as increased divorce rates, large numbers of single-parent families, both parents possibly in full-time employment, and a substantial proportion of remarriages, it seems likely that the role of the education system as an agency of socialisation will continue to increase in importance (Cox & Gunn, 1980).

A number of authors have described and emphasised the importance of school-based programmes for promoting social competence and peer relationships (e.g. Furman et al., 1989), though some authors are pessimistic about this role of the education system amidst the onslaught of the mass media, increased mobility, and the growing emphasis on individuality (Cartledge & Milburn, 1980). Certainly preventive programmes have many advantages over remedial programmes. If it is necessary to use intervention techniques then they must be used in a manner which does not stigmatise the child or isolate him or her from peers (Rook & Peplau, 1982). The obtrusive involvement of adults in social skills interventions will embarrass the child and give him or her a self-fulfilling label. The more widespread involvement of all children in skills development programmes will have a basic general utility, avoid the isolation of the troubled child, and increase the generalisation and maintenance of any benefits.

Defining withdrawal and isolation

This must inevitably involve a subjective component, a judgement concerning what constitutes a deficit and what is trained. Although social activity is generally regarded positively, some parents and teachers want a passive child. Even if these people are overruled the likelihood of success (and the ethics of an intervention in these circumstances) is doubtful.

The cause of isolation and the characteristics of the isolated child are an important consideration in devising appropriate interventions (Coie & Koeppl, 1990). Poor peer acceptance is unlikely to be a primary cause, and is often the product of a complex multiple aetiology. It can be a cause and consequence of other problems. Despite this, studies have generally been concerned with teaching the individual specific skills, often concerned with how to initiate relationships, rather than the skills and processes involved in maintaining a relationship (Duck, 1991), which provides an insight into why there have been so many problems in getting the maintenance and generalisation of training effects.

One of three main aims have characterised most social skills training studies, though some studies have used multiple criteria (Wanlass & Prinz, 1982). Unfortunately the different criteria measure quite different characteristics of a child's relationships. One approach has defined isolation in terms of quantity of interaction. For example, social isolation has been defined as interacting with peers for less than one-third of the observation period (Roopnarine & Honig, 1985). Interventions based on this approach simply attempted to increase the child's overall rate of interaction. Unfortunately relatively high rates of interaction already characterise many aggressive children and so this is not an appropriate solution in these cases.

A second approach has focused on the general qualitative patterns of behaviour that define isolation. This bears little relation to the first criterion! Poor quality of interaction would be characterised by features such as excessive aggressive behaviour. Interventions based on this perspective have typically had aims such as lowering aggression or increasing co-operative and prosocial behaviour. More recent studies of this ilk have emphasised specific social skills and problem-solving techniques (such as initiating communication or responding to aggression).

The third approach adopted has defined relationship skill deficits in terms of their social consequences. Social acceptance has been used as an indicator of social success and by implication social skill. This is often operationalised in terms of sociometric status, using a host of selection criteria such as rating for liking as a play partner. But this criterion often seems to have more to do with popularity than friendship status. As Ladd & Asher (1985) note, the improvement of trained children is often an increase in their average sociometric rating, this is not necessarily reflected in improved status on a nomination measure used to indicate best friends (e.g. Gresham & Nagle, 1980). Skills training may be better at improving levels of acceptance rather than friendship, at making children more acceptable acquaintances or "other friends" rather than best friends.

Sociometric status

Sociometric measures show a child's level of popularity rather than of the quality of his or her relationships (Hogan & Mankin, 1970). It is quite possible for a child to be extremely popular and yet not feature as any other child's best friend. Similarly, it is perfectly possible (and common) for children of average popularity to maintain their desired number of friendships at a satisfying and adequate level. Though children of low sociometric status have fewer friendships, none the less, more than half have at least one best person whom they regard as a best friend and who regards them in the same way (Parker & Asher, 1987). The utility of sociometric measures could be markedly improved by the incorporation of selection criteria which give the child an opportunity to indicate who is disliked and neglected.

The many potential ethical and practical problems of using negative criteria in sociometric instruments mean that these have rarely been used in intervention studies (Asher, 1985). This is beginning to seem overly protective. A study of preschoolers has provided evidence to show that sociometric testing, including negative nominations, does not effect subsequent peer interaction (Hayvren & Hymel, 1984). If further evidence on older groups is forthcoming this will ease the current qualms.

The direct assessment of neglected status has fared little better than the assessment of rejected status. Although potentially easier, it seems simply to have been overlooked. Standard practice is usually to infer neglect to lack of nominations from other children. This is an unfortunate practice as it seems that the direct nomination of neglected peers produces a different and more meaningful pattern of results to a calculated measure of social impact (Dygdon & Conger, 1990). The picture of the neglected child as not markedly different from the averagely popular child, and of neglected status as being a relatively unstable classification (Rubin et al., 1989), is largely built on indirect methods of assessment. Appropriate caution must consequently be exercised in accepting these conclusions, pending confirmation by more direct methods.

Despite the complexities and difficulties which abound in the use and interpretation of sociometric data, research has made it abundantly clear that it is important to distinguish between children of rejected and neglected status. These children have considerably different behavioural profiles.

Ample evidence now exists attesting to the poor relationship between social activity and sociometric status (Coie, 1985) – a worrying finding as behavioural isolation is often equated with either rejection or at least neglected status. As it is primarily rejection and associated indices of negative status that predict later adjustment (Rubin, 1985), withdrawal is not an appropriate indicator of risk at least in early and middle childhood. Attention would be better focused on aggressive or rejected children. The rate of interaction is also a poor general predictor of sociometric status. High levels can be associated with positive or negative interaction, though low levels are likely to be associated with low social acceptance (Gottman, 1977a) as they are associated with low quality of interaction – and quality of interaction (rate of giving and receiving positive reinforcements) is predictive of social status and adjustment (Hartup, Glazer & Charlesworth, 1967).

An unfortunate consequence of these many ways of defining social isolation is that there is little agreement in the literature on the criteria which constitute a genuine deficit, justify interventions, and indicate successful outcomes. It often seems to be the case that social interaction shows more change as a result of an intervention than, say, peer status. So studies targeting this appear more effective. But are changes in interaction without changes in corresponding levels of acceptance an appropriate goal? Similarly, might a small change in acceptance be better than a large change in behaviour which does not affect social status? Peer reputation is a more clearly established predictor of later adjustment. It really is very difficult comparing apples and oranges! These and many other considerations mean that there undoubtedly remain a great many methodological issues to be clarified before we fully understand what can be achieved with what form of social skills training and, importantly, why.

Focusing on the child

Amidst all these criteria it is important to be wary of losing sight of the child. Social isolation can be defined in many ways and, as Wanlass & Prinz (1982) noted, isolated children do not form an homogeneous group. Individuals differ in the level and type of social contact that they desire. A low level of interaction need not necessarily be indicative of poor peer relationships. Poor quality of interaction, social anxiety, and poor social experiences are found in children with high or low levels of interaction. Some children do not desire high levels of social interaction, others are isolated, lonely and unhappy, and still others are simply directing their attention to non-peer sources. Some children are aggressive and actively rejected, others are anxious and withdrawn or simply ignored. Some children lack social skills, and some are simply inhibited in using them. Indeed, many poorly accepted children seem blissfully unaware of this fact, they may continually annoy other children and disrupt their activities. These children misperceive how their peers evaluate their social competence and do not recognise the contribution which their own social skills have on peer reactions (Patterson, Kupersmidt & Griesler, 1990).

Detailed characteristics of populations are seldom reported and, along with initial selection differences, it means that comparing studies based on different criteria is, to say the least, problematic (Conger & Keane, 1981). The more recent emphasis is on measures to improve quality of interaction (in terms of both general quality and specific skills) rather than the sheer quantity of social interaction, though studies have attempted to produce improvement on both these measures. The rationale for this is quite simple, low levels of peer interaction need not necessarily in themselves be problematic, and simply increasing amounts of contact can produce a child regarded as disruptive and a social nuisance by other children rather than as a positive acquaintance (Walker et al., 1979). The rejected child is actively disliked by peers rather than, like the neglected child, simply ignored. Rejected children are personally blamed for their negative interactions, they are seen as intentional, the consequence of stable, personal dispositions (Waas & Honer, 1990). With this pattern of attributions it should come as no surprise that active rejection and poor quality of interaction, in comparison to simple neglect, possess greater stability across time and social groups (Coie & Kupersmidt, 1983). Rejection has significant and well-established current and future consequences for the child (Ladd, 1990).

The idea behind many approaches to intervention lies in the functions that have been attributed to relationships. For example, relationships are a training ground and so it is hardly surprising that children seen as having inadequate relationships have been regarded as being able to benefit from skills training programmes. The assumption here is that the skills deficit is maintaining or causing the presenting problem, though as we have already seen, such an assumption of causality is not always easy and it is equally possible that other constitutional or emotional problems underlie or at least contribute to observed deficits. Relatively few studies examine the role of children's emotional responses (e.g. anxiety) in social skills training (Rotheram, 1980), though it is recognised as a potential inhibiting factor. Similarly, relationships have been noted as times for emotional development and learning interpersonal trust and intimacy. Little surprise, therefore, that where this need is perceived as having been left unsatisfied that relationship therapy is considered appropriate. Implicit in this perspective is that problems are due to factors interfering with skilled performance rather than the individual lacking appropriate skills. Many therapists would be inclined to see these functions as interrelated and often specialise in a particular approach rather than using different approaches with different clients.

Approaches to therapy

A constant debate seems to rage over which treatment is best, Rutter (1975) observes that there is evidence that the many different forms of treatment are effective if used *appropriately and in the right circumstances*. A major determinant of the choice of intervention technique is the theoretical perspective, skills, and preferences of the therapist. This factor is probably considerably underestimated by the general public. A psychoanalyst is likely to interpret any of a child's problems in psychodynamic terms and consider that psychoanalysis is the appropriate therapy. In reality most therapists are (or at least claim to be) eclectic in approach and adopt very different strategies depending where they perceive the locus of the child's problems to lie. This may range from the individual child's characteristics and skills, the child's peer groups context, or the wider family relationships of the child (Sameroff & Emde, 1989).

Social skills training

Interest in interventions to alter children's style of relating to peers can be traced back at least as far as the 1930s (Renshaw, 1981), though systematic research on social skills training with children is a relatively recent endeavour. "Social skills training and research is among the most recent and most robust of the approaches to the remediation of psychological problems, the enhancement of interpersonal effectiveness, and the general improvement of the quality of life" (L'Abate & Milan, 1985, p. xi). Social skills training is concerned with the type and organisation of cognitive and behavioural skills necessary for successful social interaction. Problems can arise because of a lack of knowledge of appropriate social behaviour, lack of actual behavioural skills, or lack of ability to monitor and modify ongoing social behaviour (Mize & Ladd, 1990a). Anxiety and emotional factors, much ignored variables in social skills training, can also inhibit skilled performance (Cox & Gunn, 1980). All these factors can be incorporated in social skills training, though different approaches would be used depending on which skills are emphasised (Cartledge & Milburn, 1980). Rotheram (1980) argues for an integrated approach and that manipulating cognitive, behavioural and emotional factors on their own has consistently proven fruitless. Most social skills training originates in behavioural psychology. Some authors define social skills to include the shaping and modelling techniques of behaviour modification, others prefer to emphasise the increasingly influential cognitive–instructional aspects of social skills training.

Research on social skills training has been conducted in the last two decades (Ladd & Asher, 1985), though attempts to improve the social skills of unpopular children have been narrow in focus (Roopnarine & Honig, 1985). Generally such programmes are fairly efficacious with low accepted children, though some results have failed to find positive improvements (Burleson, 1985). Some social skills programmes also report the added bonus of improvements in the positive social behaviour of the child's non-targeted acquaintances (Cooke & Apolloni, 1976). With actively rejected children the picture is less rosy. As Bierman (1989, p. 73) notes, "No treatment has produced long-term improvements in the behavioral adjustment and peer status of rejected children, although various treatment approaches have led to specific gains in some children."

Many social skills training programmes are fairly eclectic in orientation (e.g. Avery, Rider & Haynes-Clements, 1981), though three broad approaches to intervention have often been distinguished: modelling, shaping, and coaching in its many guises (e.g. Asher, Oden & Gottman, 1977). The limitations and overlaps in this simple taxonomy, and more extensive taxonomies, have been noted by various authors (e.g. Ladd & Mize, 1983), though these classifications do reflect different theoretical origins and the system will serve as a useful structure for this exposition. The interested reader is directed to fuller accounts, such as Ladd & Mize (1983) for a more detailed analysis of the different approaches and an alternative integrated model.

The behavioural approach

Behavioural approaches to therapy have the common characteristics of an emphasis on the objective definition of problems and measurable procedures. This supposedly allows the unequivocal evaluation of the efficacy of interventions (Ross, 1978). In practice most studies have not adequately measured the generalisation and durability of treatment effects and do not give an adequate functional analysis of the relationship between trained behaviours and social consequences (Hughes & Sullivan, 1988).

The behavioural approach assumes that behavioural problems are problems of learning and that change is brought about through the same processes. For example, Solomon & Wahler (1973) found that the peers of problem children tended to focus on their negative behaviour and ignore their prosocial behaviour. By attending and responding primarily to their negative behaviour the peer group were reinforcing and hence perpetuating the behaviour. In contrast, the social behaviour of withdrawn children is increased when their social attempts are reinforced by peers (Wahler, 1967). Behaviour that is learned can be unlearned, inappropriate behaviour can be altered (extinguished or replaced), and, most importantly, it is possible to predict and control behaviour if all the relevant environmental factors are known (Apter, 1982).

The child can learn how to relate to peers through guidance, instruction and reinforcement, observing the behaviour (and its consequences) of adult and peer models, and through direct experience of social interaction (Combs & Slaby, 1977). These are also principle sources of learning in behavioural intervention programmes. Children are commonly treated individually, though many of the techniques have also been used with groups. Indeed, group therapies are one of the more successful therapeutic approaches in this context (Wilson & Hersov, 1985).

The skills taught are often selected on the basis of a comparison between what popular and unpopular children of a given age and sex are doing, or what produces positive peer reactions (see Chapter 2). It is also important to give consideration to developmental differences in the effectiveness of different techniques for teaching these various social skills. It seems highly likely that developmental considerations, especially a child's cognitive and communicative abilities influence the effectiveness of techniques (Mize & Ladd, 1990a). "Unless social skill programs are based on a developmental model which recognises intellectual, social and emotional capacities of children at various ages, the likelihood that our intervention strategies will be designed to teach children to respond as 'miniature adults' is high" (Cox & Gunn, 1980, p. 128). More specifically, in a meta-analysis of studies reporting data on social skills interventions, Schneider (1989) compared the size of effects with chronological age. From this analysis he concluded that techniques such as modelling, which require less cognitive mediation, are most effective with young preschoolers while more complex multi-technique programmes are more successful with older children. While most studies do tailor their programme to the specific client group, most studies also ignore or give minimal attention to developmental considerations and few attempt comparisons of behavioural programmes across different age groups (Furman, 1980).

Behavioural approaches are best suited to children that have specific, identifiable behavioural deficits that are causing discomfort or developmental risk (Ladd & Asher, 1985). Though as previous chapters have shown, pinning down what actually constitutes a social skills deficit (such as low rates of interaction, specific behaviours, or poor quality of interaction) or evaluating the degree of risk that deficits entail, is far from easy (Michalson, Foster & Ritchey, 1981).

Shaping

This is an operant approach to treatment – it sees the child as actively operating on his or her environment to bring about specific functional consequences. Shaping aims to gradually modify a child's behaviour in a specific desired direction by rewarding behaviours which increasingly closely approximate the desired behaviour. "Shaping is the crucial feature in the art of behaviour modification" (Yule, 1985). Behaviour therapy emphasises the functional analysis of behaviour. Behaviour is seen as a function of its consequences and hence it aims to alter the way the child operates on his or her world by altering the consequences of actions. The basic premise is that behaviours which produce rewarding consequences will strengthen and increase in frequency those that have no effect, or negative effects will reduce in frequency, sometimes termed extinction. These methods have been successfully used to increase positive social behaviour in preschoolers and to reduce aggressive behaviour (e.g. Pinkston et al., 1973). A meta-analysis of intervention studies, by Schneider & Byrne (1985), indicated that approaches using direct reinforcement to change behaviour are amongst the most powerful intervention procedures in terms of the amount of change that they produced.

Careful assessment before, during, and on termination of an intervention – and a follow-up – are important aspects of this approach (Ross, 1978). Shaping is normally applied to spontaneously occurring behaviour, though sole reliance on reinforcement procedures is difficult with extreme isolates who provide very little social behaviour to be shaped (O'Connor, 1969). Some studies have tried to get around this by providing initial coaching or modelling programmes prior to performance – more on this later. In terms of improving relationships by means of behaviour therapy, O'Connor (1969) notes that operant methods are most useful in shaping simple or broad classes of behaviour (such as time spent in interaction) rather than more complex or specific skills such as initiating interaction or resolving conflict.

Adults and peers can both serve to promote peer relationship skills (Jason & Rhodes, 1989). Indeed, Goetz, Thomson & Etzel (1975) describe a tripartite classification of withdrawal behaviour which classifies social withdrawal as pervasive (low frequency of interaction with adults and peers), withdrawal from adults (relatively higher frequency of interaction with peers than adults), or withdrawal from peers (higher rates of interaction with adults than peers). The precise nature of the child's social withdrawal determines the appropriateness of adult or peer mediated interventions. Shaping procedures have used tangible rewards and praise to gradually increase the frequency of interaction.

The case of "Ann"

A good example of social reinforcements being used to gradually shape behaviour is supplied by Allen et al. (1964). This study attempted to increase the peer attention of a four-year-old preschool girl identified as "Ann". From her first days in preschool Ann showed little attempt to initiate or respond to interaction from peers but interacted freely with adults. After six weeks in nursery school, a period considered sufficient to allow for the child to settle in, formal assessment of Ann's behaviour was made. This confirmed that Ann was socially isolated from her peers but interacted freely with the teachers. She was not maladjusted, indeed the authors note that she had a varied and well-developed repertoire of physical and mental skills that commanded teacher attention. She herself often sought and used strategies to gain the attention and interaction of teachers. For example, "With passing days she complained at length about minute or invisible bumps and abrasions" (p. 512). Unfortunately many of the attention gaining strategies were incompatible with peer play.

Five days of pre-treatment observations established a baseline for the behaviours that were to be modified: the child interacted about 10% of the time with peers and 40% of the time with the teachers. It was established that the teachers' attention acted as a positive reinforcer for the child. To modify this behaviour in the direction of more interaction with peers, the teacher rewarded the child with more attention and positive statements when she interacted with other children but not when she was alone or with an adult. Typical of shaping procedures, the precise behaviours required to be rewarded became increasingly specific. Initially simply standing close to another child would elicit reward, when this increased in frequency it provided more opportunities for playing with other children and this play lasted for longer periods of time. These then became the target behaviours and statements were directed to Ann as a group member rather than as an individual, only direct interaction was rewarded.

The intervention produced immediate and marked changes in peer and teacher directed behaviours which were maintained over the six-day intervention. After six days Ann was interacting with other children about 60% of the time and interactions with adults fell to less than 20%. The direct cause relationship between reward and the shaping of behaviour was impressively illustrated by a reversal in the procedure to restore the original reinforcement contingencies (the child being rewarded for being alone or interacting with teachers and ignored when she interacted with peers). This phase lasted five days and resulted in patterns of behaviour immediately returning to levels similar to the original baseline, less than 20% of mornings in interaction with peers and about 40% in interaction with adults. A final reversal on the seventeenth day of the intervention again rewarded the child for interacting with peers. Over the next eight days the time spent interacting with peers again increased to about 60% and the time seeking interaction with adults stabilised at about 25% of the time. The teachers now relaxed the rigid regime of reinforcement so it became more representative of that generally found in the class, though follow-up checks showed the pattern of interacting primarily with peers to be maintained over a 26-day post-intervention period. This is impressive evidence, but are these effects permanent? The issue of stability of treatment effects is a major concern associated with shaping procedures, and one to which we turn next.

Maintenance of change

Although some studies of behavioural shaping with socially ineffective children show good stability of treatment effects many months after the end of the intervention (e.g. Allen et al., 1975), many show only marginal or no significant statistical differences between groups of treated children and untreated control groups. Though studies tend to be successful in the short term, behaviour tends to return to baseline once reinforcement is terminated (e.g. O'Connor, 1972; Karoly & Harris, 1986). This is probably due, at least in part, to the brevity of many experimental intervention programmes (Combs & Slaby, 1977), though it is somewhat surprising as social interaction is supposed to be implicitly rewarding. It is also likely to be a reflection of the relatively small change reinforcement studies produce on social cognitive processes (Schneider & Byrne, 1985). A major part of the problem is probably that a limited number of skills are often taught in isolation, yet sustained interaction requires a complex set of interrelated skills (Strain & Fox, 1981). Combining shaping procedures with modelling helps to increase stability (O'Connor, 1972), perhaps by providing more subtle, holistic skill concepts. The gradual fading of reinforcement also helps to ensure that behaviour is nested within a wider, stable social context. Emphasising the role of self-reinforcement and monitoring is a means of producing longer-lasting effects, even when others ignore or punish the new behaviour (Meichenbaum, 1986).

The peer group will often function as a more natural means of delivering reinforcement and provide greater stability of outcomes (Strain & Fox, 1981). Even if the intervention is based on adults dispensing major reinforcements, ultimately peer interaction must depend on peer responses – these are the universal constituent of peer social interactions, and these are probably the crucial element in the maintenance of the benefits of an intervention. Adults are not and cannot be involved in all of a child's activities and relationships, this would be an increasingly undesirable and potentially damaging and disruptive state of affairs as the child gets older.

Modelling

Modelling, sometimes known as vicarious learning or observational learning, is the learning of behaviour through observing another person (adult or child), present or on film (in which case it is termed symbolic modelling). This is a major source of everyday social learning, and a major treatment method (Kirkland & Thelen, 1977). The process itself is often rewarded and encouraged in children. An imitator is often rewarded by his or her peers for copying them (Thelen et al., 1977). Modelling has several advantages as a technique. Because it can be via a film (symbolic modelling) rather than requiring individual therapists, it can be used on a large scale, it need not require professional administration (e.g. it can be done in the school), and can be a useful supplement to other methods.

Modelling is typically partitioned into two phases. Acquisition, the learning of a response, and performance. This procedure is often a useful initial accompaniment to a shaping programme where there is little existing behaviour to shape, as in many extreme isolates, or where the target skill is complex, as well as a valuable technique in its own right. The use of reinforcements facilitate the maintenance of changes learnt through modelling. Modelling allows the transmission of skills, the reduction of social fears which are inhibiting current performance (modelling can, of course, also serve to inhibit responses), and the facilitation of the performance of existing behaviours that occur at low rates or not at all (Bandura, 1969). The observation of a model receiving material rewards or prize has been well established as increasing performance of similar behaviours in an observer (e.g. Bandura, 1977).

A number of studies have attempted to use modelling to improve children's relationship skills. Several studies have shown children ranging from preschoolers to adolescents films of age-mates demonstrating specific social responses (which are positively received) and demonstrated modelling effects (e.g. O'Connor, 1969, 1972; Keller & Carlson, 1974; Thelen et al., 1976). The appropriateness of the model is worthy of emphasis here. This is a complex issue, though similar models are generally regarded as more informative and effective (see Schunk (1987) for a review). O'Connor's (1969) film has been successfully used with several groups of preschoolers but Furman (1980) cites a study which shows that it has none the less proved ineffective with elementary school children.

Applications of modelling

In an excellent study by O'Connor (1969), 13 socially isolated and extremely withdrawn nursery school children were identified. The children were identified on the basis of teacher nominations and behavioural observation (frequently avoiding contact by retreating into corners, closets and so on). Six of these were treated by means of a modelling procedure and the remaining children formed a no-treatment comparison group. The treated children were shown a 23-minute film containing 11 scenes in which children interacted in a nursery school setting. In each scene the child first observed and then joined in the activities. In each scene the child received positive outcomes such as peer approval (such as smiling and being talked to), acceptance into an activity, or some tangible reward such as a toy or play materials to share with the friends. The scenes were graduated in their level of threat, with early scenes being rather calm and involving only two children (such as sharing a book), later scenes involved more vigorous activities (such as tossing toys around the room) and larger numbers (up to six) of children. A narrator highlighted and emphasised the appropriateness of the models' behaviour.

Immediately after watching the films children were returned to their classrooms and their behaviour was observed. The treatment group showed an increase in their level of social interaction to that of their non-isolate peers. In fact this is a modest claim by the author, a graph in the original paper shows that they exceeded the mean number of social interactions of the non-isolated children, though no analysis of the type or quality of these interactions is made. The no-treatment children showed no improvement. Formal follow-up was not conducted, though teacher assessments of social withdrawal were obtained at the end of the school year. The teachers were uninformed as to which children had been trained and which had been in a no-treatment control condition. Only one of the six trained children was still regarded as isolated, in comparison to four of the seven children in the no-treatment condition. More systematic evidence for the maintenance over several weeks of improvements in children trained by means of modelling has been provided by later studies (e.g. O'Connor, 1972; Evers & Schwartz, 1973), though Gottman (1977b) failed to find an effect after eight weeks.

Studies which have more closely examined the content of children's social behaviour after exposure to interventions based on modelling suggest that many improvements are due to disinhibition of behaviour rather than simply copying the model. A study by Keller & Carlson (1974) used a modelling procedure to train ten isolated 3–4-year-old preschoolers in specific social behaviours. Children were shown four five-minute films which focused on one socially reinforcing behaviour from imitating, laughing and smiling, token giving, and affectionate physical contact. During sequences in the film the six-year-old models were seen performing the behaviour and receiving a positive response from peers. For comparison purposes another group of nine isolated children simply watched sequences from a nature film. The levels of interaction and the level of dispensing and receiving reinforcements were recorded before and after the treatment and in a follow-up approximately three weeks later. Although the treated children did show a stable improvement in their social behaviour in the classroom, to levels on a par with non-isolate peers, this was due to an increase in the frequency of use of behaviours already dominant in the child's pre-training repertoire (verbalisation, smiling, and imitation), not due to the use of new or previously infrequently used behaviours. In this instance modelling is serving to direct the child's attention to sources of reinforcement and hence disinhibit his or her neutral existing behaviour (Blackham & Silberman, 1975). An alternative explanation is that this procedure made explicit the functions of the behaviours that the children already possessed and were capable of using

(Ladd & Mize, 1983). It is difficult to put complex behaviour patterns into use successfully without any practice. Other approaches, such as coaching, are possibly better at encouraging the adoption and successful use of totally new and complex responses.

The two examples above have both focused on symbolic modelling. Models do, of course, also exist in real life and in the child's own classroom. Sulzer, Mayer & Cody (1968) showed that withdrawn behaviour could be improved by seating the child near a more sociable peer who serves as a model for desirable behaviour. When the model behaved in the desired way this was noted out loud by the teacher and rewarded. This is not, of course, the same as simply exposing children to live peer models. This does not necessarily seem to result in improved social behaviour skills (Strain, 1977). If it did, perhaps there wouldn't be so many isolated children in classes with many very skilled peers. One possible reason that the film used by O'Connor (1969, 1972) was more effective than many real-life examples experienced by the child is due to the narrator drawing the child's attention to appropriate skills and their consequences. Drawing the unskilled child's attention to the performance of more skilled peers could have similar effect to formal training using films (Csapo, 1972).

Combining approaches

As was noted at the beginning of this section, this technique can be usefully combined with reinforcement approaches. Indeed, modelling theory acknowledges the importance of rewards in the acquisition and performance phases of modelling (Perry & Furukawa, 1986). Imitation is more likely if a model is seen being reinforced, if the model is prestigious, of the same sex, and so on. Similarly, a learned behaviour is more likely to be performed if it is reinforced. Performance may have been considerably enhanced in the above study had such an element been included. It is, however, also important to compare to the locus and magnitude of effects produced by the different techniques. Some studies attempting comparisons have been made and it is to these that we turn next. Comparisons have also been made with a third technique, coaching (see Gresham & Nagle, 1980), and this is dealt with in the next section.

O'Connor (1972) compared the effectiveness of shaping (reinforcement contingent on peer interaction behaviour) and modelling as intervention strategies with isolated preschoolers. As in the previous study by O'Connor (1969), subjects watched either the modelling film or a control film which had been previously used. In addition, half the subjects in each of these groups were also reinforced in the classroom when they showed appropriate social orientation and interaction with peers. The results of the earlier study were replicated in the modelling condition, there was increased social interaction. Similar magnitude of effects were also observed in the control film plus shaping condition and in the modelling plus shaping condition. In other words, all the interventions were having roughly similar effects. The crucial difference was not evident until the follow-up assessments were made, at three and six weeks after the termination of the intervention. The high levels of interaction in the conditions which included modelling were maintained. In fact, in the modelling-only condition there was a further increase, while the effects in the shaping-only condition disappeared. The major advantage of modelling is its ability to maintain change – though it is also a fairly quick technique and more suitable for use in situ by classroom teachers. The film provided new social behaviours and emphasised that they will be rewarding for the child, rather than simply bolstering existing behaviour. The film also repeatedly emphasised abstract principles, such as playing together, which are often not spontaneously derived by the child in the course of shaping. The graded threat in the film scenes also helped to gradually reduce the anxiety associated with performing the social behaviours.

Coaching

This term is often used to cover the teaching of new social and cognitive skills through the direct instruction and rehearsal of specific skills. It aims to facilitate maintenance and generalisation by not only teaching skills but by promoting understanding of the skills and an ability to monitor and adapt performance (Ladd & Mize, 1983). A study by Mize and Ladd (1990a) showed that social skills training produced improvements in skills use in the classroom that correlated with improvements in the children's knowledge of friendly social strategies. The status of some unpopular children derives from their poor knowledge of how to go about making and maintaining friendships (e.g. Gottman, Gonso & Rasmussen, 1975). The approaches subsumed by this heading recognise that many behaviour problems represent complex skills deficits rather than simply inappropriate reinforcement histories or the lack of a unit of behaviour. So, for example, some children do not appreciate that they are doing something wrong, do not know what they could do that would be better or, even if they know the appropriate behaviour, are unable to produce it or are anxious about its application. Typically the child is provided with a rule or an example of an effective behaviour (the tuition phase). The child then practices the behaviour, possibly including role play (the rehearsal phase), and finally the child is given feedback, the performance is discussed and evaluated and suggestions for improvement are made (the review phase). Often the process continues by further role playing and performance evaluations. As the training is of very specific skills it is important that these are tailored for the specific client group. For example, that they are age, sex, social class and ethnic group appropriate.

As the above description implies, this approach relies more heavily than previous approaches on verbal communication. Cognitive processes are explicitly acknowledged and the child is involved as an active participant in the training (Combs & Slaby, 1977). The process has been conceptualised more in education, pedagogic terms than as therapy (Goldstein, Gershaw & Sprafkin, 1985). Because of the emphasis on verbal and cognitive factors, this approach has been mainly used on school-age children (in fact, mainly elementary school age), though similar, positive patterns of results have been reported for preschoolers (e.g. Mize & Ladd, 1990a, b).

The effects of coaching

A number of related studies have provided substantial empirical evidence about the nature and extensiveness of coaching as an intervention procedure. In an early study Gottman, Gonso & Schuler (1976) selected four third-grade girls of low sociometric status and coached two of them in social skills, the other two served were a control group and simply spent a similar amount of time with an adult. Treatment was for approximately 30 minutes per day for one week. The skills taught were selected because their importance had been established in a previous study by the authors (Gottman, Gonso & Rasmussen, 1975). Three main skills were taught, initiating interaction, referential communication, and giving and receiving positive interaction. Instruction used a variety of techniques. The first phase was a modelling procedure and used films of narrated vignettes of children joining others in ongoing activities. The second phase was direct teaching of the skills in friendship making, including role play with the coach. The third phase used various games to improve referential communication skills, the ability to take the listener's perspective. For example, the child might be asked to give instructions to a blindfold puppet navigating an obstacle course.

A follow-up assessment nine weeks after the intervention showed an improved sociometric rating for the treated children on measures of playmate and workmate preference. Similar improvements were not shown in the two children that had not received the coaching. The improved sociometric status of the treatment children was not simply a reflection of more frequent or more positive social behaviour, most notably the treated children changed the distribution of their social overtures.

A subsequent and commonly cited study of social skills training with children was conducted by Oden & Asher (1977). In this study socially isolated third and fourth graders received social skills training. The training included instruction by an adult in relevant skills concerning participation, such as initiating interaction and paying attention, co-operation and turn-taking, communication and listening skills, and "validation support", giving positive, friendly support and feedback. The child was then given the opportunity to practice the skills in the context of playing a game with a peer. The progress of the game was subsequently reviewed with the coach. Five training sessions were held over a four-week period. Children receiving social skills training subsequently showed significantly higher peer play sociometric acceptance ratings in comparison to low status children simply playing games with another child or playing solitary games. The improvement in the coached children was maintained over the course of a year. The coached children also showed an increase in the number of friendship nominations received. The lack of any improvement in a work sociometric rating showed that the game-playing skills did not generalise and produce improvement in other domains. Unfortunately this study did not find any changes in the observed positive social behaviour of the coached children. Nor were there any behavioural differences in the popular and unpopular children before the intervention – which makes it difficult to interpret the improved sociometric standing of the coached children (Putallaz & Gottman, 1981). The authors suggested that a more focused and detailed behavioural assessment could possibly establish which behaviours differ and change.

In a study by Ladd (1981) an attempt was made to refine and extend the Oden & Asher (1977) procedure. The children selected for this study were third graders of low sociometric status and poor social skills in the classroom. They were trained in pairs. Three specific skills were taught: asking questions, leading (offering useful suggestions and directions), and making supportive statements. In the first six sessions the Oden & Asher procedure was used to promote an understanding of the skills, followed by an opportunity to rehearse the skills with their training partner while supervised by the trainer. Two final sessions were used to improve skill maintenance and generalisation by asking the children to recall the skills, and encouraging them to use the skills in play situations with familiar and unfamiliar peers, and by reviewing instances in which the skills had been used with peers. Sociometric and observational assessments were conducted on completion of the training and in a follow-up session four weeks later. Significant gains in classroom peer acceptance were noted at post-test and increased through to the follow-up. Improvement was noted on two of the skills, questions and leads, the support measure was low at each time of assessment and the authors speculated that though these behaviours are valued they are used sparingly at this age.

Additional and alternative procedures

The relative effectiveness of coaching and modelling as approaches to improving social skills were examined in a study by Gresham & Nagle (1980).

The subjects of this study were third- and fourth-grade children identified as socially isolated on the basis of work and play sociometric measures. Training was generally in groups of two or three. For the modelling condition children watched a narrated film presenting scenes to highlight specific skills or coping self-statements. There was a total of six sessions over three weeks. The children in the coaching condition were instructed in an identical set of skills, given opportunity for rehearsal and discussed and received feedback on performance. A third treatment condition combined abbreviated aspects of both the modelling and coaching procedures. Assessment of treatment effects were made on five sociometric scales and four categories of behavioural observation. Observations of behaviour included rates of initiating and receiving positive and negative interaction.

Overall, behavioural and sociometric measures showed coaching and modelling were equally effective procedures for teaching social skills, though there seems little, if any, additional benefit from attempting to combine abbreviated versions of these approaches. Sociometric ratings by the class peers which evaluated the children as playmates showed all three treatment methods to be equally effective in improving social status, though like the Oden & Asher (1977) study this was not reflected in a work sociometric. Training focused on play and did not generalise to work situations.

In terms of behavioural indices, all three treatment groups showed an increase in the levels of positive behaviour received, though the increase was most marked in the modelling group. In contrast, coaching was the most effective strategy for reducing negative interactions. Gresham & Nagle (1980, p. 727) comment on their results: "It could be that modelling is more effective in increasing rates of positive peer interaction, and coaching is more effective in inhibiting or decreasing rates of negative peer interaction."

A fundamental aim of much social skills training is to alter a child's social status. This has led some authors to argue that this is most effectively achieved through controlled peer group contact rather than coaching individual children in specific skills. A study by Bierman & Furman (1984) examined the relative effectiveness of coaching and peer group contact as ways of improving the sociometric status of unaccepted fifth- and sixth-grade pre-adolescents with poor conversational skills. Treatments consisted of ten half-hour sessions over a six-week period. The children were assigned to one of four treatment conditions:

1. Individual coaching in conversational skills. This included training in skills of self-expression, questioning and giving leadership.
2. Group experience in which the children engaged in a co-operative activities with two more popular classmates. The activities centred around making a video film showing friendly interaction.
3. Conversational skills training combined with group experience. Here the

introduction of the conversational skills and the discussion and practice phases of coaching were incorporated into the first five sessions, which were used for practice before filming began. The second five sessions alternated sessions of film making and reviewing skill performance.
4. A control group received no treatment.

The effects of these treatments was assessed both immediately on completion of treatment and in a follow-up six weeks later.

The complex findings of this study indicated that both group involvement and skills training produced effects on their participants, though the nature of these effects differed. Group experience did not have any major effect on levels of skilled performance, though it did produce a temporary improvement in classroom sociometric status, rates of peer interaction at lunchtime (but not of teachers' ratings of classroom behaviour), and feelings of social efficacy effectiveness. Presumably due to the effects of modelling, opportunity to practice and be rewarded for appropriate behaviour, and the opportunity to overcome the other children's avoidance of them and disconfirm the other children's existing attitudes. But these improvements were not sustained.

Coached children showed a sustained improvement in their conversational skills and improvements in their rates of lunchtime social interaction, though in the six weeks up to the follow-up this was not reflected in changes in sociometric status. Suggesting that either (1) not enough time had elapsed for this to be reflected in these measures, or (2) a weak relationship between these measures.

Only in the group that experienced both coaching and group experience was there a general and sustained improvement in acceptance as well as in social skills and peer interaction rates through to the six-week follow-up assessment. Though this was limited to the sociometric ratings given by the non-target participants in the peer involvement task. The treatment had only contrived interaction with a limited sub-group of peers and the acceptance did not generalise to the other classmates. Emphasising the necessity of taking the social context of relationships into account.

Rejected children

Overall, the research literature paints a fairly positive picture of coaching with socially isolated children that have low popularity ratings. Unfortunately, as Bierman (1989) points out, this is not the same as coaching children that are actively rejected because of their aversive behaviour patterns. The evidence for the efficacy of coaching with these children is less clear. As Bierman (1989, p. 63) notes, "In their traditional format, coaching programs promoting positive interaction strategies are not sufficient to meet the needs of most rejected children''. To balance this conclusion it must be borne in mind that ''efforts to decrease aggressiveness or disruptiveness have been indirect and have not figured prominently in the design of most intervention programs for rejected children. Our contention is that more explicit attention to aggression and disruptiveness will result in improved intervention effectiveness'' (Coie & Koeppl, 1990). The evidence that is slowly beginning to emerge seems to support this assertion. Recent Portuguese research using coaching procedures designed specifically for use with disruptive children and adolescents has been able to show substantial amounts of voluntary participation and improvements in behaviour (Matos et al., 1990, 1991).

If the aversive behaviour is due to other difficulties, such as frustration resulting from academic difficulties, then tackling these is likely to be more productive than simply teaching social skills (Coie & Krehbiel, 1984). For rejected children with negative social behaviour both techniques to control the negative behaviour and techniques to improve social skills are necessary to bring about improvements in sociometric status. Even this is likely to produce only limited generalisation due to the reputation which the rejected child has established with peers and the consequent interpretations placed on his or her behaviour (Bierman, Miller & Stabb, 1987). None the less social skills training programmes could include an element to deal with self-control or be combined with other social learning approaches to reducing negative behaviours. Attention could then also be given to the child's social context to facilitate the generalisation and acceptance of the new behaviour patterns.

Does social skills training help promote friendship or superficial relating? As Button (1979, p. 197) notes, ''It is not too difficult to help someone to greet, meet, and converse at a personal level with other people, but the removal of an impediment alone does not compensate for the long history of not having had practice in that give and take, equal and intimate relationship that friendship implies''.

Cognitive approaches

The methods discussed in the section on behavioural interventions have been primarily concerned with modifying the child's overt behaviour and/or specific knowledge of social skills. An increasingly influential approach has aimed to move this emphasis, to give greater consideration to covert cognitive processes and patterns of social information processing (Dodge, 1985). From this perspective interest focuses not primarily on behaviour but on underlying variables such as how children identify problems and generate solutions, social perception, and the role self-reinforcement (Furman, 1984b; Meichenbaum, 1986). These processes are assumed to mediate behavioural adjustment. Some authors have speculated that much social skills training is effective largely because children gain confidence in their ability to attain interpersonal goals (Dweck, 1981; Asher & Taylor, 1981). The assumption here is that understanding the causes and consequences of behaviour will facilitate social adjustment (Hayden, Nasby & Davids, 1977). Among other considerations, the child learns that unacceptable mistakes in behaviour do not make the person less acceptable.

Although cognitive approaches represent valuable treatment methods in their own right, they have aroused considerable interest because of their potential for improving the stability and generalisation of gains achieved by other methods. For example, the teaching of probabilities attached to outcomes (rehearsal and feedback) prevents children making debilitating attributions when their newly learnt skills are unsuccessful and they experience occasional rejection (see Goetz & Dweck, 1980; Sobol & Earn, 1985b). There is also a potential benefit from training at a level of skill which is sufficiently general to be the basis for many different behavioural outcomes (Pellegrini, 1985b).

Cognitive approaches aim to teach adaptive ways of thinking which are applicable to social and personal problems. For example, delinquents show more positive and less negative social behaviour after training to enhance their social role-taking abilities (Chalmers & Townsend, 1990). Impulsive behaviour can be reduced by teaching strategies such as analysing task requirement and using verbal self-instructions to proceed slowly. Considerably more research is required in this area, especially as regards the relationship between social cognitive problem solving and behaviour.

Interpersonal cognitive problem solving

The verbal instruction approach is illustrated by the considerable literature on interpersonal problem solving programmes, and the influential work of Spivack and Shure (1974; Shure & Spivack, 1979, 1980). There are many different problem solving skills, the significance of specific skills varies with age. These skills include the ability to recognise problems, to generate alternative solutions, to see the means to achieve the desired solution, to anticipate the consequences of acts (for the child and for others), and to understand the relationship between interpersonal motives and actions. Its aim is not to find *the* solution to a problem but rather to develop a child's ability to explore possible solutions and their effects, and then to be able to select the most appropriate alternative. Communication, role taking, and the ability to compromise are obviously important factors in this goal. Spivack & Shure concentrated on developing and integrating three main skills: alternative solutions thinking, consequential thinking, and means–end thinking (though this is a higher order skill which does not emerge till middle childhood).

Intervention programmes in interpersonal problem solving produce corresponding changes in role-taking. Expertise in generating alternatives and means–end thinking has been related to group functioning in the classroom – and in general, healthy adjustment. For example, Spivack, Platt & Shure (1976) report programmes used across a wide range of ages, from preschool through to adulthood, and with both preventive and remedial aims. In a preventive programme, kindergarten children were taught a series of prerequisite thinking skills (for example, language, listening, and paying attention) and then interpersonal problem solving skills focusing on alternative solutions thinking and consequential thinking. They provided potential solutions and probable consequences for various problem situations involving peers and adults. Note that these can be quite broad goals and behaviours compared to behavioural approaches. Children showed enhanced problem solving thinking, better social adjustment, a more prosocial orientation, and higher levels of liking by peers. Impatient, impulsive, and withdrawn children showed improved, more adaptive behaviour patterns. Follow-up research after one year showed that the normal children exposed to the programme were subsequently less likely to show behavioural difficulties. It was indeed a successful preventive programme, at least over this short time period.

Unfortunately, many studies manage to improve children's problem-solving skills but without any consequent changes in their behaviour or peer relations. There are also doubts about the stability of treatment effects. These considerations have raised important doubts about the utility of the technique as an intervention strategy (e.g. Nelson & Carson, 1988). Schneider & Byrne's (1985) meta-analysis shows social cognitive approaches to be less effective than operant, modelling or coaching approaches. These variable results probably present an unduly bleak picture due to many studies being on preventive programmes (Furman, 1984b). Schneider & Byrne's analysis does indicate that programmes with "normal" children do, as one might expect from an already skilled population, produce smaller improvements.

Differences in social problem solving are most marked between popular and rejected children, with socially withdrawn children showing little difference from their more sociable counterparts (Rubin, 1985). As Rubin notes (p. 132): "By second grade . . . despite initial leanings toward adult dependent, non-assertive strategies to meet social goals, isolate children do come eventually to suggest the use of strategies identical to those suggested by average and highly sociable children. In short, the cumulative impact of consistent isolate status is practically nil." Although the cognitive characteristics of rejected and aggressive children are associated with their later problems of social adjustment, for consistently withdrawn children the problem is often one of anxiety. Social fear is associated with later internalising difficulties such as negative self-perception, social anxiety disorders, and possibly depression (Rubin et al., 1989). Therapeutic methods focusing directly on the child's social anxiety rather than social skill are the most appropriate modes of treatment for these children.

Peer-assisted interventions

Many researchers have attempted to use the child's peers in many and varied ways as agents of change (see Furman & Gavin, 1989). Although research provides some evidence for the effectiveness of these approaches, the general issue of procedural practicality has received relatively little attention (Kohler & Strain, 1990).

Although many studies have used peers in their treatment programmes, trying to change the attitudes and behaviour of the child's peer group is not common, despite the acknowledged significance of peer perceptions and behaviour for maintaining social status (Hollinger, 1987). As Price & Dodge (1989) note, "One area in which further research is especially needed is on the contributions of peers' processing and behavior to social rejection" (Price & Dodge, 1989, p. 365). Potentially this approach will aid the maintenance and generalisation of changes.

Peers have showed more interaction with a withdrawn child when reinforced, such as by teacher attention and contact (e.g. Strain & Timm, 1974), or have been coached in techniques to facilitate interaction with less skilled peers (e.g. Strain, Shores & Timm, 1977). This procedure is also effective in increasing the rate of interaction of autistic children (Ragland, Kerr & Strain, 1978) and isolated retarded children (Lancioni, 1982).

Other than these overt manipulations of peer behaviour, requiring co-operative activities to achieve goals and rewards can reduce friction and increase liking and friendship (e.g. Sherif et al., 1961). This can of course backfire if a group member can be blamed for a failure to achieve the goal. A number of subsequent studies have confirmed the utility of co-operative activities for promoting interaction and relationships in children (Orlick, 1981), though doubts remain over the stability of these effects. Utilising these techniques in standard teaching programmes will help to increase the stability of changes.

Co-operative learning programmes

The success of this technique has produced a variety of co-operative learning approaches to promote such interactions in the classroom (see Nastasi & Clements, 1991). A well-known example of such a programme is the jigsaw classroom, originally developed by Aronson et al. (1978). In this technique the material to be covered is divided among the group members. Each child has to cover a different aspect of the material. Aronson (1988) cites the example of a lesson studying the biography of Joseph Pulitzer, the publisher. The pupils in the fifth-grade classroom were in six-person groups. A biography consisting of six paragraphs covering the major aspects of his life was prepared. Each paragraph covered a different aspect of Pulitzer's life, his childhood, Pulitzer as a young man, his education, and so on. For each group, a copy of the biography was divided into its component paragraphs and each paragraph was given to a different member of the six-person group. In order to learn the full story the children had to each master their piece of the information and present it to the rest of the group. To master the paragraph they went off by themselves, though they could consult and rehearse with their counterparts in other groups. The children then returned to their groups and were given a specific amount of time to communicate their separate pieces of information. They were mutually dependent and this was emphasised by their being told that they would be tested on their knowledge. The children gradually recognise their interdependence and learn to co-operate and value every individual contribution – though it sometimes takes several days to overcome competitiveness.

There are many positive effects resulting from appropriately structured co-operative learning programmes. In addition to academic improvements (Slavin, 1983), previously isolated children become more positively regarded and develop higher self-esteem (e.g. Blaney et al., 1977), and show better role-taking abilities (Bridgeman, 1981). Slavin & Karweit (1981) found that pupils in co-operative learning programmes named more students as friends, such programmes also frequently report greater levels of liking among peers (Slavin, 1983).

Of course, not all children are able to readily manage such co-operative programmes and support and structure are important, at least initially. If these co-operative programmes are not well managed the children may fail to achieve their goals and blame this on an individual group member, thus increasing rather than reducing negative perceptions and reactions to the child.

Arranged interactions

One interesting approach has been not to manage peer interaction but simply to manage who the child interacts with. Studies show that retarded children are less well received as potential friends and that increased contact can increase this rejection (Goodman, Gottlieb & Harrison, 1972). Part of the explanation for this lies in perceived lesser ability of retarded children (Asher, Oden & Gottman, 1977). If this is the case then opportunity to interact on equal terms should improve acceptance. Supporting this, Gottlieb (1971) found that children had more positive attitudes to playing with retarded children than working with them. This same expertness factor can also be used with the isolated child. Making the isolates' talents visible to the class or teaching them a valued skill can improve their peer status.

Several studies have attempted to improve the social standing of isolated retarded children by manipulating their peer interactions. Partnering a child of low sociometric status with a more popular peer so that others observe their smooth interaction in organised co-operative group activities can facilitate the isolated child's general acceptance (Chennault, 1967), though these effects are often of limited duration (Rucker & Vincenzo, 1970). Similar attempts have been made to improve the social status of mainstreamed mentally retarded children. Again, partnering a mentally retarded child with non-retarded peers in co-operative activities. By the end of the eight-week programme improvements in sociometric status had resulted. Other research has found similar results due to co-operative peer contact with more popular peers on non-retarded socially isolated or rejected children (e.g. Lilly, 1971). A good example of such a study is that of Bierman & Furman (1984), which has been outlined in detail earlier in this chapter. Like the studies of retarded children, these interventions do improve sociometric status in the short term but have doubtful stability. The useful contribution of the Bierman & Furman study is to show that combining this approach with social skills coaching improves stability.

Younger partners

An interesting variation on the above approach has examined the behavioural benefits of arranged interaction with younger children. Many interactions with same age peers benefit the interactants differently and the child unable to hold his own becomes relegated to the social backwaters. One approach to ameliorating this situation has been to give these less socially competent children experiences and practice in successful interaction by partnering them with younger children. In an early study Koch (1935) partnered each of seven unsociable nursery school child with a sociable peer for 20 daily 30-minute play sessions with materials expected to stimulate co-operative play. A cumulative increase in sociability was noted in the isolated child.

In a similar study Furman, Rahe & Hartup (1979) partnered isolated preschoolers (four to almost six years old) with either a same-sex peer of approximately the same age or a sociable child 12–20 months younger. The child met his or her partner for ten play sessions of 20 minutes (with a change of partner after five session) over a period of 4–6 weeks. Rates of interaction in the play sessions was often over 60%, more than twice as high as that originally observed in the classroom when the children were identified as isolated. Subsequent observation of the children in the preschool classroom showed improvement in children partnered with both with same-age peers and younger children in comparison to a group not receiving any special treatment. Much of this difference is due to the amount of change in the group of children partnered with younger children. Changes in rates of peer interaction were larger and more consistent for isolates partnered with younger children. Seven of the eight children in this group improved their interaction rate by more than 50%, bringing them almost on a par with the non-isolate peers. In comparison, only three of the isolates paired with same-age peers and one of the children receiving no treatment. The play experience is effective because of its effect on reinforcement rates (e.g. helping, co-operative play), rather than altering social actions such as neutral acts or punishments. Thus, for example, reinforcement rates were increased in the treatment conditions, most markedly for children with a younger peer who increased almost threefold. As this style of behaviour characterises older children's relationships this in effect represents an increase in the maturity of relating.

The changes in behaviour recorded above did not show gradual changes over sessions, which would be consistent with a behavioural shaping of social activity, and so the authors explain improvements from interaction with younger preschoolers as apparently providing positive, better matched social experiences which the child tended not to receive in the classroom, an opportunity for assertive interactions with a higher probability of success than in the classroom. Many isolates are responsive but lack the skills to initiate and direct interactions successfully. Even relatively limited opportunity for interaction can dramatically improve their social skills. Though, as we have already noted, popular and less popular peers tend to form separate and distinct interactional subsystems (Ladd, 1983) and so lessen the possibility of such experience.

References

Aboud, F. E. (1981). Egocentrism, conformity, and agreeing to disagree. *Developmental Psychology*, **17**, 791–799.

Aboud, F. E. (1985). Children's application of attribution principles to social comparisons. *Child Development*, **56**, 682–688.

Aboud, F. E. (1988). *Children and Prejudice*. Oxford: Blackwell.

Adams, G. R. (1977). Physical attractiveness research: Toward a developmental social psychology of beauty. *Human Development*, **20**, 217–240.

Adams, G. R. & Cohen, A. S. (1974). Children's physical and interpersonal characteristics that effect student–teacher interactions. *Journal of Experimental Education*, **44**, 1–5.

Adams, G. R. & Crane, P. (1980). An assessment of parents' and teachers' expectations of preschool children's social preference for attractive or unattractive children or adults. *Child Development*, **51**, 224–231.

Adams, G. R., Hicken, M. & Salehi, M. (1988). Socialization of the physical attractiveness stereotype: Parental expectations and verbal behaviors. *International Journal of Psychology*, **23**, 137–149.

Adams, G. R. & La Voie, J. C. (1974). The effect of student's sex, conduct, and facial attractiveness on teacher expectancy. *Education*, **95**, 76–83.

Agrawal, R. (1983). A study of self-disclosure and self-concept among major castes with special reference to girl students. *Dayalbagh Educational Institute Research Journal of Education*, **1**, 22–27.

Ahrens, R. (1954). Beitrage zur entvicklung des physiognomia – und mimikerkennes. *Zeitschrift für Experimentelle und Angewandte Psychologie*, **2**, 412–454.

Ainsworth, M. D. S. (1979). Attachment as related to mother–infant interaction. In: J. S. Rosenblatt, R. A. Hinde, C. Beer & M. Busnel (Eds), *Advances in the Study of Behavior*, vol. 9. Orlando, FL: Academic Press.

Ainsworth, M. D. S. (1989). Attachment beyond infancy. *American Psychologist*, **44**, 709–716.

Ainsworth, M. D. S., Blehar, M. C., Waters, E. & Wall, S. (1978). *Patterns of Attachment: A Psychological Study of the Strange Situation*. Hillsdale, NJ: Erlbaum.

Allen, J. G. (1974). When does exchanging personal information constitute self-disclosure? *Psychological Reports*, **35**, 195–198.

Allen, K. E., Hart, B., Buell, J. S., Harris, F. R. & Wolf, M. M. (1964). Effects of social reinforcement of isolate behavior on a nursery school child. *Child Development*, **35**, 511–518.

Allen, R. P., Safer, D. J., Heaton, R., Ward, A. & Barrell, M. (1975). Behavior therapy for socially ineffective children. *Journal of the American Academy of Child Psychiatry*, **14**, 500–505.

Alley, T. R. (1981). Head shape and the perception of cuteness. *Developmental Psychology*, **17**, 650–654.

Allport, G. W. (1961). *Pattern and Growth in Personality*. London: Holt, Rinehart & Winston.

Altman, I. (1973). Reciprocity of information exchange. *Journal for the Theory of Social Behavior*, **3**, 249–261.

Altman, I. & Taylor, D. A. (1973). *Social Penetration: The Development of Interpersonal Relationships*. London: Holt, Rinehart & Winston.

American Psychiatric Association (1987). *Diagnostic and Statistical Manual of Mental Disorders* (3rd revised edn), DSM-III-R. Washington, DC: American Psychiatric Association.

Applegate, J. L., Burke, J. A., Burleson, B. R., Delia, J. G. & Kline, S. L. (1985). Reflection enhancing parental communication. In: L. E. Sigel (Ed.), *Parental Belief Systems: The Psychological Consequences for Children*. Hillsdale, NJ: Erlbaum.

Apter, S. J. (1982). *Troubled Children, Troubled Systems*. New York: Pergamon.

Arend, R., Gove, F. L. & Sroufe, L. A. (1979). Continuity of individual adaptation from infancy to kindergarten. *Child Development*, **50**, 950–959.

Argyle, M. (1988). *Bodily Communication* (2nd edn). London: Methuen.

Aristotle (1953 (first published 1934)). *Poetics and Rhetoric*. London: Dent, Dutton.

Aronson, E. (1988). *The Social Animal* (5th edn). New York: Freeman.

Aronson, E., Blaney, N., Stephan, C., Sikes, J. & Snapp, M. (1978). *The Jigsaw Classroom*. Beverly Hills, CA: Sage.

Asendorpf, J. (1986). Shyness in middle and late childhood. In: W. H. Jones, J. M. Cheek & S. R. Briggs (Eds), *Shyness: Perspectives on Research and Treatment*. New York: Plenum.

Asher, S. R. (1983). Social competence and peer status: recent advances and future directions. *Child Development*, **54**, 1427–1434.

Asher, S. R. (1985). An evolving paradigm in social skill training research with children. In: B. H. Schneider, K. H. Rubin & J. E. Ledingham (Eds), *Children's Peer Relations: Issues in Assessment and Intervention*. New York: Springer-Verlag.

Asher, S. R. (1990). Recent advances in the study of peer rejection. In: S. R. Asher & J. D. Coie (Eds), *Peer Rejection in Childhood*. Cambridge: Cambridge University Press.

Asher, S. R. & Coie, J. D. (Eds) (1990). *Peer Rejection in Childhood*. Cambridge: Cambridge University Press.

Asher, S. R. & Gottman, J. M. (1981). *The Development of Children's Friendships*. Cambridge: Cambridge University Press.

Asher, S. R. & Hymel, S. (1981). Children's social competence in peer relations: Sociometric and behavioral assessment. In: J. D. Wine & M. D. Smye (Eds), *Social Competence*. New York: Guilford.

Asher, S. R. & Parker, J. G. (1989). Significance of peer relationship problems in childhood. In: B. H. Schneider, G. Attili, J. Nadel & R. P. Weissberg (Eds), *Social Competence in Developmental Perspective*. Dordrecht: Kluwer.

Asher, S. R. & Renshaw, P. D. (1981). Children without friends: Social knowledge and social skill training. In: S. R. Asher & J. M. Asher (Eds), *The Development of Children's Friendships*. Cambridge: Cambridge University Press.

Asher, S. R. & Taylor, A. R. (1981). Social outcomes of mainstreaming: Sociometric assessment and beyond. *Exceptional Education Quarterly*, **1**, 13–30.

Asher, S. R. & Wheeler, V. A. (1985). Children's loneliness: A comparison of rejected and neglected peer status. *Journal of Consulting and Clinical Psychology*, **53**, 500–505.

Asher, S. R., Hymel, S. & Renshaw, P. D. (1984). Loneliness in children. *Child Development*, **55**, 1457–1464.

Asher, S. R., Oden, S. L. & Gottman, J. M. (1977). Children's friendships in school settings. In: L. G. Katz (Ed.), *Current Topics in Early Childhood Education*, Vol. 1. Hillsdale, NJ: Erlbaum.

Asher, S. R., Renshaw, P. D. & Hymel, S. (1982). Peer relations and the development of social skills. In: S. G. Moore & C. R. Cooper (Eds), *The Young Child: Reviews of Research*, Vol. 3. Washington, DC: National Association for the Education of Young Children.

Asher, S. R., Parkhurst, J. T., Hymel, S. & Williams, G. A. (1990). Peer rejection and loneliness in childhood. In: S. R. Asher & J. D. Coie (Eds), *Peer Rejection in Childhood*. Cambridge: Cambridge University Press.

Ashmore, R. D. & Del Boca, F. K. (1981). Conceptual approaches to stereotypes and stereotyping. In: D. L. Hamilton (Ed.), *Cognitive Processes in Stereotyping and Intergroup Behavior*. Hillsdale, NJ: Erlbaum.

Attili, G. (1989). Social competence versus emotional security: The link between home relationships and behavior problems in preschool. In: B. H. Schneider, G. Attili, J. Nadel & R. P. Weissberg (Eds), *Social Competence in Developmental Perspective*. Dordrecht: Kluwer.

Austin, A. B. & Lindauer, S. K. (1990). Parent–child conversation of more-liked and less-liked children. *Journal of Genetic Psychology*, **151**, 1, 5–23.

Avery, A. W., Rider, K. & Haynes-Clements, L. (1981). Communication skills training for adolescents. *Adolescence*, **16**, 289–298.

Bakeman, R. & Adamson, L. B. (1984). Coordinating attention to people and objects in mother–infant and peer–infant interaction. *Child Development*, **55**, 1278–1298.

Bakeman, R. & Adamson, L. B. (1986). Infants' conventionalized acts: gesture and words with mothers and peers. *Infant Behavior and Development*, **9**, 215–230.

Bakeman, R. & Brownlee, J. R. (1980). The strategic use of parallel play: a sequential analysis. *Child Development*, **51**, 873–878.

Ballard, M., Corman, L., Gottlieb, J. & Kaufman, M. T. (1977). Improving the social status of mainstreamed retarded children. *Journal of Educational Psychology*, **69**, 605–611.

Balswick, J. O. & Peek, C. W. (1971). The inexpressive male: An American tragedy. *Family Coordinator*, **20**, 363–368.

Bandura, A. (1969). *Principles of Behavior Modification*. New York: Holt, Rinehart & Winston.

Bandura, A. (1977). *Social Learning Theory*. Englewood Cliffs, NJ: Prentice-Hall.

Barenboim, C. (1981). The development of person perception in childhood and adolescence: From behavioral comparisons to psychological constructs to psychological comparisons. *Child Development*, **52**, 129–144.

Barnett, M. A. (1984). Similarity of experience and empathy in preschoolers. *Journal of Genetic Psychology*, **145**, 241–250.

Barocas, R. & Black, H. (1974). Referral rate and physical attractiveness in third-grade children. *Perceptual and Motor Skills*, **39**, 731–734.

Barrera, M. E. & Maurer, D. (1981a). Discrimination of strangers by the three-month-old. *Child Development*, **52**, 558–563.

Barrera, M. E. & Maurer, D. (1981b). Recognition of mother's photographed face by the three-month-old infant. *Child Development*, **52**, 714–716.

Barry, H., Bacon, M. K. & Child, I. L. (1957). A cross-cultural survey of some sex differences in socialization. *Journal of Abnormal and Social Psychology*, **55**, 327–332.

Bartholomew, K. (1990). Avoidance of intimacy: An attachment perspective. *Journal of Social and Personal Relationships*, **7**, 141–178.

Baumrind, D. (1967). Child care practices anteceding three patterns of preschool behavior. *Genetic Psychology Monographs*, **75**, 43–88.

Baumrind, D. (1971). Current patterns of parental authority. *Developmental Psychology Monographs*, **4** (No. 1, part 2), 1–103.

Baxter, L. A. (1984). Trajectories of relationship disengagement. *Journal of Social and Personal Relationships*, **1**, 29–48.

Becker, J. M. T. (1977). A learning analysis of the development of peer oriented behavior in nine month old infants. *Developmental Psychology*, **13**, 481–491.

Bee, H. (1989). *The Developing Child* (5th edn). New York: Harper & Row.

Belle, D. (1989). Gender differences in children's social networks and social supports. In: D. Belle (Ed.), *Children's Social Networks and Social Supports*. New York: Wiley.

Belle, D., Burr, R. & Cooney, J. (1987). Boys and girls as social support theorists. *Sex Roles*, **17**, 657–665.

Belsky, J. (1981). Early human experience: A family perspective. *Developmental Psychology*, **17**, 3–23.

Belsky, J. & Rovine, M. (1987). Temperament and attachment security in the strange situation: an empirical rapprochement. *Child Development*, **58**, 787–795.

Bem, S. L. (1974). The measurement of psychological androgyny. *Journal of Consulting and Clinical Psychology*, **42**, 155–162.

Benn, R. K. (1986). Factors promoting secure attachment relationships between employed mothers and their sons. *Child Development*, **57**, 1224–1231.

Berg, J. H. & Archer, R. L. (1980). Disclosure or concern: A second look at liking for the norm breaker. *Journal of Personality*, **48**, 2, 245–257.

Berg, J. H. & Derlega, V. J. (1987). Themes in the study of self-disclosure. In: V. J. Derlega & J. H. Berg (Eds), *Self-Disclosure*. London: Plenum.

Berg, M. & Medrich, E. A. (1980). Children in four neighbourhoods: The physical environment and its effect on play and play patterns. *Environment and Behavior*, **12**, 320–348.

Berkowitz, L. & Frodi, A. (1979). Reactions to a child's mistakes as affected by his/her looks or speech. *Social Psychology Quarterly*, **42**, 420–425.

Berndt, T. J. (1981a). Age changes and changes over time in prosocial intentions and behaviour between friends. *Developmental Psychology*, **17**, 408–416.

Berndt, T. J. (1981b). Effects of friendship on prosocial intentions and behavior. *Child Development*, **52**, 636–643.

Berndt, T. J. (1981c). Relations between social cognition, nonsocial cognition and social behavior. In: J. H. Flavell & L. Ross (Eds), *Social Cognitive Development*. Cambridge: Cambridge University Press.

Berndt, T. J. (1982). The features and effects of friendship in early adolescence. *Child Development*, **53**, 1447–1460.

Berndt, T. J. (1983). Correlates and causes of sociometric status in childhood: A commentary on six current studies of popular, rejected, and neglected children. *Merrill-Palmer Quarterly*, **29**, 439–448.

Berndt, T. J. (1985). Prosocial behavior between friends in middle childhood and early adolescence. *Journal of Early Adolescence*, **5**, 307–317.

Berndt, T. J. & Das, R. (1987). Effects of popularity and friendship on perception of the personality and social behavior of peers. *Journal of Early Adolescence*, 7, 429–439.

Berndt, T. J. & Heller, K. A. (1986). Gender stereotypes and social inferences. *Journal of Personality and Social Psychology*, 50, 889–898.

Berndt, T. J. & Hoyle, S. G. (1985). Stability and change in childhood and adolescent friendships. *Developmental Psychology*, 21, 1007–1015.

Berndt, T. J. & Perry, T. B. (1986). Children's perceptions of friendship as supportive relationships. *Developmental Psychology*, 22, 640–648.

Berndt, T. J., Hawkins, J. A. & Hoyle, S. G. (1986). Changes in friendship during a school year: Effects on children's and adolescents' impressions of friendship and sharing with friends. *Child Development*, 57, 1284–1297.

Bernstein, N. (1982). Psychosocial results of burns: The damaged self-esteem. *Clinics in Plastic Surgery*, 9, 337–346.

Berry, D. S. & McArthur, L. Z. (1986). Perceiving character in faces: The impact of age-related cranio-facial changes on social perception. *Psychological Bulletin*, 100, 3–18.

Berscheid, E. & Walster, E. (1974). Physical attractiveness. In: L. Berkowitz (Ed.), *Advances in Experimental Social Psychology* (Vol. 7). London: Academic Press.

Bhavnagri, N. P. & Parke, R. D. (1991). Parents as direct facilitators of children's peer relationships: Effects of age of child and sex of parent. *Journal of Social and Personal Relationships*, 8, 423–440.

Bianchi, B. D. & Bakeman, R. (1978). Sex-typed preferences observed in preschoolers: Traditional and open school differences. *Child Development*, 49, 910–912.

Bierman, K. L. (1989). Improving the peer relations of rejected children. In: B. B. Lahey & E. E. Kazdin (Eds), *Advances in clinical child psychology*, Vol. 12. New York: Plenum.

Bierman, K. L. & Furman, W. (1984). The effects of social skills training and peer involvement on the social adjustment of preadolescents. *Child Development*, 55, 151–162.

Bierman, K. L. & McCauley, E. (1987). Children's descriptions of their peer interactions: Useful information for clinical child assessment. *Journal of Clinical Child Psychology*, 16, 9–18.

Bierman, K. L., Miller, C. M. & Stabb, S. (1987). Improving the social behavior and peer acceptance of rejected boys: Effects of social skills training with instructions and prohibitions. *Journal of Consulting and Clinical Psychology*, 55, 194–200.

Bigelow, B. J. (1977). Children's friendship expectations: A cognitive-developmental study. *Child Development*, 48, 246–253.

Bigelow, B. J. (1980). Developmental changes in conceptual friendship expectations associated with children's friendship preferences. *Human Relations*, 33, 225–239.

Bigelow, B. J. (1982). Disengagement and development of social concepts: Toward a theory of friendship. Paper to International Conference on Personal Relationships, University of Wisconsin at Madison, July.

Bigelow, B. J. & La Gaipa, J. J. (1975). Children's written descriptions of friendship: a multidimensional analysis. *Developmental Psychology*, 11, 857–858

Bigelow, B. J. & La Gaipa, J. J. (1980). The development of friendship values and choice. In: H. C. Foot, A. J. Chapman & J. R. Smith (Eds), *Friendship and Social Relations in Children*. Chichester: Wiley.

Black, B. & Hazen, N. L. (1990). Social status and patterns of communication in acquainted and unacquainted preschool children. *Developmental Psychology*, 26, 379–387.

Blackham, G. J. & Silberman, A. (1975). *Modification of Child and Adolescent Behavior* (2nd edn). Belmont, CA: Wadsworth.

Blaney, N., Stephan, C., Rosenfield, D., Aronson, E. & Sikes, J. (1977). Interdependence in the classroom: A field study. *Journal of Educational Psychology*, **69**, 121–128.

Blehar, M. C., Lieberman, A. F. & Ainsworth, M. D. S. (1977). Early face-to-face interaction and its relation to later infant–mother attachment. *Child Development*, **48**, 182–194.

Blyth, D. A. & Foster-Clark, F. (1987). Gender differences in perceived intimacy with different members of adolescents' social networks. *Sex Roles*, **17**, 689–718.

Blyth, D. A. & Traeger, C. (1988). Adolescent self-esteem and perceived relationships with parents and peers. In: S. Salzinger, J. Antrobus & M. Hammer (Eds), *Social Networks of Children, Adolescents and College Students*. Hillsdale, NJ: Erlbaum.

Bogat, G. A., Jones, J. W. & Jason, L. A. (1980). School transitions: preventive intervention following an elementary school closing. *Journal of Community Psychology*, **8**, 343–352.

Booth, C. L., Rose-Krasnor, L. & Rubin, K. H. (1991). Relating preschoolers' social competence and their mothers' parenting behaviors to early attachment security and high-risk status. *Journal of Social and Personal Relationships*, **8**, 363–382.

Borke, A. (1971). Interpersonal perception of young children. *Developmental Psychology*, **5**, 263–269.

Boulton, M. J. & Smith, P. K. (1990). Affective bias in children's perceptions of dominance relationships. *Child Development*, **61**, 221–229.

Bower, T. G. R. (1977). *The Perceptual World of the Child*. Cambridge, MA: Harvard University Press.

Bowlby, J. (1958). The nature of the child's tie to his mother. *International Journal of Psychoanalysis*, **41**, 89–113.

Bowlby, J. (1965). *Child Care and the Growth of Love*. Harmondsworth: Penguin.

Bowlby, J. (1969). *Attachment and Loss, Vol. 1: Attachment*. London: Hogarth Press.

Bowlby, J. (1980). *Attachment and Loss (Vol. 3): Loss, Sadness, and Depression*. New York: Basic Books.

Brachfeld-Child, S. & Schiavo, R. S. (1990). Interactions of preschool and kindergarten friends and acquaintances. *Journal of Genetic Psychology*, **151**, 1, 45–58.

Brennan, K. A., Shaver, P. R. & Tobey, A. E. (1991). Attachment styles, gender and parental problem drinking. *Journal of Social and Personal Relationships*, **8**, 451–466.

Brennan, T. (1982). Loneliness at adolescence. In: L. A. Peplau & D. Perlman (Eds), *Loneliness: A Sourcebook of Current Theory, Research and Therapy*. New York: Wiley.

Brenner, D. & Hinsdale, G. (1978). Body build stereotypes and self-identification in three age groups of females. *Adolescence*, **13**, 551–562.

Bretherton, I. (1985). Attachment theory: Retrospect and prospect. Monographs of the Society for Research in *Child Development*, **50**(1–2), 3–35.

Brewer, M. B. & Mittelman, J. (1980). Effects of normative control of self-disclosure on reciprocity. *Journal of Personality*, **48**, 89–102.

Bridgeman, D. L. (1981). Enhanced role-taking through cooperative interdependence: A field study. *Child Development*, **52**, 1231–1238.

Broderick, C. B. (1966). Socio-sexual development in a suburban community. *Journal of Sex Research*, **2**, 1–24.

Brody, G. H. & Shaffer, D. R. (1982). Contributions of parents and peers to children's moral socialization. *Developmental Review*, **2**, 31–75.

Broman, S. H., Nichols, P. L. & Kennedy, W. A. (1976). *Preschool IQ: Prenatal and Early Developmental Correlates*. Hillsdale, NJ: Erlbaum.

Bronson, W. C. (1966). Central orientations: a study of behavior organization from childhood to adolescence. *Child Development*, **37**, 125–155.

Brooks, J. & Lewis, M. (1976). Infants' responses to strangers: Midget, adult, and child. *Child Development*, **47**, 323–332.

Brooks-Gunn, J. & Matthews, W. S. (1979). *He and She: How Children Develop their Sex Role Identity*. Englewood Cliffs, NJ: Prentice Hall.

Brooks-Gunn, J., Warren, M. P., Samelson, M. & Fox, R. (1986). Physical similarity of and disclosure of menarcheal status to friends: Effects of grade and pubertal status. *Journal of Early Adolescence*, **6**, 3–14.

Brown, B. (1981). A lifespan approach to friendship. *Research in the Interweave of Social Roles: Friendship*, **2**, 23–50.

Brown, R. (1988). *Group Processes: Dynamics Within and Between Groups*. Oxford: Blackwell.

Bruner, J. & Sherwood, V. (1976). Peek-a-boo and the learning of rule structures. In: J. Bruner, A. Tolly & K. Silva (Eds), *Play: Its Role in Evaluation and Development*. Harmondsworth: Penguin.

Bryant, B. (1985). The neighbourhood walk: Sources of support in middle childhood. Monographs of the Society for Research in *Child Development*, **50** (3, Serial No. 210).

Bryson, S. E., Clark, B. S. & Smith, I. M. (1988). First report of a Canadian epidemiological study of autistic syndromes. *Journal of Child Psychology and Psychiatry*, **29**, 433–445.

Buhrmester, D. & Furman, W. (1987). The development of companionship and intimacy. *Child Development*, **58**, 1101–1113.

Bukowski, W. M. & Kramer, T. L. (1986). Judgements of the features of friendship among early adolescent boys and girls. *Journal of Early Adolescence*, **6**, 331–338.

Bull, R. & Rumsey, N. (1988). *The Social Psychology of Facial Appearance*. London: Springer.

Burke, R. J. & Weir, T. (1978). Sex differences in adolescent life stress, social support, and well being. *Journal of Psychology*, **98**, 277–288.

Burleson, B. R. (1985). Communication skills and childhood peer relationships: An overview. In: M. McLaughlin (Ed.), *Communication Yearbook*, Vol. 9. London: Sage.

Burleson, B. R. & Lucchetti, A. E. (1990). Similarity–attraction revisited: Similarity in social cognition, communication skills, and communication values as predictors of friendship choices in two age groups. Fifth International Conference on Personal Relationships, Oxford University, Oxford, England. July.

Burleson, B. R., Delia, J. G. & Applegate, J. L. (1990). Effects of mothers' disciplinary and comforting strategies on children's communication skills and acceptance by the peer group. Fifth International Conference on Personal Relationships, Oxford University, Oxford, England. July.

Busk, P. L., Ford, R. C. & Schulman, J. L. (1973). Stability of sociometric choices in classrooms. *Journal of Genetic Psychology*, **123**, 69–84.

Buss, A. H. (1980). *Self-consciousness and Social Anxiety*. San Francisco, CA: Freeman.

Buss, A. H. (1986). A theory of shyness. In: W. H. Jones, J. M. Cheek & S. R. Briggs (Eds), *Shyness: Perspectives on Research and Treatment*. New York: Plenum.

Buss, A. H. & Plomin, R. (1984). *Temperament: Early Developing Personality Traits*. San Francisco, CA: Freeman.

Buss, A. H., Iscoe, I. & Buss, E. H. (1979). The development of embarrassment. *Journal of Psychology*, **103**, 227–230.

Buss, D. M. (1981). Predicting parent–child interactions from children's activity level. *Developmental Psychology*, **17**, 59–65.

Button, L. (1979). Friendship patterns. *Journal of Adolescence*, **2**, 187–199.

Byrne, D. (1961). The influence of propinquity and opportunity for interaction on classroom relationships. *Human Relations*, **14**, 63–69.

Byrne, D. (1971). *The Attraction Paradigm*. New York: Academic Press.

Byrne, D. & Griffitt, W. (1966). A developmental investigation of the law of attraction. *Journal of Personality and Social Psychology*, **4**, 699–702.

Byrnes, D. A. (1987). The physically unattractive child. *Childhood Education*, **64**, 80–85.

Cairns, R. B. (1972). Attachment and dependency: A psycho-biological and social learning synthesis. In: J. L. Gewirtz (Ed.), *Attachment and Dependency*. New York: Wiley.

Cantrell, V. L. & Prinz, R. J. (1985). Multiple perspectives of rejected, neglected and accepted children: Relation between sociometric status and behavioral characteristics. *Journal of Consulting and Clinical Psychology*, **53**, 884–889.

Carlson, C. L., Lahey, B. B. & Neeper, R. (1984). Peer assessment of the social behavior of accepted, rejected, and neglected children. *Journal of Abnormal Child Psychology*, **12**, 187–198.

Carpenter, C. J. & Huston-Stein, A. (1980). Activity structure and sex-typed behavior in preschool children. *Child Development*, **51**, 862–872.

Cartledge, G. & Milburn, J. F. (1980). *Teaching Social Skills to Children*. New York: Pergamon.

Cash, T. F. & Derlega, V. J. (1978). The matching hypothesis: Physical attractiveness among same-sexed friends. *Personality and Social Psychology Bulletin*, **4**, 1–14.

Cavior, N. & Dokecki, P. (1973). Physical attractiveness, perceived attitude similarity, and academic achievement as contributors to interpersonal attraction among adolescents. *Developmental Psychology*, **9**, 44–54.

Cavior, N. & Lombardi, D. A. (1973). Developmental aspects of judgement of physical attractiveness in children. *Developmental Psychology*, **8**, 67–71.

Cavior, N., Miller, K. & Cohen, S. H. (1975). Physical attractiveness, attitude similarity, and length of acquaintance as contributors to interpersonal attraction among adolescents. *Social Behavior and Personality*, **3**, 133–141.

Centers, L. & Centers, R. (1963). Peer group attitudes toward the amputee child. *Journal of Social Psychology*, **61**, 127–132.

Chafel, J. A. (1984a). Social comparisons by young children in classroom contexts. *Early Child Development and Care*, **14**, 109–124.

Chafel, J. A. (1984b). "Call the police, okay?": Social comparisons by young children during play in preschool. *Early Child Development and Care*, **14**, 201–216.

Chafel, J. A. (1985). Social comparisons and the young child: Current research issues. *Early Child Development and Care*, **21**, 35–59.

Chafel, J. A. (1986). A naturalistic investigation of the use of social comparison by young children. *Journal of Research and Development in Education*, **19**, 51–61.

Chafel, J. A. (1988a). The effects of two types of play settings on young children's use of social comparison. *Early Child Development and Care*, **40**, 53–75.

Chafel, J. A. (1988b). Social comparison by children: An analysis of research on sex differences. *Sex Roles*, **18**, 461–487.

Chafel, J. A. & Bahr, M. W. (1988). Observing social comparisons by young children naturalistically. *Journal of Research and Development in Education*, **21**, 49–61.

Chalmers, J. B. & Townsend, M. A. R. (1990). The effects of training in social perspective taking on socially maladjusted girls. *Child Development*, **61**, 178–190.

Chamberlin, R. W. (1977). Can we identify a group of children at age 2 who are at high risk for the development of behavior or emotional problems in kindergarten and first grade? *Pediatrics*, **59**, 971–981.

Chandler, M. J. (1973). Egocentrism and anti-social behavior: The assessment and training of social perspective taking skill. *Developmental Psychology*, **9**, 326–336.

Charlesworth, W. R. & Dzur, C. (1987). Gender comparisons of preschoolers behavior and resource utilization in group problem solving. *Child Development*, **58**, 191–200.

Charlesworth, W. R. & Hartup, W. W. (1967). Positive social reinforcement in the nursery school peer group. *Child Development*, **38**, 993–1002.

Charlesworth, W. R. & LaFreniere, P. (1983). Dominance, friendship utilization and resource utilization in preschool children's groups. *Ethology and Sociobiology*, **4**, 175–186.

Cheek, J. M., Carpentieri, A. M., Smith, T. G., Rierdan, J. & Koff, E. (1986). Adolescent shyness. In: W. H. Jones, J. M. Cheek & S. R. Briggs (Eds), *Shyness: Perspectives on Research and Treatment*. New York: Plenum.

Chelune, G. J. (1979). Measuring openness in interpersonal communication. In: G. J. Chelune (Ed.), *Self-Disclosure*. London: Jossey-Bass.

Chennault, M. (1967). Improving the social acceptance of unpopular educable mentally retarded pupils in special classes. *American Journal of Mental Deficiency*, **72**, 455–458.

Chess, S. & Thomas, A. (1982). Infant bonding: Mystique and reality. *American Journal of Orthopsychiatry*, **52**, 213–222.

Chess, S., Thomas, A. & Cameron, M. (1976). Sexual attitudes and behavior patterns in a middle-class adolescent population. *American Journal of Orthopsychiatry*, **46**, 689–701.

Clark, M. L. & Drewry, D. L. (1985). Similarity and reciprocity in the friendships of elementary school children. *Child Study Journal*, **15**, 251–264.

Clark, R. A. & Jones, J. (1990). Parental reflection enhancing communication, children's person centered communication skills, and children's success in peer relationships. Fifth International Conference on Personal Relationships, Oxford University, Oxford, England. July.

Clifford, M. & Walster, E. (1973). The effects of physical attractiveness on teacher expectations. *Sociology of Education*, **46**, 248–258.

Coates, D. L. (1987). Gender differences in the structure and support characteristics of black adolescents' social networks. *Sex Roles*, **17**, 667–687.

Cohen, L. J. (1974). The operational definition of human attachment. *Psychological Bulletin*, **81**, 207–217.

Cohn, D. A. (1990). Child–mother attachment of six-year-olds and social competence at school. *Child Development*, **61**, 1, 152–162.

Cohn, D. A., Patterson, C. J. & Christopoulos, C. (1991). The family and children's peer relations. *Journal of Social and Personal Relationships*, **8**, 315–346.

Cohn, L. D., Adler, N. E., Irwin, C. E., Millstein, S. G., Kegeles, S. M. & Stone, G. (1987). Body figure preferences in male and female adolescents. *Journal of Abnormal Psychology*, **96**, 276–279.

Cohn, N. B. & Strassberg, D. S. (1983). Self-disclosure reciprocity among preadolescents. *Personality and Social Psychology Bulletin*, **9**, 97–102.

Coie, J. D. (1985). Fitting social skills intervention to the target group. In: B. H. Schneider, K. H. Rubin & J. E. Ledingham (Eds), *Children's Peer Relations: Issues in Assessment and Intervention*. New York: Springer-Verlag.

Coie, J. D. & Koeppl, G. K. (1990). Adapting intervention to the problems of aggressive and disruptive rejected children. In: S. R. Asher & J. D. Coie (Eds), *Peer Rejection in Childhood.* New York: Cambridge University Press.

Coie, J. D. & Krehbiel, G. (1984). Effects of academic tutoring on the social status of low-achieving, socially rejected children. *Child Development*, **55**, 1465–1478.

Coie, J. D. & Kupersmidt, J. (1983). A behavioral analysis of emerging social status in boys' groups. *Child Development*, **54**, 1400–1416.

Coleman, J. C. (1980). Friendship and the peer group in adolescence. In: J. Adelson (Ed.), *Handbook of Adolescent Psychology.* New York: Wiley.

Combs, M. L. & Slaby, D. A. (1977). Social skills training with children. In: B. B. Lahey & E. E. Kazdin (Eds), *Advances in Clinical Child Psychology*, Vol. 1. New York: Plenum.

Conger, J. C. & Keane, S. P. (1981). Social skills intervention in the treatment of isolated or withdrawn children. *Psychological Bulletin*, **90**, 478–495.

Connolly, J. & Doyle, A. (1981). Assessment of social competence in preschoolers: Teachers versus peers. *Developmental Psychology*, **17**, 454–462.

Cooke, T. & Apolloni, T. (1976). Developing positive social emotional behaviors: A study of training and generalization effects. *Journal of Applied Behavioral Analysis*, **9**, 65–78.

Cooley, C. H. (1912). *Human Nature and the Social Order.* New York: Scribner.

Cooper, C. R. & Ayers-Lopez, S. (1985). Family and peer systems in early adolescence: New models of the role of relationships in development. *Journal of Early Adolescence*, **5**, 9–22.

Counts, C. R., Jones, C., Frame, C. L., Jarvie, G. J. & Strauss, C. C. (1986). The perception of obesity by normal-weight versus obese school-age children. *Child Psychiatry and Human Development*, **17**, 113–120.

Cowan, G. & Hoffman, C. D. (1986). Gender stereotypes in young children: Evidence to support a concept learning approach. *Sex Roles*, **14**, 211–224.

Cowen, E., Pederson, A., Babigian, H., Izzo, L. & Trost, M. (1973). Longterm follow-up of early detected vulnerable children. *Journal of Consulting and Clinical Psychology*, **41**, 438–446.

Cox, R. D. & Gunn, W. B. (1980). Interpersonal skills in the schools: Assessment and curriculum development. In: D. P. Rathjen & J. P. Foreyt (Eds), *Social Competence.* New York: Pergamon.

Cozby, P. C. (1972). Self-disclosure, reciprocity and liking. *Sociometry*, **35**, 151–160.

Cozby, P.C. (1973). Self-disclosure: a literature review. *Psychological Bulletin*, **79**, 2, 73–91.

Crick, N. R. & Ladd, G. W. (1990). Children's perceptions of the outcomes of social strategies: Do the ends justify being mean? *Developmental Psychology*, **26**, 612–620.

Crockett, L., Losoff, M. & Petersen, A. C. (1984). Perceptions of the peer group and friendship in early adolescence. *Journal of Early Adolescence*, **4**, 155–181.

Crockett, M. S. (1984). Exploring peer relationships. *Journal of Psychosocial Nursing and Mental Health Services*, **22**, 10, 18–25.

Cross, J. & Cross, J. (1971). Age, sex, race and the perception of facial beauty. *Developmental Psychology*, **5**, 433–439.

Crozier, R. (1979). Shyness as anxious self-preoccupation. *Psychological Reports*, **44**, 959–962.

Csapo, M. (1972). Peers models reverse the "one bad apple spoils the barrel" theory. *Teaching Exceptional Children*, **5**, 20–24.

Dakin, S. & Arrowood, A. J. (1981). The social comparison of ability. *Human Relations*, **34**, 89–109.

Davidson, B., Balswick, J. O. & Halverson, C. F. (1980). Factor analysis of self-disclosure for adolescents. *Adolescence*, **15**, 947–957.

Davis, D. & Perkowitz, W. T. (1979). Consequences of responsiveness in dyadic interactions: Effects of probability of response and proportion of content related responses. *Journal of Personality and Social Psychology*, **37**, 534–550.

Davis, J. D. (1978). When boy meets girl: Sex roles and the negotiation of intimacy in an acquaintance exercise. *Journal of Personality and Social Psychology*, **36**, 684–692.

Davis, M. H. & Franzoi, S. L. (1986). Adolescent loneliness, self-disclosure, and private self-consciousness: A longitudinal investigation. *Journal of Personality and Social Psychology*, **51**, 595–608.

Davitz, J. R. (1955). Social Perception and Sociometric choice of children. *Journal of Abnormal Social Psychology*, **50**, 173–176.

Dean, A. L., Malik, M. M., Richards, W. & Stringer, S. A. (1986). Effects of parental maltreatment on children's conceptions of interpersonal relationships. *Developmental Psychology*, **22**, 617–626.

Deaux, K. (1985). Sex and gender. *Annual Review of Psychology*, **36**, 49–81.

DeCasper, A. J. & Fifer, W. P. (1980). Of human bonding: Newborns prefer their mother's voice. *Science*, **208**, 1174–1176.

Delia, J. G. & Applegate, J. L. (1990). From cognition to communication to cognition to communication. Fifth International Conference on Personal Relationships, Oxford University, Oxford, England. July.

Denham, S. A. (1986). Social cognition, prosocial behavior, and emotion in preschoolers: contextual validation. *Child Development*, **57**, 194–201.

Denham, S. A., Renwick, S. M. & Holt, R. W. (1991). Working and playing together: Prediction of preschool social–emotional competence from mother–child interaction. *Child Development*, **62**, 242–294.

Derlega, V. J. (1988). Self-disclosure: Inside or outside the mainstream of social psychological research? *Journal of Social Behavior and Personality*, **3**, 2, 27–34.

Deutsch, M. (1973). *The Resolution of Conflict: Constructive and Destructive Processes*. New Haven: Yale University Press.

DiLeo, J. C., Moely, B. E. & Sulzer, J. L. (1979). Frequency and modifiability of children's preferences for sex-typed toys, games and occupations. *Child Study Journal*, **9**, 141–159.

Dimond, R. E. & Hellkamp, D. T. (1969). Race, sex, ordinal position of birth and self-disclosure in high school students. *Psychological Reports*, **25**, 235–238.

Dimond, R. E. & Munz, D. C. (1967). Ordinal position of birth and self disclosure in high-school students. *Psychological Reports*, **21**, 829–833.

Dion, K. K. (1972). Physical attractiveness and evaluations of children's transgressions. *Journal of Personality and Social Psychology*, **24**, 207–213.

Dion, K. K. (1973). Young children's stereotyping of facial attractiveness. *Developmental Psychology*, **9**, 183–188.

Dion, K. K. (1974). Children's physical attractiveness and sex as determinants of adult punitiveness. *Developmental Psychology*, **10**, 772–778.

Dion, K. K. (1977). The incentive value of physical attractiveness for young children. *Personality and Social Psychology Bulletin*, **3**, 67–70.

Dion, K. K. & Berscheid, E. (1974). Physical attractiveness and peer perception among children. *Sociometry*, **37**, 1–12.

Dion, K. K., Berscheid, E. & Walster, E. (1972). What is beautiful is good. *Journal of Personality and Social Psychology*, **24**, 285–290.

DiPietro, J. (1981). Rough and tumble play: A function of gender. *Developmental Psychology*, **17**, 50–58.

Dlugokinski, E. (1984). Developing cooperative school environments for children. *Elementary School Guidance and Counselling*, **18**, 209–215.

Dodge, K. A. (1980). Social cognition and children's aggressive behavior. *Child Development*, **51**, 162–170.

Dodge, K. A. (1983). Behavioral antecedents of peer social status. *Child Development*, **54**, 1386–1399.

Dodge, K. A. (1985). Facets of social interaction and the assessment of social competence in children. In: B. H. Schneider, K. H. Rubin & J. E. Ledingham (Eds), *Children's Peer Relations: Issues in Assessment and Intervention*. New York: Springer-Verlag.

Dodge, K. A. & Frame, C. L. (1982). Social cognitive biases and deficits in aggressive boys. *Child Development*, **53**, 620–635.

Dodge, K. A., Coie, J. D. & Brakke, N. P. (1982). Behavior patterns of socially rejected and neglected preadolescents: The roles of social approach and aggression. *Journal of Abnormal Child Psychology*, **10**, 389–409.

Dodge, K. A., Pettit, G. S., McClasky, C. L. & Brown, M. M. (1986). Social competence in children. *Monographs of the Society for Research in Child Development*, **51**, (2, serial No. 213).

Doise, W. & Mugny, G. (1984). *The Social Development of the Intellect*. Oxford: Pergamon.

Dornbusch, S. M., Hastorf, A. H., Richardson, S. A. & Vreeland, R. S. (1965). The perceiver and the perceived: Their relative influence on the categories of interpersonal cognition. *Journal of Personality and Social Psychology*, **1**, 434–440.

Doster, J. A. & Strickland, B. R. (1969). Perceived child-rearing practices and self-disclosure patterns. *Journal of Counselling and Clinical Psychology*, **33**, 382.

Douvan, E. & Adelson, J. (1966). *The Adolescent Experience*. New York: Wiley.

Douvan, E. & Gold, M. (1966). Modal patterns in American adolescence. In: L. W. Hoffman & M. L. Hoffman (Eds), *Review of Child Development Research*, Vol. 2. New York: Sage.

Doyle, A. B. (1982). Friends, acquaintances, and strangers: The influence of familiarity and ethnolinguistic background on social interaction. In: K. H. Rubin & H. S. Ross (Eds), *Peer Relationships and Social Skills in Childhood*. New York: Springer-Verlag.

Doyle, A. B., Connolly, J. & Rivest, L. P. (1980). The effect of playmate familiarity on the social interactions of young children. *Child Development*, **51**, 217–223.

Drewry, D. L. & Clark, M. L. (1985). Factors important in the formation of preschoolers' friendships. *Journal of Genetic Psychology*, **146**, 37–44.

Duck, S. W. (1973a). *Personal Relationships and Personal Constructs*. London: Wiley.

Duck, S. W. (1973b). Personality similarity and friendship choice: Similarity of what, when? *Journal of Personality*, **41**, 543–558.

Duck, S. W. (1975). Personality similarity and friendship choices by adolescents. *European Journal of Social Psychology*, **5**, 351–365.

Duck, S. W. (1977). *The Study of Acquaintance*. Farnborough: Saxon House.

Duck, S. W. (1982). A typography of relationship disengagement and dissolution. In: S. W. Duck (Ed.), *Personal Relationships, Vol. 4: Dissolving Personal Relationships*. London: Academic Press.

Duck, S. W. (1989). Socially competent communication and relationship development. In: B. H. Schneider, G. Attili, J. Nadel & R. P. Weissberg (Eds), *Social Competence in Developmental Perspective*. Dordrecht, Netherlands: Kluwer.

Duck, S. W. (1991). *Friends for Life* (2nd edn). Hemel Hempstead, Herts: Harvester Wheatsheaf.

Duck, S. W. & Allison, D. (1978). I liked you but I can't live with you: A study of lapsed friendships. *Social Behavior and Personality*, **6**, 43–47.

Duck, S. W. & Spencer, C. (1972). Personal constructs and friendship formation. *Journal of Personality and Social Psychology*, **23**, 40–45.

Duck, S. W., Miell, D. K. & Gaebler, H. C. (1980). Attraction and communication in children's interaction. In: H. C. Foot, A. J. Chapman & J. R. Smith (Eds), *Friendship and Social Relations in Children*. Chichester: Wiley.

Duncan, O. D., Featherman, D. L. & Duncan, B. (1972). *Socio-economic Background and Achievement*. New York: Seminar Press.

Dunn, J. (1988). *The Beginnings of Social Understanding*. Oxford: Blackwell.

Dunphy, D. C. (1972). Peer group socialization. In: F. J. Hunt (Ed.), *Socialization in Australia*. Sydney: Angus & Robertson.

Durrant, N. C. & Henggeler, S. W. (1986). The stability of peer sociometric ratings across ecological settings. *Journal of Genetic Psychology*, **147**, 353–358.

Dushenko, T. W., Perry, R. P., Schilling, J. & Smolarski, S. (1978). Generality of the physical attractiveness stereotype for age and sex. *Journal of Social Psychology*, **105**, 303–304.

Dweck, C. S. (1981). Social–cognitive processes in children's friendships. In: S. R. Asher & J. M. Gottman (Eds), *The Development of Children's Friendships*. Cambridge: Cambridge University Press.

Dweck, C. S. & Goetz, T. E. (1979). Attributions and learned helplessness. In: J. H. Harvey, W. Ickes & R. F. Kidd (Eds), *New Directions in Attribution Research* (Vol. 2). Hillsdale, NJ: Erlbaum.

Dygdon, J. A. & Conger, A. J. (1990). A direct nomination method for the identification of neglected members in children's peer groups. *Journal of Abnormal Child Psychology*, **18**, 1, 55–74.

Earn, B. M. & Sobol, M. P. (1990). A categorical analysis of children's attributions for social success and failure. *Psychological Record*, **40**, 173–185.

East, P. L. & Rook, K. S. (1992). Compensatory patterns of support among children's peer relationships: A test using school friends, nonschool friends, and siblings. *Developmental Psychology*, **28**, 1, 163–172.

Easterbrooks, M. A. & Lamb, M. E. (1979). The relationship between quality of infant–mother attachment and infant competence in initial encounters with peers. *Child Development*, **50**, 380–387.

Eckerman, C. O. & Whatley, J. L. (1977). Toys and social interaction between infant peers. *Child Development*, **48**, 1645–1656.

Eder, D. & Hallinan, M. (1978). Sex differences in children's friendships. *American Sociological Review*, **43**, 237–250.

Edinger, J. A. & Patterson, M. L. (1983). Nonverbal involvement and social control. *Psychological Bulletin*, **93**, 30–56.

Egeland, B. & Farber, E. A. (1984). Mother–infant attachment: Factors related to its development and changes over time. *Child Development*, **55**, 753–771.

Egeland, B. & Sroufe, L. A. (1981). Developmental sequence of maltreatment in infancy. *New Directions in Child Development*, **11**, 77–92.

Eggert, L. L. & Parks, M. R. (1987). Communication network involvement in adolescents' friendships and romantic relationships. In: M. McLaughlin (Ed.), *Communication Yearbook*, Vol. 10. London: Sage.

Eisenberg, N. & Miller, P. A. (1987). The relation of empathy to prosocial and related behaviors. *Psychological Bulletin*, **101**, 91–119.

Eisenberg, N., Tryon, K. & Cameron, E. (1984). The relation of preschoolers peer interaction to their sex-typed toy choice. *Child Development*, 55, 1044–1050.

Elkind, D. (1967). Egocentrism in adolescence. *Child Development*, 38, 1025–1034.

Elkind, D. (1978). Understanding the young adolescent. *Adolescence*, 13, 127–134.

Elkind, D. & Bowen, R. (1979). Imaginary audience behavior in children and adolescents. *Developmental Psychology*, 15, 38–44.

Ellis, A. & Beattie, G. (1986). *The Psychology of Language and Communication*. London: Weidenfeld & Nicolson.

Ellis, S., Rogoff, B. & Cromer, C. C. (1981). Age segregation in children's social interactions. *Developmental Psychology*, 17, 399–407.

Elovitz, G. P. & Salvia, J. (1982). Attractiveness as a biasing factor in the judgements of school psychologists. *Journal of School Psychology*, 20, 339–345.

Emihovich, C. (1986). Argument as status assertion: Contextual variations in children's disputes. *Language in Society*, 15, 485–500.

Engfer, A. (1986). Stability and change in perceived characteristics of children 4 to 43 months of age. Paper to second European Conference on Developmental Psychology, Rome. September.

Erickson, M. F., Sroufe, L. A. & Egeland, B. (1985). The relationship between quality of attachment and behavior problems in preschool in a high-risk sample. *Monographs of the Society for Research in Child Development*, 50, 147–166.

Erikson, E. H. (1963). *Childhood and Society* (2nd edn). New York: Norton.

Erikson, E. H. (1968). *Identity: Youth and Crisis*. New York: Norton.

Erwin, P. G. (1983). Attraction and friendship: A social-developmental approach. Unpublished D.Phil. Thesis, University of York, England.

Erwin, P. G. (1985). Similarity of attitudes and constructs in children's friendships. *Journal of Experimental Child Psychology*, 40, 470–485.

Erwin, P. G. & Calev, A. (1984). Beauty: More than skin deep? *Journal of Social and Personal Relationships*, 1, 359–361.

Evers, W. L. & Schwartz, J. C. (1973). Modifying social withdrawal in preschoolers: The effects of filmed modeling and teacher praise. *Journal of Abnormal Child Psychology*, 1, 248–256.

Fagot, B. I. (1977a). Consequences of moderate cross-gender behavior in preschool children. *Child Development*, 48, 902–907.

Fagot, B. I. (1977b). Variations in density: Effect on task and social behaviors of preschool children. *Developmental Psychology*, 13, 166–167.

Fagot, B. I. (1981). Continuity and change in play styles as a function of sex of child. *International Journal of Behavioral Development*, 4, 37–43.

Fagot, B. I. (1985). Beyond the reinforcement principle: Another step toward understanding sex roles. *Developmental Psychology*, 21, 1097–1104.

Fagot, B. I. & Hagan, R. (1985). Aggression in toddlers: Responses to the assertive acts of boys and girls. *Sex Roles*, 12, 341–351.

Fagot, B. I. & Littman, I. (1975). Stability of sex role and play interests, from preschool to elementary school. *Journal of Psychology*, 89, 285–292.

Fantasia, S. C., Lombardo, J. P. & Wolf, T. M. (1976). Modification of self-disclosing behaviors through modeling and vicarious reinforcement. *Journal of General Psychology*, 95, 209–218.

Fantz, R. L. (1963). Pattern vision in newborn infants. *Science*, 140, 296–297.

Feeney, J. A. & Noller, P. (1991). Attachment style and verbal descriptions of romantic partners. *Journal of Social and Personal Relationships*, 8, 187–215.

Feiring, C. & Lewis, M. (1989). The social networks of girls and boys from early through middle childhood. In: D. Belle (Ed.), *Children's Social Networks and Social Supports*. Chichester: Wiley.

Feldbaum, C. L., Christenson, T. E. & O'Neal, E. C. (1980). An observational study of the assimilation of the newcomer to the preschool. *Child Development*, **51**, 497–507.

Felson, R. B. (1985). Reflected appraisal and the development of self. *Social Psychology Quarterly*, **48**, 71–78.

Feshbach, N. D. (1978). Studies of empathic behavior in children. In: B. A. Maher (Ed.), *Progress in Experimental Personality Research*, Vol. 8. New York: Academic Press.

Festinger, L. (1954). A theory of social comparison processes. *Human Relations*, **7**, 117–140.

Festinger, L., Schachter, S. & Back, K. (1950). *Social Pressure in Informal Groups*. London: Tavistock.

Field, T. M. (1980). Preschool play: Effects of teacher/child ratios and organization of classroom space. *Child Study Journal*, **10**, 191–205.

Fincham, F. D. (1983). Developmental dimensions in attribution theory. In: J. Jaspars, F. D. Fincham & M. Hewstone (Eds), *Attribution Theory and Research: Conceptual, Developmental and Social Dimensions*. London: Academic Press.

Fine, G A. (1980). The natural history of preadolescent male friendship groups. In: H. C. Foot, A. J. Chapman & J. R. Smith (Eds), *Friendship and Social Relations in Children*. Chichester: Wiley.

Fine, G A. (1987). Friends, impression management, and preadolescent behavior. In: S. R. Asher & J. M. Gottman (Eds), *The Development of Children's Friendships*. Cambridge: Cambridge University Press.

Fishbein, M. & Ajzen, I. (1975). *Belief, Attitude, Intention and Behavior: An Introduction to Theory and Research*. Reading, MA: Addison-Wesley.

Fiske, S. T. & Taylor, S. E. (1984). *Social Cognition*. Reading, MA: Addison-Wesley.

Flavell, J. H. (1966). Role-taking and communication skills in children. *Young Children*, **21**, 164–177.

Foa, U. G. & Foa, E. B. (1971). Resource exchange: Toward a structural theory of interpersonal relations. In A. W. Siegman & B. Pope (Eds), *Studies in Dyadic Communication*. New York: Pergamon.

Fogel, A. (1979). Peer vs. mother-directed behavior in 1- to 3-month old infants. *Infant Behavior and Development*, **2**, 215–226.

Foot, H. C., Chapman, A. J. & Smith, J. R. (1977). Friendship and social responsiveness in boys and girls. *Journal of Personality and Social Psychology*, **35**, 401–411.

Foot, H. C., Chapman, A. J. & Smith, J. R. (Eds) (1980). *Friendship and Social Relations in Children*, Chichester: Wiley.

Ford, M. E. (1982). Social cognition and social competence in adolescence. *Developmental Psychology*, **18**, 323–340.

Foster, S. L. & Ritchey, W. L. (1985). Behavioral correlates of sociometric status of fourth-, fifth-, and sixth-grade children in two classroom situations. *Behavioral Assessment*, **7**, 79–93.

Foster, S. L., DeLawler, D. D. & Guevremont, D. C. (1986). A critical incidents analysis of liked and disliked peer behaviours and their situational parameters in childhood and adolescence. *Behavioral Assessment*, **8**, 115–133.

Fox, S. (1980). Situational determinants of affiliation. *European Journal of Social Psychology*, **10**, 303–307.

France-Kaatrude, A. & Smith, W. P. (1985). Social comparison, task motivation, and the development of self-evaluative standards in children. *Developmental Psychology*, **21**, 1080–1089.

Frankel, K. A. (1990). Girls' perceptions of peer relationship support and stress. *Journal of Early Adolescence*, **10**, 1, 69–88.

Fransella, F. & Bannister, D. (1977). *A Manual for Repertory Grid Technique*. London: Academic Press.

Freedman, R. J. (1984). Reflections on beauty as it relates to health in adolescent females. *Women & Health*, **9**, 29–45.

Frith, U. (1989). *Autism: Explaining the Enigma*. Oxford: Blackwell.

Fromm-Reichmann, F. (1959). Loneliness. *Psychiatry*, **22**, 1–15.

Frommer, E. & O'Shea, G. (1973). Antenatal identification of women liable to have problems in managing their infants. *British Journal of Psychiatry*, **123**, 149–156.

Furman, L. N. & Walden, T. A. (1990). Effect of script knowledge on preschool children's communicative interactions. *Developmental Psychology*, **26**, 2, 227–233.

Furman, W. (1980). Promoting social development: Developmental implications for treatment. In: B. B. Lahey & E. E. Kazdin (Eds), *Advances in Clinical Child Psychology*, Vol. 3. New York: Plenum.

Furman, W. (1984a). Some observations on the study of personal relationships. In: J. C. Masters & K. Yarkin-Levin (Eds), *Boundary Area in Social and Developmental Psychology*. New York: Academic Press.

Furman, W. (1984b). Enhancing children's peer relations and friendships. In: S. W. Duck (Ed.), *Personal Relationships, Vol. 5: Repairing Personal Relationships*. London: Academic Press.

Furman, W. & Buhrmester, D. (1992). Age and sex differences in perceptions of networks of personal relationships. *Child Development*, **63**, 103–115.

Furman, W. & Gavin, L. A. (1989). Peer's influence on adjustment and development: A view from the intervention literature. In: T. J. Berndt & G. W. Ladd (Eds), *Peer Relationships in Development*. New York: Wiley.

Furman, W., Giberson, R., White, A. S., Gravin, L. A. & Wehner, E. A. (1989). Enhancing peer relations in school systems. In: B. H. Schneider, G. Attili, J. Nadel & R. P. Weissberg (Eds), *Social Competence in Developmental Perspective*. Dordrecht, Netherlands: Kluwer.

Furman, W., Rahe, D. F. & Hartup, W. W. (1979). Rehabilitation of socially withdrawn preschool children through mixed-age and same-age socialization. *Child Development*, **50**, 915–922.

Garcia, P. A. & Geisler, J. S. (1988). Sex and age/grade differences in adolescents' self-disclosure. *Perceptual and Motor Skills*, **67**, 427–432.

Gershman, E. S. & Hayes, D. S. (1983). Differential stability of reciprocal friendships and unilateral relationships among preschool children. *Merrill-Palmer Quarterly*, **29**, 169–177.

Gesell, A. & Ilg, F. L. (1949). *Child Development*. New York: Harper & Row.

Gesell, A., Ilg, F. L. & Ames, L. B. (1965). *Youth: The Years from Ten to Sixteen* (2nd edn). New York: Harper & Row.

Gewirtz, J. L. (1976). Attachment and maternal conditioning of crying. *Human Development*, **19**, 143–155.

Giancoli, D. I. & Neimeyer, G. J. (1983). Liking preferences toward handicapped persons. *Perceptual and Motor Skills*, **57**, 1005–1006.

Gilligan, C. (1982). *In a Different Voice: Psychological Theory and Women's Development*. Cambridge, MA: Harvard University Press.

Goethals, G. R. & Darley, J. M. (1977). Social comparison theory: An attributional approach. In: J. M. Suls & R. L. Miller (Eds), *Social Comparison Processes: Theoretical and Empirical Perspectives*. Washington, DC: Hemisphere.

Goetz, T. E. & Dweck, C. S. (1980). Learned helplessness in social situations. *Journal of Personality and Social Psychology*, **39**, 246–255.

Goetz, T. E., Thomson, C. & Etzel, B. (1975). An analysis of direct and indirect teacher attention and primes in the modification of child social behavior. *Merrill-Palmer Quarterly*, **21**, 55–65.

Goffman, I. (1963). *Stigma: Notes on the Management of Spoiled Identity*. Harmondsworth: Penguin Books (1968). Originally published by Prentice Hall, Englewood Cliffs, NJ.

Gold, M. & Yanof, D. S. (1985). Mothers, daughters, and girlfriends. *Journal of Personality and Social Psychology*, **49**, 654–659.

Goldberg, S., Perrotta, M., Minde, K. & Corter, C. (1986). Maternal behavior and attachment in low-birth-weight twins and singletons. *Child Development*, **57**, 34–46.

Goldsmith, H. H., Bradshaw, D. L. & Riesser-Danner, L. A. (1986). Temperament as a potential developmental influence on attachment. *New Directions for Child Development*, **31**, 5–34.

Goldstein, A. P., Gershaw, N. J. & Sprafkin, R. P. (1985). Structured learning. In: L. L'Abate & M. A. Milan (Eds), *Handbook of Social Skills Training and Research*. New York: Wiley.

Goodman, H., Gottlieb, J. & Harrison, R. H. (1972). Social acceptance of EMRs integrated into a nongraded elementary school. *American Journal of Mental Deficiency*, **76**, 412–417.

Gottlieb, J. (1971). Attitudes of Norwegian children toward the retarded in relation to sex and situational context. *American Journal of Mental Deficiency*, **75**, 635–639.

Gottlieb, J. & Leyser, Y. (1981a). Friendship between mentally retarded and nonretarded children. In: S. R. Asher & J. M. Gottman (Eds), *The Development of Children's Friendships*. Cambridge: Cambridge University Press.

Gottlieb, J. & Leyser, Y. (1981b). Facilitating the social mainstreaming of retarded children. *Exceptional Education Quarterly*, **1**, 57–69.

Gottman, J. M. (1977a). Toward a definition of social isolation in children. *Child Development*, **48**, 513–517.

Gottman, J. M. (1977b). The effects of a modeling film on social isolation in preschool children: A methodological investigation. *Journal of Abnormal Child Psychology*, **5**, 69–78.

Gottman, J. M. (1983). How children become friends. *Child Development Monographs*, **48**, (3).

Gottman, J. M. (1986a). The world of coordinated play: same- and cross-sex friendship in young children. In: J. M. Gottman & J. G. Parker (Eds), *Conversations of Friends: Speculations on Affective Development*. Cambridge: Cambridge University Press.

Gottman, J. M. (1986b). The observation of social process. In: J. M. Gottman & J. G. Parker (Eds), *Conversations of Friends: Speculations on Affective Development*. Cambridge: Cambridge University Press.

Gottman, J. M. (1991). Finding the roots of children's problems with other children. *Journal of Social and Personal Relationships*, **8**, 441–448.

Gottman, J. M. & Parkhurst, J. T. (1980). A developmental theory of friendship and acquaintanceship processes. In: A. Collins (Ed.), *Minnesota Symposium on Child Psychology, Vol. 13: Development of Cognition, Affect and Social Relations*. Hillsdale, NJ: Erlbaum.

Gottman, J. M., Gonso, J. & Rasmussen, B. (1975). Social interaction, social competence and friendship in children. *Child Development*, **46**, 709–718.

Gottman, J. M., Gonso, J. & Schuler, P. (1976). Teaching social skills to isolated children. *Journal of Abnormal Child Psychology*, **4**, 179–197.

Grady, K. E. (1979). Androgyny reconsidered. In: J. H. Williams (Ed.), *Psychology of Women: Selected Readings*. New York: Norton.

Greenberg, M. T. & Marvin, R. S. (1982). Reactions of preschool children to an adult stranger: A behavioral systems approach. *Child Development*, **53**, 481–490.

Greenberg, M. T., Siegel, J. M. & Leitch, C. J. (1983). The nature and importance of attachment relationships to parents and peers during adolescence. *Journal of Youth & Adolescence*, **12**, 373–386.

Gresham, F. M. (1982). Social interactions as predictors of children's likeability and friendship patterns: A multiple regression analysis. *Journal of Behavioural Assessment*, **4**, 39–54.

Gresham, F. M. & Nagle, R. J. (1980). Social skills with children: Responsiveness to modeling and coaching as a function of peer orientation. *Journal of Consulting and Clinical Psychology*, **18**, 718–729.

Gronlund, N. E. (1955). The relative stability of classroom social status with unweighted and weighted sociometric measures. *Journal of Educational Psychology*, **46**, 345–354.

Gronlund, N. E. & Holmlund, W. S. (1958). The value of elementary school sociometric status scores for predicting pupils' adjustment in high school. *Educational Administration Supervision*, **44**, 225–260.

Guise, B. J., Pollans, C. H. & Turkat, I. D. (1982). Effects of physical attractiveness on perception of social skill. *Perceptual and Social Skills*, **54**, 1039–1042.

Gump, P. V. (1978). School environments. In: I. Altman & J. F. Wohlwill (Eds), *Children and the Environment*. New York: Plenum.

Guralnick, M. J. (1990). Social competence and early intervention. *Journal of Early Intervention*, **14**, 1, 3–14.

Guralnick, M. J. & Paul-Brown, D. (1984). Communicative adjustments during behavior-request episodes among children at different developmental levels. *Child Development*, **55**, 911–919.

Gurucharri, C. & Selman, R. L. (1982). The development of interpersonal understanding during childhood, preadolescence and adolescence. *Child Development*, **53**, 924–927.

Hall, E. T. (1966). *The Hidden Dimension*. New York: Doubleday.

Hall, F., Pawlby, S. J. & Wolkind, S. (1979). Early life experiences and later mothering behaviour: A study of mothers and their 20-week old babies. In: D. Shaffer & J. Dunn (Eds), *The first year of life*. Chichester: Wiley.

Hallinan, M. T. (1976). Friendship patterns in open and traditional classrooms. *Sociology of Education*, **49**, 254–265.

Hallinan, M. T. (1979). Structural effects on children's friendships and cliques. *Social Psychology Quarterly*, **42**, 43–54.

Hallinan, M. T. (1981a). Patterns of cliquing among youth. In: Foot, H. C., Chapman, A. J. & Smith, J. R. (Eds), *Friendship and Social Relations in Children*. Chichester: Wiley.

Hallinan, M. T. (1981b). Recent advances in sociometry. In: Asher, S. R. & Gottman, J. M. (Eds), *The Development of Children's Friendships*. Cambridge: Cambridge University Press.

Hallinan, M. T. & Tuma, N. B. (1978). Classroom effects on change in children's friendships. *Sociology of Education*, **51**, 270–282.

Hallinan, M. T. & Williams, R. A. (1989). Interracial friendship choices in secondary schools. *American Sociological Review*, **54**, 67–78.

Halverson, C. F. & Shore, R. E. (1969). Self-disclosure and interpersonal functioning. *Journal of Consulting and Clinical Psychology*, **33**, 213–217.

Harkness, S. & Super, C. M. (1985). The cultural context of gender segregation in children's peer groups. *Child Development*, **56**, 219–224.

Harper, L. V. & Huie, K. S. (1985). The effect of prior group experience, age, and familiarity on the quality and organization of preschoolers' social relationships. *Child Development*, **56**, 704–717.

Harper, L. V. & Sanders, K. M. (1975). Preschool children's use of space: Sex differences in outdoor play. *Developmental Psychology*, **11**, 119.

Harris, P. L. (1989). *Children and Emotion*. Oxford: Blackwell.

Hart, C. H., Ladd, G. W. & Burleson, B. R. (1990). Children's expectations of the outcomes of social strategies: Relations with sociometric status and maternal disciplinary styles. *Child Development*, **61**, 127–137.

Hartup, W. W. (1970). Peer interaction and social organization. In: P. H. Mussen (Ed.), *Carmichael's Handbook of Child Psychology* (Vol. 2). New York: Wiley.

Hartup, W. W. (1983). Peer relations. In: E. M. Hetherington (Ed.), *Handbook of Child Psychology (Vol. 4): Socialization, Personality, and Social Development*. New York: Wiley.

Hartup, W. W. (1984). The peer context in middle childhood. In: W. A. Collins (Ed.), *Development During Middle Childhood. The Years from Six to Twelve*. Washington, DC: National Academy Press.

Hartup, W. W. (1986). On relationships and development. In: W. W. Hartup & Z. Rubin (Eds), *Relationships and Development*. Hillsdale, NJ: Erlbaum.

Hartup, W. W., Glazer, J. & Charlesworth, R. (1967). Peer reinforcement and sociometric status. *Child Development*, **38**, 1017–1024.

Hartup, W. W., Laursen, B., Stewart, M. I. & Eastenson, A. (1988). Conflict and friendship relations of young children. *Child Development*, **59**, 1590–1600.

Harvey, J. H., Weber, A. L., Yarkin, K. L. & Stewart, B. E. (1982). An attributional approach to relationships breakdown and dissolution. In: S. W. Duck (Ed.), *Personal Relationships, Vol. 4: Dissolving Personal Relationships*. London: Academic Press.

Haskett, G. (1971). Modification of peer preferences of first grade children. *Developmental Psychology*, **4**, 429–433.

Haslett, B. & Bowen, S. P. (1989). Children's strategies in initiating contact with peers. In: J. F. Nussbaum (Ed.), *Life-span Communication: Normative Processes*. Hillsdale, NJ: Erlbaum.

Hastorf, A., Wildfogel, J. & Cassman, T. (1979). Acknowledgement of handicap as a tactic in social interaction. *Journal of Personality and Social Psychology*, **37**, 1790–1797.

Havighurst, R. J. (1972). *Developmental Tasks and Education*. New York: McKay.

Hay, D. F. (1985). Learning to form relationships in infancy: Parallel attainments with parents and peers. *Developmental Review*, **5**, 122–161.

Hay, D. F., Nash, A. & Pedersen, J. (1983). Interaction between six month old peers. *Child Development*, **54**, 557–562.

Hay, D. F., Pedersen, J. & Nash, A. (1982). Dyadic interaction in the first year of life. In: K. H. Rubin & H. S. Ross (Eds), *Peer Relationships and Social Skills in Childhood*. New York: Springer-Verlag.

Hayden, B., Nasby, W. & Davids, A. (1977). Interpersonal conceptual structures, predictive accuracy, and social adjustment of emotionally disturbed boys. *Journal of Abnormal Psychology*, **86**, 315–320.

Hayden-Thomson, L., Rubin, K. H. & Hymel, S. (1987). Sex preferences in sociometric choices. *Developmental Psychology*, **23**, 558–562.

Hayes, D. S. (1978). Cognitive bases for liking and disliking among preschool children. *Child Development*, **49**, 906–909.

Hayes, D. S., Gershman, E. & Bolin, L. J. (1980). Friends and enemies: Cognitive bases for preschool children's unilateral and reciprocal relationships. *Child Development*, **51**, 1276–1279.

Hayvren, M. & Hymel, S. (1984). Ethical issues in sociometric testing: Impact of sociometric measures on interaction behavior. *Developmental Psychology*, **20**, 844–849.

Hazan, C. & Shaver, P. (1987). Romantic love conceptualized as an attachment process. *Journal of Personality and Social Psychology*, **52**, 3, 511–524.

Herbert, M. (1991). *Clinical Child Psychology*. Chichester: Wiley.

Heider, F. (1958). *The Psychology of Interpersonal Relations*. New York: Wiley.

Heinicke, C. M., Diskin, S. D., Ramsey-Klee, D. M. & Given, K. (1983). Pre-birth parent characteristics and family development in the first year of life. *Child Development*, **54**, 194–208.

Hildebrandt, K. A. (1982). The role of physical appearance in infant and child development. In: H. E. Fitzgerald, B. M. Lester & M. W. Yogman (Eds), *Theory and Research in Behavioral Pediatrics* (Vol. 1). London: Plenum.

Hildebrandt, K. A. & Cannan, T. (1985). The distribution of caregiver attention in a group program for young children. *Child Study Journal*, **15**, 43–55.

Hildebrandt, K. A. & Fitzgerald, H. E. (1978). Adults' responses to infants varying in perceived cuteness. *Behavioural Processes*, **3**, 159–172.

Hildebrandt, K. A. & Fitzgerald, H. E. (1979). Facial feature determinants of perceived infant attractiveness. *Infant Behavior and Development*, **2**, 329–339.

Hildebrandt, K. A. & Fitzgerald, H. E. (1983). The infant's physical attractiveness: Its effect on bonding and attachment. *Infant Mental Health Journal*, **4**, 3–12.

Hill, C. R. & Stafford, F. P. (1980). Parental care of children: Time diary estimate of quantity, predictability, and variety. *Journal of Human Resources*, **15**, 219–239.

Hill, C. T. & Stull, D. E. (1982). Disclosure reciprocity: conceptual, and measurement issues. *Social Psychology Quarterly*, **45**, 238–244.

Hill, J. P. & Palmquist, W. J. (1978). Social cognition and social relations in early adolescence. *International Journal of Behavioural Development*, **1**, 1–36.

Hill-Beuf, A. & Porter, J. D. R. (1984). Children coping with impaired appearance: Social and psychologic influences. *General Hospital Psychiatry*, **6**, 294–301.

Hinde, R. A. (1979). *Towards Understanding Relationships*. London: Academic Press.

Hinde, R. A. (1987). *Individuals, Relationships and Culture*. Cambridge: Cambridge University Press.

Hirsch, B. J. & Rapkin, B. D. (1987). The transition to junior high school: A longitudinal study of self-esteem, psychological symptomology, school life, and social support. *Child Development*, **58**, 1235–1243.

Hobson, R. P. (1986a). The autistic child's appraisal of expressions of emotion. *Journal of Child Psychology and Psychiatry*, **27**, 321–342.

Hobson, R. P. (1986b). The autistic child's appraisal of emotion: A further study. *Journal of Child Psychology and Psychiatry*, **27**, 671–680.

Hoffman, L. R. & Maier, N. R. F. (1966). An experimental re-examination of the similarity–attraction hypothesis. *Journal of Personality and Social Psychology*, **3**, 145–152.

Hoffman, M. L. (1981a). Is altruism part of human nature? *Journal of Personality and Social Psychology*, **40**, 121–137.

Hoffman, M. L. (1981b). Perspectives on the difference between understanding people and understanding things: The role of affect. In: J. H. Flavell & L. Ross (Eds), *Social Cognitive Development*. Cambridge: Cambridge University Press.

Hoffman, M. L. (1987). The contribution of empathy to justice and moral judgement. In: N. Eisenberg & J. Strayer (Eds), *Empathy and its Development*. Cambridge: Cambridge University Press.

Hoffman, M. L. (1988). Moral development. In: M. Bornstein & M. Lamb (Eds), *Social, Emotional and Personality Development. Part 3 of Developmental Psychology: An Advanced Textbook*. London: Erlbaum.

Hogan, R. & Mankin, D. (1970). Determinants of interpersonal attraction: A clarification. *Psychological Reports*, **26**, 235–238.

Hogg, M. A. & Abrams, D. (1988). *Social Identifications*. London: Routledge.

Hollinger, J. D. (1987). Social skills for behaviorally disordered children as preparation for mainstreaming: theory, practice, and new directions. *Remedial and Special Education*, **8**, 17–27.

Hopkins, B. (1983). The development of early nonverbal communication. *Journal of Child Psychology and Psychiatry*, **24**, 131–144.

Hopkins, K. A. (1980). Why do babies find faces attractive? *Australian Journal of Early Childhood*, **5**, 25–28.

Hornstein, G. A. & Truesdell, S. E. (1988). Development of intimate conversation in close relationships. *Journal of Social and Clinical Psychology*, **7**, 1, 49–64.

Howes, C. (1988). Same- and cross-sex friends: Implications for interaction and social skills. *Early Childhood Research Quarterly*, **3**, 21–37.

Hudson, L. M., Forman, E. R. & Brion-Meisels, S. (1982). Role-taking as a predictor of prosocial behavior in cross-age tutors. *Child Development*, **53**, 1320–1329.

Hughes, J. N. & Sullivan, K. A. (1988). Outcome assessment in social skills training with children. *Journal of School Psychology*, **26**, 2, 167–183.

Hughes, R., Tingle, B. A. & Sawin, D. B. (1981). Development of empathic understanding in children. *Child Development*, **52**, 122–128.

Hunter, F. T. & Youniss, J. (1982). Changes in function of three relations during adolescence. *Developmental Psychology*, **18**, 806–811.

Huntley, D. K. & Phelps, R. E. (1990). Depression and social contacts of children from one-parent families. *Journal of Community Psychology*, **18**, 1, 66–72.

Huston, A. C. (1983). Sex typing. In: P. H. Mussen and E. M. Hetherington (Eds), *Handbook of Child Psychology (Vol. 4): Socialization, Personality, and Social Development* (4th edn). New York: Wiley.

Hymel, S. (1986). Interpretations of peer behavior: Affective bias in childhood and adolescence. *Child Development*, **57**, 431–445.

Hymel, S. & Franke, S. (1985). Children's peer relations: assessing self-perceptions. In: B. H. Schneider, K. H. Rubin & J. E. Ledingham (Eds), *Children's Peer Relations: Issues in Assessment and Intervention*. New York: Springer-Verlag.

Hymel, S. & Rubin, K. H. (1985). Children with peer relationship and social skills problems: Conceptual, methodological, and developmental issues. *Annals of Child Development*, **2**, 251–297.

Ickes, W. & Barnes, R. D. (1978). Boys and girls together – and alienated: On enacting stereotyped sex roles in mixed-sex dyads. *Journal of Personality and Social Psychology*, **36**, 669–683.

Innocenti, M. S., Stowitschek, J. J., Rule, S. & Killoran, J. (1986). A naturalistic study of the relation between preschool setting events and peer interaction in four activity contexts. *Early Childhood Research Quarterly*, **1**, 141–153.

Insko, C. A., Thompson, V. D., Stroebe, W., Shaud, K. F., Pinner, B. E. &

Layton, B. D. (1973). Implied evaluation and the similarity–attraction effect. *Journal of Personality and Social Psychology*, **25**, 297–308.

Ironsmith, M. & Poteat, G. M. (1990). Behavioral correlates of preschool sociometric status and the prediction of teacher ratings of behavior in kindergarten. *Journal of Clinical Child Psychology*, **19**, 1, 17–25.

Isabella, R. A. & Belsky, J. (1991). Interactional synchrony and the origins of infant–mother attachment: A replication study. *Child Development*, **62**, 373–384.

Jacklin, C. N. & Maccoby, E. E. (1978). Social behavior at thirty-six months in same-sex and mixed-sex dyads. *Child Development*, **49**, 557–569.

Jacobson, J. L. (1980). Cognitive determinants of wariness toward unfamiliar peers. *Developmental Psychology*, **16**, 347–354.

Jacobson, J. L. (1981). The role of inanimate objects in early peer interaction. *Child Development*, **52**, 618–626.

Jacobson, J. L. & Wille, D. E. (1986). The influence of attachment patterns on developmental changes from the toddler to the preschool period. *Child Development*, **57**, 338–347.

Jacobson, J. L., Tianen, R. L., Wille, D. E. & Aytch, D. M. (1986). Infant–mother attachment and early peer relations: The assessment of behavior in an interactive context. In: E. C. Mueller & C. Cooper (Eds), *Process and Outcome in Peer Relations*. Orlando, FL: Academic Press.

Janes, C. L., Hesselbrock, V. M., Myers, D. G. & Penniman, J. H. (1979). Problem boys in young adulthood: Teachers' ratings and twelve year follow-up. *Journal of Youth and Adolescence*, **8**, 453–472.

Jason, L. A. & Rhodes, J. E. (1989). Children helping children: Implications for prevention. *Journal of Primary Prevention*, **9**, 4, 203–212.

Johnson, D. W. & Johnson, R. T. (1983). Social interdependence and perceived academic and personal support in the classroom. *Journal of Social Psychology*, **120**, 77–82.

Johnson, F. L. & Aries, E. J. (1983). Conversational patterns among same-sex pairs of late adolescent close friends. *Journal of Genetic Psychology*, **142**, 225–238.

Johnson, M. W. (1935). The effect on behavior of variations in amount of play equipment. *Child Development*, **6**, 56–68.

Jones, G. P. & Dembo, M. H. (1989). Age and sex role differences in intimate friendships during childhood and adolescence. *Merrill-Palmer Quarterly*, **35**, 445–462.

Jones, W. H. (1989). Research and theory on loneliness: A response to Weiss's reflections. In: M. Hojat & R. Crandall (Eds), *Loneliness: Theory, Research, and Applications*. Newbury Park, CA: Sage.

Jormakka, L. (1976). The behaviour of children during a first encounter. *Scandinavian Journal of Psychology*, **17**, 15–22.

Jourard, S. M. (1958). *Personal Adjustment: An Approach Through the Study of Healthy Personality*. New York: MacMillan.

Jourard, S. M. (1959). Self-disclosure and other-cathexis. *Journal of Abnormal and Social Psychology*, **59**, 428–431.

Jourard, S. M. (1961). Self disclosure patterns in British and American college females. *Journal of Social Psychology*, **54**, 315–320.

Jourard, S. M. (1971a). *The Transparent Self*. New York: Van Nostrand.

Jourard, S. M. (1971b). *Self-Disclosure: An Experimental Analysis of the Transparent Self*. New York: Wiley.

Jourard, S. M. & Landsman, M. J. (1960). Cognition, cathexis, and the dyadic effect in men's self-disclosing behavior. *Merrill-Palmer Quarterly*, **6**, 178–186.

Jourard, S. M. & Lasakow, P. (1958). Some factors in self disclosure. *Journal of Abnormal and Social Psychology*, **56**, 91–98.

Kagan, J. (1972). Do infants think? *Scientific American*, **226**, 74–82.

Kagan, J. (1984). *The Nature of the Child*. New York: Basic Books.

Kagan, J. (1987). Perspectives on infancy. In: J. Osofsky (Ed.), *Handbook of Infant Development* (2nd edn). New York: Wiley.

Kagan, J. & Moss, H. A. (1962). *Birth to Maturity*. New York: Wiley.

Kagan, J., Kearsley, R. B. & Zelazo, P. R. (1975). The emergence of initial apprehension to unfamiliar peers. In: M. Lewis & L. Rosenblum (Eds), *Friendship and Peer Relations*. New York: Wiley.

Kandel, D. B. (1978a). Homophily, selection, and socialization in adolescent friendships. *American Journal of Sociology*, **84**, 427–436.

Kandel, D. B. (1978b). Similarity in real-life adolescent friendship pairs. *Journal of Personality and Social Psychology*, **36**, 306–312.

Kanner, L. (1943). Autistic disturbances of affective contact. *Nervous Child*, **2**, 217–250.

Karoly, P. & Harris, A. (1986). Operant methods. In: F. H. Kanfer & A. P. Goldstein (Eds), *Helping People Change: A Textbook of Methods* (3rd edn). New York: Pergamon.

Keating, D. P. & Clark, L. V. (1980). Development of physical and social reasoning in adolescence. *Developmental Psychology*, **16**, 23–30.

Kehle, T., Bramble, W. & Mason, E. (1974). Teachers' expectations: Ratings of student performance. *Journal of Experimental Education*, **43**, 54–60.

Keller, M. & Carlson, P. (1974). The use of symbolic modeling to promote social skills in preschool children with low levels of social responsiveness. *Child Development*, **45**, 912–919.

Keller, M. & Wood, P. (1989). Development of friendship reasoning: A study of interindividual differences in intraindividual change. *Developmental Psychology*, **25**, 820–826.

Kelley, H. H. (1973). The process of causal attribution. *American Psychologist*, **28**, 107–128.

Kelly, G. A. (1955). *The Psychology of Personal Constructs, Vol. 1: A Theory of Personality*. New York: Norton.

Kempler, B. (1987). The shadow side of self-disclosure. *Journal of Humanistic Psychology*, **27**, 109–117.

Kenealy, P., Frude, N. & Shaw, W. (1988). Influence of children's physical attractiveness on teacher expectations. *Journal of Social Psychology*, **128**, 373–383.

Kerckhoff, A. C. (1974). The social context of interpersonal attraction. In T. L. Huston (Ed.), *Foundations of Interpersonal Attraction*. London: Academic Press.

Kirkland, K. D. & Thelen, M. H. (1977). Uses of modelling in child treatment. In: B. B. Lahey & E. E. Kazdin (Eds), *Advances in Clinical Child Psychology*, Vol. 1. New York: Plenum.

Kleck, R. E. & De Jong, W. (1983). Physical disability, physical attractiveness, and social outcomes in children's small groups. *Rehabilitation Psychology*, **28**, 79–91.

Kleck, R. E., Richardson, S. A. & Ronald, L. (1974). Physical appearance cues and interpersonal attraction in children. *Child Development*, **45**, 305–310.

Klein, A. R. & Bates, J. E. (1980). Gender typing of games choices and qualities of boys' play behavior. *Journal of Abnormal and Social Psychology*, **8**, 201–212.

Klein, R. G. & Mannuzza, S. (1991). Long-term outcomes of hyperactive children: A review. *Journal of the American Academy of Child and Adolescent Psychiatry*, **30**, 3, 383–387.

Kleinke, C. L. & Kahn, M. L. (1980). Perceptions of self-disclosers: Effects of sex and physical attractiveness. *Journal of Personality*, **48**, 2, 190–205.

Klinnert, M. D., Emde, R. N., Butterfield, P. & Campos, J. J. (1986). Social referencing: The infant's use of emotional signals from a friendly adult with mother present. *Developmental Psychology*, **22**, 427–432.

Klos, D. S. & Loomis, D. F. (1978). A rating scale of intimate disclosure between late adolescents and their friends. *Psychological Reports*, **42**, 815–820.

Kobak, R. R. & Sceery, A. (1988). Attachment in late adolescence: Working models, affect regulation, and representation of self and others. *Child Development*, **59**, 135–146.

Kobocow, B., McGuire, J. M. & Blau, B. I. (1983). The influence of confidentiality conditions on self-disclosure of early adolescents. *Professional Psychology: Research and Practice*, **14**, 435–443.

Koch, H. (1935). The modification of unsocialness in preschool children. *Psychological Bulletin*, **32**, 700–701.

Kohlberg, L. (1969). Stage and sequence: The cognitive developmental approach to socialization. In: D. Gosling (Ed.), *Handbook of Socialization Theory and Research*. Chicago: Rand McNally.

Kohler, F. W. & Strain, P. S. (1990). Peer assisted interventions: Early promises, notable achievements, and future aspirations. *Clinical Psychology Review*, **10**, 4, 441–452.

Kon, I. S. (1981). Adolescent friendship: Some unanswered questions for future research. In: S. W. Duck & R. Gilmour (Eds), *Personal Relationships, Vol. 2: Developing Personal Relationships*. London: Academic Press.

Kon, I. S. & Losenkov, V. A. (1978). Friendship in adolescence: Values and behavior. *Journal of Marriage and the Family*, **40**, 143–155.

Konopka, G. (1983). Young girls: A portrait of adolescence. *Child and Youth Services*, **6**, 84–100.

Krantz, M. (1987). Physical attractiveness and popularity: A predictive study. *Psychological Reports*, **60**, 723–726.

Krantz, M., Friedberg, J. & Andrews, D. (1985). Physical attractiveness and popularity: The mediating role of self-perception. *Journal of Psychology*, **119**, 219–223.

Krasnor, L. R. (1982). An observational study of social problem solving in young children. In: K. H. Rubin & H. S. Ross (Eds), *Peer Relationships and Social Skills in Childhood*. New York: Springer-Verlag.

Kritchevsky, S. & Prescott, E. (1969). *Planning Environments for Young Children: Physical Space*. Washington, DC: National Association for the Education of Young Children.

Kupersmidt, J. B., Coie, J. D. & Dodge, K. A. (1990). The role of peer relationships in the development of disorder. In: S. R. Asher & J. D. Coie (Eds), *Peer Rejection in Childhood*. Cambridge: Cambridge University Press.

Kurdek, L. A. (1977). Structural components and intellectual correlates of cognitive perspective taking in first- through fourth-grade children. *Child Development*, **48**, 1503–1511.

Kurdek, L. A. & Krile, D. (1982). A developmental analysis of the relation between peer acceptance and both interpersonal understanding and perceived social self-competence. *Child Development*, **53**, 1485–1491.

Kurdek, L. A. & Rodgon, M. M. (1975). Perceptual, cognitive, and affective perspective taking in kindergarten through sixth-grade children. *Developmental Psychology*, **11**, 643–650.

L'Abate, L. & Milan, M. A. (1985). *Handbook of Social Skills Training and Research*. New York: Wiley.

Ladd, G. W. (1981). Effectiveness of a social learning method for enhancing children's social interaction and peer acceptance. *Child Development*, **52**, 171–178.

Ladd, G. W. (1983). Social networks of popular, average and rejected children in social settings. *Merrill-Palmer Quarterly*, **29**, 282–307.

Ladd, G. W. (1990). Having friends, keeping friends, making friends, and being liked by peers in the classroom: Predictors of children's early school adjustment. *Child Development*, **61**, 1081–1100.

Ladd, G. W. (1991). Family–peer relations during childhood: Pathways to competence and pathology? *Journal of Social and Personal Relationships*, **8**, 307–314.

Ladd, G. W. & Asher, S. R. (1985). Social skills training and children's peer relations. In: L. L'Abate & M. A. Milan (Eds), *Handbook of Social Skills Training and Research*. New York: Wiley.

Ladd, G. W. & Emerson, E. S. (1984). Shared knowledge in children's friendships. *Developmental Psychology*, **20**, 932–940.

Ladd, G. W. & Golter, B. S. (1988). Parents' management of preschoolers peer relations: Is it related to children's social competence? *Developmental Psychology*, **24**, 109–117.

Ladd, G. W. & Mars, K. T. (1986). Reliability and validity of preschoolers' perceptions of peer behavior. *Journal of Clinical Child Psychology*, **15**, 16–25.

Ladd, G. W. & Mize, J. (1983). A cognitive–social learning model of social skills training. *Psychological Review*, **90**, 127–157.

Ladd, G. W. & Oden, S. (1979). The relationship between acceptance and children's ideas about helpfulness. *Child Development*, **50**, 402–408.

LaFreniere, P. J. & Sroufe, L. A. (1985). Profiles of peer competence in the preschool: Interrelations between measures, influence of social ecology, and relation to attachment theory. *Developmental Psychology*, **21**, 56–69.

LaFreniere, P., Strayer, F. F. & Gauthier, R. (1984). The emergence of same-sex affiliative preferences among preschool peers: A developmental/ethological perspective. *Child Development*, **55**, 1958–1965.

Lalljee, M., Watson, M. & White, P. (1983). Some aspects of the explanations of young children. In: J. Jaspars, F. D. Fincham & M. Hewstone (Eds), *Attribution Theory and Research: Conceptual, Developmental and Social Dimensions*. London: Academic Press.

Lamb, M. E. (1974). A defense of the concept of attachment. *Human Development*, **17**, 376–385.

Lamb, M. E. (1988). Social and emotional development in infancy. In: M. Bornstein & M. Lamb (Eds), *Social, Emotional and Personality Development. Part 3 of Developmental Psychology: An Advanced Textbook*. London: Erlbaum.

Lamb, M. E. & Nash, A. (1989). Infant–mother attachment, sociability, and peer competence. In: T. J. Berndt & G. Ladd (Eds), *Peer Relationships in Child Development*. New York: Wiley.

Lamb, M. E., Easterbrooks, M. A. & Holden, G. W. (1980). Reinforcement and punishment among preschoolers: characteristics, effects, and correlates. *Child Development*, **51**, 1230–1236.

Lancioni, G. E. (1982). Normal children as tutors to withdrawn mentally retarded schoolmates: Training, maintenance, and generalization. *Journal of Applied Behavior Analysis*, **15**, 17–40.

Langlois, J. & Downs, A. (1979). Peer relations as a function of physical attractiveness. *Child Development*, **50**, 409–418.

Langlois, J. H. & Stephan, C. W. (1977). The effects of physical attractiveness and ethnicity on children's behavioral attributions and peer preferences. *Child Development*, **48**, 1694–1698.

Langlois, J. H. & Stephan, C. W. (1981). Beauty and the beast: The role of physical attractiveness in the development of peer relations and social behavior. In: S. S. Brehm, S. M. Kassin & F. X. Gibbons (Eds), *Developmental Social Psychology*. Oxford: Oxford University Press.

Langlois, J. H. & Styczynski, L. E. (1979). The effects of physical attractiveness on the behavioural attributions and preferences in acquainted children. *International Journal of Behavioural Development*, **2**, 325–341.

Langlois, J. H., Gottfried, N. W. & Seay, B. (1973). The influence of sex of peer on the social behavior of preschool children. *Developmental Psychology*, **8**, 93–98.

Langlois, J. H., Roggman, L. A. & Rieser-Danner, L. A. (1990). Infant's differential social responses to attractive and unattractive faces. *Developmental Psychology*, **26**, 153–159.

Langlois, J. H., Roggman, L. A., Casey, R. J., Ritter, J. M., Rieser-Danner, L. A. & Jenkins, V. Y. (1987). Infant preferences for attractive faces: Rudiments of a stereotype? *Developmental Psychology*, **23**, 363–369.

Lavine, L. O. & Lombardo, J. P. (1984). Self-disclosure: Intimate and non-intimate disclosures to parents and best friends as a function of Bem sex-role category. *Sex Roles*, **11**, 735–744.

Lazarus, P. J. (1982). Incidence of shyness in elementary school age children. *Psychological Reports*, **51**, 904–906.

Le Mare, L. J. & Rubin, K. H. (1987). Perspective taking and peer interaction: Structural and developmental analyses. *Child Development*, **58**, 306–315.

Lea, M. (1979). Personality similarity in unreciprocated friendships. *British Journal of Social and Clinical Psychology*, **18**, 393–394.

Ledingham, J. E. & Younger, A. J. (1985). The influence of the evaluator on assessments of children's social skills. In: B. H. Schneider, K. H. Rubin & J. E. Ledingham (Eds), *Children's Peer Relations: Issues in Assessment and Intervention*. New York: Springer-Verlag.

Lee, L. (1984). Sequences in separation: A framework for investigating endings of the personal (romantic) relationship. *Journal of Social and Personal Relationships*, **1**, 49–74.

Lerner, R. M. (1982). Children and adolescents as producers of their own development. *Developmental Review*, **2**, 342–370.

Lerner, R. M. & Karabenick, S. A. (1974). Physical attractiveness, body attitudes, and self-concept in late adolescents. *Journal of Youth and Adolescence*, **3**, 307–316.

Lerner, R. M. & Korn, S. J. (1972). The development of body-build stereotypes in males. *Child Development*, **43**, 908–920.

Lerner, R. M. & Lerner, J. V. (1977). Effects of age, sex, and physical attractiveness on child–peer relations, academic performance, and elementary school adjustment. *Developmental Psychology*, **13**, 585–590.

Lever, J. (1976). Sex differences in the games children play. *Social Problems*, **23**, 478–487.

Levinger, G. (1983). Development and change. In: H. Kelley et al. (Eds), *Close Relationships*. New York: Freeman.

Levinger, G. & Levinger, A. C. (1986). The temporal course of close relationships: Some thoughts about the development of children's ties. In: W. W. Hartup & Z. Rubin (Eds), *Relationships and Development*. Hillsdale, NJ: Erlbaum.

Lewin, K. (1931). Environmental forces in child behavior and development. In:

C. Murchison (Ed.), *A Handbook of Child Psychology*. Worcester, MA: Clark University Press

Lewin, K. (1936). Some social-psychological differences between the United States and Germany. *Character and Personality*, **4**, 265–293.

Lewis, M. & Brooks, J. (1974). Self, others and fear: Infants' reactions to people. In: M. Lewis & L. A. Rosenblum (Eds), *The Origins of Fear*. New York: Wiley.

Lewis, M. & Brooks, J. (1978). Self knowledge and emotional development. In: M. Lewis & L. A. Rosenblum (Eds), *The Development of Affect*. New York: Plenum.

Lewis, M. & Feiring, C. (1989). Early predictors of childhood friendship. In: T. J. Berndt & G. W. Ladd (Eds), *Peer Relationships in Child Development*. New York: Wiley.

Lewis, M., Young, G., Brooks, J. & Michalson, L. (1975). The beginnings of friendship. In: M. Lewis & L. A. Rosenblum (Eds), *Friendship and Peer Relations*. London: Wiley.

Li, A. K. (1984). Peer interaction and activity settings in a high density preschool environment. *Journal of Psychology*, **116**, 45–54.

Lieberman, A. F. (1977). Preschooler's competence with a peer: Relations with attachment and peer experience. *Child Development*, **48**, 1277–1287.

Lilly, M. S. (1971). Improving social acceptance of low sociometric status, low achieving students. *Exceptional Children*, **37**, 341–347.

Lindzey, G. & Borgatta, E. F. (1954). Sociometric measurement. In: G. Lindzey (Ed.), *Handbook of Social Psychology*, Vol. 1. Cambridge, MA: Addison-Wesley.

Littlefield, R. P. (1974). Self-disclosure among some Negro, White, and Mexican-American adolescents. *Journal of Counselling Psychology*, **21**, 133–136.

Livesley, W. J. & Bromley, D. B. (1973). *Person Perception in Childhood and Adolescence*. London: Wiley.

Lockheed, M. E. (1985). Sex and social influence: A meta-analysis guided by theory. In: J. Berger & M. Zeldich (Eds), *Status, Attributions, and Reward*. San Francisco: Jossey-Bass.

Lockheed, M. E. (1986). Reshaping the social order: The case of gender segregation. *Sex Roles*, **14**, 617–628.

Lockheed, M. E. & Klein, S. S. (1985). Sex equity in classroom organization and climate. In: S. Klein (Ed.), *Handbook for Achieving Sex Equity Through Education*. Baltimore, MD: John Hopkins University Press.

Lombardo, J. P. & Wood, R. D. (1979). Satisfaction with interpersonal relations as a function of level of self-disclosure. *Journal of Psychology*, **102**, 21–26.

Loo, C. M. (1972). The effects of spatial density on the social behavior of children. *Journal of Applied Psychology*, **2**, 372–381.

Lord, C. (1984). The development of peer relations in children with autism. In: F. J. Morrison, C. Lord & D. P. Keating (Eds), *Applied Developmental Psychology*, Vol. 1. Orlando, FL: Academic Press.

Lorenz, K. (1943). Die angeborenen formen möglicher erfahrung. *Zeitschrift Tierpsychologie*, **5**, 235–409.

Luft, J. (1970). *Group Processes: An Introduction*. Palo Alto, CA: National Press.

Luft, J. (1984) *Group Processes*, 3rd edn. Palo Alto, CA: Mayfield.

McArthur, L. Z. (1982) Physical attractiveness and self attribution. *Personality and Social Psychology Bulletin*, **8**, 460–467.

McCall, G. J. (1982). Becoming unrelated: The management of bond dissolution. In: S. W. Duck (Ed.), *Personal Relationships, Vol. 4: Dissolving Personal Relationships*. London: Academic Press.

McCarthy, B. (1981). Studying personal relationships. In: S. W. Duck & R. Gilmour

(Eds), *Personal Relationships, Vol. 1: Studying Personal Relationships*. London: Academic Press.

Maccoby, E. E. (1980). *Social Development: Psychological Growth and the Parent–Child Relationship*. New York: Harcourt Brace Jovanovich.

Maccoby, E. E. (1988). Gender as a social category. *Developmental Psychology*, **24**, 755–765.

Maccoby, E. E. (1990). Gender and relationships: A developmental account. *American Psychologist*, **45**, 4, 513–520.

Maccoby, E. E. & Jacklin, C. N. (1974). *The Psychology of Sex Differences*. Stanford, CA: Stanford University Press.

Maccoby, E. E. & Jacklin, C. N. (1980). Sex differences in aggression: A rejoinder and reprise. *Child Development*, **51**, 964–980.

Maccoby, E. E. & Jacklin, C. N. (1987). Gender segregation in childhood. In: E. H. Reese (Ed.), *Advances in Child Development and Behavior*, Vol. 20. New York: Academic Press.

Maccoby, E. E. & Martin, J. A. (1983). Socialization in the context of the family: parent–child interaction. In: E. M. Hetherington (Ed.), *Handbook of Child Psychology, Vol. 4*. New York: Wiley.

McFall, R. M. (1982). A review and reformulation of the concept of social skills. *Behavioural Assessment*, **4**, 1–33.

McGrew, W. C. (1972a). Interpersonal spacing of preschool children. In: J. S. Bruner & K. J. Connolly (Eds), *The Development of Competence in Early Childhood*. London: Academic Press.

McGrew, W. C. (1972b). Aspects of social development in nursery school children, with emphasis on introduction to the group. In: N. Blurton-Jones (Ed.), *Ethological Studies of Child Behaviour*. London: Cambridge University Press.

McGuire, J. M. (1973). Aggression and sociometric status with preschool children. *Sociometry*, **36**, 542–549.

McGuire, K. D. & Weisz, J. R. (1982). Social cognition and behavior correlates of preadolescent chumship. *Child Development*, **53**, 1478–1484.

McHale, S. M., Simeonsson, R. J., Marcus, L. M. & Olley, J. G. (1980). The social and symbolic quality of autistic children's communication. *Journal of Autism and Developmental Disorders*, **10**, 299–310.

Mackie, M. (1973). Arriving at "truth by definition": The case of stereotype inaccuracy. *Social Problems*, **20**, 431–447.

MacMillan, D. L. & Morrison, G. M. (1980). Correlates of social status among mildly handicapped learners in self-contained special classes. *Journal of Educational Psychology*, **72**, 437–444.

MacPherson, J. C. (1984). Environments and interaction in rows-and-column classrooms. *Environment and Behavior*, **16**, 481–502.

Maier, R. A., Holmes, D. L., Slaymaker, F. L. & Reich, J. N. (1984). The perceived attractiveness of preterm infants. *Infant Behavior and Development*, **7**, 403–414.

Main, M. & Cassidy, J. (1988). Categories of response to reunion with the parent at age 6: Predictable from infant attachment classifications and stable over a 1-month period. *Developmental Psychology*, **24**, 415–426.

Main, M. & Weston, D. R. (1981). The quality of the toddler's relationship to mother and to father: Related to conflict and the readiness to establish new relationships. *Child Development*, **52**, 932–940.

Main, M., Kaplan, N. & Cassidy, J. (1985). Security in infancy, childhood, and adulthood: A move to the level of representation. Monographs of the Society for Research in *Child Development*, **50** (whole No. 209), 66–104.

Mand, C. L. (1974). Rediscovering the fourth "R". *Theory into Practice*, 13, 245-251.

Marsh, D. T., Serafica, F. C. & Barenboim, C. (1981). Interrelationships among perspective taking, interpersonal problem-solving, and interpersonal functioning. *Journal of Genetic Psychology*, 138, 37-48.

Martin, C. L. & Little, J. K. (1990). The relation of gender understanding to children's sex-typed preferences and gender stereotypes. *Child Development*, 61, 1427-1439.

Martin, G. B. & Clark, R. D. (1982). Distress crying in neonates: Species and peer specificity. *Developmental Psychology*, 18, 3-9.

Martinek, T. (1981). Physical attractiveness: Effects on teacher expectations and dyadic interactions in elementary age children. *Journal of Sport Psychology*, 3, 196-205.

Masters, J. C. (1971). Social comparison by young children. *Young Children*, 3, 37-60.

Masters, J. C. & Furman, W. (1981). Popularity, individual friendship selection and specific interaction among children. *Developmental Psychology*, 17, 344-350.

Masters, J. C. & Wellman, H. M. (1974). The study of human infant attachment. *Psychological Bulletin*, 81, 218-237.

Matas, L., Arend, R. A. & Sroufe, L. A. (1978). Continuity of adaptation: Quality of attachment and later competence. *Child Development*, 49, 547-556.

Matos, M. G., Fonseca, V., Belo, J. & Oliveira, L. (1990). Social skills training with behaviorally disordered adolescents: A skill deficit and contextualist approach. Paper to the 20th European Congress on Behaviour Therapy, Paris, September.

Matos, M. G., Fonseca, V., Belo, J. Oliveira, L., Gaspar, A., Jesus, L., Lebre, P. & Miguel, P. (1991). Social skills training: A skill deficit and contextualist approach. Paper to the Annual Conference of Counselling Psychology Section of the British Psychological Society, Birmingham. June.

Matthews, K. A., Batson, C. D., Horn, J. & Rosenman, R. H. (1981). Principles in his nature which interest him in the fortune of others . . . The heritability of empathic concern for others. *Journal of Personality*, 49, 237-247.

Mead, G. H. (1934) *Mind, Self, and Society*. Chicago, Chicago University Press.

Medrich, E. A., Rosen, J., Rubin, V. & Buckley, S. (1982) *The Seriousness of Growing Up: A Study of Children's Lives Outside School*. Berkeley, CA: University of California Press.

Meichenbaum, D. (1986). Cognitive behavior modification. In: F. H. Kanfer & A. P. Goldstein (Eds), *Helping People Change: A Textbook of Methods* (3rd edn). New York: Pergamon.

Meisel, C. J. & Blumberg, C. J. (1990). The social comparison choices of elementary and secondary school students: The influence of gender, race, and friendship. *Contemporary Educational Psychology*, 15, 2, 170-182

Melikian, L. H. (1962). Self-disclosure among university students in the Middle East. *Journal of Social Psychology*, 57, 257-263.

Michalson, L., Foster, S. L. & Ritchey, W. L. (1981). Social skills assessment of children. In: B. B. Lahey & E. E. Kazdin (Eds), *Advances in Clinical Child Psychology*, Vol. 4. New York: Plenum.

Miller, C. (1984). Self schemas, gender and social comparison: A clarification of the related attributes hypothesis. *Journal of Personality and Social Psychology*, 46, 1222-1229.

Miller, J. B. (1889). Memories of peer relations and styles of conflict management. *Journal of Social and Personal Relationships*, 6, 487-504.

Mize, J. & Cox, R. A. (1990). Social knowledge and social competence: Number and quality of strategies as predictors of social behavior. *Journal of Genetic Psychology*, 151, 1, 117-127.

Mize, J. & Ladd, G. W. (1990a). Toward the development of successful social skills training for preschool children. In: S. R. Asher & J. D. Coie (Eds), *Peer Rejection in Childhood*. New York: Cambridge University Press.

Mize, J. & Ladd, G. W. (1990b). A cognitive social learning approach to social skills training with low-status preschool children. *Developmental Psychology*, **26**, 3, 388–397.

Mohan, J., Sehgal, M. & Bhandari, A. (1982). Sociometric status, personality, academic achievement and personal problems. *Indian Psychological Review*, **22**, 20–29.

Montemayor, R. & Eisen, M. (1977). The development of self-conception from childhood to adolescence. *Developmental Psychology*, **13**, 314–319.

Montemayor, R. & Flannery, D. J. (1989). A naturalistic study of the involvement of children and adolescents with their mothers and friends: Developmental differences in expressive behavior. *Journal of Adolescent Research*, **4**, 3–14.

Montemayor, R. & Van Komen, R. (1985). The development of sex differences in friendship patterns and peer group structure during adolescence. *Journal of Early Adolescence*, **5**, 285–294.

Moore, G. T. (1986). Effects of the spatial definition of behavior settings on children's behavior: A quasi-experimental field study. *Journal of Environmental Psychology*, **6**, 205–231.

Moore, R. W. & Young, D. (1978). Childhood outdoors: Toward a social ecology of the landscape. In: I. Altman & J. F. Wohlwill (Eds), *Children and the Environment*. New York: Plenum.

Moore, T., Pepler, D., Weinberg, B. & Hammond, L. (1990). Research on children from violent homes. *Canada's Mental Health*, **38**, 19–23.

Morris, W. & Nemcek, D. (1982). The development of social comparison motivation among preschoolers: Evidence of a stepwise progression. *Merrill-Palmer Quarterly*, **28**, 413–425.

Morton, T. L. (1978). Intimacy and reciprocity of exchange: A comparison of spouses and strangers. *Journal of Personality and Social Psychology*, **36**, 72–81.

Mosatche, H. & Bragonier, P. (1981). An observational study of social comparison in preschoolers. *Child Development*, **52**, 376–378.

Moss, H. A. (1967). Sex, age and state as determinants of mother–infant interaction. *Merrill-Palmer Quarterly*, **13**, 19–36.

Mueller, E. & Brenner, J. (1977). The origins of social skills and interaction among playgroup toddlers. *Child Development*, **48**, 854–861.

Mueller, E. & Lucas, T. (1975). A developmental analysis of peer interaction among toddlers. In: M. Lewis & L. A. Rosenblum (Eds), *Friendship and Peer Relations*. London: Wiley.

Mulcahy, G. A. (1973). Sex differences in patterns of self-disclosure among adolescents: A developmental perspective. *Journal of Youth and Adolescence*, **2**, 343–356.

Murgatroyd, S. (1980). *Helping the Troubled Child*. London: Tavistock.

Murphy, M., Nelson, D. & Cheap, T. (1981). Rated and actual performance of high school students as a function of sex and attractiveness. *Psychological Reports*, **48**, 103–106.

Murray, R. (1974). The influence of crowding on children's behavior. In: D. Cantor & T. Lee (Eds), *Psychology and the Built Environment*. London: Architectural Press.

Murstein, B. I. (1977). The stimulus-value-role theory of dyadic relationships. In:

S. W. Duck (Ed.), *Theory and Practice in Interpersonal Attraction*. London: Academic Press.

Murstein, B. I. (1986). *Paths to Marriage*. London: Sage.

Muss, R. E. (1982). Social cognition. *Adolescence*, **17**, 499–525.

Nastasi, B. K. & Clements, D. H. (1991). Research on cooperative learning: Implications for practice. *School Psychology Review*, **20**, 1, 110–131.

Nelson, G. & Carson, P. (1988). Evaluation of a social problem-solving skills program for the third- and fourth-grade students. *American Journal of Community Psychology*, **16**, 79–99.

Nelson, J. & Aboud, F. E. (1985). The resolution of social conflict among friends. *Child Development*, **56**, 1009–1017.

Nelson, K. (1981). Social cognition in a script framework. In: J. H. Flavell & L. Ross (Eds), *Social Cognitive Development*. Cambridge: Cambridge University Press.

Nelson, K. & Gruendel, J. (1979). At morning it's lunchtime: A scriptal view of children's dialogues. *Discourse Processes*, **2**, 73–94.

Newcomb, A. F. & Brady, J. E. (1982). Mutuality in boys' friendship relations. *Child Development*, **53**, 392–395.

Newcomb, A. F., Brady, J. E. & Hartup, W. W. (1979). Friendship and incentive conditions as determinants of children's task-oriented social behavior. *Child Development*, **50**, 878–881.

Newson, J. & Newson, E. (1976). *Seven Years Old in the Home Environment*. London: Allen & Unwin.

Nolen-Hoeksema, S. (1987). Sex differences in unipolar depression: Evidence and theory. *Pychological Bulletin*, **101**, 259–282.

Norrell, J. E. (1984). Self-disclosure: Implications for the study of parent–adolescent interaction. *Journal of Youth and Adolescence*, **13**, 163–178.

Nowicki, S. & Oxenford, C. (1989). The relation of hostile nonverbal communication styles to popularity in preadolescent children. *Journal of Genetic Psychology*, **150**, 39–44.

O'Connor, R. (1969). Modification of social withdrawal through symbolic modeling. *Journal of Applied Behavior Analysis*, **2**, 15–22.

O'Connor, R. (1972). Relative efficacy of modeling, shaping, and the combined procedures for modification of social withdrawal. *Journal of Abnormal Psychology*, **79**, 327–334.

Oden, S. & Asher, S. R. (1977). Coaching social skills for friendship making. *Child Development*, **48**, 495–506.

O'Donnell, L. & Stueve, A. (1983). Mothers as social agents: structuring the communities activities of school aged children. In: H. Z. Lopata & J. H. Pleck (Eds), *Jobs and Families*. Greenwich, CT: JAI

Ogbu, J. U. (1981). Origins of human competence: A cultural–ecological perspective. *Child Development*, **52**, 413–429.

Olson, J. M. & Hazlewood, D. (1986). Relative deprivation and social comparison: An integrative perspective. In: J. M. Olson, C. P. Herman & M. P. Zanna (Eds), *Relative Deprivation and Social Comparison*. London: Erlbaum.

Olweus, D. (1980). Familial and temperamental determinants of aggression behavior in adolescents – a causal analysis. *Developmental Psychology*, **16**, 644–660.

O'Neill, M., Fein, D., Velit, K. M. & Frank, C. (1976). Sex differences in preadolescent self-disclosure. *Sex Roles*, **2**, 85–88.

Oppenheimer, L. & Thijssen, F. (1983). Children's thinking about friendships and its relation to popularity. *Journal of Psychology*, **114**, 69–78.

Orlick, T. D. (1981). Positive socialization via cooperative games. *Developmental Psychology*, **17**, 426–429.

Papini, D. R., Farmer, F. F., Clark, S. M., Micka, J. C. & Barnett, J. K. (1990). Early adolescent age and gender differences in patterns of emotional self-disclosure to parents and friends. *Adolescence*, **25**, 959–976.

Park, K. A. & Waters, E. (1989). Security of attachment and preschool friendships. *Child Development*, **60**, 1076–1081.

Parke, R. D. & Bhavnagri, N. P. (1989). Parents as managers of children's peer relationships. In: D. Belle (Ed.), *Children's Social Networks and Social Supports*. New York: Wiley.

Parke, R. D. & Sawin, D. B. (1975). Infants' characteristics and behavior as elicitors of maternal and paternal responsivity in the newborn period. Cited by S. S. Brehm, S. M. Kassin & F. X. Gibbons (Eds) (1981), *Developmental Social Psychology*. Oxford: Oxford University Press.

Parke, R. D. & Slaby, R. G. (1983). The development of aggression. In: E. M. Hetherington (Ed.), *Handbook of Child Psychology, Vol. 4: Socialization, Personality, and Social Development*. New York: Wiley.

Parker, J. G. & Asher, S. R. (1987). Peer relations and later personal adjustment: Are low accepted children at risk? *Psychological Bulletin*, **102**, 357–389.

Parker, J. G. & Gottman, J. M. (1989). Social and emotional development in a relational context. In: T. J. Berndt & G. W. Ladd (Eds), *Peer Relationships in Child Development*. New York: Wiley.

Pastor, D. L. (1981). The quality of mother–infant attachment and its relationship to toddlers' initial sociability with peers. *Developmental Psychology*, **17**, 326–335.

Paterson, R. J. & Moran, G. (1988). Attachment theory, personality development, and psychotherapy. *Clinical Psychology Review*, **8**, 611–636.

Patterson, C. H. (1974). *Relationship Counselling and Psychotherapy*. Harper & Row.

Patterson, C. J., Kupersmidt, J. B. & Griesler, P. C. (1990). Children's perceptions of self and of relationships with others as a function of sociometric status. *Child Development*, **61**, 1335–1349.

Patterson, C. J., Vaden, N. A. & Kupersmidt, J. B. (1991). Family background, recent life events and peer rejection during childhood. *Journal of Social and Personal Relationships*, **8**, 347–361.

Patterson, G. R. (1986). Maternal rejection: Determinant or product for deviant child behavior. In: W. W. Hartup & Z. Rubin (Eds), *Relationships and Development*. Hillsdale, NJ: Erlbaum.

Patterson, M. L. (1988). Functions of nonverbal behaviour in close relationships. In: S. W. Duck (Ed.), *Handbook of Personal Relationships*. Chichester: Wiley.

Patzer, G. L. (1985). *The Physical Attractiveness Phenomenon*. London: Plenum.

Patzer, G. L. & Burke, D. M. (1988). Physical attractiveness and Child Development. In: B. B. Lahey & E. E. Kazdin (Eds), *Advances in Clinical Child Psychology*, Vol. 11. New York: Plenum.

Pedersen, D. M. & Higbee, K. L. (1969). Personality correlates of self-disclosure. *Journal of Social Psychology*, **78**, 81–89.

Peery, J. C. (1980). Neonate and adult head movement: No and yes revisited. *Developmental Psychology*, **16**, 245–250.

Pellegrini, D. S. (1985a). Social cognition and competence in middle childhood. *Child Development*, **56**, 253–264.

Pellegrini, D. S. (1985b). Training in social problem solving. In: M. Rutter & L. Hersov (Eds), *Child and Adolescent Psychiatry* (2nd edn). Oxford: Blackwell.

Pellegrini, D. S. (1986). Variability in children's level of reasoning about friendship. *Journal of Applied Developmental Psychology*, 7, 341–354.

Pellegrini, R. J., Hicks, R. A. & Meyers-Winton, S. (1979). Situational affective arousal and heterosexual arousal: Some effects of success, failure, and physical attractiveness. *Psychological Record*, 29, 453–462.

Pennebaker, J. W., Hendler, C. S., Durrett, M. E. & Richards, P. (1981). Social factors influencing absenteeism due to illness in nursery school children. *Child Development*, 52, 692–700.

Peplau, L. A. & Perlman, D. (1982). Perspectives on loneliness. In: L. A. Peplau & D. Perlman (Eds), *Loneliness: A Sourcebook of Current Theory, Research and Therapy*. New York: Wiley.

Perry, D. G., Perry, L. C. & Weiss, R. J. (1989). Sex differences in the consequences children anticipate for aggression. *Developmental Psychology*, 25, 312–319.

Perry, M. A. & Furukawa, M. J. (1986). Modeling methods. In: F. H. Kanfer & A. P. Goldstein (Eds), *Helping People Change: A Textbook of Methods* (3rd edn). New York: Pergamon.

Pettit, G. S., Dodge, K. A. & Brown, M. M. (1988). Early family experience, social problem solving patterns, and children's social competence. *Child Development*, 59, 107–120.

Pettit, G. S., Harrist, A. W., Bates, J. E. & Dodge, K. A. (1991). Family interaction, social cognition and children's subsequent relations with peers at kindergarten. *Journal of Social and Personal Relationships*, 8, 383–402.

Pfluger, L. W. & Zola, J. M. (1974). A room planned by children. In: G. Coates (Ed.), *Alternative Learning Environments*. Stroudsburg, Penn.: Dowden, Hutchinson, and Ross.

Phinney, J. S. (1979). Social interaction in young children: Initiation of peer contact. *Psychological Reports*, 45, 489–490.

Phinney, J. S. & Rotheram, M. J. (1980). Influence of sex of speaker and respondent on the type and success of young children's social overtures. Paper to British Psychological Society Developmental Section Annual Conference, Edinburgh. September.

Phyfe-Perkins, E. (1980). Children's behavior in preschool settings: A review of research concerning the influence of the physical environment. In: L. G. Katz (Ed.), *Current Topics in Early Childhood Education*, Vol. 3. Norwood, NJ: Ablex.

Piaget, J. (1959). *The Language and Thought of the Child*. London: Routledge.

Piaget, J. (1970). Piaget's theory. In: P. H. Mussen (Ed.), *Carmichael's Manual of Child Psychology*. New York: Wiley.

Piaget, J. (1977) (originally published 1932). *The Moral Judgement of the Child*. Harmondsworth: Penguin.

Pianta, R. C., Sroufe, L. A. & Egeland, B. (1989). Continuity and discontinuity in maternal sensitivity at 6, 24, and 48 months in a high risk sample. *Child Development*, 60, 481–487.

Pinkston, E., Reese, N., LeBlanc, J. & Baer, D. (1973). Independent control of a preschool child's aggression and peer interaction by contingent teacher attention. *Journal of Applied Behavior Analysis*, 6, 115–124.

Pittenger, J. B., Mark, L. S. & Johnson, D. F. (1989). Longitudinal stability of facial attractiveness. *Bulletin of the Psychonomic Society*, 27, 171–174.

Plog, S. C. (1965). The disclosure of self in the United States and Germany. *Journal of Social Psychology*, 65, 193–203.

Plomin, R. & Daniels, D. (1986). Genetics and shyness. In: W. H. Jones, J. M. Cheek & S. R. Briggs (Eds), *Shyness: Perspectives on Research and Treatment*. New York: Plenum.

Porteus, M. A. (1979). Survey of the problems of normal 15 year olds. *Journal of Adolescence*, **2**, 307–323.

Post, B. & Hetherington, E. M. (1974). Sex differences in the use of proximity and eye contact in judgement of affiliation in preschool children. *Developmental Psychology*, **10**, 881–889.

Pratap, S. & Bhargava, G. (1982). Self-disclosure as related to personality. *Indian Journal of Clinical Psychology*, **9**, 233–236.

Prescott, E. (1973) *Who Thrives in Daycare?* Pacific Oaks College, 714 West California Boulevard, Pasadena, CA 91105. Mimeograph.

Prescott, E. (1978). Is day care as good as home? *Young Children*, January, 13–19.

Price, J. M. & Dodge, K. A. (1989). Peers' contributions to children's social maladjustment: Description and intervention. In: T. J. Berndt & G. W. Ladd (Eds), *Peer Relationships in Child Development*. New York: Wiley.

Putallaz, M. (1983). Predicting children's sociometric status from their behavior. *Child Development*, **54**, 1417–1426.

Putallaz, M. (1987). Maternal behavior and children's sociometric status. *Child Development*, **58**, 324–340.

Putallaz, M. & Gottman, J. M. (1981). An interactional model of children's entry into peer groups. *Child Development*, **52**, 986–994.

Putallaz, M., Costanzo, P. R. & Smith, R. B. (1991). Maternal recollections of childhood peer relationships: Implications for their children's social competence. *Journal of Social and Personal Relationships*, **8**, 403–422.

Quay, L. C., Weaver, J. H. & Neel, J. H. (1986). The effects of play materials on positive and negative social behaviors in preschool boys and girls. *Child Study Journal*, **16**, 67–76.

Quilitch, H. R. & Risley, T. (1973). The effects of play materials on social play. *Journal of Applied Behavioral Analysis*, **6**, 575–578.

Radke-Yarrow, M., Cummings, E. M., Kuczynski, L. & Chapman, M. (1985). Patterns of attachment in two- and three-year olds in normal families with parental depression. *Child Development*, **56**, 884–893.

Ragland, E. U., Kerr, M. M. & Strain, P. S. (1978). Behavior of withdrawn autistic children: Effects of peer social initiations. *Behavior Modification*, **2**, 565–578.

Rathjen, D. J. (1980). An overview of social competence. In: D. P. Rathjen & J. P. Foreyt (Eds), *Social Competence*. Oxford: Pergamon.

Reaves, J. Y. & Friedman, P. (1982). The relationship of physical attractiveness and similarity of preferences to peer affiliation among Black children. *Journal of Negro Education*, **51**, 101–110.

Renshaw, P. D. (1981). The roots of current peer interaction research: A historical analysis of the 1930s. In: S. R. Asher & J. M. Gottman (Eds), *The Development of Children's Friendships*. Cambridge: Cambridge University Press.

Renshaw, P. D. & Asher, S. R. (1982). Social competence and peer status: The distinction between goals and strategies. In: K. H. Rubin & H. S. Ross (Eds), *Peer Relationships and Social Skills in Childhood*. New York: Springer-Verlag.

Renshaw, P. D. & Asher, S. R. (1983). Children's goals and strategies for social interaction. *Merrill-Palmer Quarterly*, **29**, 353–374.

Rheingold, H. L. & Cook, K. V. (1975). The content of boys' and girls' rooms as an index of parents' behavior. *Child Development*, **46**, 459–463.

Rholes, W. S. & Ruble, D. N. (1984). Children's understanding of dispositional characteristics of others. *Child Development*, **55**, 550–560.

Richardson, S. A. (1971). Children's values and friendships: A study of physical disability. *Journal of Health and Social Behavior*, **12**, 253–258.

Richardson, S. A., Ronald, L. & Kleck, R. E. (1974). The social status of handicapped and non-handicapped boys in a camp setting. *Journal of Special Education*, **8**, 143–152.

Richardson, S. A., Goodman, N., Hastorf, A. & Dornbusch, S. (1961). Cultural uniformity in reaction to physical disabilities. *American Sociological Review*, **26**, 241–247.

Richey, M. H. & Richey, H. W. (1980). The significance of best-friend relationships in adolescence. *Psychology in the Schools*, **17**, 536–540.

Richmond, V. P. (1984). Implications of quietness: Some facts and speculations. In: J. A. Daly & J. C. McCrosky (Eds), *Avoiding Communication*. Beverly Hills, CA: Sage.

Ricks, D. M. & Wing, L. (1976). Language, communication and the use of symbols in normal and autistic children. In: L. Wing (Ed.), *Early Childhood Autism* (2nd edn). Oxford: Pergamon.

Rivenbark, W. M. (1971). Self-disclosure patterns among adolescents. *Psychological Reports*, **28**, 35–42.

Robins, L. N. (1966). *Deviant Children Grow up: A Sociological and Psychiatric Study of Sociopathic Personality*. Baltimore: Williams & Wilkins.

Roff, J. D. & Wirt, R. D. (1984). Childhood aggression and social adjustment as antecedents of delinquency. *Journal of Abnormal Child Psychology*, **12**, 111–126.

Roff, M. (1961). Childhood social interactions and young adult bad conduct. *Journal of Abnormal and Social Psychology*, **63**, 333–337.

Roff, M. (1963). Childhood social interactions and young adult psychosis. *Journal of Clinical Psychology*, **19**, 152–157.

Roff, M., Sells, S. B. & Golden, M. M. (1972). *Social Adjustment and Personality Development in Children*. Minneapolis: University of Minnesota Press.

Rook, K. S. & Peplau, L. A. (1982). Perspectives on helping the lonely. In: L. A. Peplau & D. Perlman (Eds), *Loneliness: A Sourcebook of Current Theory, Research and Therapy*. New York: Wiley.

Roopnarine, J. L. (1985). Changes in peer-directed behavior following preschool experience. *Journal of Personality and Social Psychology*, **48**, 740–745.

Roopnarine, J. L. (1987). Social interaction in the peer group: Relationship to perceptions of parenting and to children's interpersonal awareness and problem solving ability. *Journal of Applied Developmental Psychology*, **8**, 351–362.

Roopnarine, J. L. & Honig, A. S. (1985). The unpopular child. *Young Children*, **40**, 59–64.

Root, J. (1977). The importance of peer groups. *Educational Research*, **20**, 22–25.

Roscoe, B., Callahan, J. E. & Peterson, K. L. (1985). Physical attractiveness as a potential contributor to child abuse. *Education*, **105**, 349–353.

Rose, A. S. (1991). The role of physical attractiveness in social interaction. Unpublished dissertation, Manchester Polytechnic, England.

Rose, S. A., Blank, M. & Spalter, I. (1975). Situational specificity of behavior in young children. *Child Development*, **46**, 464–469.

Rosenfeld, L. B. (1979) Why am I afraid to tell you who I am? *Communication Monographs*, **46**(1), 63–74.

Rosenfeld, H. M. & Jackson, J. (1965). Temporal mediation of the similarity-attraction hypothesis. *Journal of Personality*, **33**, 649–656.

Rosenthal, M. K. (1973). Attachment and mother–infant interaction: Some research impasses and a suggested change in orientation. *Journal of Child Psychology and Psychiatry and Allied Disciplines*, **14**, 201–207.

Rosenthal, R. (1973). The pygmalion effect lives. *Psychology Today*, **7**, 56–63.

Rosenthal, R. & Jacobson, L. (1968). *Pygmalion in the Classroom*. New York: Holt, Rinehart & Winston.

Ross, A. O. (1978). Behavior therapy with children. In: S. L. Garfield & E. Bergin (Eds), *Handbook of Psychotherapy and Behavior Change*. New York: Wiley.

Ross, H. S. & Lollis, S. P. (1989). A social relations analysis of toddler peer relationships. *Child Development*, **60**, 1082–1091.

Ross, M. B. & Salvia, J. (1975). Attractiveness as a biasing factor in teacher judgments. *American Journal of Mental Deficiency*, **80**, 96–98.

Rotenberg, K. J. (1984). Sex differences in children's trust in peers. *Sex Roles*, **11**, 953–957.

Rotenberg, K. J. (1986). Same-sex patterns and sex differences in the trust-value basis of children's friendship. *Sex Roles*, **15**, 613–626.

Rotenberg, K. J. & Mann, L. (1986). The development of the norm of reciprocity of self-disclosure and its functions in children's attraction to peers. *Child Development*, **57**, 1349–1357.

Rotenberg, K. J. & Sliz, D. (1988). Children's restrictive disclosure to friends. *Merrill-Palmer Quarterly*, **34**, 203–215.

Rothbart, M. K. (1986). Longitudinal observation of infant temperament. *Developmental Psychology*, **22**, 356–365.

Rothenberg, B. B. (1970). Children's social sensitivity and the relationship to interpersonal competence, intrapersonal comfort, and intellectual level. *Developmental Psychology*, **2**, 335–350.

Rotheram, M. J. (1980). Social skills training programs in elementary and high school classrooms. In: D. P. Rathjen & J. P. Foreyt (Eds), *Social Competence*. New York: Pergamon.

Rotheram-Borus, M. J. & Phinney, J. S. (1990). Patterns of social expectations among Black and Mexican-American children. *Child Development*, **61**, 2, 542–556.

Rubin, K. H. (1972). Relationship between egocentric communication and popularity among peers. *Developmental Psychology*, **7**, 364.

Rubin, K. H. (1973). Egocentrism in childhood: A unitary construct? *Child Development*, **44**, 102–110.

Rubin, K. H. (1978). Role-taking in childhood: Some methodological considerations. *Child Development*, **49**, 428–433.

Rubin, K. H. (1982). Non-social play in preschoolers: Necessary evil? *Child Development*, **53**, 651–657.

Rubin, K. H. (1983). Recent perspectives on sociometric status in childhood: Some introductory remarks. *Child Development*, **54**, 1383–1385.

Rubin, K. H. (1985). Socially withdrawn children: An "at risk" population? In: B. H. Schneider, K. H. Rubin & J. E. Ledingham (Eds), *Children's Peer Relations: Issues in Assessment and Intervention*. New York: Springer-Verlag.

Rubin, K. H. & Daniels-Beirness, T. (1983). Concurrent and predictive correlates of sociometric status in kindergarten and grade one children. *Merrill-Palmer Quarterly*, **29**, 337–352.

Rubin, K. H. & Hayvren, M. (1981). The social and cognitive play of preschool-aged children differing with regard to sociometric status. *Journal of Research and Development in Education*, **14**, 116–122.

Rubin, K. H. & Maioni, T. L. (1975). Play preference and its relationship to egocentrism, popularity and classification skills in preschoolers. *Merrill-Palmer Quarterly*, **21**, 171–179.

Rubin, K. H. & Mills, R. (1988). The many faces of social isolation in childhood. *Journal of Consulting and Clinical Psychology*, **56**, 916–924.

Rubin, K. H. & Pepler, D. J. (1980). The relationship of child's play to social-cognitive growth and development. In: H. C. Foot, A. J. Chapman & J. R. Smith (Eds), *Friendship and Social Relations in Children*. Chichester: Wiley.

Rubin, K. H., Daniels-Beirness, T. & Hayvren, M. (1982). Correlates of peer acceptance and rejection in early childhood. *Canadian Journal of Behavioral Sciences*, **14**, 338–349.

Rubin, K. H., Hymel, S. & Mills, R. (1989). Sociability and social withdrawal in childhood: Stability and outcomes. *Journal of Personality*, **57**, 237–255.

Rubin, K. H., Hymel, S., LeMare, L. & Rowden, L. (1989). Children experiencing social difficulties: Sociometric neglect reconsidered. *Canadian Journal of Behavioural Sciences*, **21**, 94–111.

Rubin, Z. (1980). *Children's Friendships*. London: Fontana.

Rubin, Z. (1982). Children without friends. In: L. A. Peplau & D. Perlman (Eds), *Loneliness: A Sourcebook of Current Theory, Research and Therapy*. New York: Wiley.

Rubin, Z. & Sloman, J. (1984). How parents influence their children's friendships. In: M. Lewis (Ed.), *Beyond the Dyad*. New York: Plenum.

Ruble, D. (1983). The development of social comparison processes and their role in achievement-related self-socialization. In: E. T. Higgins, D. N. Ruble & W. W. Hartup (Eds), *Social Cognition and Social Development*. Cambridge: Cambridge University Press.

Ruble, D. N., Feldman, N. S. & Boggiano, A. K. (1976). Social comparison between young children in achievement situations. *Developmental Psychology*, **12**, 192–197.

Ruble, D. N., Boggiano, A. K., Feldman, N. S. & Loebl, J. H. (1980). Developmental analysis of the role of social comparison in self evaluation. *Developmental Psychology*, **16**, 105–115.

Rucker, C. N. & Vincenzo, F. M. (1970). Maintaining social acceptance gains made by mentally retarded children. *Exceptional Children*, **36**, 679–680.

Rumsey, N., Bull, R. & Gahagan, D. (1986). A developmental study of children's stereotyping of facially deformed adults. *British Journal of Psychology*, **77**, 269–274.

Russell, A. (1984). A social skills analysis in childhood and adolescence using symbolic interactionism. *Youth and Adolescence*, **13**, 73–92.

Russell, A. & Finnie, V. (1990). Preschool children's social status and maternal instructions to assist group entry. *Developmental Psychology*, **26**, 603–611.

Russell, D., Cutrona, C. E., Rose, J. & Yurko, K. (1984). Social and emotional loneliness: An examination of Weiss's typology of loneliness. *Journal of Personality and Social Psychology*, **46**, 1313–1321.

Rutter, M. (1975). *Helping Troubled Children*. Harmondsworth: Penguin.

Rutter, M. (1978). Diagnosis and definition. In: M. Rutter & E. Schopler (Eds), *Autism: A Reappraisal of Concepts of Treatment*. New York: Plenum.

Rutter, M. (1979). *Fifteen Thousand Hours: Secondary Schools and Their Effects on Children*. London: Open Books.

Saegert, S., Swap, W. & Zajonc, R. B. (1973). Exposure, context and interpersonal attraction. *Journal of Personality and Social Psychology*, **25**, 234–242.

Sagi, A. & Hoffman, M. L. (1976). Empathic distress in newborns. *Developmental Psychology*, **12**, 175–176.

Salvia, J., Algozzine, R. & Sheare, J. B. (1977). Attractiveness and school achievement. *Journal of School Psychology*, **15**, 60–67.

Sameroff, A. J. & Emde, R. N. (1989). *Relationship Disturbances in Early Childhood*. New York: Basic Books.

Samuels, C. & Ewy, R. (1985). Aesthetic perception of faces during infancy. *British Journal of Developmental Psychology*, **3**, 221–228.

Sanders, K. M. & Harper, L. V. (1976). Free play fantasy behavior in preschool children: Relations among gender, age, season, and location. *Child Development*, **47**, 1182–1185.

Santrock, J. & Ross, M. (1975). Effects of social comparison on facilitative self control in young children. *Journal of Educational Psychology*, **67**, 193–197.

Sarnoff, I. & Zimbardo, P. G. (1961). Anxiety, fear, and social affiliation. *Journal of Abnormal and Social Psychology*, **62**, 597–605.

Savin-Williams, R. C. (1979). Dominance hierarchies in groups of early adolescents. *Child Development*, **50**, 923–935.

Savin-Williams, R. C. (1980). Social interactions of adolescent females in natural groups. In: H. C. Foot, A. J. Chapman & J. R. Smith (Eds), *Friendship and Social Relations in Children*. Chichester: Wiley.

Scarr, S. (1968). Environmental bias in twin studies. *Eugenics Quarterly*, **15**, 34–40.

Scarr, S. & Kidd, K. K. (1983). Developmental behavior genetics. In: M. M. Haith & J. J. Campos (Eds), *Handbook of Child Psychology: Infancy and Developmental Psychobiology* (Vol. 2). New York: Wiley.

Schachter, S. (1951). Deviation, rejection, and communication. *Journal of Abnormal and Social Psychology*, **46**, 190–207.

Schachter, S. (1959). *The Psychology of Affiliation*. London: Tavistock.

Schaffer, H. R. (1971). *The Growth of Sociability*. Harmondsworth: Penguin.

Schaffer, H. R. & Emerson, P. E. (1964). The development of social attachments in infancy. *Monographs of the Society for Research in Child Development*, **29**, (3, serial No. 94).

Schiff, W., Blackburn, H., Cohen, F., Furman, G., Jackson, A., Lapidos, E., Totkin, H. & Thayer, S. (1980). Does sex make a difference? Gender, age, and stimulus realism in perception and evaluation of aggression. *American Journal of Psychology*, **93**, 53–78.

Schneider, B. H. (1989). Between developmental wisdom and children's social skills training. In: B. H. Schneider, G. Attili, J. Nadel & R. P. Weissberg (Eds), *Social Competence in Developmental Perspective*. Dordrecht, Netherlands: Kluwer.

Schneider, B. H. & Byrne, B. M. (1985). Children's social skills training: A meta-analysis. In: B. H. Schneider, K. H. Rubin & J. E. Ledingham (Eds), *Children's peer relations: Issues in Assessment and Intervention*. New York: Springer-Verlag.

Schneider, B. H., Rubin, K. H. & Ledingham, J. E. (Eds) (1985). *Children's Peer Relations: Issues in Assessment and Intervention*. New York: Springer-Verlag.

Schofield, J. W. (1981). Complementary and conflicting identities: Images and interaction in an interracial school. In: R. Asher & J. M. Gottman (Eds), *The Development of Children's Friendships*. Cambridge: Cambridge University Press.

Schofield, M. J. & Kafer, N. F. (1985). Children's understanding of friendship issues:

Development by stage or sequence? *Journal of Social and Personal Relationships*, **2**, 151–165.

Schultz, N. R. & Moore D. (1986) The loneliness experience of college students: sex differences. *Personality and Social Psychology Bulletin*, **12**(1), 111–119.

Schultz, N. R. & Moore, D. (1989). Further reflections on loneliness research. In: M. Hojat & R. Crandall (Eds), *Loneliness: Theory Research and Applications*. Newbury Park, CA: Sage.

Schunk, D. H. (1987). Peer models and children's behavioral change. *Review of Educational Research*, **57**, 149–174.

Schwartz, S. & Johnson, J. H. (1985). *Psychopathology of childhood* (2nd edn). New York: Pergamon.

Sedlak, A. J. & Kurtz, S. T. (1981). A review of children's use of causal inference principles. *Child Development*, **52**, 759–784.

Selman, R. L. (1976). Social cognitive understanding: a guide to educational and clinical practice. In: T. Lickona (Ed.), *Moral Development and Behavior: Theory, Research and Social Issues*. New York: Holt, Rinehart, Winston.

Selman, R. L. (1980). *The Growth of Interpersonal Understanding*. New York: Academic Press.

Selman, R. L. (1981). The child as a friendship philosopher: A case study in the growth of interpersonal understanding. In: S. R. Asher & J. M. Gottman (Eds), *The Development of Children's Friendships*. Cambridge: Cambridge University Press.

Serbin, L. A., Tonick, I. J. & Sternglanz, S. H. (1977). Shaping cooperative cross-sex play. *Child Development*, **48**, 924–929.

Serbin, L. A., Connor, J. M., Burchardt, C. J. & Citron, C. C. (1979). Effects of peer presence on sex-typing of children's play behavior. *Journal of Experimental Child Psychology*, **27**, 303–309.

Serbin, L. A., Sprafkin, C., Elman, M. & Doyle, A.-B. (1984). The early development of sex differentiated patterns of social influence. *Canadian Journal of Social Science*, **14**, 350–363.

Shaklee, H. (1983). Sex differences in children's behavior. *Advances in Developmental and Behavioral Pediatrics*, **4**, 235–285.

Shantz, C. U. (1975). The development of social cognition. In: E. M. Hetherington (Ed.), *Review of Child Development Research*, vol. 5. Chicago: University of Chicago Press.

Shantz, C. U. (1983). Social cognition. In: P. H. Mussen (Ed.), *Handbook of Child Psychology*, Vol. 3. New York: Wiley.

Shantz, D. W. (1986). Conflict, aggression and peer status: an observational study. *Child Development*, **57**, 1322–1332.

Shapiro, B. Z. (1977). Friends and helpers: When ties dissolve. *Small Group Behavior*, **8**, 469–478.

Sharabany, R., Gershoni, R. & Hofman, J. E. (1981). Girlfriend, boyfriend: Age and sex differences in intimate friendship. *Developmental Psychology*, **17**, 800–808.

Shatz, M. & Gelman, R. (1973). The development of communication skills: Modifications in the speech of young children as a function of the listener. *Monographs of the Society for Research in Child Development*, **38** (whole no. 152).

Shaver, P. & Hazan, C. (1989). Being lonely, falling in love: Perspectives from attachment theory. In: M. Hojat & R. Crandall (Eds), *Loneliness: Theory, Research, and Applications*. Newbury Park, CA: Sage.

Shaver, P. & Rubenstein, C. (1980). Childhood attachment experience and adult loneliness. In: L. Wheeler (Ed.), *Review of Personality and Social Psychology*. Beverly Hills, CA: Sage.

Shea, J. (1981). Changes in interpersonal distances and categories of play behavior in the early weeks of preschool. *Developmental Psychology*, **17**, 417–425.

Sheehan, R. & Day, D. (1975). Is open space just empty space? *Day Care and Early Education*, **3**, 10–13, 47.

Sherif, M. & Sherif, C. W. (1953). *Groups in Harmony and Tension: an Integration of Studies in Intergroup Relations*. New York: Harper & Row.

Sherif, M., Harvey, O. J., White, B. J., Hood, W. E. & Sherif, C. W. (1961). *Intergroup Conflict and Cooperation: The Robbers Cave Experiment*. Norman, Oklahoma: University of Oklahoma Press.

Shrum, W., Cheek, N. H. & Hunter, S. M. (1988). Friendship in school: gender and racial homophily. *Sociology of Education*, **61**, 227–239.

Shultz, T. R., Fisher, G. W., Pratt, C. C. & Rulf, S. (1986). Selection of causal rules. *Child Development*, **57**, 143–152.

Shure, M. B. (1963). Psychological ecology of a nursery school. *Child Development*, **34**, 979–992.

Shure, M. B. & Spivack, G. (1979). Interpersonal cognitive problem solving and primary prevention: Programming for preschool and kindergarten children. *Journal of Clinical Child Psychology*, **8**, 89–94.

Shure, M. B. & Spivack, G. (1980). Interpersonal problem-solving as a mediator of behavioral adjustment in preschool and kindergarten children. *Journal of Applied Developmental Psychology*, **1**, 29–44.

Sigelman, C. K., Miller, T. E. & Whitworth, L. A. (1986). The early development of stigmatizing reactions to physical differences. *Journal of Applied Developmental Psychology*, **7**, 17–32.

Sigman, M., Mundy, P., Sherman, T. & Ungerer, J. (1986). Social interactions of autistic, mentally retarded and normal children and their caregivers. *Journal of Child Psychology and Psychiatry*, **27**, 647–656.

Simmons, C. H. & Sands-Dudelczyk, K. (1983). Children helping peers: Altruism and preschool environment. *Journal of Psychology*, **115**, 203–207.

Simmons, R. G. & Rosenberg, F. (1975). Sex, sex roles, and self-image. *Journal of Youth and Adolescence*, **4**, 229–258.

Simmons, R. G., Rosenberg, F. & Rosenberg, M. (1973). Disturbance in the self-image at adolescence. *American Sociological Review*, **38**, 553–568.

Sinha, V. (1969). Nature of self-disclosure among students. *Agra University Journal of Research* (letters), **17**, 43–46.

Sinha, V. (1972). Age differences in self-disclosure. *Developmental Psychology*, **7**, 257–258.

Sinha, V. & Tripathi, A. D. (1975). Personality differences of high and low self-disclosers in interpersonal communications. *Psycho-lingua*, **5**, 35–41.

Siperstein, G. N. & Bak, J. J. (1989). Social relationships of adolescents with moderate mental retardation. *Mental Retardation*, **27**, 5–10.

Skoe, E. E. & Ksionzky, S. (1985). Target personality characteristics and self-disclosure: An exploratory study. *Journal of Clinical Psychology*, **41**, 14–21.

Skypeck, G. (1967). Self-disclosure in children ages six through twelve. Unpublished Masters thesis, Florida University.

Slavin, R. E. (1983). When does cooperative learning increase student achievement? *Psychological Bulletin*, **94**, 429–445.

Slavin, R. E. & Karweit, N. (1981). Cognitive and affective outcomes of an intensive student team learning experience. *Journal of Experimental Education*, **50**, 29–35.

Sluckin, W., Colman, A. M. & Hargreaves, D. J. (1980). Liking words as a function of the experienced frequency of their exposure. *British Journal of Psychology*, **71**, 163–169.

Sluckin, W., Miller, L. B. & Franklin, H. (1973). The influence of stimulus familiarity/novelty on children's expressed preferences. *British Journal of Psychology*, **64**, 563–567.

Smetana, J. G. & Letourneau, K. J. (1984). Development of gender constancy and children's sex-typed free play behavior. *Developmental Psychology*, **20**, 691–696.

Smith, J. & Krantz, M. (1986). Physical attractiveness and popularity in children: A methodological refinement and replication. *Journal of Genetic Psychology*, **147**, 419–420.

Smith, P. (1974). Aspects of the playgroup environment. In: D. Cantor & T. Lee (Eds), *Psychology and the Built Environment*. London: Architectural Press.

Smith, P. K. (1978). A longitudinal study of social participation in preschool children: Solidarity and parallel play re-examined. *Developmental Psychology*, **14**, 517–523.

Smith, P. K. & Connolly, K. (1972). *Ethological Studies of Child Behavior*. Cambridge: Cambridge University Press.

Smith, P. K. & Connolly, K. J. (1980). *The Ecology of Preschool Behavior*. Cambridge: Cambridge University Press.

Smith, P. K. & Green, M. (1975). Aggressive behavior in English nurseries and play groups: Sex differences and response of adults. *Child Development*, **46**, 211–214.

Smollar, J. & Youniss, J. (1982). Social development through friendship. In: K. H. Rubin & H. S. Ross (Eds), *Peer Relationships and Social Skills in Childhood*. New York: Springer-Verlag.

Snoek, D. & Rothblum, E. (1979). Self-disclosure among adolescents in relation to parental affection and control patterns. *Adolescence*, **14**, 333–340.

Snow, M. E., Jacklin, C. N. & Maccoby, E. E. (1983). Sex of child differences in father–child interaction at one year of age. *Child Development*, **54**, 227–232.

Snyder, M. & Uranowitz, S. W. (1978). Reconstructing the past: Some cognitive consequences of person perception. *Journal of Personality and Social Psychology*, **36**, 941–950.

Snyder, M., Tanke, E. & Berscheid, E. (1977). Social perception and interpersonal behavior: On the self-fulfilling nature of social stereotypes. *Journal of Personality and Social Psychology*, **35**, 656–666.

Sobol, M. P. & Earn, B. M. (1985a). What causes mean: An analysis of children's interpretations of the causes of social experience. *Journal of Social and Personal Relationships,* **2**, 137–151.

Sobol, M. P. & Earn, B. M. (1985b). Assessment of children's attributions for social experiences: Implications for social skills training. In: B. H. Schneider, K. H. Rubin & J. E. Ledingham (Eds), *Children's Peer Relations: Issues in Assessment and Intervention*. New York: Springer-Verlag.

Social Trends (1991). Volume 21. London: Central Statistical Office, HMSO.

Solomon, R. W. & Wahler, R. G. (1973). Peer reinforcement control of classroom problem behavior. *Journal of Applied Behavior Analysis*, **6**, 49–56.

Spence, S. H. (1987). The relationship between social-cognitive skills and peer sociometric status. *British Journal of Developmental Psychology*, **5**, 347–356.

Spivack, G. & Shure, M. B. (1974). *Social Adjustment of Young Children: A Cognitive Approach to Solving Real Life Problems*. San Francisco, CA: Jossey-Bass.

Spivack, G., Platt, J. J. & Shure, M. B. (1976). *The Problem Solving Approach to Adjustment*. San Francisco, CA: Jossey-Bass.

Sroufe, L. A. (1979). The coherence of individual development. *American Psychologist*, **34**, 834–841.

Sroufe, L. A. (1983). Infant–caregiver attachment and patterns of adaptation in preschool: The roots of maladaptation and competence. In: M. Perlmutter (Ed.), *Minnesota Symposium on Child Psychology*, Vol. 16. Hillsdale, NJ: Erlbaum.

Sroufe, L. A. (1985). Attachment classification from the perspective of infant–caregiver relationships and infant temperament. *Child Development*, **56**, 1–14.

Sroufe, L. A. & Fleeson, J. (1986). Attachment and the construction of relationships. In: W. W. Hartup & Z. Rubin, (Eds), *Relationships and Development*. Hillsdale, NJ: Erlbaum.

Sroufe, L. A. & Jacobvitz, D. (1989). Diverging pathways, developmental transformations, multiple etiologies and the problem of continuity in development. *Human Development*, **32**, 196–203.

Sroufe, L. A., Schork, E., Motti, F., Lawroski, N. & LaFreniere, P. (1984). The role of affect in social competence. In: C. Izard, J. Kagan & R. Zajonc (Eds), *Affect, Cognition and Behavior*. Cambridge: Cambridge University Press.

Steinberg, L. D. & Silverberg, S. (1986). The vicissitudes of autonomy in early adolescence. *Child Development*, **57**, 841–851.

Stengel, E. (1971). *Suicide and Attempted Suicide*. Harmondsworth: Penguin.

Stokols, D. (1972). On the distinction between density and crowding. *Psychological Review*, **79**, 275–277.

Strain, P. S. (1977). Effects of peers' social initiations on withdrawn preschool children: Some training and generalization effects. *Journal of Abnormal Child Psychology*, **5**, 445–455.

Strain, P. S. & Fox, J. J. (1981). Peers as behavior change agents for withdrawn classmates. In: B. B. Lahey & E. E. Kazdin (Eds), *Advances in Clinical Child Psychology*, Vol. 4. New York: Plenum.

Strain, P. & Timm, M. (1974). An experimental analysis of social interaction between a behaviorally disordered preschool child and her classroom peers. *Journal of Applied Behavior Analysis*, **7**, 583–590.

Strain, P. S., Shores, R. E. & Timm, M. A. (1977). Effects of social initiations on the behavior of withdrawn preschool children. *Journal of Applied Behavior Analysis*, **10**, 289–298.

Strayer, F. F. (1980). Social ecology of the preschool peer group. In: A. Collins (Ed.), *Minnesota Symposium on Child Psychology, Vol. 13: Development of Cognition, Affect and Social Relations*. Hillsdale, NJ: Erlbaum.

Styczynski, L. (1976). Effects of physical characteristics on the social, emotional, and intellectual development of early schoolage children. Unpublished PhD thesis, University of Texas at Austin.

Sullivan, H. S. (1953). *The Interpersonal Theory of Psychiatry*. New York: Norton.

Suls, J. (1986). Comparison processes in relative deprivation: A lifespan analysis. In: J. M. Olson, C. P. Herman & M. P. Zanna (Eds), *Relative Deprivation and Social Comparison*. London: Erlbaum.

Suls, J. & Sanders, G. (1979). Social comparison processes in the young child. *Journal of Research and Development in Education*, **13**, 79–89.

Sulzer, B., Mayer, G. R. & Cody, J. J. (1968). Assisting teachers with managing classroom behavioral problems. *Elementary School Guidance and Counselling*, **3**, 40–48.

Sussman, S., Mueser, K. T., Grau, B. W. & Yarnold, P. R. (1983). Stability of females, facial attractiveness during childhood. *Journal of Personality and Social Psychology*, **44**, 1231–1233.

Tajfel, H. (1982). Social psychology of intergroup relations. *Annual Review of Psychology*, **33**, 1–39.

Takac, R. & Benyamini, K. (1989). Criteria for children's adjustment in school, peer group, and youth movement. *School Psychology International*, **10**, 257–263.

Tesch, S. A. (1983). Review of friendship development across the lifespan. *Human Development*, **26**, 266–276.

Tesser, A., Campbell, J. & Smith, M. (1984). Friendship choice and performance: Self evaluation maintenance in children. *Journal of Personality and Social Psychology*, **46**, 561–574.

Thelen, M. H., Fry, R. A., Dollinger, S. J. & Paul, S. C. (1976). Use of videotaped models to improve interpersonal adjustment of delinquents. *Journal of Consulting and Clinical Psychology*, **44**, 492.

Thelen, M. H., Kirkland, K. D., Dollinger, S. J. & Paul, S. C. (1977). On being imitated: Effects on reward and reward value of the imitator. *Journal of Research in Personality*, **11**, 101–109.

Thomas, A., Chess, S. & Birch, H. G. (1970). The origin of personality. *Scientific American*, **233**, 102–109.

Thompson, R. A. & Lamb, M. E. (1984). Infants, mothers, families and strangers. In: M. Lewis (Ed.), *Beyond the dyad*. New York: Plenum.

Thompson, R. A., Lamb, M. E. & Estes, D. (1982). Stability of mother–infant attachment and its relationship to changing life circumstances in an unselected middle-class sample. *Child Development*, **53**, 144–148.

Thompson, S. K. (1975). Gender labels and early sex role development. *Child Development*, **46**, 339–347.

Thorndike, R. L. (1968). A review of *Pygmalion in the Classroom*. *American Educational Research Journal*, **5**, 4, 708–711.

Thorne, B. (1986). Girls and boys together . . . but mostly apart: Gender arrangements in elementary schools. In: W. W. Hartup & Z. Rubin (Eds), *Relationships and Development*. Hillsdale, NJ: Erlbaum.

Tieger, T. (1980). On the biological bases of sex differences in aggression. *Child Development*, **51**, 943–963.

Tracy, R. L. & Ainsworth, M. D. S. (1981). Maternal affectionate behavior and infant–mother attachment patterns. *Child Development*, **52**, 1341-1343.

Tripathi, A. D. (1979). A psychological study of personality traits of high self-disclosers and its clinical importance. *Indian Journal of Clinical Psychology*, **6**, 81–82.

Trnavsky, P. A. & Bakeman, R. (1976). Physical attractiveness: Stereotype and social behaviour in preschool children. Paper presented at the meeting of the American Psychological Association, Washington. August.

Troy, M. & Sroufe, L. A. (1987). Victimization among preschoolers: Role of attachment relationship history. *Journal of the Academy of Child and Adolescent Psychiatry*, **26**, 166–172.

Tuma, N. & Hallinan, M. T. (1979). The effects of sex, race and achievement in school children's friendships. *Social Forces*, **57**, 1265–1285.

Turiel, E. (1983). Interaction and development in social cognition. In: E. T. Higgins, D. N. Ruble & W. W. Hartup (Eds), *Social Cognition and Social Development*. Cambridge: Cambridge University Press.

Tversky, A. & Kahneman, D. (1974). Judgement under uncertainty: heuristics and biases. *Science*, **185**, 1124–1131.

Unger, R. K. (1979). *Female and Male*. New York: Harper & Row.

Vandell, D. L. (1977). Boy toddlers' social interaction with mothers, fathers and peers. Unpublished Doctoral dissertation, Boston University.

Vandell, D. L. (1979). Effects of a playgroup experience on mother–son and father–son interaction. *Developmental Psychology*, **15**, 379–385.

Vandell, D. L. (1980). Sociability with peer and mother during the first year. *Developmental Psychology*, **16**, 335–361.

Vandell, D. L. & Mueller, E. C. (1980). Peer play and friendships during the first two years. In: H. C. Foot, A. J. Chapman & J. R. Smith (Eds), *Friendship and Social Relations in Children*. London: Wiley.

Vandell, D. L. & Wilson, K. S. (1982). Social interaction in the first year: Infants' social skills with peers versus mothers. In: K. H. Rubin & H. S. Ross (Eds), *Peer relationships and social skills in childhood*. New York: Springer-Verlag.

Vandell, D. L. & Wilson, K. S. (1987). Infants' interactions with mother, sibling, and peer: Contrasts and relationships between interaction systems. *Child Development*, **58**, 176–186.

Vandell, D. L., Wilson, K. S. & Buchanan, N. R. (1980). Peer interaction in the first year of life: An examination of its structure, content and sensitivity. *Child Development*, **51**, 481–488.

Van Vliet, W. (1981). The environmental context of children's friendships: An empirical and conceptual examination of the role of child density. *EDRA – Environmental Design Research Association*, No. 12, 216–224.

Van Vliet, W. (1986). The methodological and conceptual basis of environmental policies for children. *Prevention in Human Services*, **4**, 59–78.

Vaughn, B. & Waters, E. (1981). Attention structure, sociometric status and dominance. *Developmental Psychology*, **17**, 275–288.

Veroff, J. (1969). Social comparison and the development of achievement motivation. In: C. P. Smith (Ed.), *Achievement-related Motives in Children*. New York: Russell Sage.

Volkmar, F. R., Sparrow, S. S., Goudereau, D., Cicchetti, D. V., Paul, R. & Cohen, D. J. (1987). Social deficits in autism: An operational approach using the Vineland Adaptive Behavior Scales. *Journal of the American Academy of Child Psychiatry*, **26**, 156–161.

Vondracek, F. W. (1969). The study of self-disclosure in experimental interviews. *Journal of Psychology*, **72**, 55–59.

Vosk, B. N., Forehand, R. & Figueroa, R. (1983). Perception of emotions by accepted and rejected children. *Journal of Behavioural Assessment*, **5**, 151–160.

Waas, G. A. & Honer, S. A. (1990). Situational attributions and dispositional inferences: The development of peer reputation. *Merrill-Palmer Quarterly*, **36**, 2, 239–260.

Wada, M. (1986). Effects of liking, interpersonal distance, and topics on nonverbal behaviours and self-disclosure. *Japanese Journal of Experimental Social Psychology*, **26**, 1–12.

Wahler, R. G. (1967). Child–child interactions in five filed settings: Some experimental analyses. *Journal of Experimental Child Psychology*, **5**, 278–293.

Walden, T. A. & Field, T. M. (1990). Preschool children's social competence and production and discrimination of affective expressions. *British Journal of Developmental Psychology*, **8**, 1, 65–76.

Waldrop, M. F. & Halverson, C. F. (1975). Intensive and extensive peer behavior: Longitudinal and cross-sectional analyses. *Child Development*, **46**, 19–26.

Walker, H. M., Greenwood, C. R., Hops, H. & Todd, N. (1979). Differential effects of reinforcing topographic components of social interaction. *Behavior Modification*, **3**, 291–321.

Wallace, M. (1991). Social comparison processes in children. Unpublished dissertation, Manchester Polytechnic, England.

Wallander, J. L. & Hubert, N. C. (1987). Peer social dysfunction in children with developmental disabilities: Empirical basis and a conceptual model. *Clinical Psychology Review*, **7**, 2, 205–221.

Wallerstein, J. S. & Kelly, J. B. (1980). *Surviving the Breakup: How Children and Parents Cope with Divorce*. New York: Basic Books.

Wanlass, R. L. & Prinz, R. J. (1982). Methodological issues in conceptualizing and treating childhood social isolation. *Psychological Bulletin*, **92**, 39–55.

Warr, P. B. (1965). Proximity as a determinant of positive and negative sociometric choice. *British Journal of Social and Clinical Psychology*, **4**, 104–109.

Waters, E. & Sroufe, L. A. (1983). Social competence as a developmental construct. *Developmental Review*, **3**, 79–97.

Waters, E., Vaughn, B. & Egeland, B. (1980). Individual differences in infant–mother attachment relationships at age one: Antecedents in neonatal behavior in an urban, economically disadvantaged sample. *Child Development*, **51**, 203–216.

Waters, E., Wippman, J. & Sroufe, L. A. (1979). Attachment, positive affect, and competence in the peer group: Two studies in construct validation. *Child Development*, **50**, 821–829.

Weinraub, M. & Brown, L. M. (1983). The development of sex role stereotypes in children: Crushing realities. In: V. Ranks & F. Rothblum (Eds), *The Ailing Feminine Stereotype: Sex Roles and Women's Mental Health*. New York: Springer.

Weinstein, C. S. (1977). Modifying student behavior in an open classroom through changes in physical design. *American Educational Research Journal*, **14**, 249–262.

Weinstein, C. S. (1979). The physical environment of the school. *Review of Educational Research*, **49**, 577–610.

Weisfeld, G. E., Muczenski, D. M., Weisfeld, C. C. & Omark, D. R. (1987). Stability of boys' social success among peers over an eleven year period. *Human Development*, **18**, 58–80.

Weiss, R. S. (1973). *Loneliness: The Experience of Emotional and Social Isolation*. Cambridge, MA: MIT Press.

Weiss, R. S. (1989). Reflections on the present state of loneliness research. In: M. Hojat & R. Crandall (Eds), *Loneliness: Theory, Research, and Applications*. Newbury Park, CA: Sage.

West, L. W. (1970). Sex differences in the exercise of circumspection in self-disclosure among adolescents. *Psychological Reports*, **26**, 226.

West, L. W. (1971). A study of the validity of the self-disclosure inventory for adolescents. *Perceptual and Motor Skills*, **33**, 91–100.

West, L. W. & Altman, H. A. (1987). The inventory of communication patterns for adolescents (ICPA). *Canadian Journal of Counselling*, **21**, 4–17.

West, L. W. & Zingle, H. W. (1969). A self-disclosure inventory for adolescents. *Psychological Reports*, **24**, 439–445.

Wheeler, L. & Zuckerman, M. (1977). Commentary. In: J. M. Suls & R. L. Miller (Eds), *Social Comparison Processes: Theoretical and Empirical Perspectives*. Washington, DC: Hemisphere.

Wheeless, L. R. & Grotz, J. (1977). The measurement of trust and its relationship to self-disclosure. *Human Communications Research*, **3**, 250–257.

White, R. W. (1959). Motivation reconsidered: The concept of competence. *Psychological Review*, **66**, 297–333.

White, R. W. (1972). *The Enterprise of Living: Growth and Organisation in Personality*. New York: Holt, Rinehart & Winston.

Whiting, B. B. & Edwards, C. P. (1973). A cross-cultural analysis of sex differences in the behavior of children aged 3–11. *Journal of Social Psychology*, **91**, 171–188.

Whiting, B. B. & Edwards, C. P. (1988). *Children of Different Worlds*. Cambridge, MA: Harvard University Press.

Wiener, J. (1987). Peer status of learning disabled children and adolescents: A review of the literature. *Learning Disabilities Research*, 2, 2, 62–79.

Williamson, J. A. & Campbell, L. P. (1985). Parents and their children comment on adolescence. *Adolescence*, 20, 745–748.

Wilson, P. & Hersov, L. (1985). Individual and group psychotherapy. In: M. Rutter & L. Hersov (Eds), *Child and Adolescent Psychiatry* (2nd edn). Oxford: Blackwell.

Wing, L., Yeates, S. R., Brierly, L. M. & Gould, J. (1976). The prevalence of early childhood autism: Comparison of administrative and epidemiological studies. *Psychological Medicine*, 6, 89–100.

Wolfe, M. (1978). Childhood and privacy. In: I. Altman & J. F. Wohlwill (Eds), *Children and the Environment*. New York: Plenum.

Wright, P. H. (1982). Men's friendships, women's friendships and the alleged inferiority of the latter. *Sex Roles*, 8, 1–20.

Wright, P. (1988). Interpreting research on gender differences in friendship: A case for moderation and a plea for caution. *Journal of Social and Personal Relationships*, 5, 367–373.

Young, R. D. & Avdzej, A. (1979). Effects of obedience–disobedience and obese–non-obese body type on social acceptance by peers. *Journal of Genetic Psychology*, 134, 43–51.

Youngblade, L. M. & Belsky, J. (1989). Child maladjustment, infant–parent attachment security and dysfunctional peer relationships in toddlerhood. *Topics in Early Childhood Special Education*, 9, 1–15.

Younger, A. J., Schwartzman, A. E. & Ledingham, J. (1986). Age related differences in children's perceptions of social deviance: Changes in behavior or perspective? *Developmental Psychology*, 22, 531–542.

Youniss, J. & Smollar, J. (1985). *Adolescent Relations with Mothers, Fathers, and Friends*. Chicago: University of Chicago Press.

Youniss, J. & Volpe, J. (1978). A relational analysis of children's friendships. In: W. Damon (Ed.), *New Directions for Child Development*, Vol. 1. San Francisco: Jossey-Bass.

Yule, M. (1985). Behavioural approaches. In: M. Rutter & L. Hersov (Eds), *Child and Adolescent Psychiatry* (2nd edn). Oxford: Blackwell.

Zahn, G. L., Kagan, S. & Widaman, K. F. (1986). Cooperative learning and classroom climate. *Journal of School Psychology*, 24, 351–362.

Zahn-Waxler, C. & Radke-Yarrow, M. (1982). The development of altruism: Alternative research strategies. In: N. Eisenberg (Ed.), *The Development of Prosocial Behavior*. New York: Academic Press.

Zajonc, R. B. (1968). Attitudinal effects of mere exposure. *Journal of Personality and Social Psychology Monograph Supplement*, 9, 1–27.

Zakin, D. F., Blyth, D. A. & Simmons, R. G. (1984). Physical attractiveness as a mediator of the impact of early pubertal changes in girls. *Journal of Youth and Adolescence*, 13, 439–450.

Zimbardo, P. G. (1977). *Shyness: What It Is, What to do About It*. New York: Jove.

Zimbardo, P. G., Pilkonis, P. A. & Norwood, R. M. (1975). The social disease called shyness. *Psychology Today*, 8, 68–72.

Zimbardo, P. G. & Radl, S. L. (1981). *The Shy Child*. New York: McGraw-Hill.

Index

KING ALFRED'S COLLEGE
LIBRARY